MW00914457

Business to Business Direct Marketing

Third Edition

Bernie Goldberg

&

Tracy Emerick

DIRECT MARKETING PUBLISHERS

DEDICATION

This book is dedicated
to all business-to-business direct marketers --
we hope you can profit and learn
from each other.

Published by
DIRECT MARKETING PUBLISHERS
1304 University Drive
Yardley, PA 19067
(215) 321-3068 FAX (215) 321-9647
ISBN # 1-879644-06-1

Note: The pronouns he and his are used consistently
throughout this book to enhance its readability.
These references were not intended to be interpreted
literally.

Table of Contents

Introduction

If you have been asked to supervise or manage direct marketing activities in your company, you already know that there seems to be more problems than solutions. In a lot of ways, direct marketing is like a decision tree or maze -- the more you get into it, the more difficult it becomes.

The good news is that you're not alone. Almost everyone who starts down the road of using direct mail, telemarketing, or direct response advertising has faced the same problem. The bad news is that all of the available instructional materials and texts are geared towards consumer marketing.

As we began to implement business-to-business direct marketing programs, we felt alone and like pioneers. There is very little written on the subject and seminars and programs we attended were not geared to our needs. That's why we developed this book. If you feel like us, this book will give you a basis for understanding and implementing business-to-business direct marketing.

You can become an expert in the direct marketing field if you spend about two years making mistakes. You will still have to learn by your own mistakes even with this book as a guide, but there is no reason not to profit from the same mistakes that have been made by others.

Volumes have been written and are continually being developed on the subject of direct marketing. All devote 90% of their time to reaching the consumer, and may only address selling to other businesses in one chapter.

The focus on consumer direct marketing is well justified. At this printing, there are about 90 million households and over 240 million people in the United States that businesses are trying to reach through direct marketing. In addition, the concepts initially developed in America are growing at a phenomenal rate in other countries. Meanwhile, the business marketer is looking at a universe of somewhere between 10 and 12 million companies in the United States. Just looking at the numbers, a book is doing a reasonable job if it spends 10% on how to market to other businesses ... right?

You can't fault the other books; most are very good. The easy action and opportunity for direct marketing experts is in consumer direct marketing. In addition, marketing to the consumer has a long head start and more documented experience than selling to other businesses. However, all businesses are engaged in direct marketing even though they may call it something different.

It is the complexity of targeting consumers in their place of business that makes direct marketing to business so difficult. The segmentation techniques used in the consumer world don't work when selling to other businesses. The large universe in the consumer world allows you to make mistakes and still have almost an unlimited group to sell to.

On the other hand, because most businesses only sell to smaller segments of a particular business market, the number of targets is limited. The range of experimentation is reduced and you must develop better measurement and testing techniques to be successful. We were unable to find any book that really addressed these complex issues. The more we discussed the subject, the more we were convinced that a complete text on business-to-business direct marketing really needed to be written.

This book first differentiates consumer direct marketing from business-to-business direct marketing. It focuses on the needs of the business marketer. Business marketing is more difficult to plan and evaluate, especially if you are using a field sales force. Throughout this book, we focus on how to work with a field sales organization and be successful with direct marketing. We have dedicated a whole chapter to lead generation for field sales.

How to create and use a database to effectively control your efforts is also stressed and examined. Given the limited size of the business universe and the higher cost of identifying prospects, database marketing is absolutely critical.

Planning and measurement are the cornerstones to successful direct marketing. You will not only find the techniques and processes to allow you to succeed in these areas, but also the actual cases and formulas to make these approaches come alive.

Every business is looking at two major growth areas in direct marketing: telemarketing and cataloging. You will find comprehensive chapters devoted to each of these topics. Among many other findings, you will discover whether you are already in the catalog business and don't know it. And, you will also be able to decide whether you are using telesales or telemarketing.

If you gain one idea per chapter, your effectiveness as a manager can improve your overall results and enhance your position within your company. We hope you can learn from all of our mistakes and successes.

Bernie Goldberg & Tracy Emerick

About the Authors

Bernard A. Goldberg

Bernie Goldberg spent ten years at IBM Corporation in marketing and sales of small to medium computer systems. Bernie was one of the top sales people and later a top sales manager for the company. In addition, he spent two years in sales training and marketing planning. In his last position with IBM in 1979, he managed a pioneering facility in direct marketing and telemarketing. Like most of us, he started in business-to-business direct marketing with no experience and no prior training. Because of Bernie's prior sales background he has empathy and understanding for the field sales organization.

Prior to IBM, Bernie spent four years in the army immediately after receiving his Bachelor of Arts degree from C.W. Post College.

After IBM, Bernie's entrepreneurial spirit fostered two different telemarketing companies. He has specialized in all aspects of business-to-business direct marketing. He is a frequent speaker at direct marketing and telemarketing meetings and has written numerous articles on both subjects. He has also served as Vice Chairman and Programming Chairman of the Business-to-Business Council of the Direct Marketing Association. In addition to this book, Bernie also wrote *How to Manage and Execute Telephone Selling* and *The Lead Generation Handbook* and publishes bimonthly *The Business Marketing Note Pad*.

Bernie is currently president of his own consulting firm, B. A. Goldberg Consulting, in Yardley, Pennsylvania. A native of Amityville, New York, Bernie, a father of three daughers, resides with his wife in Yardley, Pennsylvania.

J. Tracy Emerick

Tracy Emerick is the Transition Doctor. Since 1973 he has assisted many companies as they move from traditional marketing to direct and database marketing. He is both a consultant and a practitioner. He is now aiding companies in the transition from traditional and database marketing to internet marketing, a complicated transition that requires companies to restructure their organizations and redefine their marketing strategies.

Tracy's transition knowledge comes from a renegade potpourri of work and educational experiences. Work experiences range from field sales to company president, consulting to Global 2000 companies and start-up entrepreneurs in industries from no-tech to high tech, public utilities to not-for-profit. He has served on the faculty of three universities and three professional seminar companies. Tracy has a bachelor's degree in Philosophy and a Masters and Ph.D. in Business Administration.

Tracy is a Senior Fellow of the International Society for Strategic Marketing. The New England Direct Marketing Association selected him Direct Marketer of the Year in 1996. He is past chairman of the Business-to-Business Council of the Direct Marketing Association, winner of an Echo Award and recipient of the Henry Hoke Award for direct marketing excellence.

Tracy is a founder and principal of Taurus Direct Marketing, formed in 1981, a direct marketing agency. He is also the founder and president of Receptive Marketing, Inc., formed in 1994, which provides database enabled use of the internet for e-commerce and online lead and customer management.

Chapter One:
Business-to-Business Overview

Consumer vs. Business-to-Business Direct Marketing

Is there really a difference between direct marketing to consumers at home and direct marketing to prospects at their place of business? Let's examine both situations through the best understood method of direct marketing - direct mail advertising - and see whether there is a basic difference.

The consumer receives his or her own mail from a mail box. In most cases, the target or addressed recipient sees each piece of mail and makes a decision whether to open and read the message. Often, this involves a quick sorting between bills and what is perceived to be personal mail in one stack, and advertising solicitations of all kinds in another. This process generally takes place where there is a counter and a trash can. All too often from the marketer's point of view, the consumer will toss the advertising mail, unopened, directly into the trash can.

In the consumer area, getting the mail opened and responded to is the major challenge. It is relatively easy to address and reach prospects. With the constant refinement of technology, thousands of lists are available that allow you to target your prospect by first and last name. It isn't necessary to address your message to 'Occupant'. While the rate of change of addresses in the consumer world is estimated at about 15% per year, new postal address change systems that enable marketers to keep track of those changes are widely used.

Now let's look at the environment for receiving direct mail advertising in the work place. In many businesses, a mail room or mail clerk receives the mail and is responsible for sorting and distributing it to the appropriate parties. In a large company, it is likely that assistants will open the mail. They will evaluate the message you are attempting to deliver and determine if their executives should read the mail pieces.

Therefore, two potential screens for direct mail solicitations exist in the business world that don't impede the consumer mail marketer. First, the mail room may misroute or be instructed to throw out advertising mail, especially duplicate copies. Second, the administrative assistants filter out matters considered not essential to their superior's performance. Unsolicited direct mail is often perceived to be a waste of time, so the secretary or administrative assistant throws it out.

In addition to these screens, there is another, more fundamental problem facing the business-to-business marketer. As we all know, business is in continuous motion and the only thing constant is change. Your prospect, the target you want to reach, is the individual whose job responsibilities are best aligned to your offer. Changing jobs or responsibilities is very common. The rate of change in the job function you're trying to reach can easily be 40% to 50% per year. Therefore, addressing your prospect by name and ensuring that you are really reaching the right person in the right job, is much more difficult in the business arena.

Before we define direct marketing and apply it to the business environment, let's take a quick look at other methods of marketing to businesses and see if they differ from consumer marketing. The process of direct response advertising in magazines, newspapers and other media are similar in both marketplaces. However, the creative approach used in the other media for business-to-business marketing can be substantially different than it is for consumer marketing. We will focus on those areas later in this book.

Telemarketing has additional considerations worth reviewing when contrasting consumer with business-to-business markets. The consumer is normally reachable from 5:00 to 9:00 in the evening, and all day on weekends.

Usually, you're trying to reach any adult in the household, so if someone answers you can probably get a decision on your offer. In most cases, you're selling a product so the consumer can simply say yes or no to your offer. Rescheduling the call to reach the appropriate individual is not necessarily based on a specific time that the individual will be available. A structured rescheduling approach over a planned number of contacts can be very successful. You don't have to try to accommodate 'on demand rescheduling' -- someone asking you to call back at a specific time on a specific day.

Business-to-business telemarketing introduces the villain, 'Bobby Barrier', whose only mission in life is to ensure that no salesperson reaches the decision maker. Telemarketing program design has to circumvent 'Bobby' and allow you to talk to your prospect. Plus you must plan on calling at times when your prospect is most likely in the office and available to talk. In most cases, your target will not be the first person to answer the phone. You'll probably go through two or more individuals before you reach your target. Moreover, due to constant responsibility changes, often the appropriate decision maker has been misidentified and you will have to begin anew attempting to contact the correct individual. It is also likely that upon reaching your target directly over the phone, you'll have to reschedule the call at a specific time and day in order for your prospect to agree to hear your message.

Technology further complicates the problem. Voice mail, for example, is a significant barrier that makes it even more difficult to contact the business target.

Let's put it in perspective: Most of the concepts of direct marketing that work in motivating an individual to respond in the consumer world will also work in the business world. After all, the business person is also a consumer. However, a major difference you need to evaluate relates to whose money you are asking your prospect to spend. In the consumer environment, you're asking your prospect to spend their own funds on your offer. In the business world, you are asking an individual to commit corporate funds.

So the real differences in the two marketplaces involve the accessibility of the prospects and their financing or money sources. Obviously, the size of the two markets is also substantially different. The challenge you face is getting your message in front of the individual who can make a decision on your offer.

In this book, we will focus on techniques that have been effective in using direct marketing to sell products or services from one business to another. First, let's get a better understanding of what we mean by direct marketing.

Direct Marketing Defined

There are many definitions for direct marketing. We believe that direct marketing:

Explores, tests, and substantiates methods of :

- *Prospecting*
- *Qualifying*
- *Closing*

exclusive of a face-to-face contact by a salesperson.

A more complete explanation of direct marketing can be found in Illustration 1-1. We have further simplified the definition into six understandable elements described in Illustration 1-2. The first element of this definition states that direct marketing is part of a planned marketing program and will often include a series of contacts.

Direct marketing activity can employ various media forms but it always seeks to produce a lead or an order. **Direct marketing will call its identified target to perform some action.**

The creation and maintenance of a database is an integral aspect of direct marketing. *Database* has become the most used and probably the most misunderstood term in marketing and direct marketing. In marketing, a ***database*** is the structure for storing and controlling the relationship information between a company and its customers.

As part of the same example displayed in Illustration 1-2, *Direct Marketing Magazine* has established a definition of database that is easy to understand.

DIRECT MARKETING - What is it?

An aspect of total marketing -
not a fancy term for mail order

Marketing is all activities which move goods and services from seller to buyer. Direct marketing has the same broad function except that direct marketing requires the existence and maintenance of a database to:

- Record names of customers, expirations, and prospects
- Provide a vehicle for storing, then measuring, results of advertising - - usually direct-response advertising
- Provide a vehicle for storing, then measuring purchasing performance
- Provide a vehicle for continuing direct communication by mail and/or phone

Thus

DIRECT MARKETING is interactive, requiring a database for controlled activity using mail, phone, or through other media, selected on the basis of previous results.

DIRECT MARKETING makes direct response advertising generally desirable because response (inquiries or purchasing transactions) can be recorded in a database for building the list, providing marketing information.

DIRECT MARKETING plays no favorites in terms of methods of selling, of which there are only three:

a) The buyer seeks the seller - retailing, exhibits
b) The seller seeks the buyer - personal selling
c) The buyer seeks the seller by mail or phone - mail order

DIRECT MARKETING requires that a response or transaction at any location be recorded in a computer database or other format.

DIRECT MARKETING can be embraced by any kind of business as defined by the U.S. Census Standard Industrial Classification System.

DIRECT MARKETING is an interactive system of marketing that uses one or more advertising media to produce a measurable response and/or transaction at any location.

Illustration 1-1: Direct Marketing definition from *Direct Marketing Magazine*.

The Definition of Direct Marketing

- **An organized and planned system of contacts**

- **Using a variety of media -- seeking to produce a lead or an order**

- **Developing and maintaining a database**

- **Measurable in costs and results**

- **Effective in all methods of selling**

- **Expandable with confidence**

Illustration 1-2:   A simplified definition of Direct marketing.

Direct marketing will develop and maintain a database which:

- *Provides names of customers or prospects*
- *Is a vehicle for storing and measuring responses*
- *Is a vehicle for storing and measuring purchases*
- *Is a vehicle for continuing direct communication to the prospects, respondents and customers*

Let's examine each of the elements of this database definition and again differentiate business-to-business from consumer direct marketing.

- **A database provides names of customers or prospects.**

    People used to think that buying a mailing list was all that was necessary to create a database. The world has become more sophisticated, and technology allows us to do a much better job of building complete information repositories. The original mailing list is important and becomes a part of the database, but information involving the activity of that list is also essential.

    At this printing, the U.S. consumer universe consists of over 280 million people in about 90 million households. The business world is not as easily counted. While it is safe to say that there are over 17 million business names in the U.S., each company may have

---

The Definition of Direct Marketing with Database Defined

- An organized and planned system of contacts

- Using a variety of media -- seeking to produce a lead or an order

- Developing and maintaining a database

  - **Providing names of customers and prospects**

  - **Vehicle for storing and measuring responses**

  - **Vehicle for storing and measuring purchases**

  - **Vehicle for continuing direct communication**

- Measurable in costs and results

- Effective in all methods of selling

- Expandable with confidence

Illustration 1-3: The definition of direct marketing and database.

several operating business names. Different company names and abbreviations for the same company complicate matters. For example, 3M Corporation has several identities:

> 3M
> Three M
> Minnesota Mining and Manufacturing Company
> 3M Company
> 3M Inc.
> 3M Corporation

These six identities for the same company do not include the seemingly endless name permutations on the divisional and subsidiary level. All of these company name variations make tracking a purchaser or a respondent much more difficult in the business-to-business universe. Addresses, executive names, and phone numbers complicate the problem. Plus, list compilers each have different counts of businesses and business executives for the same type of business lists to be purchased.

As you can see a company may be a complex web of divisions and subsidiaries and purchasing decisions delineated in various ways. An extremely sophisticated database capable of tracking and reporting these relationships may be beyond your immediate grasp. But don't be daunted; always capture the information. It is still very difficult to maintain the hierarchy of business and who owns what, but as programming and hardware power advances you may need to establish the various relationships to target your offer to the appropriate universe. In fact, you're likely to need to reach both the decision makers and the influencers to sell your product or service, and you should start capturing that information immediately.

Business-to-business list management is more difficult than consumer list management. Business addresses may be 4, 5 or 6 lines long including internal 'mail stop' addresses. List selection by title - never a consideration in consumer list selection - can be tricky because an individual's title often carries different weight from company to company. By comparison, a consumer list normally has 3 line addresses and you can usually count on reaching the decision maker or key influencer.

- **A database is a vehicle for storing and measuring responses.**

Once you reach the target and get a response to your offer, create a record of that response and any previous purchasing history. The database should enable you to track each contact and each response.

Your customers have established a relationship with you and have a lower degree of fear, uncertainty and doubt (FUD). They know who you are, what you sell, and the quality of your products. More importantly, they have demonstrated a need for your products or services by purchasing in the past. The best source of additional business is former customers. Many companies forget that prospects who responded, but did not purchase from prior campaigns, are also excellent sources of additional business. They have established some relationship with you and should not be ignored.

- **A database is a vehicle for storing and measuring purchases.**

Once prospects respond to a direct marketing program, you want to track their responses to see if they become buyers.

Direct marketing programs often use the initial response rate as the sole measurement criteria. Cost per respondent or lead, which is the effective measurement from initial response, is an important first part of the program's measurement criteria. By tracking and measuring the responses, cost per respondent or lead can be established. However, cost per respondent will not help you measure the *profitability* of your program. To evaluate the ultimate success of the program, you should measure the respondent through the entire sales cycle and determine the cost per order, average order size, and lifetime value.

When someone initially responds to a direct marketing program, it is referred to as the *front -end* of the program. The prospect has responded but whether they will actually purchase the product or service is still unclear. The *back-end* of the program refers to the conversion of a respondent to a buyer and a repeat buyer. In direct selling programs, where the response is actually an order, the front-end and back-end can be the same.

A program can seem attractive at the front-end in terms of cost per respondent. It may be a failure when the cost per order and average order size is reviewed.

- **A database is a vehicle for continuing direct communication to the prospects, respondents, and customers.**

The database should provide a sustained and complete ability to contact the:

a) Initial list of prospects
b) Respondents
c) Buyers

The need to track the status of each contact while measuring the results of each effort makes this process complicated.

Direct marketing is measurable in both its costs and its results, (see Illustration 1-2). In the consumer universe, a buying decision usually occurs within one contact or call. A business-to-business transaction may have an *influencer* who selects a product, but a different person who makes the actual buying decision. The size of the expenditure can affect the length of time it takes to get a decision. This multilevel decision process often precludes a single contact from generating an order.

In lead generation programs, trying to establish buyers and cost per buyer can be very frustrating (see Chapter 3). Several factors affect this.

- The purchase may occur in the future.
- The respondent and the buyer may be different people.
- The name of the company that actually responds or buys can be difficult to track.

Direct marketing can serve in all methods of selling. In a retail setting, where the buyer seeks the seller, coupons and special offers can drive traffic into the retail center. Or a salesperson may use direct marketing as a lead generation vehicle in order to get a face-to-face appointment. Soliciting the prospects to buy through the telephone or mail, which is similar to the consumer mail order business, is another possibility.

One of the key benefits of direct marketing is that a successful technique can be expanded with confidence. Results should be predictable. If something worked before at a certain volume or rate, you should be able to get similar results, other factors being equal.

Illustration 1-4 depicts the five basic functions or elements that must be controlled to effectively implement direct marketing.

- **Database**

  We defined and discussed the elements of the database. A more detailed discussion will follow in Chapter 4.

- **Promotional Material**

  Specialized promotional material that seeks to produce a response, either a lead or an order, is required. We have frequently seen pro-

Illustration 1-4: The five required elements of direct marketing.

grams in which technical specification material and brochures were redeployed for use in generating sales leads. This material was created as collateral to assist the field sales force; it was not designed to create a response, and is unlikely to do so.

A comment we often hear is: "My business is different. I tried direct marketing, and it didn't work." When the prior attempts are examined, no effort to provide specialized promotional material is evident.

• **Controls and Analysis**

An effective direct marketing program measures both costs and results. Costs are usually pretty easy to monitor, but in the business-to-business environment it is surprisingly difficult to measure the results of the program.

The different company names and abbreviations make tracking difficult. It is not unusual to have a prospect fill out a response device while away from the office. They may or may not include their company name. If the company name is provided, it may be abbreviated or given differently than other names for the same company that are already on the list.

In several programs in which we participated, leads were given to the salespeople with company names listed and the orders were placed with different company names. The orders were actually placed through a leasing company and became impossible to link to the original lead.

The decision process frequently extends beyond the initial contact and the eventual order may not occur during the original time period designated by the campaign's planners. Lead programs in high technology industries can have selling cycles of months and years. Management wants to measure the success of the lead efforts in weeks, so the lead programs are never successful.

Frequently a company assigns purchasing agents. The respondent and the purchaser may be different people. This creates similar measurement problems to those we discussed earlier with different company names. Purchasing agents can further complicate the tracking process because ongoing direct marketing programs targeted to customers can be aimed at the wrong individual. The purchasing agent is normally told to place the order and may not have the money, authority, need, or desire for additional products or services.

Companies will often have different phone numbers for the corporate offices and the individual employees. Therefore, using a phone number as a controlling identifier will not work. Many companies use *direct-inward-dialing (DID)*. This service, available from your local phone company, will give people a direct line to their office that can still go through the company switchboard.

Companies have frequent changes in responsibility and a respondent today may not be the appropriate target tomorrow. This tends to be the most difficult problem in business marketing. It is worthwhile to retain title information on responses to help identify the appropriate target within the company as individuals move around.

It is possible to receive multiple responses from the same company that only generate one order. This can occur as purchase decisions are centralized and pooled to take advantage of volume discounts. Multiple influencers can also cause this to happen.

- **Fulfillment**

Delivering the offer made in the direct marketing promotion is called *fulfillment*. The ability to deliver your promise is key to successful direct marketing.

Providing fulfillment includes such simple yet essential steps as ensuring that the toll-free number used in the promotion is answered. There have been situations where the advertising department forgot to notify the switchboard, customer service department, or outside service that a promotion had been run. You can imagine the way the incoming calls were handled.

Prospects might respond to your promotion and ask for additional information. Responding to this kind of inquiry is another form of fulfillment.

Sending leads to the salesperson and having him follow-up is, again, a form of fulfillment. This seems obvious enough, but in our experience, you can never assume anything when planning or instituting a lead generation program for a field sales force.

Within a true mail order operation, fulfillment involves shipping the product and handling billing, collections, returns, and inventory control.

- **Marketing**

   Marketing has two distinct areas that must be addressed to ensure the success of direct marketing.

   The first area to address in marketing is the integration of the direct marketing program into the existing marketing channel. This is the *tactical* use of direct marketing; how you will implement direct marketing with the current approach to selling.

   The *strategic* use of direct marketing relates to the long term efforts and results that will be experienced.

   Both the strategic and tactical ramifications of direct marketing should be evaluated and reviewed prior to beginning a direct marketing project.

A key to the success of the direct marketing effort is having a complete and detailed business plan prior to the start of the project. You can't measure the success of a program if you're not certain of your objectives. This business plan should focus on each of the five elements of direct marketing.

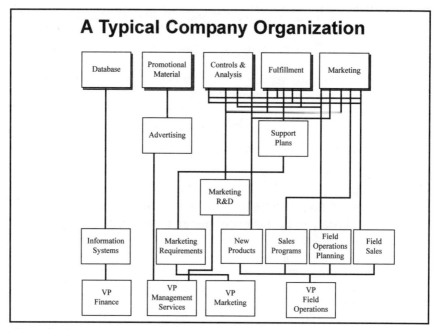

Illustration 1-5: A typical company and the organization that relates to the five elements of direct marketing.

Complete control over each element is required and you must have the ability to react to the changing business environment. In most businesses, the five elements report to different units of the organization and are controlled by managers and executives who are not directly involved in the direct marketing effort.

Look closely at Illustration 1-5 and you'll probably see shades of your own organization. With this 'spaghetti chart' organization, you tend to spend more time selling people internally than executing direct marketing. Plan a means to control these five elements of direct marketing prior to implementing a program.

The Universe

There are many definitions for the targets we are trying to reach with the direct marketing effort. Let's review the universe concept as it is pictured in Illustration 1-6.

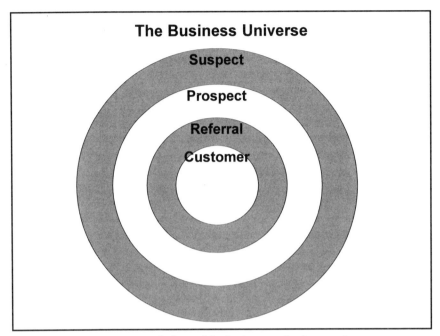

Illustration 1-6: A conceptual view of the business-to-business universe.

Imagine the business-to-business universe as a funnel that you are viewing from above. The entire funnel is made up of suspects.

A *suspect* is no more than a business name. We understand that many businesses operate under more than one name; even an abbreviation of a name can be considered a different suspect.

Prospects comprise the next ring inside the funnel. A prospect is a suspect that meets your predetermined qualification criteria. You might want to include prospects in an ongoing marketing program. You probably only want to reach each establishment once, although it may do business under many different names. Your qualification criteria may also be specific to a certain decision-maker or individual within the prospect's business.

Referrals are prospects of such high quality that you want to refer them to someone for immediate action. They form the next ring. You may send the referral to a salesperson for disposition or try to generate an order immediately. In the past, we've found that the term 'lead' was used synonymously with referral. The referral term should not be confused with occasions when one prospect or customer refers you to another prospect or customer.

The *Customer* is contained in the inner most ring and is the smallest group of the universe. This term describes individuals who have purchased products or services from you.

Most businesses spend a great deal of their resources attempting to locate prospects in the suspect universe (Illustration 1-7). In reality, each compa-

Illustration 1-7: Where most businesses spend resources.

ny should spend as little effort as possible on suspects and focus attention on:

1) Customers
2) Referrals
3) Prospects

An interesting point has been raised by some of our clients. Frequently, the individual responsible for implementing a direct marketing program has been instructed to eliminate customers and known referrals from the list. In the business-to-business arena, no computer program can eliminate all cus-

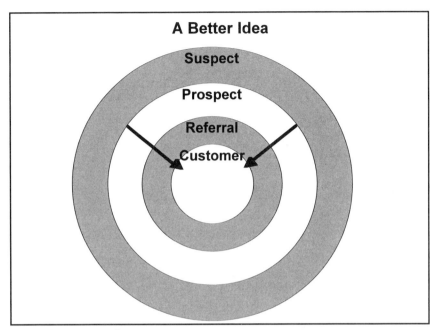

Illustration 1-8: Another way to generate customers.

tomers and active referrals from any list, due to the name variation problem. Some duplication and mistaken contacts are unavoidable.

We have graphically looked at the business-to-business universe as a funnel. As you know, as the neck of a funnel narrows, the pressure increases. It is impossible not to get the rings towards the center of the funnel wet.

In other words, when designing a selective direct marketing program, anticipate that everyone will hear of your offer, not just a few. A program that could have a negative effect on your customers and active referrals should be carefully evaluated. Direct marketing should generate a lead or an order, not hurt business.

When you attempt to eliminate certain names because of the impact direct marketing will have on selected groups, you're trying to avoid getting that group wet. You can restrict the offer to certain prospects or customers easier than you can eliminate their names. You should be able to explain or justify an offer that does not include your customers; it is not unusual to have special terms and conditions that restrict an offer from being used by certain people.

The Objective

Targets can fall into one of four categories (Illustration 1-9).

1) Prospects or suspects who are not qualified and not interested are relatively easy to eliminate from further activity. They will not respond to direct marketing contacts or advertising and require no further action at this time.

2) The not qualified yet interested group can be a terrible drain on resources if you are doing a lead generation program and sending the leads to a sales force for follow-up. These prospects tend to ask many questions with no intention to purchase the product or service you are offering. One of a sales manager's most difficult tasks is to ensure that sales people don't spend their time with this group. A salesperson has to deal with rejection all day long. This type of prospect is a false oasis in the desert of rejection. The prospect will talk to the salesperson and ask lots of questions, but rarely buy anything.

3) The not interested yet qualified prospect can be another big drain on resources. We often hear salespeople say they have found a great prospect. Which is a better place to spend time?

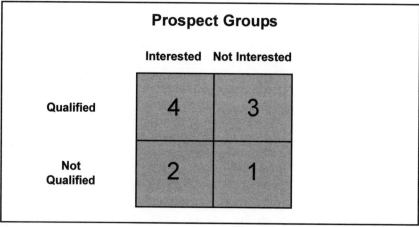

Illustration 1-9: Another way of looking at the business-to-business universe.

a) Convincing a prospect who is interested in your product or service that they can actually use it; that is, taking the interested prospect and making him qualified.

Or

b) Convincing the prospect who is qualified that they *should be* interested in your product or service.

Either situation is difficult and time consuming.

4) The group you need to work on is both qualified and interested in your product or service. We are all trying to find the qualified and interested prospect, the referral. You can apply our definitions to the four categories of prospects (Illustration 1-10).

The ideal situation is to expend your most expensive resource, salespeople, on the group in the upper left corner of the grid; the qualified and interested group. Cultivate the interested and not qualified group, and the not interested and qualified group, with various direct response promotional efforts that are less costly than a sales force. Develop a conditioning and regeneration program to move this group along through the sales cycle.

When a prospect becomes a referral, both interested and qualified, the name should be turned over to the sales organization. The objective is to provide

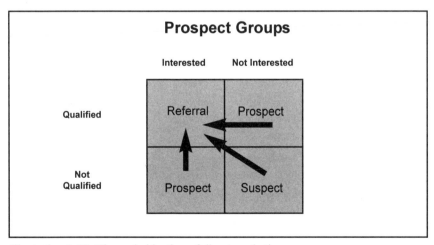

Illustration 1-10: The real objective of direct marketing.

only referrals to the sales force. Bear in mind the other groups will provide future referrals. Your direct marketing program should convert these prospects into referrals.

The Buying Decision

People go through a number of steps when they decide to buy anything. Sometimes the buying decision is made very quickly and the prospect does-n't really understand the entire decision process. Focus on each step of the process to ensure you create an environment that will encourage your prospects or referrals to purchase the product or service you are offering.

The buying decision can be visualized as a pyramid (Illustration 1-11). One of the cornerstones of the structure is Need. *Need* can be defined as a problem that prospects have to address. For example, prospects that are having difficulty generating invoices in a timely manner have a need for an invoicing system. The need is not for a particular product, but for a solution to a problem.

The other cornerstone of the buying decision is Desire. Again, the desire is not for your product, but for a solution that will solve the problem or satisfy the need. In this case, the prospect wants to find a better way to invoice.

Once need and desire are established, your prospect must justify making a change to address the need. Justification is not always financial; emotion plays a very important role in the buying decision. Your prospect has to be assured that making a change is going to be worthwhile.

Your prospect will study various ways for meeting their need by examining solutions or various approaches. Thus far into the buying decision, the project has not involved a specific vendor but has centered on how to solve a specific problem.

After your prospect understands their desire to fill a need, have justified making a change, and have researched alternatives, they must believe that making a change to meet their needs is feasible within the environment. Will the change to meet the need adversely affect the company? Will the cure kill the patient?

Once your prospect has evaluated each element, they are prepared to make a buying decision. It may seem farfetched to expect each buying decision

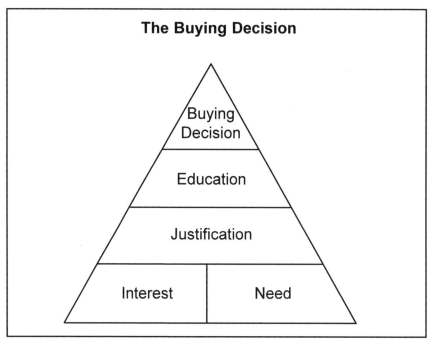

Illustration 1-11: The buying decision as created in the mind of the prospect.

to be this complicated. The whole process may take only a few moments in the mind of your prospect. The order of activity may be different, but we all go through this process whenever we purchase anything.

It is after you make the buying decision that you select a vendor and a product. You may select product before vendor, but you always make the buying decision first. The following defines a process that prospects go through to make a purchase.

- **Decide to Buy**
  Need and interest must be established.

- **Select Vendor**
  Awareness, liking, and preference must be established.

- **Select Product**
  Need must be fulfilled and justified with the best possible solution.

Some direct marketing programs seem to be aimed at the vendor and product areas of the buying process. The assumption is that the prospect has already made the buying decision. In fact, most of the time, the material used in the direct marketing effort is all product oriented and isn't designed to produce a lead or an order. This is especially true in the technology product arena.

We believe it is always worthwhile to create or affirm the buying decision in all contacts. Need and desire are the cornerstones of the ultimate sale. Evaluate your existing mail pieces and advertising. See which of these areas you're addressing. You may be missing an important opportunity by not focusing on the buying decision.

Relationship Marketing

The pressure on businesses to find alternative methods for dealing with their business customers has increased substantially in the last decade. According to the latest statistics, the cost of an industrial face-to-face call has increased from around $97 in 1977 to over $400 today and is still climbing. The Marketing Challenge (Illustration 1-12) shows that using a 20% cost of selling/marketing as an average percentage of gross revenue, reveals significant disparity between the rising cost of the sales call, and the revenue required to support that call.

In 1977 the revenue necessary to sustain the average sales call, assuming a 20% cost of selling, was less than $500. Today, more than $2,000 in revenue is required to support that same sales call using the 20% assumption criteria. The area between the revenue at inflation and the revenue at 20%, in Illustration 1-12, represents the *pressure* or disparity that businesses are faced with when selling to other businesses.

There are a number of ways to deal with this continuing problem. The easiest method is to increase prices to maintain profits. However, competitive pressures make it difficult to increase prices at a level high enough to offset the escalating costs of selling. Another more popular method, has been to curtail or abandon selling efforts to smaller customers, or for less expensive products.

As companies feel the pressure to address the escalating cost of sales, they begin to explore alternatives for selling to smaller customers and for selling less expensive products. Many companies cannot afford even one sales call to a customer who is spending less than $2,000.

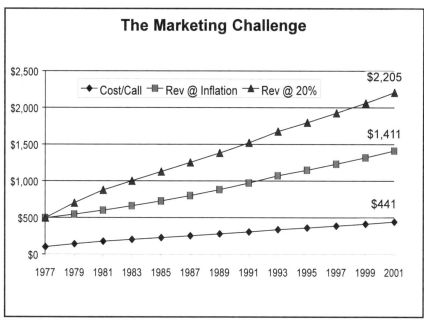

Illustration 1-12: The cost of face-to-face selling.

Historically, it was the salesperson's responsibility to maintain the relationship with a company's customers. Successful salespeople maintain a vast inventory of information about their customers. Each sales representative maintains a file containing the historical relationship of their company and their customers. In fact, these files are handed down from one salesperson to another as territories or responsibilities change. In some cases, the salesperson's file is the most complete historical record available detailing the relationship between the customer and the company.

We've asked a number of salespeople in our seminars why they maintain extensive customer files. Here are some of their responses.

- I want a complete history of everything the customer has done with me, so I can understand how the customer thinks.
- My file contains letters, notes from calls, and copies of all orders, so I can reconstruct the activity between us.
- I don't trust my company to maintain files; they have lost orders and letters in the past.
- If I know all the activity that has transpired in the past, I can use that information to construct what I should do next.

- If I leave the company, I may want to market to my customers in my new job. A good customer file will give me a basis for future activity.

The answers run the gamut from security to opportunity. The underlying reason for maintaining customer files is that salespeople know the key to selling is establishing and maintaining a relationship with their customers and prospects. The files document that sustained relationship.

Good salespeople will continue to maintain the history of their relationships in their own files. The real question is: How can we, as companies, maintain the same historical record for all our customers? This question becomes more critical as we assess alternative methods of dealing with various customer segments.

Some companies instruct their clerical staff to develop and maintain complete customer files. Over time these files become too full and older infor-

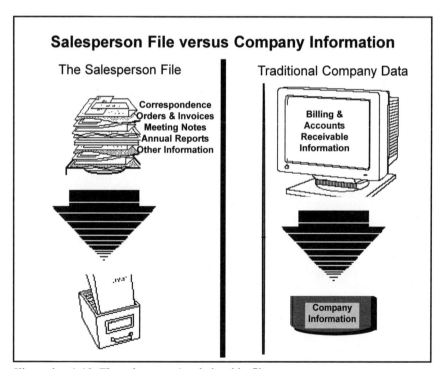

Illustration 1-13: The salesperson's relationship file.

mation is often purged. In addition, these files often only contain contact information in which the customer initiated the contact. The file may not contain all contact initiated by the company.

It is quite common to have a customer file in accounting or administration detailing order and billing information. Another customer file in sales and marketing may contain correspondence and contacts with the customer. Still another customer file maintained by the salesperson has all the information above as well as notes and miscellaneous information the salesperson has developed concerning that customer.

The files maintained by accounting and sales administration will generally be well-organized and standardized. However, they will not be complete. The salesperson's files will be complete, but individualized by the salesperson making them difficult for someone else to use. There may be scarce information available about smaller customers.

It is interesting that there tends to be a direct relationship between how frequently customers are contacted and how often they buy. The best customers are often those who have received the best sales and support services from the company.

As selling costs continue to grow, the number of customers that a company can afford to have salespeople call on, will continue to decline. Smaller customers become too expensive to service with a salesperson. As a result, the historical record of the relationship with that customer, maintained by the salesperson, is lost.

It is almost a self-fulfilling prophecy that smaller customers remain small or even become non-customers over time. The company ultimately loses its relationship with these customers. Does this mean that businesses cannot afford to deal with smaller customers?

Not necessarily. Direct marketing, teleselling, and the internet are ideal methods to sustain and enhance the relationship between a company and its customers. However, in business-to-business selling, some form of database will be required to record and identify the marketing relationships.

Traditional consumer selling is frequently a one-shot approach. That is, the company makes an offer for a product, and does or does not make the sale. Often, there is no need or desire to maintain a sustained relationship with the customer. Like retail selling, the consumer marketer will attempt to drive a new customer for each order. Because of the relatively large size of the consumer universe, it is both reasonable and affordable to drive a new customer for each order.

Business marketers can't afford to regenerate new customers for each order. Most businesses are selling to a limited universe, which tends to be relatively small. The best opportunity for a company is to establish long term relationships with their customers.

Some form of database is necessary to sustain the relationship in business-to-business marketing. This database can be as simple as the sales files described earlier. It doesn't always have to be executed on a large mainframe computer and cost hundreds of thousands of dollars. Earlier we stated that a direct marketing database will:

- Contain the names, addresses, titles, and phone numbers of contacts you want to reach via direct mail, telephone or some other direct marketing format.
- Have the capability to record all responses.
- Have the capability to record all purchases.
- Provide the capability to sustain communication and selling activity for all names on the database and record each contact.

This is done by the salesperson in their desk file. It just makes good business sense to develop a history of the relationship between a company and its customers. Unfortunately, as the company grows, the ability to maintain a manual database becomes impossible. And, because most companies have data processing report to the financial area of the company, computerized databases for marketing purposes become a low priority.

The direct marketing database can become very complex, as there are a large number of data elements related to the selling process. Illustration 1-14 identifies some of the tables in one database model.

This is not to suggest that each company develop such a sophisticated database immediately. However, every business selling to other businesses should plan to develop a complete marketing database over time. It should not suspend any current marketing efforts to enhance general customer relationships for the sake of database development. It should be evolutionary.

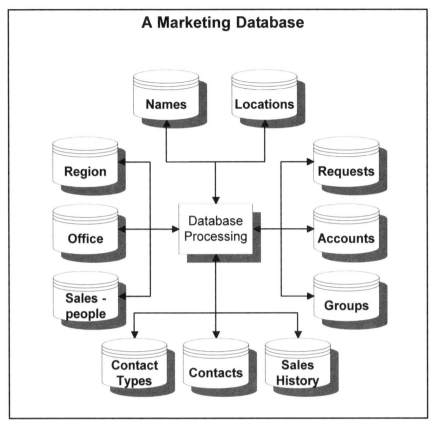

Illustration 1-14: A database model.

A number of effective, inexpensive and easy-to-use computerized database programs are available that allow the marketing and sales department to use personal or desktop computers to satisfy their database needs. These programs make it relatively easy to implement the database described on page 27. Armed with a marketing database, whether manual or fully automated, relationship marketing can be expanded to include all customers.

As you'll note from Illustration 1-15, the results of one marketing activity should trigger the next marketing activity. The ongoing transactions in the relationship should control the ongoing marketing activity.

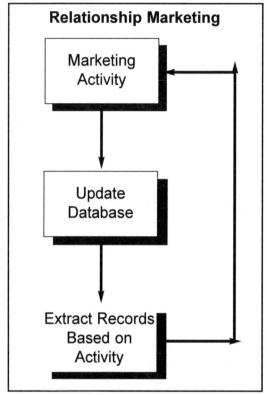

Illustration 1-15: Relationship Marketing.

When marketers know all the products purchased by customers, they can design a direct mail program or telesales program in which those customers are periodically contacted and solicited for additional sales based on what they have purchased in the past. Direct mail can be personalized and created via a word-processing system. Telesales contacts can be made which review prior activity and develop new needs based on the relationship. Customers can be made to feel like they are receiving personal attention. The *relationship* is being sustained.

All customers can be scored based on the recency of their last purchase, how often they purchase and the total sales dollars expended. This **RFM** (recency, frequency and monetary) approach can be used to identify the best selling opportunities and periodic contact schedules can be established. For example, based on purchase history, the marketer can schedule each customer to receive a contact monthly, bi-monthly, quarterly, semi-annually, or annually. Teleselling and face-to-face selling, can be used to create a 'personal' contact.

In a recent project with a company that identified the need to focus on enhancing its customer relationships, all sales were made using telesales. Each customer was scored (A,B,C and D), and a planned contact level was identified for each category. Direct mail was used to enhance the relationship, but telesales was used as the fundamental selling channel. The company was able to double its sales and, as importantly, double the number of customers purchasing annually by simply increasing the contact level. The company focused on enhancing its relationship with its customers.

Business-to-business catalogs and telephone selling seem to be the most frequently used formats for dealing with smaller customers and lower average order sizes. New internet and World Wide Web communication methods can further augment these efforts. These are effective approaches to continuing the concept of relationship marketing and they should enjoy continued growing success. These formats capitalize on the customer relationship that has developed over time.

Another format that should be explored is a direct marketing newsletter. This newsletter has the ultimate objective of selling products and services. It shouldn't contain pictures of buildings and information about the personnel of the business. The newsletter should help the customer understand additional benefits they can derive by using the company's products and services. Such a newsletter can be produced and delivered electronically at minor expense. Most importantly, it should continue to ask the customer to order throughout the document. You may also want to consider using the newsletter as a mini-catalog followed by periodic telesales.

Relationship marketing is not a new concept; successful salespeople have used it for years. What has changed is the cost of having salespeople deal with customers, the availability of high technology tools to enhance the sales relationship, and the increased level of competition forcing better relationships for business survival. Teleselling and Internet communication are the ideal vehicles to enhance and sustain the relationship at an affordable cost-per-contact. The very survival of a business depends on its ability to enhance and sustain customer relationships.

Relationship marketing, and the increased costs of having a salesperson contact customers and prospects, is the driving force behind the phenomenal growth of telephone selling and Internet marketing. In fact, you're probably reading this book because you're faced with the challenge of sustaining your customer relationships at a lower cost.

A Six-Step Selling Process

Recently one of my clients identified a six-step selling process which seems to accurately reflect selling to other businesses. What makes this selling process unique is the addition of a step to deal with the multiple decision-makers involved in business buying decisions.

Penton Information Service (Cleveland, OH - 216-696-7000), estimates that there are three to five people involved in business purchase decisions. In larger companies this is even higher with many companies forming buying teams to evaluate various alternatives prior to making a decision.

Illustration 1-16 identifies a six step selling process. All too often businesses attempt through their communications to bridge the six steps in one leap. Many companies don't even recognize the multiple steps involved in selling.

1) **Need** - The prospects have identified a problem that needs attention. They recognized that this problem needs to be solved and are willing to commit resources to investigate potential solutions. The prospects realizes that the problem they've identified can be solved, and they want to pursue a solution. In their mind, they can justify making a change to resolve a problem because they have identified their need.

2) **Interest** - The prospect understands some potential solutions to the problem or need. The prospect has developed an interest in their own mind. They have responded to an offer or requested information. All too often, lead generation managers conclude based on answers to a series of questions, that there is need and interest present independent of the prospects feelings. It is too easy to conclude based on research information that a company can justify making a change. Need and interest must be established and *agreed to by the prospect* at the onset of a realistic selling opportunity.

3) **Proliferation** - This is the step that is often overlooked in selling to other businesses. Salespeople have long recognized the need to identify and sell all the decision-makers and influencers involved in the buying decision. The larger the size of the transaction the more likely that multiple influencers are going to be involved. This important step must be clearly recognized and acknowledged. Face-to-face, tele-selling, and internet marketing campaigns should all reflect how the

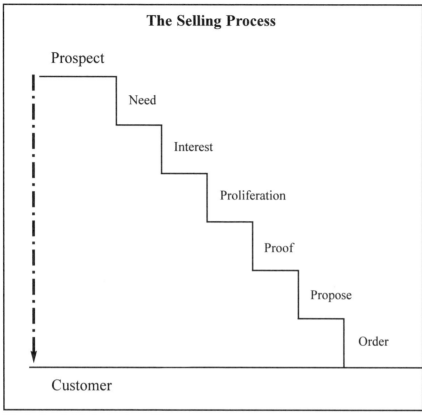

Illustration 1-16: A six step selling process

selling process will be proliferated to include all of the impacted personnel within the prospect company. It's a step that has always been part of the process, but never clearly identified as a unique element. Once identified, it will be easier to address. Instead of only planning to establish need and desire on the part of a single contact, we'll begin to design programs to address all people involved.

4) **Proof** - Once you have interest and need established and have begun to proliferate a decision to make a change, you'll have to prove the value of buying your products. A demonstration or trial of the product, as well as cost analysis, will probably have to occur to help the prospects overcome their natural fear of the unknown. Fear, uncertainty and doubt (FUD) have to be overcome prior to a buying decision. Many corporate decisions involve multiple people simply to help

overcome FUD. You may need to provide proof several times because of proliferation. However, you may be able to plan for a single proof event for the entire group.

5) **Propose** - Contracts, order forms, and/or proposals are presented to the prospects. In the real world of selling, you have probably been proposing and selling all along. This may be not be a formal step, but it is still a required element in the selling process. You have to ask for the order.

6) **Order** - A signed contract, purchase order or check has been received from the customer.

Quite often these steps are not unique events, but rather elements in the sales process that can all be resolved in one sales call. Unfortunately, in selling to businesses, the process will most often involve multiple contacts and people.

Salespeople have learned from experience that it is virtually impossible to move a prospect directly to being a customer in one step. Direct marketing needs to follow the sales approach and gradually move prospects closer to becoming customers. Communication needs to be designed and executed with offers that gradually move prospects along the selling process (Illustration 1-17). All too often we try to tell the prospect what and why they should buy, instead of why they should take the next step in the selling process.

Remember that the proliferation step is the most often ignored and could be the most difficult portion of the process. It is the clear recognition of this step that will allow you to plan and execute programs to sell all of the potential influencers involved.

Business-to-Business Overview Summarized

So far we have reviewed the major distinctions between consumer and business direct marketing. Throughout the remainder of this book we will frequently contrast specific differences in marketing between these two universes. The fundamental differences in the two marketplaces are the accessibility of the prospect, and their financing or money sources.

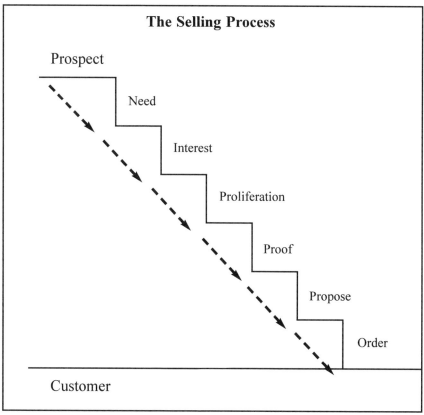

Illustration 1-17: Taking one step at a time.

Direct marketing has five basic elements and you must control all to suc-ceed. The five elements -- database, promotional material, controls and analysis, fulfillment, and marketing -- were described in detail and will be covered at length throughout this book.

The business universe was defined and consists of four major groups:

- Suspects
- Prospects
- Referrals
- Customers

We defined these major groups and then explained the objectives of direct marketing.

The buying decision was explained - how prospects evaluate and ultimately decide on purchasing products. Central to this discussion is our belief that communications to the business universe should address the buying decision as well as vendor and product selection.

The complexity of business direct marketing is amplified by the lack of company information available after salespeople are eliminated from the support equation. Salespeople tend to be less organized and focused and therefore maintain information in random unorganized files. They are responsible for developing and maintaining the company/customer relationship and sometimes refuse to help the corporation build complete databases of important information.

Finally, the concept of relationship marketing and improving customer sales was discussed in detail. Teleselling and internet communication are ideal ways to enhance and improve customer relationships. Some form of a database is required to use relationship marketing.

As you expand the use of business direct marketing, keep in mind that the sales process typically involves multiple steps which have to be negotiated prior to expecting a buying decision. We discussed a six step selling process you may want to consider in your planning and execution.

Throughout the remainder of this book, the focus will be on practical concepts that you can implement immediately. We'll use actual examples and case studies to illustrate our point. This chapter is our way of establishing common ground and definitions that will act as a foundation for other concepts and techniques.

All good direct marketing has to start with a complete and well documented business plan. So let's examine business planning next.

Chapter Two:
Direct Marketing Planning

Why Plan?

To execute effective direct marketing, the most important element is the development of a business plan before starting any program. The business plan is the definition of your objectives and the method of measuring the success of your activities. Throughout this chapter, we will define and display all of the elements in your business plan, including the essential tools you can use to create your own: outlines, flowcharts, budget sheets and the formula for determining them.

Too many books on marketing, advertising, and direct marketing contain an obligatory chapter on business planning. Typical presentations on this subject tend to be about as exciting as watching paint dry. However, don't let past dull recitations on abstract business theory lessen your zeal to master the business plan. No subject is more vital in determining the success or failure of a marketing effort. Let us show you a practical guide on how to develop and execute a business plan for business-to-business direct marketing. We conclude this chapter with an actual business plan.

The best direct marketing business plans can be read and understood by someone who doesn't know a thing about your business. Perhaps the most difficult part of developing the plan is keeping it simple enough for someone outside your organization to understand.

Writing a detailed business plan may not seem like the best use of your time because you probably already think that you know everything about your business. *Business planning* is putting on paper all the facts you have at your disposal.

In many instances, in order to implement your strategy and tactics you'll need outside help. The aid of an agency, consultant or list broker may be required. The business plan can be a tool to quickly and inexpensively bring these people up to speed on the specifics of your business.

There are many purposes for a business plan. Internal support will have to be briefed on your plans and assumptions. You can use it to remind you of your original objectives after the project is complete.

Your management should be given the completed plan prior to starting any activity. By ensuring that everyone has the same understanding and expectations, your project will have a higher chance of success.

The business plan will contain several major sections that can be categorized into the following areas:

- Company Background
- Organization Charts
- Current Costs and Budgets for Sales
- Direct Marketing
- Intensive Planning
- Strategies
- Measurements
- Tactics

Company Background

The background of the business encompasses many areas. Begin your plan with a brief history of your company and explain the key reasons for its suc-

---

Outline of Business Background

1) Background
   A) History of the company

   B) Product overview
      1) Type of products
      2) Product mix
      3) Revenue by product

   C) Marketplace
      1) The market
      2) Target individuals by product
         a) Decision makers
         c) Influencers
      3) Revenue by market segment

   D) Competition

   E) Current and prior channels of distribution
      1) Current channels by product
      2) Sales people overview
         a) Type of sales organizations
         b) Reporting structures
         c) Personalities
      3) Prior experience with direct marketing
      4) Pricing per channel
         a) Discounts allowed
         b) Pricing and strategy overview
      5) Revenue by channel of distribution

Illustration 2-1: Outline of Business Background.

cess. Remember, you're trying to write a plan for someone who doesn't know anything about your company.

You'll be tempted to avoid writing the history of your company. You may think this subject is too basic and superfluous. We have found that by forcing a review of the past, you can build a better foundation for activity in the future. Founders of businesses had great ideas and products. As time goes by, many companies may stray from the things that made them successful in the past. Reviewing the past history of the business may open doors that were accidentally shut.

Next, write a review of the products or services offered by your company. Try to address product evolution and how you obtained your current product mix. If your business has product areas or groups, review the major areas as well as the specific types of products. Don't try to address the marketplace or current marketing strategy. Focus on the product, product features, and product benefits you offer your customers. You will focus on the marketplace and marketing strategy later. Again, keep in mind that whoever is reading your plan may not know your company, your industry, or the problem that the product is designed to solve.

If you ask your colleagues or friends to read this section of the plan, pay close attention to the questions they ask. If the products are not clear, try redefining them again.

Don't try to describe every item of inventory. Focus on the major product categories and what these do for your customers.

Try to present the sales mix and percentage of sales for which each major product group is responsible. Real dollars and percentages of the total are very helpful. A comparison of the last few years of activity can help to show product trends. The average order size and number of orders by product group are important data to analyze in establishing strategy.

Now that you've examined the products and share of revenue, review the market and marketplace. A thorough study of the market is helpful in evaluating strategies and objectives. Review the markets for your products and product groups without focusing on your current marketing strategy. Just as you avoided strategy discussions in the product review, focus on the market and marketplace separately.

The purpose of the market section is to explain the size and composition of your marketing opportunity. You want to review the size of the market and the number of opportunities for you to sell your product. Business counts by Standard Industry Classifications (SIC), North American Industry Classification System (NAICS), geography, and business size are important. List brokers can be helpful in quantifying your marketing opportunity.

Within the marketplace overview, a section should identify the individuals you're trying to reach. Identify each product group's target individuals. Focus on the potential customers for your products; how they think and act; and how they make buying decisions.

Include a description of each major decision maker, including personality similarities and organization reporting structures. As discussed in Chapter 1, a unique characteristic of the business market is the multiple levels involved in the purchasing decision.

In your review of the individuals involved in the buying process, focus on influencers as well as decision-makers. If selling your products involve both decision makers and influencers, try to describe their individual functions and how they interact. Describe how these players fit into the organization and how they affect the buying decision. Examining the general personalities of all of these individuals can help you evaluate new or existing strategies. Keep in mind that different product groups may have different buying decision structures.

Now write a similar analysis for your market and market distribution. Include total revenue by market segment and percentages of revenue from market segments. By listing comparative information over several years you will notice trends in the marketplace.

The revenue analysis by market may not always be appropriate. Some companies have an unusual distribution of business. For example, if 25% of your sales comes from one or two accounts, your marketplace is different than a traditional company. This non-typical distribution will distort any analysis and will not be helpful in directing future marketing efforts. However, you should try to identify the unique characteristics of your offering that have caused the unusual distribution. There may be a special benefit that can allow you to expand your business substantially.

Try to review the average volume of a customer in both dollars sold and number of orders. Later, when we review the need for direct marketing, the customer volume data could become very important.

Competitive products and services can affect your ability to generate sales. Incorporate a detailed analysis of competition into your business plan. If possible, try to evaluate why the competition is succeeding or failing. Competitive pricing and offers can be key ingredients in the direct marketing program you develop. The competitive analysis should focus on the various product and market segments. If your competitors differ by region, be sure to review how this will affect your ability to sell in each area.

Now that you've examined the product and the market, evaluate the strategy and channels you've used to sell your products to that market. In this section, review your current and past approaches to selling to the market.

Relate how the current approach and channels of distribution have evolved. Each channel of distribution should be reviewed and explained. Understanding the current sales process and channels of distribution are critical to the success of your direct marketing efforts. How the current process works will be critical to any new programs you try.

If salespeople are involved, whether your own or other distributors, they can affect direct marketing. The sales force's personalities, compensation, and motivation, are important elements to consider when you implement direct marketing.

Describe the reporting structure of your sales organization. The way they are managed is critical to how you'll introduce and manage your direct marketing program. If you or your company has had a prior experience with direct marketing, document the program and results. Salespeople are like elephants, they never forget. More importantly, they never forgive. Chapter 3 reviews how to implement direct marketing with the sales force.

An important and integral part of your business plan explains how you will introduce the direct marketing plan to the current channels of distribution. Prior activities can dramatically influence the reception of your current program.

As you discuss the different channels of distribution, review the pricing, discounts offered, and gross revenue by channel. Again, list comparative information for several years to help identify any trends. Average revenue per order and number of orders is useful information to include.

If pricing differs by channel of distribution, explain why. The different pricing structure can be an indication of how different offers may be received by your market. You should understand why different customers are paying different prices for the same products.

Similarly, if selling strategies differ by channel, explain why. These different strategies can indicate strategies to test within an integrated direct marketing program.

Organization Charts

After you've reviewed the background of the business, an explanation of the organization should be included in the business plan.

Develop a current organization chart that identifies your functions and where you fit into the company. More importantly, focus on the organization as it controls the five elements necessary for direct marketing. The five elements were presented in Chapter 1 and are restated here:

1. Database
2. Promotional Materials
3. Control and Analysis
4. Fulfillment
5. Marketing

Direct marketing will frequently report to multiple areas of a company. You may not be able to change the structure, but you should certainly be aware of it.

You'll have to coordinate support for all the functions prior to starting a direct marketing project. We have often seen direct marketing managers spend precious time trying to internally "sell" or gain the proper support from others in the company after the project has started. Measurement and implementation will become very difficult without support from data processing and controls and analysis personnel.

Current Costs and Budgets for Sales

So far, most of the information that you have been documenting should be easily available within your company. In fact, there may already be a business plan that you've been able to use. The budgets for the current sales approaches are also pretty easy to establish. Get as much detail as possible on this subject. The key measurement to the success of direct marketing is profitability. If you can produce an order for less than the current approach, the program will probably be considered successful.

Most companies do not measure sales costs on a cost per order or cost per item basis. On the other hand, direct marketing is measurable and normally focuses on the cost per order or cost per item sold. Striking a comparison to measure the success of your program against historical information can be difficult.

Once you've established the selling budget for the year, some simple math will help you establish the overall cost per order or cost per item.

Refer to your background section to get the total number of items sold for the last year. Then determine your total sales expense by reviewing the budget.

Sales Expense ÷ Number of Orders = Sales Cost per Order

By dividing the sales expense dollars by the number of orders, you can determine the overall cost per order. This is a good place to start. However, it can be seriously distorted by more expensive products.

Now, establish the percentage of revenue that is used for sales expense. Divide the sales expense by the total revenue. Again, reviewing both the product and market sections, you can establish the actual dollars of sales expense per order and per item sold. You'll probably be surprised how expensive generating orders has become.

Sales Expense ÷ Total Revenue = % of Revenue used for Sales Expense

As we mentioned earlier, comparative results over several years can show interesting trends. Over time, you'll begin to get a better sense as to what has been happening to selling expenses.

We have always found that the less expensive products and smaller customers are allocated sales expenses that are not realistic. That is to say, you may find only fractions of a dollar allocated to certain products for sales expense. Certain customers may be allocated sales expenses that amount to less than the cost of one phone contact per year.

This exercise in establishing the cost per order or the cost per item often focuses attention on where you need direct marketing support. You will learn where costs have escalated to a point where profitable selling has become prohibitive. It is easy to get top level management to commit to a program to save money and reduce costs.

If you're using a sales force to sell, try to establish the cost of the order, average order size and cost per sales call. This is difficult to do and will require you to convince management to agree with certain assumptions. If you can establish the cost per sales call, your direct marketing objectives will be easier to establish and justify.

The use of personal computers and spread sheets has made life a lot easier. We can model and change assumptions with ease and examine the impact of our changes. There are a number of ways to establish the cost per sales call. We'll examine one from which you may want to create a spread sheet model. This approach is an example that you can expand or contract based on your own requirements.

First, establish the total revenue and marketing costs for the period you will use to establish the cost per sales call. Try to use a 12 month period and plan your results on an annual basis. Next identify the total number of salespeople you have in your company. Do not include management or field support personnel. These and other 'overhead' costs will be included within the total marketing costs.

Total Marketing Costs ÷ Number of salespeople = Cost per Salesperson

By dividing the total marketing costs by the number of salespeople, you'll establish the cost per salesperson per year. We have frequently encountered sales executives who maintain that they're paying their sales forces strictly on a commission basis, therefore the commissions are the only cost for the salespeople. This ignores the other costs involved in promoting and supporting the products.

If you're only using a sales force, the only time you have an opportunity to sell is when the salesperson makes contact with your customers or prospects. Marketing expenses should be apportioned to all of the salespeople, since this will give you a much better indication of your true selling costs.

Now use your background section to get the total number of orders generated. Establish the average order size next by dividing the total revenue by the number of orders.

Now determine the average revenue and the average number of orders per salesperson. To do this, divide the revenue by the number of salespeople. Then divide the total revenue by the total number of orders.

So far the data you've been creating has been based on numbers you can easily verify. You haven't made any assumptions, except to use all marketing expenses to determine the cost per salesperson per year. If your management is uncomfortable with this approach, ask them to give you the average earnings per year per salesperson. If you double this figure, to allow for support, expenses, fringe benefits, and general and administrative costs, it may be easier to develop your plan. This approach isn't as accurate as the first method, but it will still give you a basis from which to work. *Remember to document how you arrived at the cost per salesperson per year.*

Now that you know the average cost per salesperson, the average number of orders per salesperson, and the average revenue per order, you can begin to establish cost per sales call.

Much of the information you will generate on the cost per sales call will be based on assumptions that are difficult to verify. Try to be as conservative as possible. Use multiple sources for your data and be sure to document how and why you made a certain assumption. Review your assumptions with management and be flexible enough to make changes based on their suggestions.

You should also establish the average number of face-to-face sales calls made per business day. Most companies believe they average between three and four face-to-face sales calls per day. The same research used to establish the cost of an average face-to-face sales call referenced in Chapter 1, also estimates an average of 2.1 sales calls per day per salesperson.

Salespeople spend time traveling to and from the call, planning the call and creating call reports and orders. When you consider all the other activities required of the salesperson, three to four calls per day may be overly optimistic.

Salesperson Cost Worksheet

A) Total annual revenue _____

B) Total annual marketing expenses _____

C) Total number of orders _____

D) Total number of salespeople _____

E) Revenue per salesperson per year
   $(A \div D = E)$ _____

F) Cost per salesperson per year
   $(B \div D = F)$ _____

G) Average order size
   $(A \div C = G)$ _____

H) Average # of orders per salesperson
   $(C \div D = H)$ _____

I) Average # of sales calls per day
   (Based on assumption) _____

J) Number of business days per year
   per salesperson (Normally 200-220) _____

K) Number of sales calls per year per
   salesperson $(J \times I = K)$ _____

L) Cost per sales call
   $(F \div K = L)$ _____

M) Number of sales calls per order
   $(K \div H = M)$ _____

N) Closing rate
   $(H \div K = N)$ _____

Illustration 2-2: Salesperson Cost Worksheet.

The actual number of selling days per year is an interesting and sometimes very depressing fact of business. There are 365 days per year. 104 are weekends (52x2). This leaves 261 available selling days. When you subtract vacations (average 10 days) and holidays (average 10 days) and personal days (average 6 days) you'll have only 235 potential selling days per year.

This 235 days equals only 19.6 selling days per month. Now estimate the number of days taken from selling time for meetings, administrative work in the office, training, and recognition events and you'll probably end up with 200 to 220 days available for selling per year. And 220 days of selling per year equals only 18.3 selling days per month.

Using an average of three sales calls per day, the average salesperson makes 660 sales calls per year. Four sales calls per day would equal 880 sales calls per year. Although this number is usually far lower than the number of calls management thought were being made, it is probably overstated. Averaging three or four calls per day doesn't recognize the independence of the sales force and their tendency to play golf, tennis, and socially spend time with their customers.

The worksheet in Illustration 2-2 gives a simple format for establishing the cost per sales call. With the information you can also establish the cost per order by dividing total expenses by total orders. To determine your average cost per sales call, divide the average cost per salesperson per year by the average number of sales calls. To establish the number of sales calls per order, divide the number of sales calls per year by the number of orders per year. Finally, identify your closing rate by dividing the number of orders by the number of sales calls. Closing rate is the percentage of sales calls that result in an order.

Your cost per sales call may surprise you and your management. As we mentioned in Chapter 1, the average cost of an industrial sales call across most industries is over $400. In our experience this cost has frequently been much higher. Knowing how expensive it has become to make a sales call can help you establish where direct marketing can most help your company.

If the average cost of a sales call is $400, and your allowable sales expense was 20% of revenue, you would have to generate a $2,000 order for every 5 sales calls. This is determined by dividing the cost per sales call by the allowable percentage of revenue for selling expenses. This assumes that you're experiencing a 100% closing rate -- an impossible objective. Therefore, you will probably determine that there are certain products and market segments to which you can no longer sell using the traditional salesperson.

Knowing the facts -- the costs and the budgets -- can help you establish a better direction for your program. You'll also establish some measurement criteria that can help evaluate the success of your program.

Direct Marketing: Section of Business Plan

The purpose of this section of your business plan is to establish why you're going to use direct marketing. You should identify the problem that direct marketing will solve. The product, market, and marketing strategy sections establish what and to whom you're selling. The budgets and costs section establishes your current costs and will probably highlight the areas that need support.

Describe in clear terms what you plan to do with direct marketing and why. If you're planning a lead generation program, describe what you're planning to do and what you hope to accomplish.

Make sure you describe the universe you're trying to reach (prospects), the group that you want to respond (referrals), and finally who will buy (customers). List brokers and list salespeople can help you understand the size and composition of your target universe.

There are some interesting techniques you can use to establish why and where you need direct marketing support. One approach is to use *Intensive Planning*. This is a concept that encourages communication, problem definition, and problem resolution.

Intensive Planning

Intensive planning sessions normally involve all of the individuals in a particular function. It should be done off-site in an informal and relaxed environment. Normally the session will take two full days. We have run sessions for all the top management in a company to identify programs

---

Planning Session Rules

- Only one person may speak at a time.
- Everyone is equal; positions within the company are forgotten.
- All problems are to be stated in complete sentences
  -- no abbreviations -- and should state cause and effect.
- If anyone leaves the room, all planning stops.
- The person with the marker is in charge.
- All participants must unanimously agree to include a problem.

Illustration 2-3: Intensive Planning Session Rules.

that will allow the company to attain its objectives. The same type of session has effectively helped a sales unit identify programs to allow it to reach its objectives.

The planning session needs to be coordinated and controlled by an outside individual. Consultants, experienced in this type of planning, are excellent session moderators. The moderator and senior manager or executive should meet prior to the planning session and establish who should participate and the short and long-term objectives to be planned during the session.

The planning session should convene where there can be no interruptions. Meals should be available to keep breaks to a minimum. The rooms used for the planning sessions should have a lot of wall space, as you'll be writing on flip charts and hanging the results on the walls. You'll also need two flip chart easels, flip chart paper, masking tape, and several different colored markers.

Once everyone is present, the senior manager or executive starts the session by reviewing the objectives for the unit. These objectives should be both short-term (next 12 months) and long-term (next 3 years). The objectives should be written on a flip chart prior to the session. The objectives are taped to the wall after they have been reviewed and explained by the senior manager. The senior manager will become a participant in the planning session after the objectives are presented. They will only have a single vote equal to any other member of the group.

The rules for the planning session are very simple:

- Each person has one vote, regardless of their level or position within the company.

- All problems are written in complete sentences stating a cause and effect.

- In order for a problem to be included in the final planning document, all participants must agree to include it.

- There is only one speaker at a time, and no side conversations.

- The person with the writing marker is in charge.

On the first day the members will identify only the problems that interfere with their objectives. On the second day, the participants will group the problems and create action plans to solve them.

After the objectives are reviewed, the group will define all the problems that prevent them from attaining their objectives. No problem is too small as long as the group unanimously agrees to include the problem.

One participant is appointed to act as moderator and given the marker. The moderator position is rotated periodically. Initially, the outside participant who controls the session should moderate the session. The two flip chart stands are set up in the front of the room. All problems the group agrees to include are listed on one chart. Each problem and each chart are numbered. The other easel is used as a scratch pad until the problem is written clearly, in a complete sentence, and is one the whole group agrees to include.

One speaker at a time states a problem in a complete sentence defining both its cause and effect. It is very difficult to discuss problems without trying to solve them; strong control must be exercised to focus only on identifying problems.

If the problem is that the sales force needs qualified leads, a more complete statement should be established. For example: The sales force needs qualified leads to sell in order to meet this year's sales objectives. The cause and effect are defined. When you read this problem later in the day or at some point in the future, it will be easy to understand what was meant.

Sales Problems			
Problems	**Actions**	**Who**	**When**
2,41,43	Align sales compensation programs to ensure consistency.	SJ	12/1
4,6	Establish accurate forecasting system.	TM	5/1
1,21,89	Develop hiring program to add 1 salesperson per month starting 6/1.	SJ	6/1

Illustration 2-4: Example of action plans from planning session.

The problem is written on the scratch flip chart. After clearly stating the problem, the group discusses the problem. If there is unanimous agreement, the problem is copied to the final charts.

As a final chart fills, it is removed from the easel and taped to the wall. The charts and problems should be kept in order. By keeping the problems in clear view, the group can refer to the charts and ensure no duplication. The complete sentence, cause and effect, makes understanding the problem easy.

The problem definition phase is the longest and toughest part of the planning session. It should continue until all the problems are described and written on the charts. It is not unusual to have more than 100 problems. Frequently, the problem definition phase will go late into the evening because only one day has been allocated for this phase.

The group dynamics and communication forced during the problem definition phase can be as important as the actual problem resolution.

During the second day, all the problems are grouped into several broad categories. Training, Communication, Compensation, Personnel, and Engineering are some groups, but you should create your own groups. There are no rules for which problem goes in which group. One problem can appear in more than one group. It is easier to use a specific colored marker to identify each group, and to write the group next to the problem number.

After each problem is grouped, you can begin to establish action plans to solve the problems. Every problem has to fall within a group, or have its own group. Some problems will be outside the sphere of control of the participants and cannot be solved. These are environmental issues and should be grouped within a special group called Environment.

Additional charts are then created for each group. Each problem number is listed. When the charts are later transposed and typed, the group resolution charts should contain the complete problem description.

Obviously, you can't solve the problems in a two-day planning session. However, you can establish action plans with target dates for completion and the individuals who are responsible. The set of charts listing the action program, target dates and responsible individual becomes your activity plan for the future.

The planning session helps you identify all of the problems that prevent you from reaching your objectives. The activity programs that come from this session should resolve most of those interferences.

If a session like this is conducted with sales, advertising, data processing, and marketing, the reasons to use direct marketing will be very clear. More importantly, everyone signs up to be part of the solution. You will get great support for all the required elements of direct marketing and everyone will know why you're doing the project.

It is critical that all the parties who will be involved understand and agree to the direct marketing program. Throughout this book we continually stress the need to communicate why and how you'll implement direct marketing. The biggest cause for failure in any direct marketing project is an unrealistic expectation level at the onset.

Strategies

The primary differences between strategies and tactics are scope and the dimension of the undertaking. *Tactics* are the things we do to execute a strategy. A *strategy* defines where you would like to go over the longer term. The strategy is the war while tactics are the individual battles.

So far you have identified the background of your company, its organizational structure, its current costs, and why you need direct marketing. You are now ready to establish long-term goals and objectives. For example, you may decide to reduce sales expenses from 20% of revenue to 18%. More realistically, you may only want to hold sales expenses at a certain rate, while costs are escalating. High technology companies have been trying to address the dual problem of increasing selling expenses and decreasing revenue per product. Retail distribution, catalog selling, direct mail, teleselling and internet marketing are becoming more common in the high technology area because of reduced revenue per product.

As you establish your strategy, remember that you must consider its long-term implications. You may want to test and evaluate whether another channel of distribution is appropriate. Direct marketing to sell the product may be reasonable, but you may have to introduce these programs in steps.

During the strategy review, focus only on determining the direction in which you want to move over the long term. Avoid establishing media and direct marketing applications; they are the tactics. For example, you may want to establish a database for ongoing direct contacts. This is a strategy. Buying database software, writing procedures to enter the data, and deciding which names will go into the database are all tactics. Shifting business to e-commerce to reduce sales costs is a strategy. Developing web site ideas and electronic customer communication methods are tactics.

To help you focus on your strategies, review the section of your business plan in which you stated why you needed direct marketing. Now you must establish a plan for testing and evaluating whether direct marketing can work for your company.

Measurements

How you will measure your direct marketing program must be determined before you define all the elements that must be executed. In selling to the consumer, marketers appreciate that most buying decisions are made in a relatively short period. Most of the time, the targeted consumer can make the decision. The environment for selling to businesses is quite often more complicated. A single selling cycle can span many weeks and months.

If you won't find out whether a prospect has purchased for several months, how will you measure the success of your efforts? Simply design a program that allows you to measure the project in stages, and evaluate your success against interim objectives. Your business plan should contain these complete objectives for front and back-end results. Measuring response expectations and actual results to the initial offering can indicate whether your program will succeed. Keep in mind, however, that the ultimate measurement will be purchases.

First prepare a complete financial operating plan for each aspect of your direct marketing program. Include the costs and expected results of the program. As you execute different parts of the plan, you can compare results to expectations.

We have seen companies execute programs that could never succeed because of impossibly high expectations. It seems as if every executive expects a 20% response in the mail. High results (20% response is basically unrealistic) may be possible, but shouldn't be required in order for a program to be successful.

Another gratifying result of all of your planning is that you don't have to implement a program with unreasonable expectations. Just take your ultimate objective, and plan backwards. If you need an order cost of $200, you can establish a financial and operating plan that produces that kind of result.

You may not realize how low an order rate you actually need to create a successful program.

Let's look at a direct response ordering program:

Average order	$400.00
Allowable sales expense rate	20%
Allowable sales expense dollars	$80.00
Cost per 1000 pieces mailed	$750.00
Required order rate ($.75/$80)	.94%

Let's assume that we are trying to sell a $400 average order. If our planned sales expense is 20%, we can spend $80 per order. If we're spending $750 per 1000 pieces to mail to the universe, a 1% response will produce 10 orders per 1000 pieces mailed. The total selling expense will be $75 per order. To arrive at the minimum acceptable order rate, you establish the cost per contact ($750 ÷ 1000 = $.75) and then divide by the allowable sales expense dollars. In our example this is 0.94%.

This was a very simple example that didn't consider returned orders, bad payment or any other fulfillment factors to complicate matters. However, it does illustrate how as little as a 1% response may be all you need to conduct a successful direct response ordering program.

Lead generation programs, or those campaigns that have multiple steps before closing the sale, are more difficult to measure but can also be planned using the same techniques. Along with the previous measurements given, you must add the cost of sales calls and the anticipated closing rates to arrive at the complete cost per order.

Here is a simple example of a measurement plan for lead generation:

Average order	$5000.00
Allowable sales expense rate	20%
Allowable sales expense dollars	$1000.00
Cost per sales call	$250.00
Closing rate	30%
Salesperson cost per order	$833.33
Allowable cost per direct mktg lead	$176.67
% Respondents qualified as leads	40%
Allowable cost per respondent	$70.80
Cost per 1,000 pieces mailed	$750.00
Required response rate	1.06%

A number of elements will have to be measured to verify whether this plan succeeded. The first and easiest piece will be to establish the response rate to the mailing. If you get 1.06% response or better, you're ahead of your planned expectations. If 40% of the respondents qualify as referrals and are sent to the sales force, you again are ahead of the plan. If your initial response rate was higher, but your qualification rate lower, you can still be ahead of the plan. As long as you produce a qualified lead for $176.67 or less, you are meeting the plan.

In both examples, the program was successful if we could produce about 1% response. This response rate is reasonable and attainable for most programs. If you present a detailed plan that focuses on cost per order, you'll probably succeed. Lead programs have their own set of measurement problems that will be discussed in Chapter 3.

Establishing the Required Response Rate

When you're asked to plan your next direct marketing campaign, how will you project the response rate? Guess? Assume about 1% because that's what everyone else does? Accept your boss's estimate and expectation of 5% because they think that's what it will be? You could get lucky and be close in guessing the rate, but there is a better way.

We suggest that you plan programs not by intuitively identifying projected responses, but by identifying the required response in order to meet the business objective.

Establish an allowable or expected direct marketing cost per order to help you identify the required number of orders you have to obtain to pay for the campaign.

In Illustration 2-5, the average order allows $600 in lead generation expense. If you allow 20% of revenue as the allowable direct marketing expense, you can identify the allowable expenses per order generated.

We always use 1,000 names mailed or promoted to develop the required response level. You can use the actual number you plan to mail in developing your objectives. As you can see, we used $1.00 per piece and established the promotion expenses at $1,000. In order to meet the allowable selling expense plan, this program must produce 1.67 orders.

Once you have identified the required orders, you can work backwards to establish the number of leads and finally the number of responses required to meet your objectives.

In the Sample Plan, we have assumed that this is a lead generation program and that 20% of the leads will close to an order. Therefore, it will take five leads for each order. In addition, only 60% of the responses will convert to leads, requiring 13.92 responses per order.

If you're designing a lead generation program to produce highly closeable leads, not every response will become a lead. Those responses that aren't leads immediately may be able to convert to leads in the future if you implement an ongoing campaign to condition and sell them.

As you can see "*back-planning*" this program identifies the required response rate. In the Sample Plan, the 1.39% is somewhat high and may be difficult to achieve. The list promoted and offer made to the

Sample Plan	
Average new customer	$3,000
Allowable lead expense %	20%
Allowable lead expenses	$600
Contribution	$2,400
Number mailed	1,000
Cost per mailing	$1.00
Mailing cost	$1,000
Required orders	1.67
Closing ratio	20%
Required leads	8.35
% Leads of response	60%
Required response	13.92
Required response %	1.39%

Illustration 2-5: Example of back-planning.

prospect will greatly influence the level of response. We continually stress the importance of the offer.

By changing only one element you'll see the impact it can have on required response. If you reduce the cost per piece mailed from $1.00 to $.75, the required response rate drops to 1.04%. Increase the average order from $3,000 to $3,500 (you can control the average order with the offer you make) and the response drops to 1.19%. Change the closing ratio from 20% to 25% and the response rate drops to 1.11%. Send more of the responses out as leads, 65% instead of 60% and the response rate drops to 1.29%.

We think that the best plan comes from optimizing several elements slightly to get the best results. Change the cost per piece to $.90, increase the average order to $3,200 and change the closing ratio to 22% and the required response drops to .99% – just under 1%. And these slight modifications are probably achievable.

Armed with this kind of planning before you start, you can determine the promotion budget, the size of the sale the offer must generate, and the quality of the lead you require. Besides answering the response rate question, you will actually plan the program instead of having it plan you.

XYZ Coffee Service Business Plan

If this approach to planning seems a little far-fetched or difficult to grasp, let's look at a real life example. We recently created a business plan that established the required response rates in a lead generation program for a sales force using only telemarketing. The company sold a coffee service to other businesses using sales representatives. The objective of the program was to generate sales leads that were interested in trying the coffee service. The difference between telemarketing and telesales will be completely defined later in this book. For this example, telemarketing was used to generate leads for the sales force. If the sale is completed over the phone teleselling is being used.

XYZ Coffee Service Current Sales Approach

Average Earnings per Salesperson $25,000

Multiplier to include General, Administrative

& Management Costs in Average Earnings	2.00
Total Cost per Salesperson per year	$50,000
Average Customer Expenditures per year	$1,200
Annual New Sales Quota per Salesperson	$144,000
Average New Customers per Month per Salesperson	10
New Customers per Year per Salesperson	120
Average Face to Face Sales Calls per Week	21
Sales Calls per Year (Assume 48 Weeks allowing for Vacation and Holidays)	1,008
Sales Calls per Month	84
Closing Ratio (Orders per Month/Sales Calls per Month)	11.90%
Cost per Sales Call	$49.60
Cost per Order	$416.67

Lifetime Value of the Customer		
% Loss of Customers per Year		30.00%
Value Year 1	$1,200	
Value Year 2	$840	
Value Year 3	$588	
Total for 3 Years		$2,628

% Cost of Sales of 1st Year Revenue	34.70%
% Cost of Sales of Total Revenue	15.90%

Anticipated Results with Telemarketing

Planned Closing Ratio of Leads Generated From Telemarketing	30.00%
Number of Calls to Non-Ordering Prospects (Trial Service is delivered by Service Rep Salesperson calls near end of trial to convert)	1

Number of Calls to Purchaser	2
(Sales Rep has to make a second call to get contract signed)	
Total Face to Face Sales Calls per Order	4.3
(Prospect Calls/Closing Ratio less 1 Call who became a purchaser plus Purchaser Calls)	
Total Salesperson Cost per Order	$213.28
(Total Face To Face Calls multiplied by Current Cost per Sales call)	
Cost of Trial of Service	$35.00
(Cost delivering & picking up equipment and cost of coffee)	
Total Cost of Trials per Order	$116.67
(Cost of Trials divided by Closing Ratio)	
Total Selling Cost per Order	$329.95
(Cost of Salesperson plus Cost of Trials)	
Allowable Direct Marketing Cost per Order	$86.72
(Current Cost per Order less Total Selling Cost with Telemarketing)	
Telemarketing Cost per Hour	$30.00
(This assumes a $3.00 cost per follow up phone call)	
Names Consumed per Hour	10
% of Consumed that are Completed	65.00%
Number of Completed Calls per Hour	6.5
Required Orders per Hour	0.35
Required Response Rate of Original List	3.50%
Required Response Rate of Completed Calls	5.38%

In creating this business plan, management was unable or unwilling to reveal the entire marketing budget so we used the average earnings of the salesmen for our budgeting calculations. The cost of one salesperson was estimated at $25,000 per year. This number was doubled to $50,000 to approximate the true cost of the average salesperson per year. It was interesting to observe that even with this company's extremely low cost per sales call figure, the average cost of an order was still fairly high.

The average customer historically spent about $100 per month or $1,200 annually.

Each salesperson had an annual sales quota for new business of $144,000. We divided the above $1,200 by this $144,000 to get the annual new customer objective of 120 customers per salesperson. We then divided 120 by 12 months to get the monthly quota of 10 new customers.

Given that the average salesperson made 21 sales calls per week, we then multiplied 21 by 48 weeks to establish 1,008 sales calls per year. The 48 weeks allowed for vacations and holidays. It really didn't allow for sick, personal, and other time off. Although somewhat overstated, these were management's numbers, and the credibility of our plan meant more than fighting for a more conservative estimate. Finally, we divided the 1,008 calls per year by 12 to establish the monthly sales call volume of 84 calls per month.

Once we knew the total number of calls and the total number of orders per month, it was fairly easy to establish the closing ratio, cost per sales call, and cost per order. The closing ratio is established by dividing the number of orders by the number of sales calls ($10 \div 84 = 11.90\%$). The cost per sales call is established by dividing the annual cost per salesperson by the number of sales calls made per year ($50,000 \div 1008 = \$49.60$). The cost per order can be established two different ways with the same results. (1) Divide the annual cost of the salesperson by the number of orders per year ($50,000 \div 120 = \$416.67$). (2) Divide the cost of the sales call by the closing ratio ($49.60 \div 11.90\% = \$416.81$). There is a slight difference due to rounding.

Many businesses fail to examine the costs of acquiring a customer against the lifetime value of that customer. It is unfair to judge a program against only the first year's sales of a customer if that customer will continue to purchase products for a longer period. In this example, customer turnover or attrition rate was about 30% per year. Therefore, the average customer will last somewhat longer than three years. When considering turnover and lifetime values of customers, keep in mind that the turnover rate is always on the remaining balance, therefore it will never drop completely to zero.

The turnover rate of 30% was used to establish the value of the customer for the next three years. Although this was understating the lifetime value of the customer, it did allow us to work with a more realistic estimate of revenue from each customer. In addition, we didn't use present value techniques to establish the real return on investment. So being a little off in the value estimate was balanced against the missing factors of cash flow and net present value of money.

In year 1 the customer contributes $1,200 in revenue. The year 2 value is 70% (100% - 30% = 70%) of the $1,200 or $840. Year 3 is 70% of the $840 or $588. As you can see, the number will never equal zero. For our example we stopped the revenue, for evaluation purposes, after three years and totaled the revenue at $2,628.

The cost of selling can now be compared to both the annual revenue and the lifetime revenue of each customer. The annual revenue comparison shows that the cost of selling is almost 35% of the first year's revenue. This would make the cost of selling prohibitive in most businesses and suggests that you can't afford to sell. When the comparison is extended to include the lifetime value, it is about 16% of sales. This is a more realistic selling expense.

As you can see, it takes a great deal of work to establish the costs of current approaches to selling before you begin to develop the direct marketing approach. But you really should be armed with sales costs on a current basis to objectively compare them with your direct marketing results. Most sales executives are not aware of how expensive it has become to close an order.

XYZ Coffee Telemarketing Plan

We first established that the quality of the lead we wanted to generate should be able to close at a 30% rate. After some prospect qualification on the telephone, we were planning to telemarket an offer for a one month free trial of the coffee service. Prior experience with trial service had shown these offers to close at about 30%. The trial service would be delivered by the sales representative. If a prospect didn't order, it was felt that the salesperson would only have to make a single sales call to determine that the prospect would not become a customer. Prospects that became customers required a second call to have the service contract signed.

To establish the total number of face-to-face calls required for this program we added together the total number of prospecting calls that didn't order and the number of calls to customers who did order. It took one call to determine the quality of the prospect and 30% of the calls made would yield a customer. Therefore, 1 ÷ 30% = 3.33 sales calls to qualify prospects and one additional call to the customer who bought. The total number of sales calls required was 4.3 per sale.

To establish the cost of the sales calls we multiplied the current sales call cost by the total number of sales calls required per customer. Therefore, 4.3 x $49.60 = $213.28 in salesperson selling costs for each order. In addition, there was a cost to have the trial coffee service installed. The cost per trial service was $35.00. The total cost for trial service was established by dividing the single cost per service by the closing ratio. The total cost of the trials was $116.67 ($35.00 ÷ 30%).

The total sales expense per order was the sum of the salesperson costs and the cost of the trials. The total sales expense was $329.95 ($213.28 + $116.67). We then established the allowable direct marketing expense, $86.72, by subtracting the total planned selling expense from the current selling expenses ($416.67 - $329.95).

Because telemarketing was going to be used to generate the trials, we had to establish its cost. (We go into more detail in a later chapter on how to plan a telemarketing program.) For this example, we used the cost per telemarketing hour of $30.00. We expected to consume ten names per hour of activity and 65% of the consumed names were completed contacts. Therefore, we anticipated 6.5 completed contacts per hour. A *completed contact* is contacting the prospect and getting a decision on the offer.

We then established how many acceptances we needed to generate for each hour of activity by dividing the cost per hour by the allowable direct marketing expense. We needed to generate .35 orders per hour ($30.00 ÷ $86.72). Once we knew the completed number of contacts per hour, and the number of orders required per hour, we established the required response rate for both the total number of records used, and the actual number of people contacted with telemarketing. From the original list, this program required a 3.5% response rate (.35 ÷ 10) and of the total contacts, 5.4% (.35 ÷ 6.5).

This was a program designed only for telemarketing and the response rate required to make the program successful was modest. This type of planning can help adjust expectation levels that may not be realistic.

Even before you get into the specifics of your program, measurement has to be considered and evaluated. First, you have to determine how you'll measure the program, and how much you can afford to spend. With a firm understanding of the tolerable selling costs, you can design and plan the direct marketing effort.

Tactics

As you define the actual direct marketing tactics you'll be using, be sure you document and chart the flow of the program. *The biggest single problem we've encountered in direct marketing programs is not anticipating all the necessary and possible alternative steps.* A complete flowchart will force you to consider all of the alternatives.

You're designing an operating system when you design a direct marketing program. The database, promotional material, controls and analysis, fulfillment and marketing integration must be anticipated. By developing a complete flow of the activities, you will be forced to anticipate all of the possible alternatives. As part of the flowchart, you should consider time frames and contingencies that can affect the program.

As you can see in Illustration 2-6, you should first anticipate what lists you will use and where you will get them. These lists will then be merged to create a single mailing list. Eliminate the duplicate names on this list. Duplicates are expensive and can have a seriously adverse effect on your prospects, especially if you will be using telemarketing.

At the same time that the lists are merged and the duplicate records are eliminated, the list should be source coded to allow measurement. In our example, we planned to test three groups of customer lists and two outside lists for the direct marketing project. Each of the five lists had to be coded with special sourcing information to allow measurement.

The mail was then dropped to all of the prospects. The prospect could respond by mail or through an inbound toll-free number. These respondents were processed and, if possible, eliminated from the telephone marketing list. We recognized that a prospect who had already responded might still receive a phone call. The script was designed to address this situation.

Acceptances were sent a trial of the product and a portion of those who accepted were scheduled for a follow-up telephone selling call 14 days after the trial was mailed. The trials that did not receive a phone call received mail reminders. This was a method to test the impact of the second phone call. The second phone call also provided information on why the prospect was rejecting the trial and not purchasing the product. Any prospect that decided to purchase the product was shipped the remainder of the order and added to the customer file.

Prospects who did not respond to the mailing and who had a phone number, received a telemarketing call 15 days after the mail was dropped. If the prospects accepted the offer, they were processed similarly to the mail acceptances as described in the preceding paragraph.

From the acceptances, telemarketing and follow-up telephone calls, and other information, a complete prospect database was established for future activity. A business plan was developed from the flowchart to establish a methodology to measure the program.

The business plan for direct mail is done based on experience and known costs. Begin the business planning process with the total number of records on each list. You have to know how many of each group will be used for direct marketing. If you already have had experience with a particular list segment, use those results during the planning process. Certain segments of the customer list may perform better than others. In our example, the different response rates were based on our experience with that type of list. The total response rate, which is the weighted average for all of the list segments, was also calculated by dividing the total number of responses by the total number mailed. The total response is the sum of the response for each list category.

The total responses by list segment and total for the test are easily established using the projected response rates. Again, experience with various list segments can be used to project the closing ratio of each group of respondents. You can determine the weighted average closing ratio by dividing the total number of orders by the total number of respondents. The total number of orders is the sum of the orders for each group.

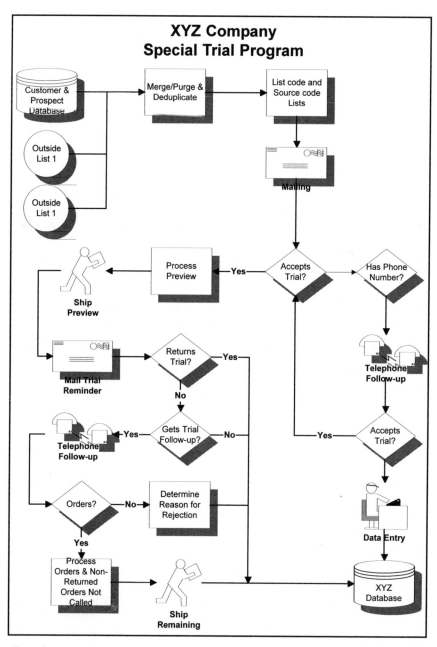

Illustration 2-6 A Sample Flowchart.

The cost for the mail is used to calculate the mailing cost for each segment of the list. The total cost is the sum of the costs by list category. Now you can easily establish the cost per responder and the cost per order.

Now that you have planned your direct mail campaign you can use a similar approach to plan your telemarketing and telephone sales activity. As you'll note from the plan, only a small portion of the list (Cust A & Cust B) had phone numbers and could be used for telemarketing. From those records that are contacted via telephone, we established the respondents and orders from telemarketing by using the same methodology employed for direct mail. As we discuss in Chapter 6, only a percentage of the list we start with will be able to be contacted with telemarketing. Note that only the total number of records used for telemarketing is included in the Total column. As you'll note in the phone activity portion of the plan, the total column reflects 5,459 total contacts, 1,411 total trials and 283 total orders.

Now let's return to our XYZ Direct Marketing example. After the initial offer to try XYZ's coffee, we planned follow-up phone calls to those prospects who accepted the offer, to try to convert the trials into orders. We used the number of anticipated contacts per hour to determine the number of calling hours required for both the initial and subsequent follow-up calling. Using the $35.00 per calling hour cost, we established the cost per responder (trial) and the cost per order.

XYZ Direct Marketing Program

	Cust A	Cust B	Cust C	List 1	List 2	Total
Mail Activity						
Tot Rec on list	1,299	6,500	6,500	4,500	2,500	21,299
Mail Response Rate	3.00%	2.00%	2.00%	1.00%	1.00%	1.73%
Total Resp/Trials	39	130	130	45	25	369
Proj Conv Mail Trial	25.00%	20.00%	20.00%	20.00%	20.00%	20.60%
Mail Orders	10	26	26	9	5	76
Mail Cost/1000	$400					
Mail Costs	$520	$2,600	$2,600	$1,800	$1,000	$8,520
Cost per Responder	$13.33	$20.00	$20.00	$40.00	$40.00	$23.09
Cost per Order	$52.00	$100.00	$100.00	$200.00	$200.00	$112.00
Phone Activity						
% of List Contactable	70.00%	70.00%	0.00%	0.00%	0.00%	70.00%
Total Contacts	909	4,550	0	0	0	5,459

% Request Trials	30.00%	25.00%	25.00%	20.00%	20.00%	25.85%
Telemktg Trials	273	1,138	0	0	0	1,411
% of Trials Converting	20.00%	20.00%	20.00%	20.00%	20.00%	20.00%
Number of Orders	55	228	0	0	0	283
Telemktg Contact/Hour	8	8	8	6	6	
No. of Init Telemktg Hrs	114	569	0	0	0	683
No. Prev F/U Telemktg Hrs	34	142	0	0	0	176
Total Telemktg Hrs	148	711	0	0	0	859
Cost/Telemktg Hr	$35.00	$35.00	$35.00	$35.00	$35.00	$35.00
Total Telemktg Costs	$5,180	$24,885	$0	$0	$0	$30,065
Cost per Trial	$18.97	$21.87	$0.00	$0.00	$0.00	$21.31
Cost per Order	$94.18	$109.14	$0.00	$0.00	$0.00	$106.24

Mail & Phone Combined

Total Previews	312	1,268	130	45	25	1,780
Total Orders	65	254	26	9	5	359

Costs

Direct Marketing	$5,700	$27,485	$2,600	$1,800	$1,000	$38,585
Cost of Goods	$4,875	$19,050	$1,950	$675	$375	$26,925
Cost of Previews	$6,240	$25,360	$2,600	$900	$500	$35,600
Commissions	$3,510	$13,716	$1,404	$486	$270	$19,386
Total Costs	$20,325	$85,611	$8,554	$3,861	$2,145	$120,496

Costs per Order	312.69	337.05	329	429	429	335.64
Revenue per Order	$900	$900	$900	$900	$900	$900

Gross Revenue	$58,500	$228,600	$23,400	$8,100	$4,500	$323,100
Contribution	$38,175	$142,989	$14,846	$4,239	$2,355	$202,604
% Rev as Contribution	65.00%	63.00%	63.00%	52.00%	52.00%	63.00%

At this point, we have established the combined anticipated results of the program. Next, we combined the results by list segment, and then calculated totals for the entire program. We summarized the total number of orders and previews by type of media and list segment.

Next we figured the costs for the direct marketing effort. We also calculated the cost of goods for orders, the cost of goods for the previews, and any commissions paid for orders by list segment.

Finally, we totaled all the costs for the project by list segment. We determined the cost per order by dividing the costs per order by the total number of orders. The gross revenue was calculated by multiplying the revenue per order by the total number of orders. The costs are subtracted from the revenue to determine the contribution by list segment. By dividing the contribution by the revenue, we determined the percent of contribution.

Contribution is the amount of gross profit made by a specific activity. In many companies, this is the method of measuring the effectiveness of any marketing program. In essence, it is the gross profit of a project after allowing for cost of goods and cost of selling including commissions. It doesn't normally include general and administrative expenses or other overhead items. The concept of contribution is more fully described in Chapter 8.

By tracking the costs and results by list segment, the effectiveness of each list and facet of the marketing program can be accurately evaluated. You'll be able to determine if the overall program was a success or failure, and which portions of your target audience were more profitable than others.

Ongoing Direct Marketing Program Planning

Once you have established the background and strategy for your direct marketing programs, each new program you execute is much easier to plan. You still want to focus on the definitions of the prospect, offer, and universe you're trying to contact, but you don't have to spend much time on the historical issue. In addition, most of your anticipated results will be based on the experiences you've had in other direct marketing efforts.

We have included a sample plan of an ongoing program for you to use as a model.

Acme Computer Corporation
Marketing and Sales Department
Sales Operating Guide

Section: **Sales Programs**
S/G: Shared Data Program   S/G #: 20-05

This guideline identifies and explains a special marketing program to generate sales leads and expand the customer base. The program uses direct
marketing to make the offer to an appropriate group of prospects, and then
leads are given to the salesperson for follow-up. Generic product names
(A,B,C etc.) have been used to avoid trademark issues.

1.0   Objective

This program is designed to develop qualified sales leads for the
salespeople to pursue. A special offer is used to get the prospect
involved and interested in Acme Computer Company. Because it
has been determined that selling a relational database as a concept
is very difficult, this promotion emphasizes the need to share information when several computers are involved. The concept of purchasing equipment has a higher perceived level of risk and is more
difficult to sell. This promotion is targeted to reduce risk and make
the decision to try an ACC system virtually painless. The offer is
targeted to make the prospect feel accepting the offer is similar to
accepting the free 30-day post installation trial they receive when
they acquire software.

After indicating an interest and concern in sharing information, the
prospect is offered the opportunity to install an Acme Computer
AC300 system for 30 days and find out for himself how easy and
flexible sharing data is with an Acme Computer System.

The Acme Computer system will be installed by the customer after
some training and assistance by Acme Computer personnel. The
system will be installed using communication and the initial target
audience will be primarily the Product A user who is also using
Personal Computers (PC's).

Section: **Sales Programs**
S/G: Shared Data Program   S/G #: 20-05

2.0 The Universe

2.1 The universe of prospects for this promotion consists of three unique groups of people.

2.1.2 Businesses that have only a Product A host system installed and are also sharing information with a network of PC's.

2.1.2 Businesses that have a Product A system, a Product B system, and a network of PC's sharing information.

2.1.3 Businesses that have a Product B host system installed, and are also sharing information with a network of PC's.

2.2 The primary target in each group of prospects is the executive or manager responsible for the data processing installation.

2.3 The prospect's objectives in accepting the free trial offer are to:

2.3.1 Determine if they can share data across multiple hosts and users.

2.3.2 Decide if Acme Computer has a potential solution for sharing data problems.

2.3.3 Test new technology and a relational database easily by installing the AC300.

2.3.4 Educate himself and his staff on an available approach for solving both current and future problems.

2.3.5 Enable users to see their own applications running with the AC300.

2.3.6 Be shown how to use simple query and 4GL approaches to access data without having to write application programs.

2.3.7   Learn first hand what is required to install hardware.

Installing hardware has been perceived as difficult and hard to learn to use. The trial program will give the prospect an opportunity to disprove this perception.

3.0 Prospect Qualification
A qualified prospect is one who:

3.1   Is currently using PC's and any of the following hosts:
Product A
Product B
Product C
Product D

3.2   Can provide a potential connection to their existing computer network and additional programmer support to implement the AC system if they are using a Product A or Product B host.

3.3   Can identify an application that will be used for data sharing after the trial.

3.4   Has reasonable credit worthiness.

3.5   Is an end-user. VAR's and resellers are excluded.

3.6   The ACC salesperson will obtain the following additional qualification information:

3.6.1   Types of hosts.

3.6.2   Number of hosts at the site.

3.6.3   Number of hosts to be used during the trial installation.

3.6.4   The application for data sharing after the trial.

Section: **Sales Programs**
S/G: Shared Data Program   S/G #: 20-05

  3.6.5   A schedule to implement the trial and the application.

  3.6.6   Application alternatives other than the ACC solution.

  3.6.7   The method of payment for the solution after the trial.
          (The availability of funding.)

  3.6.8   Agreement from the prospect that they understand the
          costs associated with continuing to use the AC system.

  3.6.9   The authority of the prospect to accept the trial.

  3.6.10 The decision criteria and names of those who will
          decide to purchase the AC system after the trial.

  3.6.11 A letter of commitment signed by the prospect. This
          letter will identify the ACC responsibilities for the
          trial, and prospect responsibilities to implement the
          trial.

  3.6.12 The criteria for evaluating the trial and what it will
          take to convince the prospect to continue using an AC
          system.

4.0 Offer

  4.1   Free trial of AC300 for 30 days.

  4.2   System will be installed for sharing of data between PC's and
        supported hosts.

  4.3   ACC will provide training, system, installation support and
        guidance on conversion of data files to the AC300.

  4.4   Prospect will provide:

        4.4.1   Files for use on the AC300.

      4.4.2   Users who will be trained by the prospect with ACC assistance.

      4.4.3   Site and site preparation including electrical and environmental changes if needed.

      4.4.4   Communication facilities.

      4.4.5   Host and PC's to work with the AC300. The PC will have a minimum configuration of at least 233mz with 400 megabytes free.

5.0   Direct Marketing Approach

    5.1   Flowchart Explanation

      5.1.1   Lists will be acquired for targeting the offer and the direct marketing program. The internal lists of prior respondents and customers will be used as the base list to start all activities. The Computer Intelligence Corporation (CIC) list of Product A systems will also be used. A subscription list of Product A systems will be acquired for direct mail and telemarketing activities.

             A Publisher's Professional list or Gary Slaughter Compiled list will be used.

             The lists will be name-directed whenever possible. The target contact will be the director or manager of data processing.

             Additional lists will be tested to include Product B sites. The same list sources will be used but will specifically be targeted for Product B. During the initial mailings, only Product A users and Telco managers will be used.

Section: **Sales Programs**
S/G: Shared Data Program   S/G #: 20-05

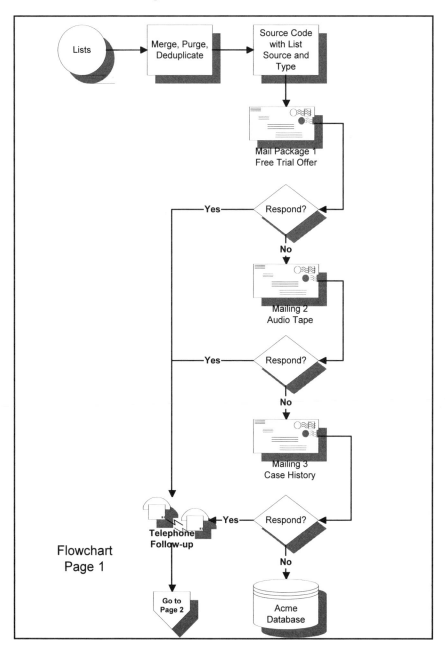

Section: **Sales Programs**

S/G: Shared Data Program   S/G #: 20-05

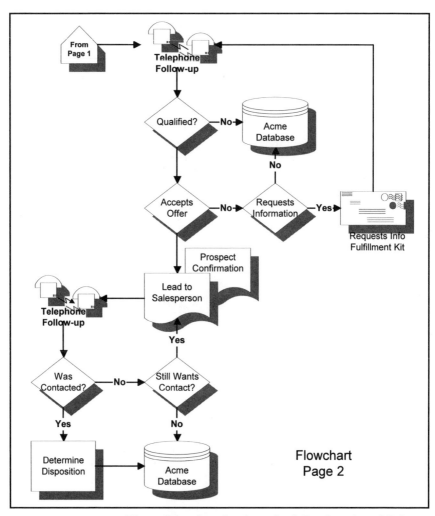

If possible, sites that have both Product A and B hosts will be identified and coded on the list to allow testing of all types of prospects.

If telemarketing is used, the combined unduplicated list will be sent to a service bureau specializing in appending phone numbers to the record. This will be

Section: **Sales Programs**
S/G: Shared Data Program   S/G #: 20-05

done in parallel to the mailing. This process normally takes about two weeks and is about 50% effective on the list supplied to the service bureau.

5.1.2 The lists will be sent to an outside service bureau and combined to eliminate duplicate names and sites. The primary list will be the Acme Computer customer list, followed by the former respondent list. CIC will be next in the hierarchy and the subscription lists will be last.

5.1.3 The service bureau will code each record with the list source:

List Source	System	Code
Acme Computer Customer	Unknown	ACC0
Acme Computer Customer	Product A	ACC1
Acme Computer Customer	Product B	ACC2
Acme Computer Customer	Product C	ACC3
Acme Computer Customer	Other	ACC4
Acme Computer Prospect	Unknown	ACP0
Acme Computer Prospect	Product A	ACP1
Acme Computer Prospect	Product B	ACP2
Acme Computer Prospect	Product C	ACP3
Acme Computer Prospect	Other	ACP4
CIC	Unknown	CIC0
CIC	Product A	CIC1
CIC	Product B	CIC2
CIC	Product C	CIC3
CIC	Other	CIC4
Name of Publication	Unknown	SU10
Name of Publication	Product A	SU11
Name of Publication	Product B	SU12
Name of Publication	Product C	SU13
Name of Publication	Other	SU14

Acme Computer will only offer complete coverage in selected cities. The list will be extracted to only include selected sectional centers that are geographi-

Section: **Sales Programs**
S/G: Shared Data Program   S/G #: 20-05

cally within the covered areas. This will be explained in a memo prior to the mailing.

5.1.4   All of the un-duplicated names will be mailed package number 1.

5.1.5   Respondents to the first mailing will be sent to the local sales office for telemarketing and actual follow-up.

5.1.6   Nonrespondents to the mailing will be mailed package number 1 again. This will be mailing #2.

5.1.7   Respondents to the second mailing will be sent to the local sales office for telemarketing and face-to-face sales follow-up.

5.1.8   Nonrespondents to the second mailing will be mailed a third mailing package.

5.1.9   A database will be developed and only those records that are the property of Acme Computer will be included (Acme Computer Customers, Acme Computer Prospects, CIC).

5.1.10 If the prospect is qualified during the telemarketing effort, the prospect will be offered a visit from an ACC salesperson to review the free trial program and discuss how it can be implemented. The mail solicitations will offer the prospect the opportunity to try the AC system for 30 days free. The salesperson will determine the prospect's qualification level in order to receive the free trial.

5.1.11 The prospect may refuse the offer and ask for additional information. This group will be fulfilled with an information package.

Section: **Sales Programs**

S/G: Shared Data Program   S/G #: 20-05

Ten days after the information package is mailed, this group will be recontacted via telemarketing to try to convert them into sales leads.

5.1.12 The names of unqualified prospects and those prospects that refuse the offer will be updated on the database and held for possible future activity.

5.1.13 Accepters of the offer will receive a letter confirming their acceptance, and giving the name of the salesperson or sales manager by whom they will be contacted.

A sales lead will be sent to the salesperson. Both the confirmation letter and lead will be mailed within two business days of the initial contact.

5.1.14 All leads will be recontacted via telemarketing 30 to 45 days after they were mailed to determine the disposition of the situation. If the lead wasn't contacted by a salesperson, they will be offered the opportunity to be contacted.

5.1.15 If the prospect wants to be recontacted, the lead's name will be telephoned to the regional director and mailed the same day.

5.1.16 If the prospect was contacted, the disposition will be determined and the database updated.

6.0   Financial Projections

Anticipated Results

Number of Records for Analysis	20,000
% of Records lost via merge, purge, de-duplicate	25.00%
Number of records lost via merge, purge, de-duplicate	5,000
Records receiving pre-mailing	15,000

Section: **Sales Programs**
S/G: Shared Data Program   S/G #: 20-05

Group	AC Prosp	Dec Prof	CMP	Total
Mail				
Total Records - Mail #1	3,000	10,000	2,000	15,000
Mail Resp Rate	1.00%	1.00%	1.00%	1.00%
Total Respondents	30	100	20	150
% Leads of Respondents	60%	60%	60%	60%
Leads	18	60	12	90
% Trials of Leads	60%	60%	60%	
Trials	11	36	7	54
% Orders of Trials	30%	30%	30%	
Orders	3	11	2	16
Total Records - Mail #2	2,970	9,900	1,980	14,850
Mail Resp Rate	1.00%	1.00%	1.00%	1.00%
Total Respondents	30	99	20	149
% Leads of Respondents	60%	60%	60%	60%
Leads	18	59	12	89
% Trials of Leads	60%	60%	60%	
Trials	11	35	7	53
% Orders of Trials	30%	30%	30%	
Orders	3	11	2	16
Total Records - Mail #3	2,940	9,801	1,960	14,701
Mail Resp Rate	1.00%	1.00%	1.00%	1.00%
Total Respondents	29	98	20	147
% Leads of Respondents	60%	60%	60%	60%
Leads	17	59	12	88
% Trials of Leads	60%	60%	60%	
Trials	10	35	7	52
% Orders of Trials	30%	30%	30%	
Orders	3	11	2	16
Total Mail Results (3 Mailings)				
Respondents	89	297	60	446
Leads	53	178	36	267
Trials	32	106	21	159
Orders	9	33	6	4
Total Mail Results (2 Mailings)				
Respondents	60	199	40	299
Leads	36	119	24	179
Trials	22	71	14	107
Orders	6	22	4	32

Costs
Mail Costs
Cost per Direct Mail Piece for Package 1 (w/postage) $1.89

Section: **Sales Programs**
S/G: Shared Data Program   S/G #: 20-05

Cost per Direct Mail Piece for Package 2 (w/postage)	$2.89
Cost per Direct Mail Piece for Package 3 (w/postage)	$1.89
Cost per Literature Fulfillment Kit	$3.00
Cost per Lead Confirmation Mailing	$1.50

List Costs

Cost per Name with Processing	$0.15
Cost per Name for Phone number	$0.30
Cost per Lead Processed	$1.50

Telemarketing Costs

Cost per Telephone Call	$5.00

One Time Costs

Development	$20,000

List

Initial Name	$0.00	$4,500.00	$900.00	$5,400.00
Phone Number	$0.00	$0.00	$0.00	$0.00
Lead Processing	$79.50	$267.00	$54.00	$400.50
Total List Costs	$79.50	$4,767.00	$954.00	$5,800.50

Direct Mail

Package #1	$5,670.00	$18,900.00	$3,780.00	$28,350.00
Package #2	$8,670.00	$28,900.00	$5,780.00	$43,350.00
Package #3	$5,670.00	$18,900.00	$3,780.00	$28,350.00
Lit Req Fulfill	$51.00	$177.00	$36.00	$264.00
Lead Confirmation	$79.50	$267.00	$54.00	$400.50
Total Mail Costs	$20,140.50	$67,144.00	$13,430.00	$100,714.50

Telemarketing Costs

Lead F/U Call	$445.00	$1,485.00	$300.00	$2,230.00
Tot Telemktg Cost	$445.00	$1,485.00	$300.00	$2,230.00

Development Costs				$20,000.00
Total Costs	$20,665.00	$73,396.00	$14,684.00	$128,745.00
Total Leads	53	178	36	267
Total Trials	32	106	21	159
Total Orders	9	33	6	48
Cost per Lead	$389.91	$412.34	$407.89	$482.19

Section: **Sales Programs**
S/G:　　Shared Data Program　　　　　　　　　　S/G #: 20-05

Cost per Trial	$645.78	$692.42	$699.24	$809.72
Cost per Order	$2,296.11	$2,224.12	$2,447.33	$2,682.19
Avg Order Size	$95,000	$95,000	$95,000	$95,000
Total Revenue	$855,000	$3,135,000	$570,000	$4,560,000
% Rev/Direct Mktg	2.42%	2.34%	2.58%	2.82%

List

Initial Name	$0.00	$3,000.00	$600.00	$3,600.00
Phone Number	$0.00	$0.00	$0.00	$0.00
Lead Processing	$54.00	$178.50	$36.00	$268.50
Total List Costs	$54.00	$3,178.50	$636.00	$3,868.50

Direct Mail

Package #1	$5,670.00	$18,900.00	$3,780.00	$28,350.00
Package #2	$8,583.30	$28,611.00	$5,722.20	$42,916.50
Package #3	$0.00	$0.00	$0.00	$0.00
Lit Req Fulfill	$72.00	$240.00	$48.00	$360.00
Lead Confirmation	$54.00	$178.50	$36.00	$268.50
Total Mail Costs	$14,379.30	$47,929.50	$9,586.20	$71,895.00

Telemarketing Costs

Lead F/U Call	$300.00	$995.00	$200.00	$1,495.00
Tot Telemktg Cost	$300.00	$995.00	$200.00	$1,495.00
Development Costs				$20,000.00
Total Costs	$14,733.30	$52,103.00	$10,422.20	$97,258.50
Total Leads	36	119	24	17
Total Trials	22	71	14	107
Total Orders	6	22	4	32
Cost per Lead	$409.26	$437.84	$434.26	$543.34
Cost per Trial	$669.70	$733.85	$744.44	$908.96
Cost per Order	$2,455.55	$2,368.32	$2,605.55	$3,039.33
Revenue per Order	$95,000	$95,000	$95,000	$95,000
Total Revenue	$570,000	$2,090,000	$380,000	$3,040,000
% Rev/Direct Mktg	2.58%	2.49%	2.74%	3.20%

Section: **Sales Programs**
S/G: Shared Data Program   S/G #: 20-05

7.0 Direct Mail Copy Platforms

   7.1 Package #1 - Initial Free Trial Offer

      This package will create a high impact, perhaps in a three dimensional format. It will introduce the concept of sharing data, and call the prospect to respond to Acme Computer to have a salesperson visit, and explain how the prospect can take advantage of the free trial offer.

      This mail package will paint a conceptual picture of the sharing data problem and convince the prospect that they are experiencing this problem. After reading the mail package, the prospect will want to learn more about how the Acme Computer system can help solve the data sharing problem.

      The proliferation of PC's magnifies the intensity of the data sharing problem, and the prospect should be interested in learning how to resolve this issue.

      The target group of data processing managers receives mail from a large number of vendors, and this mail piece will have to break through the clutter.

      The response vehicle will be a *BRC* (Business Reply Card) or *BRE* (Business Reply Envelope) which will supply a minimum of qualification information. A toll free phone number, e-mail address, and Web site might also be utilized.

   7.2 Package #2 - Audio tape free trial offer

      This package will create a high impact, perhaps in a three dimensional format. It will introduce the concept of sharing data and call the prospect to respond to Acme Computer by allowing a salesperson to visit and explain how to take advantage of the free trial. Package #2 will follow mailing package #1 by about three weeks.

      This package might also be tested as a stand-alone mailing.

This mail package will also paint a conceptual picture of the sharing data problem and convince the prospect that they are experiencing a similar problem. After reading the mail package, the prospect will want to learn more about how the Acme Computer system can help solve any data sharing problem.

The proliferation of PC's magnifies the intensity of the data sharing problem, and prospects should be interested in learning how to resolve this issue.

The target group of data processing managers receives mail from a large number of vendors, and this mail piece will have to break through the clutter.

The response vehicle will be a BRC or BRE which will supply a minimum of qualification information. A toll free phone number, e-mail address, and web site might also be utilized.

7.3 Package #3 - Offering Free Trial of AC300

This package also will create a strong impact, perhaps in a three dimensional format. It too will introduce the concept of sharing data, and call the prospect to respond to Acme Computer by allowing a salesperson to visit and explain how the prospect can take advantage of the free trial. The third package will follow mailing package #2 by about three weeks. This package might also be tested as a stand-alone mailing.

This mail package will paint a conceptual picture of the sharing data problem and the prospect will identify with or feel he has the problem too. After reading the mail package, the prospect will want to learn more about how the Acme Computer system can help solve their data sharing problem.

The continuing proliferation of PC's magnifies the intensity of the data sharing problem, and they should be interested in learning how to resolve this issue.

Section: **Sales Programs**
S/G: Shared Data Program   S/G #: 20-05

The target group of data processing managers receives mail from a large number of vendors, and this mail piece will have to break through the clutter.

The response vehicle will be a BRC or BRE which will supply a minimum of qualification information. A toll free phone number, e-mail address, and web site might also be utilized.

7.4 Lead Confirmation Mailing

This mailing will confirm to the prospect that they will be contacted by an AC sales representative soon who will explain the free trial of the AC300 system.

The purpose of this mailing is to open a door of communication if the salesperson is late in getting back to the prospect. It acknowledges that AC knows the prospect has accepted their offer.

7.5 Send Literature Fulfillment

Package #1 initially will be used to fulfill literature requests. Ultimately a separate package to fulfill literature requests will be developed.

We used an outline format for this business plan in order to make additional programs easy to test and document. You should try to establish a consistent format for developing your own follow-up programs.

Planning Summarized

By now your business plan looks like a major tome. It contains as much as you'll ever want to know about your company, why you need direct marketing, and what results you expect from the direct marketing program. As we said at the start of this chapter, reading about business planning isn't very exciting. Most of the information is common sense and has probably already been developed within your company.

The development of the program you're going to implement is the only fun part of planning. It may seem easier to just start doing something, but without prior planning, your chances for failure are very high. Much of the remainder of this book describes different tactical approaches to implementing business-to-business direct marketing.

By forcing yourself to examine the basics of your business, you'll ensure that the implementation of direct marketing will have the highest chance to succeed. Your company organization may require unique implementation considerations and reporting programs. Establishing the current selling costs will allow you to effectively measure and evaluate the direct marketing effort. Finally, the overall planning phase will help clarify why you need direct marketing and what results you should expect.

Once you've developed a documented direct marketing business plan, it will be easy to communicate your program to others within your company and to outside vendors you might need. In addition, the documented plan will give you a basis from which to build new programs.

We know how hard it is to read about planning, but using some of the examples we've given, we hope you find the actual planning phase easier to accomplish. Don't sell business planning short. The effort you spend up front could be the best investment you'll make to ensure that your direct marketing program is successful.

Chapter Three:

Lead Generation Programs

Real World

Generating sales leads for a field sales force may be the most frustrating direct marketing campaign to launch. As the direct marketing manager, usually you have no control over the ultimate success of the project and it's almost impossible to measure the results. Let's discuss ways to improve this situation.

Virtually every business-to-business direct marketing professional can tell war stories of attempted lead generation projects that were never continued because the program's results couldn't be measured. The reason lead programs can be difficult to measure is due to not understanding the environment. We, the communications and direct marketing departments, perceive our mission to be to help the sales force by generating sales leads. Yet, the field organization frequently has a different perception of our role. They feel it's "the staff at headquarters, in their ivory towers" versus "the field

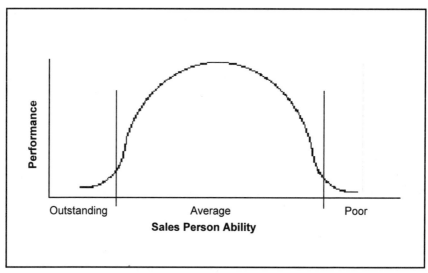

Illustration 3-1: The bell-shaped curve as it relates to a typical sales force.

force, where the rubber meets the road." If you examine the field's side of the story, their perception is often partially accurate.

Most lead generation program failures occur due to one or two fatal flaws. First, in many instances, the direct marketing program is designed with little or no input from the field sales force. As a result the field feels suspicious, distrustful and downright hostile. They think we have only encumbered them with additional reporting requirements and a lot of paper work and supposed leads whose value has not been explained.

Second, lead generation programs are often designed for the outstanding performers of the sales force. This group will make anything work and often doesn't need any help. We ask this group to qualify and sell the lead and then report back on the success of the lead program. This poor targeting has probably done more damage to lead programs than any other factor.

Why? The performance of a sales organization will normally fall into a bell-shaped curve, similar to Illustration 3-1. The left end of the curve, the outstanding salesperson, needs little or no help. However, if sent leads, this group is most likely to follow-up and even generate orders. They are not at all threatened by outside help and support.

The right end of the curve, the poor salesperson, wants help but has trouble accepting it. He is threatened and constantly looks for excuses. His excuse for failure will be directed at the poor leads we are sending to him.

The group in the middle, the average salesperson, is where your program should be targeted. If you can move this group to the left, even a small amount, you can have a dramatic impact on the success of your company.

Our goals in this chapter are to explain how you can make a lead generation program work; how you can build measurement programs on the quality and results of the lead program that you can control; and how you can solicit and get the support of the sales force in your program.

The Use of Sales Time

The statement, "the only real resource we have in business is time," could not be more appropriately applied than in sales. The effective use of time is the key to the salesperson's success. The more time the salesperson has in front of a prospect or customer, the better the odds of making a sale.

Sales managers have to be very selective when they require the sales force to perform functions that take them away from contact with prospects or customers.

A well-known high technology company measures their entire field force at least annually to determine how time is being used. The results are used to determine what resources are needed for products and services and how the organization might be improved. The company's field reporting system determined that only 33% of work time was being spent face-to-face with customers. It is alarming to find that two-thirds of the sales force's time was being spent in non-customer related activities.

This situation sounds extreme. Yet, you may be surprised to learn that within your own company your sales force may actually spend only half their time in front of customers. Vacations, holidays and personal time off probably take more than one month out of every year away from available time to sell. Consider the sales contests and travel awards you run and you probably lose another week or two. Education and product training time also take away selling time from the sales force. Factor in the weekly sales meetings, and time devoted to writing reports and special projects and it is easy to see how as much as 50% of available selling time can be lost.

We've already mentioned that the average cost of a sales call continues to escalate. The cost of the sales call is approximately $400.

When you couple this high cost with how little time salespeople actually spend in front of customers and prospects, Illustration 3-2 becomes even more meaningful. This diagram illustrates that most selling time is spent finding qualified prospects and making them aware of your offerings.

Your objective is to invert the way sales time is spent to correspond with Illustration 3-3. Direct marketing should be used to move the prospect through the identification, qualification, awareness and interest stages. Of

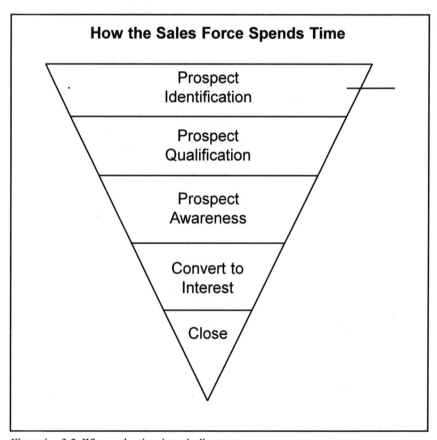

Illustration 3-2: Where sales time is typically spent.

course the salespeople will not be completely eliminated during these stages, but their involvement should be reduced substantially.

If this is such a simple concept, why then isn't it happening naturally? Any salespeople will readily agree that prospect identification and qualification isn't something they like to do. The sales force would prefer to have these functions done for them. Why then do we have such a difficult time implementing lead generation programs with the sales force?

No one has a complete answer to this difficult question. We speculate that the sales force doesn't believe that anyone can perform this function as well as they do and their performance is ultimately based on new leads. They don't trust anyone else to do their job, especially management staff who

Illustration 3-3: Where we would like sales time spent.

don't have regular contact with the field. Also, often their prior experience with leads hasn't been good. Finally, the sales force typically creates the time to do the identification and qualification phases. If the sales force had an adequate and ongoing supply of highly qualified referrals, their opinions and work habits might change. This is not a short-term problem with short-term answers.

Lead Generation Questions

As you begin to plan your lead generation program, you will need to resolve a number of critical questions. Illustration 3-4 identifies the six major issues.

1) What is a good lead?

Some of the experiences we had in designing this lead program at another high-tech company will probably sound familiar to you.

The lead program was a test to support 90 salespeople in five branch offices. The salespeople were responsible for selling new account, first-time users of computer systems. During the design phases of the project, we brought 16 of the salespeople together to get their opinions on several issues.

The 16 salespeople were asked to define a good lead. We wrote the definitions on charts as the salespeople gave their requirements. When we were finished there were 21 different definitions of a good lead.

It is intriguing that while the success of any lead program will ultimately be judged by the quantity and quality of the leads generated, we have yet to get a group of salespeople to agree on the definition of a good lead. On only one point do they agree: A good lead is one that closes. Salespeople feel that we direct marketers should be able to foretell that a specific lead will purchase a product or service.

Later, we will discuss some issues you need to address to establish the quality of a sales lead. During the planning session for this

---

Lead Program Questions to Resolve

1) What is a good lead?

2) How many leads are enough?

3) Which is worse -- no leads or too many?

4) How do you track leads?

5) What about turnover?

6) How do you get feedback?

Illustration 3-4: The six major issues involved in a lead generation program.

example program, we ultimately agreed that a good lead was one that would specifically answer the following questions based on the sales group's predetermined qualifications:

- Were they evaluating a hardware/software purchase for administrative support personnel within the next 12 months?
- When were they planning to acquire the system?
- How many administrative support people did they have?
- Had they added any administrative support personnel in the last 12 months?
- Did they anticipate adding administrative support people in the next 12 months?
- Did they have an Accounts Receivable problem?
- Did they have an Inventory Control problem?

Any prospect who was evaluating a product in the next 12 months was considered a lead and sent to the sales force. The salespeople had determined that they wanted an opportunity to sell any prospect who was in the process of product evaluation. This was a serious flaw in the structure of this program and will be discussed later.

2) How many leads are enough?

This question is also very difficult to get a consensus opinion from the sales force. They all agree that marketing should just send them the sales leads and they will handle them.

The same group of salespeople originally said that they wanted as many as 20 leads per day. We had discussed with them our plan to use direct mail and telemarketing to generate the leads. Our plan was to give them their required number of leads every day. This was a new concept to the sales force; they had never experienced a sustained and ongoing flow of leads.

The sales force we were dealing with was selling computer systems including both hardware and software. Like most significant capital equipment decisions, it took at least three sales calls to sell the product. Given 20 leads per day, each salesperson would have to make 20 follow-up calls to qualify the lead and schedule an appointment. If each phone call took only 15 minutes, the sales force had just signed up for five hours of telemarketing every day. We were able to convince the sales force to take only three sales leads per day.

This ultimately proved to be about three times as many leads as the salespeople could handle. A lot of the problems associated with the leads really tied back to our definition of a good lead. In a 90-day period, we generated over 12,000 leads for the 90 salespeople.

The correct number of leads is directly related to the quality of follow-up required and the number of orders you want to generate as a result of the lead program. As discussed in the business planning chapter, the key to the success of any program is the expectation level. You'll never be able to completely replace the identification and qualification functions of the sales force. In the beginning, you should anticipate that only a small portion of the salesperson's business will come from the lead program. As the program gains credibility, you can expect a higher contribution from the leads.

3) Which is worse -- No leads or too many?

We have constantly asked this question of direct marketing executives and sales executives alike. The answers seem to follow a pattern.

The sales executive, sales manager, and salesperson always answer that no leads are the worse alternative. The sales force only wants an opportunity to sell; they never think about the issue of being unable to follow up on a lead. A lead to a salesperson means a potential order, and that is all he considers.

On the other hand, the direct marketer knows it's almost impossible to measure the results of a lead program. Generating excess leads only complicates the problem.

In addition, when you send too many leads to the sales force, all the leads become poor quality. The sales force can't handle the volume, therefore the leads can't be that good. Too many leads is normally a turn off to the sales organization. They perceive all the leads to be of lower quality and tend not to follow up, or they screen the leads and follow up selectively. This type of program tends to be non-recoverable; you can't expect the sales force to ever accept the leads positively in the future.

A final point about too many leads: a prospect who has been promised that a salesperson will call, expects to be contacted. When you fail to follow up, how do you think this prospect feels about your company and products? Quite probably he will be upset and may never do business with you. We call the concept of sending too many leads to follow up "poisoning your universe."

Obviously, the right number of leads is the amount on which the sales force can consistently follow up. No leads, although probably better from a direct marketing point of view, will yield no business. Too many leads can destroy the opportunity for the direct marketing program to succeed.

4) How do you track leads?

Within this issue are a number of points that need special attention for a successful generation program.

- **There must be specific objectives.**

    Lead programs frequently fail because of unrealistic expectations. For example, only a portion of the leads will actually be followed up and only a portion of the leads followed up will actually buy.

    Our experience indicates that about 15% of sales leads are contacted by a salesperson. Even in the best of situations, you can expect only about 30% of the leads that are generated to be followed up. This sounds somewhat absurd, but nevertheless it's true. Salespeople will attempt to reach a prospect and if they are unable to contact the individual after several attempts, they will move on to someone else.

    In the best of programs we are surprised to receive a 40% follow up rate. We have seen follow up levels below 10%, especially if you are providing leads to a third-party sales force. We believe that the most difficult aspect in creating a lead generation program is getting the salespeople to follow-up.

    Only a certain amount of leads actually followed up will buy. Perhaps you're expecting 25% of the leads to close. With excellent cooperation from the sales force you get 40% follow up. That means you will actually achieve 12% of the leads closing. Not a bad program, but if you expected 25% to close, the program will be perceived as a failure.

    You must get everyone involved in the program to agree on very specific objectives. Objectives should be directly tied to revenue and orders. All too often lead generation program objectives are tied to the number of responses and leads and the program is not measured based on revenue and orders. Senior management is ultimately interested in bottom-line results, not the activity generated from the lead generation campaign. If you don't measure the campaign to include orders and revenue, it will probably never be considered a success.

One way to mitigate this situation is to set expectations, measure results, and report qualified leads. Generation of qualified leads, unlike sales, is under your control.

- **There must be commitment.**

Once you've established reasonable expectations for the lead program, everyone involved needs to commit to the project. Frequently, the direct marketer is behind a project, but sales and sales management haven't truly signed up. Only when everyone involved in the project agrees to meet specific expectations and responsibilities does the effort stand a chance to succeed.

Commitment to the lead program must begin with the salesperson, and continue all the way up to the V.P. of sales. The best situation is to have the sales organization involved in the design of the program. The more ownership the sales organization has, the higher the odds for success.

The lead program cannot succeed without feedback on the quality of the leads and how they can be improved. If management and the sales force aren't committed to giving feedback and helping to track the leads, the program will fail.

As we'll discuss later, you can design measurement campaigns which provide feedback directly from the prospect and have a measurement valve that isn't so dependent upon the salesperson. We suggest you plan on feedback from both the salespeople and the prospect.

- **The system must be heuristic.**

Heuristic means to teach yourself and to learn from experience. With specific agreement to realistic objectives, commitment to follow up the leads and provide feedback, the program can become heuristic. As you learn about the quality and quantity of the leads program, you can use the feedback to improve and make the program better. Similar to the computers used in recent man vs. computer chess competitions, the lead system can continue to learn from itself.

These issues truly affect our ability to track and understand the results of the lead generation program. Before you start the project, the issue of tracking the results needs to be resolved. When we looked back on this program we ultimately made substantial changes because we didn't originally anticipate these issues. However, we constantly had to return and resell management on why the project needed to be continued and expanded.

5) What about turnover?

The real question is: What happens to your leads when the salesperson leaves? In most programs we've reviewed, the leads leave with the salesperson. It is not uncommon for sales representatives to keep copies of leads or enter the lead information in a database.

Leads are expensive. After the lead has been followed up only once, it has become downright valuable. You probably have invested $300 to $500 in each lead. It is difficult to generate a qualified lead for less than $150. Part of designing your lead program must address the inevitable turnover within the field force and what will happen to the leads.

6) How do you get feedback?

As we mentioned earlier, feedback is one of the most critical elements in the ultimate success or failure of the lead program. The design of the lead document can radically affect the feedback of the program.

For example, the way you communicate the lead to the salesperson must make it easy for them to provide feedback. If you're still distributing your leads on paper, the lead document must be easy for the salesperson to return.

To facilitate analysis, once the document or lead information is returned, you may want to establish a coding plan to enable the salesperson to quickly identify the quality of the lead.

In our example program we established several questions with coded answers that allowed us to evaluate the lead and recognize any additional activity required to help convert the lead to an order.

Lead Qualification Reporting

Disposition Codes

1) Actively working - prospect has agreed to further contacts.
2) Prospect not handled by this location.
3) Prospect referred to another location.
4) Prospect ordered.
5) Already a customer.
6) Prospect rejected us:
   a) They are too small
   b) We are too expensive
   c) We are not competitive
   d) Performance
   e) Deferred decision
   f) Satisfied with current
   g) Other
7) Prospect wants to be deleted from our files.
8) Prospect bought competition within the last year.
9) Unable to contact the prospect within the last 30 days.
10) Other - _____
   _____

Lead Quality Analysis

Likelihood to buy
1) Definitely will buy
2) Probably will buy
3) Uncertain
4) Probably won't buy
5) Definitely won't buy

Likelihood to buy from you
1) Definitely will buy
2) Probably will buy
3) Uncertain
4) Probably won't buy
5) Definitely won't buy

Timing to buy
1) Immediate
2) Less then 3 months
3) Less then 6 months
4) Less then 1 year
5) One year or more
6) Probably won't

 Disposition Code

 Likelihood to buy

 Likelihood to buy from you

 Timing to buy

Illustration 3-5: A typical lead quality reporting mechanism.

Illustration 3-5 depicts the reporting system we designed. Unfortunately, we had to change the salesperson's lead form three times to include this system. It is always difficult to change a program after it has started. By anticipating how you'll receive feedback about the lead, you can avoid problems in the future.

Using lead forms in past years, salespeople only had to fill in the appropriate codes and return the copies to the lead generation center. All the lead information was included on the form but the salespeople were asked to update outdated information. We anticipated giving the salespeople and the sales manager a copy of the lead. Forms made that task easy. As we all know, computers and other capital equipment aren't sold on the first sales call. We provided an extra copy to report the initial call disposition and the final disposition of the lead. We even provided a binder with tabs to make territory organization easier.

The internet and sales automation systems now make it easier for the salesperson to get information about their prospects. One would think that it would also be easier to get feedback. Salespeople are uncomfortable providing management and headquarters with information about their customers, prospects and territories. Automation has not seemed to improve our ability to track and accurately measure sales leads. As we'll discuss, the best source of measurement and information about lead programs will probably come from direct contact with the prospect.

In the electronic lead management era, you can use a similar coding system as described earlier to facilitate feedback information from the salespeople.

The feedback on lead quality is as important as the lead generation itself. Most times this is an area that is overlooked. You can't measure and control a program without information on the lead and the effectiveness of the program.

Lead Quality

As we said, every salesperson has a different definition of a good lead. They rarely agree on criteria and have a difficult time expressing what qualities constitute a qualified lead.

To establish what makes a lead qualified, you must consider four categories. These categories are especially helpful if you're going to use telemarketing to qualify the lead prior to making a sales call.

As an aside, one of the problems in using telemarketing is the ease in which you can get additional information. Often people confuse lead generation and market research when performing the lead qualification process. Always ask yourself whether the information you're requesting is really necessary to establish if a prospect is qualified as a sales lead.

The major categories to use in lead qualification are :

> **Money**
> **Authority**
> **Need**
> **Desire**

Hopefully, if the prospect is interested in your product or service, they can afford to purchase from you. In reality, there are three areas that can help financially justify almost any business decision:

1) *Displaceable Expenses*: Dollars already being expended for similar or like services. You may find displaceable expenses in related areas of the business, as well as in the primary area you're trying to address.

2) *Avoidable Expenses*: Dollars that the company can avoid having to spend in the future, if they buy your solution.

3) *Increased Revenue and Business Growth*: Dollars that the company might generate due to better procedures or approaches to their business. This area is often addressed as intangible. Many business decisions are made on emotion based on the intangible value to be derived. For example, a computer that allows instant access to order status will improve customer satisfaction and service. It is very difficult to attribute savings or revenue to improved customer service. However, we cannot overlook these 'intangibles' as a primary justification.

As you try to establish the ability of a company to buy your solution, don't get bogged down with unnecessary details. Sometimes it's nice to have additional facts, but they don't really improve the quality of the lead. Sales managers often forget that the salespeople will generate their own level of information. You invest too much time getting unnecessary details just to qualify the sales lead.

Authority is often difficult to establish. To determine if the person to whom you're trying sell to has the authority to buy from you, is tough. Ego being what it is, some business people cannot admit to people outside their own company that they have limited power. Lead quality normally suffers the most in this area. Many techniques can be tried to subtly establish buying authority. However, the best method is to ask the prospect directly if they can make the decision to buy your product or service.

Establishing need is the area we all tend to over complicate. Try to limit your questions and probes to one or two major criteria. Keep in mind that you're trying to qualify a sales lead that will be followed up by a salesperson. The salesperson will sell the product or service. Many companies perform too much market research under the guise of trying to determine prospect need.

Finally, a lead isn't qualified until the prospect has accepted the offer and agreed to see a salesperson. During the example program, we initially sent a prospect's name to the sales force when the prospect indicated plans to purchase in the next 12 months. The prospect did not indicate any desire to talk to the salesperson. Obviously, when the salesperson called, the prospect wasn't certain of the purpose of the call. The quality of the lead was immediately questionable in the mind of the salesperson.

The whole process of establishing lead quality should be started in a meeting with the salespeople. Write the four major categories on a white board and ask the sales force what one single question in each area, if answered, would help to confirm the quality of the lead. You'll ultimately get more than one question. To eliminate the other questions, try to determine if the information is absolutely necessary to establish the qualification of the lead.

You can sometimes resolve the money, authority, and desire issues with one question that introduces the price of your product and an offer. Prospects may respond that they can't afford it or that they have to talk to someone else before deciding. Remember, a prospect isn't qualified unless they agree to become a referral.

Lead Qualification -
The Prospect Is The Only One That Counts!

Very often lead generation programs include a qualifying step to determine if the respondent merits a follow-up by a salesperson. This qualifying step is targeted to ensure that the prospect is qualified based on our criteria. When do we consider the interest and desire of the prospect?

Does the prospect have the money to afford your proposition? The underlying assumption to this qualification issue is that the prospect has some expectation as to the cost of your product or service. In many lead generation programs, companies avoid price discussions for fear of reducing the response. You can introduce price in relation to monthly terms or the minimum price required for your basic unit. We are not advocating baiting your prospects, but by identifying some price point, you'll eliminate the totally unqualified response.

Does your respondent have the authority to participate in the buying decision for your product? Most leads are not qualified because the respondent doesn't have the authority. As many as 85% of unqualified leads are attributed to this area. We do not advocate asking prospects a lot of questions to empirically determine whether they are qualified. Authority is the exception. We suggest that all lead generation efforts include a basic question to determine the decision authority of the respondent. One question that works particularly well for us is:

Which of the following best describes your involvement in a decision to acquire _____?

   1)   You make the decision.
   2)   You investigate and recommend.
   3)   The decision is made elsewhere in the company.

It always surprises us how often this qualification question is answered. This question does work effectively in establishing authority.

Non-decision makers should not be sent to salespeople for follow-up activity. If the prospect answers with a 3, ask for the name and phone number of the person who is responsible. If the respondent is not involved in the decision, you'll never get a salesperson to follow-up. This group of respondents will require a fulfillment approach other than a face-to-face contact.

Does the prospect have a need or problem that your product can fulfill? In order to sell anything a prospect must have a problem or need that your product or service will address. Need is not necessarily product related. A company having a problem collecting accounts receivables may find a computer useful in helping to solve this problem. The need isn't for the computer, but to improve accounts receivable.

Finally, does your prospect have a desire to find a solution to their need or problem? Once a prospect recognizes that a problem exists, unless they have demonstrated a desire to overcome the need, they are not qualified. A prospect must accept an offer to do something, demonstrating desire.

Many companies will develop sophisticated questionnaires to determine if a prospect should be contacted by a salesperson. These companies believe that to be considered a lead, a prospect must meet certain pre-established criteria.

A few years ago we learned a very valuable lesson. Prospects who don't meet our qualification criteria will often buy. Back in the mid 70's while selling computers, we often thought that a business had to have at least 1 million in annual sales to afford a computer. We uncovered a prospect in the fuel oil business who was much smaller, yet decided to buy a computer. Should we have refused the order?

This seems like an absurd question, yet so many lead programs focus on data like annual sales, instead of money, authority, need and desire. These programs try to capture information that will reveal if the prospect has money and need. If the criteria is met, these same lead generation programs will offer the prospect an opportunity to be contacted by a salesperson. Sometimes, the prospect will not even be offered the opportunity to accept or reject a sales call. Instead, a decision will be made by the empirical value of the data and the *lead* will be forwarded to the salesperson.

These kinds of respondents are not leads and will tend to destroy lead generation programs. **The prospect who doesn't acknowledge that they are a lead, is not a lead.**

The key to successful lead generation efforts will often rest on the offer you make to the respondent. The most prevalent offer made in lead generation programs is to have a salesperson contact the prospect. The next most often used offer is to provide additional information. Neither of these offers alone will help qualify a lead.

The best leads will generate a respondent who recognizes a problem, wants to solve the problem, and has some understanding of how much a solution might cost. In addition, this respondent will have the authority to pursue a solution to the problem. Most qualifications can be resolved in a well-conceived offer.

An offer that promises a salesperson contact to describe XYZ computer will not generate well-qualified respondents. Similarly, promising information about the XYZ computer will generate questionable quality respondents. You can strengthen the quality of the respondent by identifying the price of the computer and how it will help the business.

For example, our XYZ computer can help you reduce your accounts receivable by 20% and cost as little as $250 per month - Respond today for a free operations analysis of your business.

This offer establishes a potential benefit and cost in the mind of the prospect. You don't have to ask questions about sales or accounts receivable. By identifying a benefit and cost, respondents can determine if they are qualified.

As mentioned earlier, we believe the most important consideration is whether the prospect thinks they are qualified. If a prospect is convinced they have a problem and can appreciate the cost of the solution and afford it, who cares what the data indicates? The prospect -- not the data -- is going to buy. Of course prospects who can't pass credit checks can be a problem, but we would rather deal with a few credit problems than prospects who have not indicated a desire to make a change.

In our early experiences in lead generation we were also enamored with using data to evaluate lead quality. We even sent prospects who only wanted additional information to the sales force as leads. These programs ultimately failed. How the prospect judges their level of interest and need are really the only important ingredients in developing high quality leads.

Telephone is an excellent medium for qualifying respondents to convert them to leads. Because this medium is so interactive, we will often go too far in data gathering and lose sight of the lead generation objective.

Lead generation programs will often become market research projects. Direct marketers have to guard against this phenomenon. We believe that telephone should be used to qualify respondents, but only by making a well-conceived offer. Only questions that establish money, authority, need and desire should be asked. These issues can most often be established in the offer and one question about decision authority.

The best leads are those that have the prospect convinced they are qualified. Once you begin to focus on generating this kind of lead, the number of leads you send to the field will go down, but the number of leads that convert to orders will go up. Your sales force will be happier.

Lead Generation Offers

You don't want to confuse activity with results. Generating lots of sales leads may not be the best way to generate lots of orders. In fact, too many leads can often mean lower sales productivity. In addition, excess leads typically annoy the sales force and create resentment towards the entire lead effort.

Many lead generation efforts never focus on the offer or activity that is required of the prospect. As mentioned earlier, the two most over-used offers in business marketing are asking the prospect if they would like additional information or if they would like to be contacted by a salesperson. Both situations will not ensure high quality leads.

If you plan to offer additional information as the primary offer, why not just send the information as part of the original promotion?

As an aside, very often the information fulfillment kits containing the additional information are not developed with an eye towards producing a lead or an order. These information packages are typically too technical and don't really sell the prospect on making a change. Most tend to be very feature-oriented with very little effort aimed at selling the products benefits.

Offering a salesperson is like offering a prospect a ten-inch railroad spike and two pound sledge hammer. If they respond to the direct marketing promotion, you'll send them the spike and hammer. The prospect can place the spike in the center of their head and hit it with the hammer. Odds are pretty good that prospects will not respond to this offer. Offering to have a salesperson call on a prospect is often perceived to be as painful as the spike and hammer. Most prospects are not anxious to receive a sales call.

We have found that the best approach is to offer prospects the effect or results of a sales visit. For example, you can offer a prospect the opportunity to receive a survey of his business. This connotes a valuable service that the prospect will receive, and also defines what the salesperson will do upon visiting the prospect.

Most of us fear and resent salespeople. We seem to always take information delivered by the salesperson with a 'grain of salt'. If we have a prior relationship with a company, it is easier to put trust in the salesperson. In a new relationship, a certain amount of fear and distrust is normal. A visit by a salesperson who is trying to sell you his wares is not always perceived positively.

Develop your offers to include some explanation of the financial investment required. This will help you screen away prospects who do not have money or need. By also focusing on the benefits of the product, you can help create need and desire.

We don't know any way to test desire other than to make the prospect a clear, concise offer. Prospects who respond to the offer, and qualify their decision authority, should be high quality leads. Information collectors and less qualified respondents will automatically screen themselves out.

Some of the most exciting offers that generate response and high quality prospects involve a qualification process for a free trial. Not all prospects automatically receive the free trial, but all have to qualify for the offer. The offer should contain the ultimate investment required and an explanation of how the product will help the prospect. Respondents expect to be contacted to achieve their qualification status. The salesperson following up on this kind of lead has a great way to start his dialogue and insure some credibility.

We have used offers that promote surveys, business analysis and free-premiums. All were meant to make the selling and qualification effort easier for the salesperson.

In one situation, we offered a computerized analysis of the company's needs. The salesperson would arrive at the prospect's location with a laptop computer programmed to provide an analysis of potential savings available to the prospect if they elected to purchase. High-tech analysis can elicit significant credibility from prospects.

Your offer should promote what the salesperson will do for the prospect. By focusing on the results of the sales call, the prospect can overcome his natural reluctance and understand why it is in his best interests to spend time with a salesperson.

As you evaluate lead generation offers, examine promotions you receive. Most will offer additional information about products and services. Some will offer to have salespeople contact you to provide this additional material. Very few will actually offer you anything exciting. Notice the promotions that catch your interest. Odds are pretty high that you become interested in those offers that promise you something of value, minimize your risk, and offer you an opportunity to advance within your company.

Lead generation is no different than any other direct marketing program. You're asking a prospect to make a buying decision, albeit to just evaluate your product, without seeing, hearing, touching, feeling, or tasting it. Your offer has to overcome the prospect's natural fear, uncertainty and doubt (FUD). That same prospect has even greater FUD of salespeople.

As you design the lead program, begin to evaluate offers that will make it easy for prospects to respond and qualify themselves. Keep in mind the natural fear of salespeople and design programs that focus on real benefits the prospect will realize by responding. If you only offer information you will not establish true desire. Instead, you will attract information collectors. Many managers are quite interested in things they will never buy.

Unfortunately, when lead generation programs are designed, the only offers that managers find available are to send information or a salesperson to the prospect. Most managers believe that it shouldn't take a lot of thought to develop an offer that will allow a salesperson to call on the prospect. The results of this kind of thinking have done a lot to create high quantity and low quality leads. Remember: the ultimate objective is to produce orders -- not leads.

The Sales Attitude

Illustration 3-6 lists the traits that make up a good salesperson. As sales managers, these are the characteristics we look for when hiring a salesperson. These traits are common in the successful salesperson.

Every sales manager has their own opinion regarding the characteristics desirable in the perfect salesperson. The list in Illustration 3-6 reflects the characteristics mentioned by sales managers we have interviewed. The real issue is the difference between the actual definition of direct marketing (see Illustration 3-7) and the salesperson's attitude toward it.

Generalizations are always dangerous, but bear in mind the target is the average salesperson. The sales attitude is built around a very large, yet fragile ego. It is hard for salespeople to accept that you can find a prospect in their territory that they didn't already know about. Our requirement to track the lead and determine its quality goes directly against the key elements of the sales attitude. An individual who hates paperwork, is protective of his territory and does nothing unless it produces a personal gain, is not likely to help you measure and control the lead program.

The Sales Attitude
(Or what traits make a good salesperson)

- Is greed motivated.

- Has a large ego.

- Hates paperwork.

- Is protective of territory.

- Won't do anything that doesn't provide a personal gain.

- Is an overachiever.

Illustration 3-6: The sales attitude.

The Sales Attitude	**Direct Marketing**
• Is greed motivated.	• An organized and planned system of contacts
• Has a large ego.	• Using a variety of media -- seeking to produce a lead or an order
• Hates paperwork.	
• Is protective of his territory.	• Developing and maintaining a data-base
• Won't do anything in which he doesn't see a personal gain.	• Measurable in costs and results
• Is an overachiever.	• Effective in all methods of selling
	• Expandable with confidence

Illustration 3-7: The contrast between the sales attitude and the definition of direct marketing.

Direct marketing people and salespeople have very different views on the objectives of direct marketing. The grid in Illustration 3-8 shows how direct marketing views its mission. Now review Illustration 3-9 to see how the salesperson views the same objective.

Direct marketing's objective is to reduce the cost of selling. We want sales-people to spend more time in better selling opportunities. Clearly, part of the direct marketing program is to sell the sales staff on this objective.

The sales attitude can seriously affect the success of the direct marketing program. Without the support of the sales force, we will never be able to measure the success of the project. When you design the lead generation program, you should consider how the salesperson will perceive your efforts.

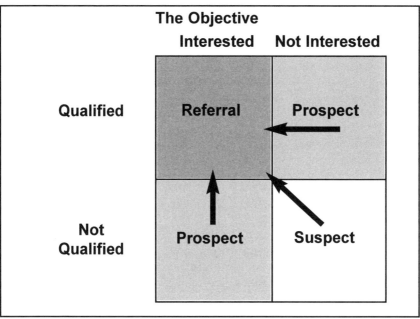

Illustration 3-8: The real objective of direct marketing.

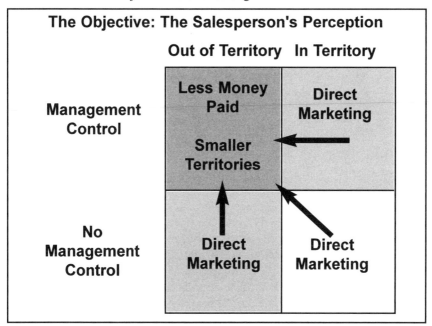

Illustration 3-9: The salesperson's perception of direct marketing.

Lead Management

You must design your lead management system to capture information for measuring and tracking leads. Over the years, many systems have been created and refined to generate information about lead disposition. It seems that every company initially goes through the same process. Illustration 3-10 shows the typical lead tracking approach.

The key element is the chastisement of the sales organization when the lead information isn't returned. This is especially difficult if more leads were generated than the sales organization could follow-up. The more pressure that is put on the organization to return the lead information, the more likely the data will be inaccurate.

Here's a typical scenario: The pressure is applied to the sales force to return the lead information. The sales force reacts to the pressure by taking all the leads and coding them as bad leads.

Lead management is frustrating and difficult. Many companies give up and send leads without any attempt to measure the results. Most of the time, when direct mailing to prospects, objectives are not set. And measurement is even less likely. The typical tracking system is only used in less than 50% of the leads generated.

We encourage people to continue to work with the sales force on measuring lead quality. However, you might consider also asking the *prospect* what finally happened. Illustration 3-11 indicates an approach that could give you the lead quality information you require.

It may be hard to believe, but when this approach has been used we have found less than 50% of the leads generated were ever followed up by the sales force. This really isn't a condemnation of the sales force, but a reflection on the reality of the environment. If more sales leads are generated than can be followed up, when we contact the prospect and find a vast majority not being attended to, we only confirmed that too many leads were generated. Additionally, the salesperson probably tried to reach the prospect on more than one occasion. After several attempts, the salesperson pursued something else. In the crush of business, the lead may get lost. Following-up with the prospect allows you to determine the final outcome. If the lead wasn't contacted, you is still may have a sales opportunity.

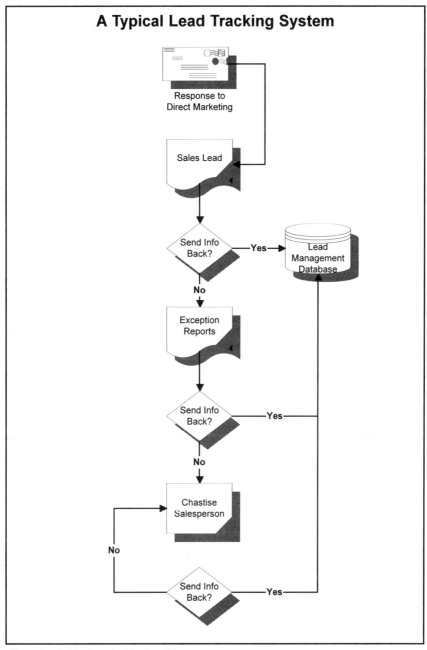

Illustration 3-10: A typical lead tracking system.

The best source of measuring lead programs is the respondent. You will learn the effectiveness of the lead program and the effectiveness of the selling effort by the field sales force.

Every time we have contacted leads after they have been sent to the field force, we are surprised at the high number that were never contacted by salespeople. This is often caused by several factors:

- The salespeople are not happy with the quality of leads from prior programs. They have pre-judged the current leads and determined it is not in their best interest to waste time contacting poor quality leads again.

- The salespeople have received too many leads to follow-up. This is one of the most common problems. The salespeople do not have enough time to contact all of the leads and will often make arbitrary judgments about lead quality. They will elect to contact only a few prospects. The rest will never be contacted and are often returned coded as bad leads.

- The salespeople have unsuccessfully attempted to contact the prospect several times. We know from our experience in telephone selling that only about 25% of dialings in the business world will result in a completed call. Most salespeople will call prospects at convenient times during the day. Convenient to the salesperson, not to the prospect. If they leave a return phone number, the salesperson will probably not be available when the prospect does call back. And if a salesperson makes 3 or 4 attempts and doesn't get through, they will probably give up and move on to other opportunities. Leads that the salesperson is unable to contact will often be returned as poor quality leads.

- The salesperson is already aware of the lead. Some leads will be returned by the salesperson because they are familiar with the company. They may never contact the respondent and simply return the lead, often coding it as poor quality.

Salespeople have difficulty acknowledging that you can find a prospect in their territory that they didn't already know about. They feel that to do so is to admit someone else has done a better job than they have. It is an ongo-

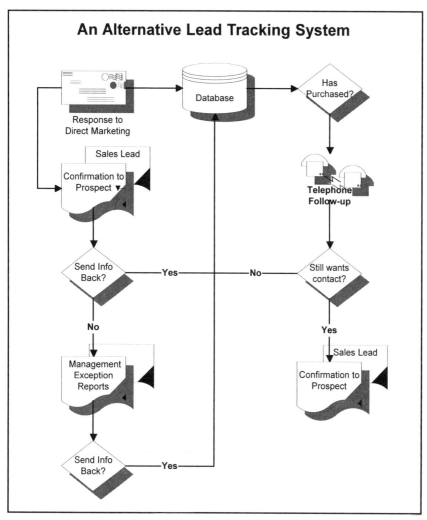

Illustration 3-11: An alternative lead tracking system.

ing struggle to convince the sales force that you are working -- not competing -- with them.

Once you execute a lead generation program and make an offer to a prospect, that prospect deserves your continued attention. If you have made a significant offer and a prospect has accepted, failure to contact the prospect can do great long-term harm to your company.

It is important your company develop and maintain a direct relationship with the prospect as well as asking a salesperson to do so.

Mail, FAX or e-mail the prospect a confirmation of their response and tell them which sales office you have asked to contact them. By doing so, you are building the relationship between your company and the prospect. You will also gain the ability to go back directly to the prospect to find out if a salesperson contacted them. The prospect probably responded to your promotion because they had an interest in your company and products -- not because of a relationship they had with a salesperson. You should maintain the relationship the prospect started.

Lead measurement and tracking need to be considered in the initial program design. Establish a lead tracking system which is based on sales force interaction and direct contact with the prospect. You will get invaluable information on the quality and quantity of sales follow-up. You also will gain great insight into what and why prospects are buying, including your competition.

Scoring

With the example lead generation program, lead quality became a major issue. The sales force had asked for many more leads than they could possibly follow up. Ultimately we returned to the drawing table to try to define a good lead.

During the telemarketing effort we had the communicator input prospect responses directly into a database. This database was then used to determine the quality of the prospect and to insure only those prospects who qualified as leads or referrals were offered a salesperson visit.

As we have discussed, relying on prospect information to qualify a lead is not the ideal method for ensuring interested and qualified referrals. Prospects who understand the costs of a transaction and the benefits they will receive from accepting your offer are qualified. Many companies still insist on contacting the prospect and scoring the quality of the lead. We have all gone through this learning process.

The example program communicators were part-time employees who were not knowledgeable in the product line. They had been trained in good telephone techniques and the telephone call was completely scripted. The script itself was manual using a flip card approach, but the scheduling and data capture were interactive with the computer.

This script was developed with the sales staff and focused on screening prospects before the leads were sent to a salesperson for follow-up. Initially, a lead was sent out for any prospect that was in the process of evaluating a system within three months regardless of the prospect's desire to see a salesperson. We used binary decision-making; that is, by answering a yes or no question, the prospects qualified themselves. If the prospect was making a decision within six months, they were automatically qualified, and offered a salesperson contact. If the decision was to be made within three months, the lead was sent to the salesperson, regardless of whether they agreed to see a salesperson.

If a purchase was planned for the future, the other qualification criteria was examined to determine if the prospect should be offered a salesperson. Again, all the questions were binary. The prospect answered yes or no to meet the criteria. The prospect's answers to certain questions determined if a salesperson would call on that prospect.

When the script was developed, we didn't understand or relate to the MAND concept (money, authority, need, desire) that was discussed earlier. The sales force asked for three sales leads per day. If the prospect had answered certain questions, the sales force wanted to have that prospect as a lead. We quickly had severe lead quality problems. Many prospects were evaluating inexpensive products that cost approximately $2,000. The smallest systems we sold were then priced at about $15,000. The salespeople were unhappy with the leads.

Using the manual scripting technique, you really don't have many options on lead qualification. You can link different binary decisions, but the qualification process becomes more and more difficult to implement.

The salespeople asked for fewer leads that were of higher quality. We tried to define 'higher quality,' but had the same problem of defining a good lead. Which was better: A prospect making a decision in 90 days or less who only had one administrative person; or a prospect not making a decision for more than six months who had eight administrative people?

A Lead Qualification Scoring Approach

Computer Decision		Clerical Employees		Total Employees	
Immediate	35	6 or more	15	100+	15
Less then 3 mos	25	3 to 6	10	50 to 99	10
3 to 6 mos	15	2	5	25 to 49	5
6 to 12 mos	10	1	0	less than 25	0
Unsure	5	0	(10)		
Not evaluating	0				

Added Clerical In Last Year		Will Add Clerical		Accounts Rec'vble	
Yes	10	Yes	15	Yes	10
No	0	No	0	No	0

Inventory Growth		Using Data Proc		Annual Sales	
Yes	10	Purch Sys>1 yr	5	25 million+	10
No	0	Purch Sys<1 yr	(10)	1 to 25 million	5
				500k to 1 mill	0
		Serv Bureau	15	less than 500k	(5)
		Not Satisfied	15		

Illustration 3-12: A lead scoring system.

We began to evaluate the relationship of the answers to the qualification questions. This relative lead qualification procedure was a tremendous breakthrough, and finally allowed us to differentiate between prospects and referrals.

We established point values for each answer and were able to score the lead. The scoring system in Illustration 3-12 is an example of the algorithms we used.

This system is almost impossible to implement with a manual script and a communicator trying to score manually while on the phone. The ideal situation would allow the prospect to be scored during the phone call and enable the score to be used to determine the appropriate offer.

We worked with the sales force to establish the values for each answer. Bear in mind that the best scoring system will change and be modified as you learn from leads you've already generated. We went back and scored all the leads we generated prior to the scoring system introduction, and found the average lead to be worth about 20 points. Qualified leads required a score of at least 40 points.

We automated the scheduling process of the telemarketing calls and gave each communicator access to a common database. We used a relative approach to determine lead quality and the appropriate offer that would be made to the prospect. The database evaluated the answers in real time during the telemarketing calls. If the prospect crossed a certain threshold, the offer was made. For the first time we could actually differentiate between prospects and referrals.

A prospect was one who scored between 20 and 39 points. Referrals had to score more than 39 points. We also decided that a single question could not qualify a referral. The average referral or lead had a score of 47 points after we introduced the scoring qualification system. More importantly, the salespeople now liked 65% of the leads and were unhappy with only 35%. Before we implemented the scoring system, the sales force disliked 65% of all leads generated.

We have used scoring algorithms in many other programs with the same kinds of results. When we work with clients to define the values for scoring, no one question will qualify a prospect to be a referral. The MAND concept makes it easier to decide what questions to ask. It is very difficult to implement a scoring system to determine the offer without communicators interacting with a database during the telephone call. However, scoring after the fact can be valuable to determine lead quality, the results of your offers, and list usage.

Scoring solves many problems but creates a whole new set of challenges, which can become opportunities. In the past, every prospect who met a certain criteria was sent to the sales force for action. With scoring, you identify the best referrals to send to the salespeople. You also identify a group qualified as prospects, but not qualified enough to be leads. What do you do with this group to ultimately turn them into leads and customers? In a later section we discuss an alternative using conditioning and regeneration.

You can accomplish similar scoring results by using two step mailing techniques. Initial respondents are mailed a second piece which has qualification information that can be returned. After the second response, the prospect can be considered a lead. Obviously, this technique will substantially reduce the number of leads sent to the salespeople.

Remember, we continue to stress that it really isn't important what we think of a prospect's qualifications; it is only important what the prospect thinks about their needs and ability to pay for a solution to their problems.

The ultimate qualified lead is a prospect who understands their problem, recognizes that there are potential solutions, has a preliminary idea of how much a solution will cost and is prepared to spend money to implement a solution.

We think that once a prospect is interested in addressing a problem, we should offer them an opportunity to self-assess their needs. Rather then offering information or a salesperson, we should offer them a method to self evaluate the size and scope of their needs.

Tools that help prospects self-assess their needs are not as threatening as offering a salesperson and typically draw more responses. More importantly, they allow the prospect to qualify themselves and give them a reason for answering those annoying qualifying questions.

An insurance company offered prospects *The Executive Guide to Evaluating Your Pension Plan.* This inexpensive brochure provided a series of questions telling the prospect how to evaluate their existing or planned pension program. A hardware manufacturer created *The PC Configuration Planner* which allowed prospects to build a computer and determine the elements best suited for their needs. Another company offered a *Calculator* which allowed the prospects to determine their needs by answering a series of questions.

All of these tools provided enough information for the prospect to determine whether they had a need and should look for a solution. Each offered a follow-on step which allowed the prospect to receive a professional assessment from the company offering the tool, in other words, a sales call. Think about the improved quality of these leads where the prospect has already determined their need, has a general idea of costs and wants to take the next step.

Several companies have developed computer models that provide analysis of a prospect company's needs. The prospect is offered the opportunity to provide some limited data from which they will receive a valuable analysis. The marketers are able to obtain required qualification information and give the prospect something of value in return.

You can create self-assessment offers that will allow the prospect to qualify and increase overall response. By adding a follow-on phone call to each respondent, you can convert many of these prospects into highly qualified leads.

Quite often one of the steps in the selling process includes a demonstration. Another PC company did a program offering "The Business Communication Kit" which allowed self-assessment as well as demonstrations. Prospects were asked to send in a minimal amount of information for which they received a personalized kit demonstrating the value and use of desktop publishing and desktop presentations.

All too often the data captured through lead generation questioning is not perceived as accurate by the salespeople. They are suspicious of the accuracy of the information and attempt to verify it themselves. Quite often, when they find an inconsistency, they use it to "expose" the poor quality of the lead generation program. Gathering the data quickly becomes a no-win situation.

Rather than asking a series of questions which allow you to assess the size of the prospect, self-assessment allows them to verify their own needs. Instead of asking for the annual sales or revenue, why not show the prospect potential savings based on their annual sales or allow them to score their needs based on annual revenue?

Offer is the ultimate lead qualification element. If you identify a minimum price and convince a prospect that they have a need, if the prospect responds, they will be qualified. We prefer to design multi-step campaigns which allow the prospect to self-assess their needs and understand the basic costs in making a change prior to offering a salesperson. And when you do offer a salesperson, make sure you identify the benefit the prospect will receive from participating in the sales call.

Multiple Steps in Lead Generation Programs

You can use several direct marketing steps, prior to involving a salesperson, to better qualify each prospect. A respondent to multiple steps in a program has indicated a better understanding of the solution to their problem and a stronger interest in moving forward.

Many companies use multiple step promotions to qualify advertising inquiries. According to many salespeople, advertising has always produced leads of suspicious quality. Many salespeople refuse to follow-up these leads, particularly those generated by the reader service cards, often referred to as bingo cards. To better qualify these respondents and produce quality leads, a fulfillment kit calling for a second response is often added to the process. Only those prospects responding to the fulfillment kit are considered leads and forwarded to a salesperson.

The technique of using a fulfillment kit to create the lead is often called a two-step program. The first step is the generation of the initial response and fulfillment with an information kit, the second step is the response from the kit.

Unfortunately, many of the fulfillment kits that are used to satisfy the requests for information are designed to convey product features and not to generate high quality sales leads. But those prospects that do respond to these kits are acutely interested and should be relatively high quality leads. Many times these leads suffer only because the respondent does not have the authority to make a decision.

The concept of using the two-step approach to qualify advertising respondents has led us to using multiple step programs to qualify all respondents. More and more of the programs we see use multiple step activities to move the prospect closer to a buying decision and produce higher quality leads.

Offering a fulfillment kit which actively moves the prospect closer to the buying decision, and then following up with either a phone call or another mailing will often produce great leads. Each step serves to eliminate less qualified prospects and encourage those interested and qualified to move closer to buying.

Complicated products like machine tools, electronic equipment, and computer software and hardware, will often require multiple steps to describe

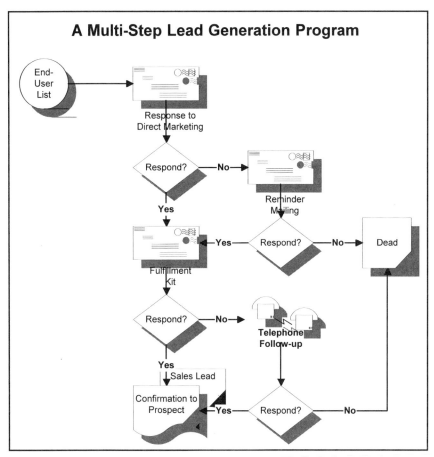

Illustration 3-13: A multi-step lead generation program.

the benefits of the product and motivate a prospect to become a lead. Today's technology makes it possible to produce personalized letters based on the unique characteristics and status of each prospect. Telephone can be used to augment the direct mail effort and further clarify the offer and generate leads.

In Illustration 3-13, the prospect is offered a fulfillment kit. If they fail to respond to the initial mailing, a reminder is used to generate as much response as possible.

The fulfillment kit is designed to explain the benefits of becoming a customer and to make another offer encouraging the prospect to respond again. The second response will become a qualified lead. A significant effort should be devoted to creating the fulfillment kit. It will become your primary offer in the initial promotion. It should offer a significant benefit to the prospect.

After making another strong offer in the fulfillment kit, you can use telephone selling to further qualify prospects who requested the kit but failed to respond a second time.

This multiple step program recognizes the reality of how business executives gradually make a buying decision. The program combined direct mail and telephone to ensure that the prospect was ultimately converted to a qualified sales lead.

Current technology makes it possible to manage prospects through different stages and ensure the appropriate communication is created and delivered. Although you can implement this approach internally, several service bureaus and direct marketing companies specialize in this type of sustained marketing activity.

As we have mentioned several times, most leads are not followed up by salespeople. You run the risk of creating long-term image problems in your market when respondents are not contacted.

Prospects who are responding to your direct marketing efforts are indicating a desire to have a relationship with your company. Although you may be dependent on the salesperson to develop, maintain and sustain the relationship, the prospect indicates an interest initially in a relationship with your company -- not the salesperson. This is often a difficult concept to explain to the sales force. Many salespeople believe that the prospect is really interested in having a relationship with them personally, and these salespeople are often reluctant to allow you to participate in that relationship.

If the salesperson fails to contact the prospect, you will have an unsatisfactory situation which you can't resolve. Rather than allowing this problem to fester, we often suggest that you maintain the relationship directly with the prospect.

As you generate a lead, you can maintain the relationship by confirming the lead with the prospect and opening a communication channel between the prospect and your company. If the prospect is not contacted by the salesperson, you can provide the prospect with a name and phone number to reopen the dialogue directly with your company.

Think about your reaction if you were to request information and contact from a potential vendor. No one bothers to contact you. You'll probably have a long memory and never forget how poorly you were treated.

Now imagine your reaction if that same company instead sent you a letter or e-mail confirming your request and giving you the name and phone number of the salesperson who would be contacting you. The correspondence also gave you the name of a manager you could contact if you were at all dissatisfied with the salesperson assigned to your account. This kind of lead confirmation opens the dialogue between a company and its prospect. It develops a positive relationship which may encourage the prospect to buy in the future, if not now!

Illustration 3-14 shows a fax confirmation used to notify the prospect of the salesperson responsible for handling the inquiry. We have effectively used FAX and e-mail, as well as mail, to deliver the confirmation. The object is to maintain the relationship between your company and the prospect that was initiated by the prospect's response.

Establishing Objectives for a Lead Generation Program

Lead generation programs frequently fail because companies do not establish reasonable and realistic objectives for the number of leads required. If you ask a sales executive how many leads they would like to see provided from a lead generation program, the answer will inevitably be as many as possible. . . the more the better. With 'concrete' objectives like this, is it any wonder that so many lead programs never get beyond the test phase?

You can plan better lead generation programs and establish objectives based on the number of orders and revenue required.

Using the Lead Requirements Worksheet (Illustration 3-15), you can quickly establish the leads required per salesperson and, by multiplying that number by the number of salespeople, the total number of leads required for the program.

Direct Marketing Publishers
1304 University Drive
Yardley, PA 19067

Date: 9:30 a.m., Thursday, November 21, 1998

To: Joe Sample, President
             Sample Company
             111 Any Street
             Anytown, XX 99999
             Phone: (123) 456-7890 Fax: (123) 456-7891

From: Bernie Goldberg
             Phone (215) 321-3068   Fax: (215) 321-9647

Pages: Including this cover sheet: 1

I appreciate your recent request for information and request to have one of our consultants perform a sales and lead generation audit. You should be contacted in the next few days by:
             Sam Salesperson
             Direct Marketing Publishers
             123 Anystreet
             Anytown, XX 99999
             Phone (123) 860-5200

The sales manager for your area is Dennis Johnson . If you have not been contacted within the next two days, please call him at (123) 860-5200 or call us at (800) 123-4567.

Illustration 3-14: A fax lead confirmation.

It is unreasonable to expect a lead generation program to account for all of the business generated by the salespeople. Most salespeople will continue to generate their own opportunities and close business regardless of lead activity.

The place to start to establish the lead volume that will be required is with the annual quota or sales objective expected from each salesperson.

You should estimate the percentage of the annual quota that the salesperson will close without a lead generation program. Prior average sales perfor-

Lead Requirements Worksheet

A) Annual sales quota/objective per salesperson _____

B) Percent sales quota achieved without leads _____

C) Sales revenue achieved without leads *(B x A)* _____

D) Sales revenue required from leads *(A - C)* _____

E) Sales revenue achieved without leads *(B x A)* _____

F) Sales revenue required from leads *(A - E)* _____

G) Average revenue per order from leads _____

H) Number of orders from leads required *(F ÷ G)* _____

I) Percentage of leads that order _____

J) Number leads required per salesperson *(H x I)* _____

Illustration 3-15: Lead Requirements Worksheet.

mance can often indicate the sales that can be obtained without a new lead program.

Simple math will allow you to calculate the revenue you can anticipate. Regardless of what your average order has been in the past, a different offer can change its size.

The Lead Requirements Worksheet needs a planned average order to determine the number of leads required. You can use your current average order as determined using the Salesperson Cost Worksheet from Chapter 2 or the average order expected from the offer made in the direct marketing program.

By dividing the required revenue from the lead program by the average order, you'll establish the number of orders required from your lead program.

You can establish the number of leads that are required per salesperson by estimating the percentage of leads that order. This will give you a better set of lead objectives than might have been set in the past.

When you complete the Lead Requirements Worksheet, you also identify the quality of the leads you require. By establishing the anticipated closing rate and size of the order, you have identified a substantial part of the direct marketing program. You have established the list and offer requirements and probably even the promotional concept that you'll use.

A word of caution: In Chapter 2 we identified the number of available sales calls per salesperson per year as well as the cost per sales call. As you plan the lead generation program, you should evaluate the number of sales calls that a salesperson can make per year. It is not unusual to initially plan a lead program that requires more sales resources than might be available. If this occurs, you'll have to modify the closing ratio of your leads or the size of the order.

Plan your lead programs to produce results that are realistic and attainable. If you establish a required number of orders and revenue, you'll establish a program that can be measured and controlled. The program will have a better chance to succeed.

Conditioning and Regeneration

Most companies have a limited universe within the business-to-business arena. A prospect is very valuable and, even if one does not buy from you now, they may buy from you in the future. When you talk to the sales organization, you learn that a prospect takes time to nurture and sell. Selling through direct marketing is the same. Once a prospect is identified, you should continue to market this prospect even if they became a lead and was sent to the sales force. This sustained selling activity is a form of *conditioning*. Repeated attempts to motivate the prospect to respond through direct mail and telephone selling is *regeneration*.

During the example lead program, we learned there is a difference between prospects and referrals. When operating a lead generation program, the referrals are sent to the sales force and prospects are nurtured and conditioned into referrals. We also know that not all the leads will be followed up with the same quality.

We designed a direct mail program that involved multiple contacts spread over a three to four month period. After the prospects or referrals were identified, they were mailed a conditioning series of mail pieces to move them along through the sales cycle. The series was not product oriented. It focused on the buying decision. Need and desire were the themes used throughout the series. Cost justification, application needs and identification, and computer uses were the topics of three of the pieces in the series. All the pieces asked the prospect to get involved with the material. They all contained involvement devices.

Prospects and referrals were tested to determine the effectiveness of this approach. Lead quality improved dramatically and the sales force wanted to add their own prospects to the existing database to have them receive the mail series.

In prolonged selling situations it is difficult to ensure that there is ongoing communication to keep the prospect moving forward. We think you can design a sustained direct marketing campaign that continues to reinforce your company/prospect relationship and enhance the selling effort. This is an unusual direct marketing program because its goal is to maintain the relationship instead of moving the prospect to immediate action.

You can develop a lead and proposal follow-up program which ensures complete handling of every active transaction. Although most of us rely on field and telephone follow-up, many active transactions are never fully contacted. Follow-up and phone calls always seem to become a lower priority.

Direct mail can be an effective tool to ensure complete follow-up of all active prospects and deliver a powerful message. These letters sell added value and services and enhance the relationship. You can create a series of letters from various departments of your company explaining how they'll work with the prospect as they become a customer.

You can create these letters internally and use a personalized or window envelope. In Illustration 3-16, the first letter will be sent about two weeks after the original lead or proposal.

You can create a letter from the customer service manager explaining how their department supports accounts. The letter could start like this: We understand you are considering purchasing a system from ABC company, and as the manager of customer support, we wanted to explain how we are prepared to support you.

The tone of all of the letters should be warm and conversational. The more personal the letter, the better. Because this campaign will be difficult to measure, it should be designed to make the prospect comfortable with your company. The letters should stress the benefits a customer receives in doing business with your company. The timing between letters should be two weeks to one month depending on the anticipated length of the selling cycle.

Other letters can also be sent from the senior executives of manufacturing stressing quality, research and development explaining how new products are continually developed, Administration

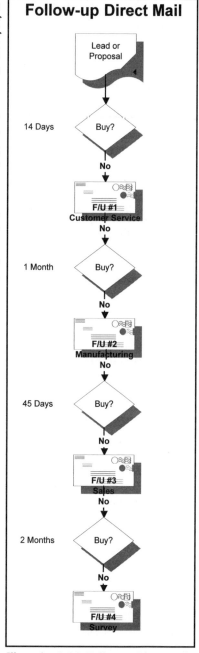

Illustration 3-16: Follow-up Direct Mail.

focusing on how you are organized to support your customers; and Sales to identify pre-sale and post-sales support.

The final letter might be from your CEO and contain a survey type questionnaire trying to determine what has happened and why. The letter will have a response form allowing the prospect to tell you how they feel about your company and the way they've been handled.

You can always add letters and communication if the sales cycle turns out to be longer. We think this campaign should be designed to enhance and help the field salesperson by building and maintaining the relationship.

Conditioning and regeneration are key elements to continuing to work the prospect and referral universe. If you're unable to close the business today, this technique allows you to get the business in the future. Good salespeople perform this function independently. When a salesperson identifies a qualified prospect, they begins to work to sell that prospect over time. The salesperson will send literature, letters and make many phone calls until the prospect succumbs to their efforts. Tenacity is a trait we all look for in a good salesperson.

We should learn from our sales force. This repetitive activity works in direct marketing as well as in direct selling. The sales force should be consulted to determine those techniques that are successful. You should try to implement a uniform system to condition prospects to become referrals and to regenerate referrals into customers over time.

Lead Generation - Two Big Pitfalls

The vast majority of promotion expense in businesses selling to other businesses is in generating sales leads for the field salesperson. Lead generation is the most difficult direct marketing program to successfully implement. In fact, it is unusual to find a lead generation program that has sustained itself for more than a year or two.

Prospects will often respond to a direct marketing program and never receive additional information or follow-up. I have found that less than 30% of leads sent to salespeople are ever contacted. Illustration 3-17 demonstrates what can occur if information is not fulfilled in a timely manner to prospects and customers.

Illustration 3-17: The other side of fulfillment.

Lead generation programs often make promises but never deliver. I think there are two problems that you should be aware of before implementing a lead generation program. The first is the normal delay that the prospect will experience from response to receipt of information. The second is whether the salesperson ever contacts the prospect and how you'll measure their sales activity.

Even in the best scenario, a prospect who becomes interested in your product or service, and who responds to the promotion will have to wait two weeks or more before receiving the information they request.

Even in a well-planned and executed fulfillment operation, a prospect will suffer some delay between response and receipt of information. There are obvious delays caused by fulfillment operations and postal handling. In other environments, information requests have not been completely planned for and are handled ineffectively.

Delays in handling responses will cause the prospect to cool or even forget that they responded. It is even possible for the prospect to pursue a competitive alternative while waiting to receive information.

The sooner information can be fulfilled, the higher the odds of closing the sale.

If you are generating sales leads for salespeople, you are never certain of the quality and timeliness of the follow-up. Many salespeople will pre-judge lead quality based on their own subjective evaluation. In some cases, those leads that the salespeople feel are poor quality may never receive any follow-up. In addition, a salesperson has their own priorities and may not execute a follow-up contact to your leads as quickly as you would like.

Most salespeople don't like sales leads. When was the last time you heard a salesperson say: Those were great leads, send me more! The more typical reaction seems to be: Those were awful leads, and the only good ones were prospects that I already knew about.

Most salespeople feel threatened by leads and will typically condemn lead generation activity as a waste of the company's money. It is very difficult to get the salesperson to return any information concerning lead disposition or follow-up.

You should design a fulfillment program that puts information in the hands of your prospects as soon as possible. If you can turn around information the same day, do it.

The information kit you use to fulfill information requests should be designed to generate a lead or an order. Existing material or brochures should not be mailed in an effort to save costs.

Even if you plan to send the respondent to your sales force as a lead, send a complete information kit to him as well. You are never certain that the sales force will follow up quickly or completely. I suggest to my clients that they not only send an information kit, but a letter explaining who the prospect can contact if they aren't contacted soon by the sales force.

As we mentioned earlier, lead management programs should be designed to have the prospect tell you about selling activity. So many lead programs ultimately fail because management is unable to get the salesperson to report on lead quality and disposition.

Prospects responding to direct marketing are indicating an interest in your company. Most respondents would like to start a relationship with the company, yet most businesses rely on the salesperson to develop and sustain that relationship. You can help the salesperson and your company if you also maintain some relationship with your respondents.

You can use direct mail promotion to fulfill the initial inquiry along with sending the lead to the salesperson. Even if the salesperson fails to follow-up, you'll be assured of a contact. A telephone call after the lead has been generated can be made in the guise of customer service to help measure the effectiveness of the lead program.

The sustained use of direct mail can also be used to maintain a relationship with the respondent and help move the prospect further towards buying your products or services.

There are many challenges in developing and executing lead generation programs. The two pitfalls described have traditionally created some of the most obvious reasons for failure. As you plan your next campaign, consider the timely follow-up of information to your respondents and how you will ensure that the salesperson fulfills as you have promised. As you plan solutions to these troublesome areas, you will begin to take positive steps towards better lead generation efforts.

Lead Programs Summarized

In this chapter we talked about the inconsistencies in lead follow up, the difficulty in lead definition, and how to implement leads with the sales force. Whenever you implement a lead program, you try to reduce the cost of selling by improving the effectiveness of the sales force. The lead program has to work as a tool for the sales force. It should not be perceived by the salespeople as an alternative to their efforts. Nothing will destroy the effectiveness of the project faster than if the salespeople feel that you are trying to replace them with direct marketing. Work with your sales organization to create the lead program to make their jobs easier rather than eliminate them.

When the decision is made to implement the lead program, do not reduce commissions or territories. For the lead program to be successful, you need the support of the salespeople. Anything that affects their perception of the direct marketing effort in a negative way, should be avoided at all costs. Sell the direct marketing program to the sales force. If mail is being used, send a copy of the piece to the homes of the salespeople. Put them on your list.

In order to measure the effectiveness of the lead program, you must have feedback. Salespeople perform a variety of activities. Unfortunately, their highest priority will not be to give you information on the quality of the leads. You should design a lead tracking and management system to control the distribution and reporting of the leads. Ask sales management to get involved and help with reporting. However, do not chastise the salespeople for not returning sales leads. Consider positive actions such as contests for the most leads followed up. Make sure you publicize sales successes from the sales leads. Nothing will motivate a salesperson to follow up the leads more than sales success.

Design a way to ask the prospect directly what has happened. Special offers that give a premium for buying as a result of the offer is an interesting method to measure the conversion of leads to orders. Giving a coupon or special discount to the prospect also will help measure some of the conversions.

A questionnaire or telephone call after the lead is generated is an ideal way to determine lead quality and lead conversion. Go directly to the referral and ask about the quality of the lead follow up. You can find out what the prospect bought, if anything; why the prospect bought or didn't buy; and you can determine if that prospect is still a sales opportunity for you.

We gave you a worksheet that can help you determine the number of leads required from the lead program. Many programs ultimately suffer or fail because management has unreasonable expectations.

One final point: Any information you have on the prospect or referral should be sent to the salesperson. Don't hide any data. Most salespeople are entrepreneurs and like to have complete control of their accounts.

Chapter Four:
Database

Consumer Versus Business Databases

Through the years consumer direct marketing companies have become unbelievably accurate in building databases and targeting specific customers and prospects. As time goes on, the consumer world enjoys unending advancements in their ability to build and maintain databases. As good as we have become in the consumer arena, we have not enjoyed similar growth in the business-to-business market.

There is a significant difference between the two markets and many of the major differences involve the capture and storage of information electronically. In addition, when a consumer changes their address, they will file a change of address notification through the National Change of Address (*NCOA*) system of the U.S. Postal Service. The rate of change is relatively stagnant at about 15% per year and we can keep track of who is moving and where they are going thanks to the NCOA.

Consumer address information is three to four lines of data and relatively homogeneous. The direct marketing community has developed sophisticated record identification techniques based on match-code formulas that allow us to be over 95% accurate. In general we can build and maintain consumer databases with uncanny accuracy.

There are companies that specialize in merging files and purging duplicates ("merge/purge"). An example of the consumer match code is:

Zip code	the first 5 positions
Last name	3 characters - usually the first, third and fourth because the second position is often a vowel which is frequently an error during data entry.
First name	1 character - the first initial
Unit number	2 characters of the unit number of the address - there are algorithms for separating street address into unit, directional, and street address.
Street name	3 characters - usually the first, third and fourth because the second position is often a vowel which is frequently an error during data entry.
Check digit	1 character - an algorithm assigns an additional character based on the information.

There are different variations of this approach which create 14 to 17 position match codes that can be 95% to 97% accurate.

The business address can be six or seven lines of information including contact name, title, company, division, street address, mail stop, city, state and zip code. Techniques that work well in the consumer world are not as effective in the business environment.

Company house files are developed based on information provided by respondents. Many people are lazy and will often abbreviate company names and make the matching even more unlikely. It is impossible to train data entry personnel to solve the problem because customers and prospects provide inaccurate abbreviations when they respond.

Creating an alias file, which could help identify the accurate company name, is almost impossible. Business marketing is much more difficult than similar consumer efforts, and the company name problem is often at the core of most issues.

Match coding which ignores the company name doesn't work because many companies can be located within the same office building, plant or warehouse. Therefore using a person's name and address could invalidate the matching algorithm with multiple people having similar names at the building address. The World Trade Center in New York or your local office park are good examples of why this solution won't work.

Most business people do not notify the postal service when they change jobs, titles or functions and therefore NCOA isn't nearly as effective in the business world. We really don't know the rate of change in the business world. In many of our seminars we'll ask the audience about the rate of change and often find 35% to 50% have changed within the last 12 months.

Match-code algorithms are not as effective in the business world, due to the company naming problems. We will typically only match 50% to 65%. In addition, the consumer world is characterized by a one-to-one relationship: one home address, one targeted decision maker. The business world is one-to-many. One company has many potential decision makers. Maintaining information about multiple people who often change responsibilities within companies is almost impossible.

The business buying decision will often involve multiple people (Illustration 4-1) and a bad decision can result in a poor employee perception, negative evaluation or worse. We will often have to target multiple people within the same company in order to get a buying decision.

Unlike the consumer world where we can target our customer directly, many business managers and executives will have individuals responsible for screening their mail and phone calls. The one-to-many problem is magnified by these barriers and can make the building and maintaining of the business database even more difficult.

All too often the business world is further complicated by multiple locations or divisions within the same enterprise. You may receive an order from an individual in one location, requiring that it be shipped to another location and has to mail the invoice to a third address. As you can see, tracking the relationships of the multiple locations and individuals can be a daunting, if not impossible, task.

As business people change, what happens to order history? Because of the relative simplicity of the consumer world, sales history can be maintained for as long as a company feels appropriate. If sales history is tied to individual buyers, the significant rate of change will obsolete the information within a year or two. On the other hand if you maintain order history at the company level, you really don't have information about the buyer.

We have encountered situations where a company found that their customer contact had changed and deleted the sales history for that customer when they eliminated the contact. This situation might be acceptable if you're selling consumable supplies, but if you're selling capital equipment, the product is still probably being used and sales history should be maintained.

As we will discuss, the derivation of your company's computer systems will often effect the information available in your marketing database. Unfortunately, many existing computer systems only store one contact name for an account and the name is most often the person responsible for paying the bill (accounts payable) not the person who ordered.

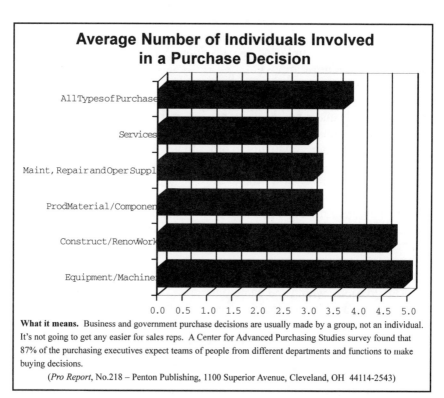

What it means. Business and government purchase decisions are usually made by a group, not an individual. It's not going to get any easier for sales reps. A Center for Advanced Purchasing Studies survey found that 87% of the purchasing executives expect teams of people from different departments and functions to make buying decisions.

(*Pro Report*, No.218 – Penton Publishing, 1100 Superior Avenue, Cleveland, OH 44114-2543)

Illustration 4-1: People involved in a business decision according to Penton Publishing.

The business decision process adds another level of complexity that is different than consumer marketing. The business buying decision can involve several groups with different levels of authority:

Decision Maker
Recommender
Influencer
Information Gatherer
Consultant
Purchaser
User

In addition, there is no standard title coding. A vice president in one company may be the senior decision maker while the same title in other companies is far less influential. The finance community has often assigned a vice-president title to salespeople to facilitate their discussions with customers and prospects.

The amount of information required in the business world is significantly greater than in consumer marketing. Many consumer databases can be handled with straight-forward data processing files that have little or no relationship with other files or information. The one-to-one relationship simplifies the database. The business world requires a relational database which is difficult to build and maintain.

System Evolution

The original reason a company implemented their computer systems often has a significant effect on information that is available and the ease in capturing additional data. Traditional company organization structures, as illustrated in 4-2, focused application needs within each department.

Computers were originally sold to automate the accounting functions with a company. General ledger, accounting, payroll, inventory control, billing and accounts receivable were on the forefront of data processing applications. Thousands of computers were installed, perhaps in your company, to automate these basic administrative tasks. As you'll notice in Illustration 4-3, systems seem to have evolved starting with accounting based applications.

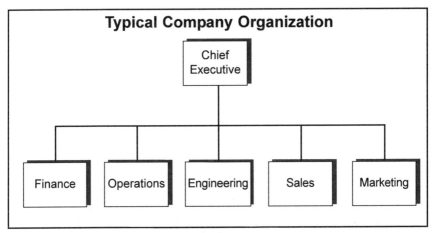

Illustration 4-2: Traditional company organization structure.

The information in these early applications was originally stored on punch cards, then magnetic tape and ultimately via direct access storage ("disk storage"). The configuration of the information was in a flat file. All of the necessary information was stored within the record. In addition, the files were identified within the computer programs, therefore making a change to the structure of the information required all of the computer programs that dealt with that information to be modified.

Once these computer programs were written and operating, data processing departments have been reluctant to change. These systems operate quite well and why run the risk of fixing something that isn't broken.

As you examine accounting derived systems, you realize that there was never a reason to store much information about customers. The focus of the system is internal to the company. Besides sending an invoice or bill to the appropriate individual, the accounting system doesn't require customer information. In most of these systems it isn't possible to separate the first and last names of the contact.

From time to time you may have requested a simple change to your company's customer file, like adding an additional contact. The typical response from the Information department is "that sounds like a great idea but it will take us two years." The information professionals aren't being cute but rather recognize in the older systems, often referred to as legacy systems, that every program has to be examined to ensure the change to file will not impact their ability to operate.

Information System Evolution

- **Accounting**
  - Flat file derived
  - Manage financial areas
  - little or no customer information

- **Operations**
  - Some database
  - Internal productivity driven
  - Little or no customer information

- **Sales & Marketing**
  - Requires database
  - Satisfy customer needs first - external orientation
  - Accounting & operations are by-products
  - Flexible

Illustration 4-3: Information system evolution.

Computer programs are traditionally written to manage files whose records have specific characteristics. If the record format is changed, the computer programs that are used with that record will all have to be modified. It is not unusual, as a system evolves, to have hundreds of computer programs involved in the processing of information. Introducing a new piece of information, such as the average earnings per household, could require a major programming effort. This big "change" is not to create the new information, but to modify the existing programs to handle this new piece of data.

Traditional computer programs deal with fixed length and formatted files. Your data processing department is probably using programs and files. In addition, if your company is a long-time user of data processing, you probably have a number of program applications based on flat-file processing (*Legacy Systems*). This doesn't mean that your data processing system is antiquated, but just reflects the natural business perspective of, if it isn't broken, why fix it. Your data processing department is never starved for things to do. Updating an application that is working always will be assigned a lower priority than installing new applications or fixing existing programs that are not functioning properly.

Technology improvements through the 1980's allowed companies to begin to use technology in the operational area of the company. Applications to help schedule work, manage jobs and deal with production optimization were introduced and expanded. Many companies began to open new horizons with computers but still remained focused on improving the internal operations of the company.

The accounting system required billing and product information but had little use for who was actually making the purchase decision. Most accounting oriented systems are only capable of maintaining the contact name of the person responsible for paying the bill. Frequently the name doesn't contain title or other contact information.

Operations has even less need for customer information as these systems are again internally focused. Although many operational systems utilize a database, the focus of the applications is to solve internal operational problems, not deal with customers.

As data processing equipment technology has improved, so have the programming and processing techniques. In the 1990's and beyond, the state-of-the-art has evolved to computer programs that can deal with data independently of the programs. This means that the computer programs don't care about the format of the information. A series of utility programs have evolved to manage data independently of the application programs. These database management systems (**DBMS**) allow the data processing departments to write programs that will not have to be modified when information is added or changed within the system.

Most database management systems will allow an unsophisticated user to perform their own inquiries into the computer without the aid of the data processing department. This new technology has great promise in being able to reduce the backlog of new applications to be developed by the data processing department. More importantly, it will put the power of the computer into the hands of the end-users without having to make them computer programmers.

A computer database program to manage information is a relatively new concept. Most companies are not yet using this new technique; more than likely they are still using application programs and files to manage their information. It is ironic that while the cost and effort to convert existing applications to a database management system may be prohibitive, the cost of the actual DBMS program is fairly modest.

Technological enhancements over the last few years have produced a whole new set of applications. Because the data is now randomly available and the computer is powerful enough to process one transaction at a time, *on-line transaction processing applications* have evolved. This new application series has placed added demands on data processing to provide data instantly.

When many computer programs originally were written, the available data and necessary reports were perceived to be relatively fixed. If the programmer who initially designed the system didn't anticipate a requirement for information in the future, that information became very difficult to obtain. Data availability was controlled by the computer and data processing department, not the user of the information. This accounts for the usage explosion of personal computers within business. End-users were frustrated with the "long" delivery time from data processing. They wanted to control their own information and not be limited in what information they could receive.

Database management systems offer a way to solve the problems of both the user and the data processing department. Still, business decision-makers are faced with some very difficult questions:

1) Which database management system suits our needs?

2) Does the economic benefit of transferring information to the user outweigh the cost of the additional computer power needed for rapid information delivery?

3) How difficult will it be to convert to a database management system?

The 1990's has seen an explosion of the use of database systems. Marketing and sales departments, long frustrated by the data processing and Information Technology (*IT*) departments within their companies, have ventured out on their own and implemented a myriad of database and sales automation applications. These free-standing systems are typically not tied to the billing and accounting information. Most maintain information about the contacts within customers and prospects independent of the order processing and accounts receivable functions.

The organization chart, as in Illustration 4-4, develops silos of information to meet the individual department needs and tends to place the customer in the chasm created by different information systems. Customers cannot get all the information they require from a single contact. As you can see in Illustration 4-5, each department typically needs different elements of customer information. Almost as disconcerting is that the various sources of information (Illustration 4-6) are all different and disconnected.

Because most data processing centers are still using programs and files to process information, greater care in planning for the data requirements of your direct marketing program will be needed. As we discussed in Chapter 1, you must have five specific elements (Illustration 4-7) for a successful direct marketing program.

Two of these elements are directly related to our discussion:

- **Database**

- **Controls & Analysis**

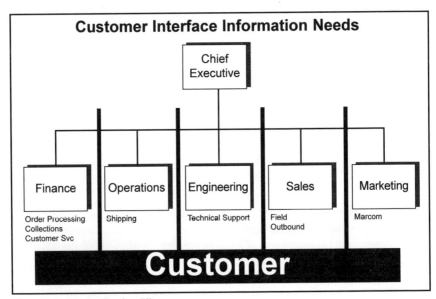

Illustration 4-4: Application Silos.

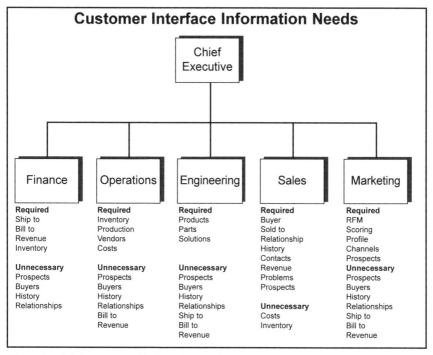

Illustration 4-5: Departmental information needs.

Let's again examine the various parts of the direct marketing database:

- **A database provides names of customers or prospects.**

  The original name and address list is an important part of the database, but all of the activity relating to each of the names on that list is also essential.

- **A database is a vehicle for storing and measuring responses.**

  Once you've reach the targets you identified and they respond to your offer, the database should provide the ability to track each contact and each response.

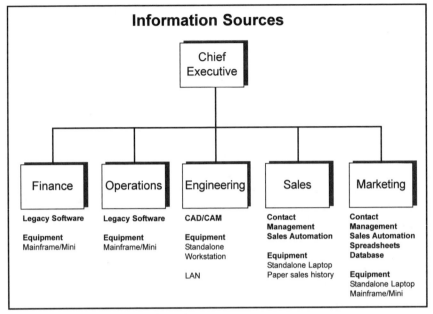

Illustration 4-6: Departmental information sources.

- **A database is a vehicle for storing and measuring purchases.**

Now that you know if a prospect has responded to your direct marketing program, you want to track whether these respondents actually become buyers.

The back-end conversion of respondents to orders is the key measurement in evaluating the success of the direct marketing program. By tracking the actual respondents who purchase, you can establish the cost per order and the average order size.

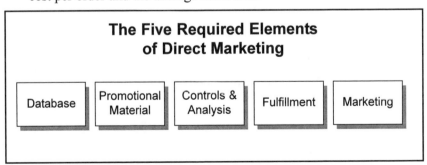

Illustration 4-7: The required elements of direct marketing.

The Definition of Direct Marketing with Database Defined

- An organized and planned system of contacts

- Using a variety of media -- seeking to produce a lead or an order

- Developing and maintaining a database

  - **Providing names of customers and prospects**

  - **Vehicle for storing and measuring responses**

  - **Vehicle for storing and measuring purchases**

  - **Vehicle for continuing direct communication**

- Measurable in costs and results

- Effective in all methods of selling

- Expandable with confidence

Illustration 4-8: The definition of direct marketing and database.

A database is a vehicle for continuing direct communication to the prospects, respondents, and customers.

The database should allow you to have a sustained and complete ability to contact the initial list of prospects, the group that responded, and the group that became customers.

As you can see, the measurement and controls of the direct marketing program are directly tied to the database. It is very challenging to anticipate the information you'll have to capture to measure and evaluate the program, prior to starting the project. Because most data processing departments are using programs and files as opposed to database management systems, adding or changing data is more difficult.

Building a Relational Database

Relational database technology now allows you to separate your data into unique elements and only store one version of information for multiple

Traditional Flat File Processing

Account #	Name & Address	Contact	Phone #

Date	Description	Amount	Disposition

Date	Description	Amount	Disposition

Date	Description	Amount	Disposition

Illustration 4-9: Flat File Processing.

uses. For example, you can create a single company name and address that can be used for contacting multiple people within that company. If the address changes, you only have to make the address change once for all contacts within the company.

Information in a relational database is stored in *tables*. The database table contains *columns*, that are similar to the fields in a normal data processing file. The members of the table are called *rows*. These are similar to the records in standard data processing files. Key fields are data elements that link information in separate files to make updating easier.

In the past, if you needed to capture multiple options for a specific question that allowed more than a single response, you probably created a separate 'bucket' for each possible response. Illustration 4-9 depicts a single record that has been designed to accommodate 3 orders. The 3 sets of information about the 3 orders become a part of each customer record. As you can see, to capture this information with traditional file processing, a separate bucket for each order is necessary. Additionally, if the customer purchases a 4th time, you would have to either eliminate one of the prior orders or change all the programs and files involved.

Relational Processing

Location Table

Account #	Name & Address	Phone #
Account #	Name & Address	Phone #
Account #	Name & Address	Phone #

Names Table

Account #	Contact	Phone #
Account #	Contact	Phone #
Account #	Contact	Phone #

Activity Table

Account #	Contact	Date	Description	Amount	Disposition
Account #	Contact	Date	Description	Amount	Disposition
Account #	Contact	Date	Description	Amount	Disposition

Illustration 4-10: Relational Processing.

In a relational database, you would create a separate table for orders and link them together using a common key.

For example, suppose you have given your prospects the following response choices in a mailing: receive additional information; attend a seminar; be contacted by a salesperson; or be added to a mailing list. Prospects will often select more than one option. To capture this information with traditional file processing, a separate bucket for each option was necessary. Additionally, if you offered another option on a subsequent program, you would have to change all of the files and programs involved.

Using a relational database (Illustration 4-10), a table for prospect requests is created and linked via a common element in the *Names* table. Normally, the common element is a name number. Each separate request is entered into the activity table. New or additional requests are added independent of prior activities.

Location addresses are stored in a separate table and individuals are related to the location table by a common location identifier. If the address changes, only the location table needs to be changed. Each individual's contact address is automatically updated by the change.

Lists

As we mentioned earlier, some direct marketers consider their lists to be the complete database. In reality, the list is just the initial building block of the database.

There are basically five kinds of lists:

- House or Customer lists
- Compiled lists
- Respondent lists
- Subscription or Membership lists
- Combined Databases

Each list has different characteristics that may make it a worthwhile list for your business to use. The lists you select for your direct marketing effort will be the single most important decision in determining the success or failure of the project.

In real estate, there are three things that are important in a piece of property:

1) Location
2) Location
3) Location

Direct marketing has a similar series of important elements:

1) List
2) List
3) List

To underscore the importance of the list, carefully consider this direct marketing axiom: an outstanding offer made in an outstanding package to a poor list will produce poor results. On the other hand, a mediocre offer, in a mediocre package made to a good list will probably produce good results.

Let's look at the different kinds of lists and their characteristics:

House or Customer Lists: These are people that have previously responded to you or have already become customers. This is the most valuable list source you have and will produce the highest results when used in a direct marketing project.

Develop as much geographic, demographic and psychographic information as possible on your house lists. The more information you have on people who have already bought from you, the easier it will be to select prospects who may buy from you. There is a scientific computer method, called regression analysis, available to review customers and determine their areas of similarity. This technique will use mathematical algorithms to determine the important similar traits exhibited by a group of customers. If you have about 1,000 or more customers, regression analysis can be an interesting and exciting approach to help determine what your customers have in common. You can get additional information about regression analysis techniques from your local college statistics department or by contacting the Direct Marketing Association, 1120 Avenue of the Americas, New York, NY, 10036-6700.

The existing sales force, if you have one, can be very helpful in establishing a profile of likely prospects to purchase your products or services. Again, people who have already purchased your products are the best indicator of others who should be your customers.

House lists, particularly if you're billing the customer, are fairly current and up to date. These lists will normally contain phone numbers and name and title information. Depending on the product you're selling, the contact name and title may or may not be appropriate for your needs. Depending on your company's credit policies, your house lists may not contain industry and sizing information. Your customer list may contain shipping and billing information and may not contain the contact you're looking for.

Evaluate your house lists for applicability to your needs. House lists are excellent sources for cross-selling, upgrading, and generating repeat business. They consist of customers with whom you have already established a working relationship. Capitalize on that relationship in your direct marketing programs.

Compiled Lists: There are many companies that compile and develop lists as their primary business. You're probably familiar with the Dun and Bradstreet (D&B) and InfoUSA. Both are well-known business information provides. Some list compilers have specialized in specific market niches. They may use direct mail and telephone interviewing to build and verify the information. You can even contract with a list compiler to build a unique list to meet your special needs.

Compiled lists are typically used by marketers to fulfill a unique requirement, so compiled list owners normally append some additional information to the basic name and address. Most use SIC codes as a primary segmentation tool. Frequently, compiled lists will have more than one contact per business. Some of the major list compilers have built total lists of all available businesses with some sizing and other demographic information.

Compiled lists are normally updated on a periodic basis, usually annually or bi-annually. Some lists are compiled from the yellow pages, therefore they are only updated once per year. With the frequent changes of title and position in American industry, compiled lists tend to be outdated by 20% to 40%. The basic sizing and segmentation data doesn't change significantly.

Compiled lists are excellent resources when you are looking for additional information to help you target a promotion. If you want to reach a segment of the market that can only be identified by very specific criteria, compiled lists are probably your best source.

Respondent Lists: People who have previously purchased or responded to direct marketing are more likely to respond to direct marketing again. Direct marketers commonly weigh the value of a respondent in terms of how *recently* they have responded, how *frequently* they have responded, and the *monetary* value of their purchase. This concept is called **RFM (Recency, Frequency and Monetary)**. Catalog marketers are very familiar with this concept and frequently score their lists using RFM techniques.

Other direct marketers will frequently rent their respondent lists to others. Renting lists can provide excellent opportunities for you to sell your products or services. You will have to evaluate the type of products the respondents purchased on these lists, and the similarity between those products and yours. Business list brokers can provide valuable insight into list usage by other marketers and recommendations based on their years of experience in the list rental business.

In most cases, respondent lists do not contain very much additional information concerning the prospect or company beyond RFM. It is unusual for the respondent list to contain a phone number.

Respondent lists can be fairly current, depending on the group that you decide to rent. The more recently the respondents purchased, the more accurate the list will be. If the list is aged, you run the risk of not being able to reach many names on the list. An aged list will probably contain incorrect and old contact information. Contacts that can't be reached or confirmed because of bad information are commonly called *Nixies*.

Subscription and Membership Lists: This group of lists consists of people who have demonstrated an affinity with a common set of interests. In the business community, a group that subscribes to a trade journal probably has an interest in that activity. By advertising, mailing, or phoning the members of this group, you are targeting the identified interest. This type of affinity is called a *psychographic characteristic* -- how people feel about things. Membership and subscription lists consist of people who have made a conscious decision to participate. They raised their hands and said, I want to belong.

Membership lists may contain industry, sizing, and other pertinent information. Most frequently, these lists only contain name and address data, though telephone numbers may be available. These lists may be out of date. Frequently, the name and address information on membership lists are not purged and kept current.

Subscription lists usually only contain name, title, and address information. The publication is being sent to the name on a periodic basis, and therefore the name and address information is accurate. Most subscription lists do not include telephone numbers, titles or industry information.

There are two types of subscriptions:

Paid Subscription: The subscriber has paid to receive the publication. Although there is very little additional information available about the subscriber, they paid to belong to this group. Paid subscriptions might also be classified as respondent lists because they are direct response purchasers.

Controlled Subscription: This is a free subscription. The reader fills out an application to qualify to receive the publication. Controlled subscription publication lists have additional information and can be segmented and targeted better than paid subscription lists. Although, because it is free, the reader may not have as strong an affinity towards the product as the paid subscriber.

Combined Databases: In the last few years, the list industry has created still another type of list. Using sophisticated data processing techniques, the largest list managers have created large combined lists of people who responded to multiple campaigns or subscribe to a number of publications. For example, a large magazine publisher handling a number of different publications can create a combined list containing all of the subscriber names identifying which publications they receive.

Combined database lists are being developed to include multiple subscription, multiple membership and multiple respondent files. The characteristics of this list should be similar to those of the type of list on which the combined information is based. In many cases you can select multiple affinities therefore identifying even better names to promote.

Because the list manager is attempting to create a more valuable list type, many of the names have been enhanced to include business size, type and other pertinent demographic information. Many have phone numbers.

Selecting the appropriate type of list will depend on the direct marketing promotion. Each list type has its own advantages. As you design your direct marketing program, we suggest you test different lists and list types to determine your most effective list source.

Combining Lists

In the business-to-business environment there are over 70,000 lists available. It is impossible to know about every list. As part of your direct marketing business plan, you will identify the most likely prospect for your products. After you define your marketing program, you may want to consider using a list broker to help you select and evaluate the most useful lists.

Once you select the various lists you plan to use, your database effort will begin. Using various computer routines, you'll want to combine the lists and eliminate duplicate records to the best of your ability. De-duplicating in the business-to-business environment is more difficult than when marketing to consumers.

Even screening by telephone number, which you may or may not have, will not guarantee the elimination of duplicate records. Many businesses provide direct phone numbers for individuals and a different phone number for the company. On the other hand, some businesses only have a central phone number. It is impossible to use the phone number to accurately eliminate duplicates.

Based on our experience, the best de-duplication routines will be only about 60% effective in the business-to-business environment. Consider using an outside service to eliminate duplicates and combine the lists. Each record should be updated to reflect the list from which it came. This will allow you to perform an analysis of each list source.

If you're planning to use telemarketing, you may want to send the combined, de-duplicated list to a service bureau to have the phone numbers appended to the record. These same service bureaus can also add industry, sizing and other demographic information to your list.

What started as a simple mailing list, is now growing into a database containing other valuable pieces of information. At this point, you can fulfill the first requirement of the direct marketing database - - you can reach a group of prospects or customers. Frequently, this is where the database effort ends. We often find internal databases that have no measurement information about respondents or purchasers. It is also fairly common to find that the respondents from a mail campaign were never recorded and sent to the field force for handling.

Measuring Response

Your data processing department may not be able to handle additional information because of the modifications required by their existing programs. If an application system is being designed to support your needs, you should evaluate all of the additional information required for your database.

The database should be capable of measuring that group of people who responded to the direct marketing promotion. This sounds simple, but it can prove to be very difficult depending on your direct marketing program type. As you define your database requirements for the data processing department, make sure they understand that you'll need to identify respondents and, ultimately, buyers.

Lead generation and traffic building programs (those campaigns that ask prospects to respond by going to a specific location) are difficult to measure. You may have to design a special method to capture respondent information. Special coupons or premium offers that are only available as a result of the direct marketing program can be useful in establishing measurement information.

As you design your database requirements, you may want to include:

> Type of contact
> Date of contact
> Response date
> Response request (what did the prospect ask for)
> Response source (mail, phone, internet, trade show)
> Response subsource (specific campaign, program)

This information can be helpful in evaluating the success of your program, and determining your next logical step. By building a transaction file detailing the activity and results, you'll be able to follow the sales cycle from start to finish.

If you are only making one contact per prospect, this information is not difficult to record. The situation gets more complex and difficult if multiple contacts and types of contacts are used for the same list. For example, you may decide to mail to several different titles in the same business. Tracking responses from this program can become difficult.

Lead generation programs get more complicated because you involve a variable that you can't control -- the salesperson. That is why lead programs need to be both measured and controlled.

Being able to measure respondents is easier in the consumer environment because the list is simpler. The consumer will frequently purchase as the response, therefore you don't have to deal with a response and purchase separately. Business-to-business is more complicated because there is no easy way to manage the name; the decision cycle is longer, more complicated and may have more than one player. All of these factors require a more sophisticated database in business marketing than in the consumer world.

Measuring Purchases

As we mentioned earlier, the real measurement of the success of any direct marketing program is the ultimate cost per order and the profitability of the program. But if the measuring of a respondent can get difficult, the measuring of a purchase can become impossible.

Frequently, a prospect will respond to a direct marketing program with a different company name than the name used during the purchase. A prospect may respond to the offer as an individual, yet the purchase is actually made by the company.

Your database must first measure respondents and then those respondents that ultimately convert to orders. If you're selling a product directly and not using a sales force, the problem is a little less difficult. You will ultimately know that a sale took place. In a lead generation program, you may never find out that there was a sale.

Several methods can help you measure the actual purchases made because of the direct marketing program.

- Make a special offer only available through the direct marketing program. If this offer is fulfilled, you'll know that the order came as a direct result.

- Ask the customer after they buy, how they heard of your company and the primary reason they purchased.

- Pay special incentives to the distribution channel for ordering through the direct marketing program.

- Use a computer matching routine to identify orders from direct marketing.

- If you are using a sales force, ask the salespeople what has happened.

Don't limit your measurement program to these ideas. Include measurement as part of the creative process in designing your direct marketing program.

In a lead generation program, the problem of measuring sales is frustratingly complicated. The salespeople do not like to admit that you helped them. They are reluctant to give credit to the direct marketing program for the sale. In addition, many leads are not even followed up by the salespeople. The same techniques described above for measuring orders can also be used to measure the effectiveness of your salespeople. Frequently, direct marketers elect to ask the sales force to evaluate the quality of the leads. This seems to be the least effective technique for evaluating the success of the direct marketing program.

You may want to add the following information to your database to help you evaluate purchases:

> Date of purchase
> Product purchased
> $ Amount purchased
> Method of purchase (retail, salesperson, direct)

Continuing Communication

Any respondent to your direct marketing programs -- whether for information or actual purchases -- will become your best opportunity for additional response in future programs. The respondent list could become one of your most valuable assets.

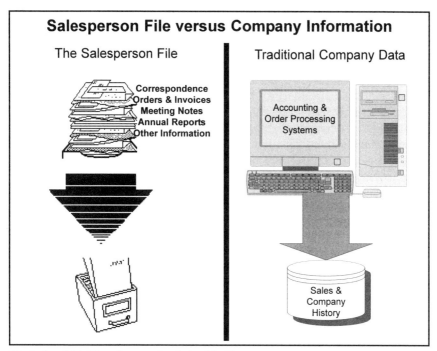

Illustration 4-11: The salesperson's relationship file.

In Chapter 1, we discussed the difference between information maintained by salespeople about their customer relationships and the information typically kept by the company (Illustration 4-11). The database you develop will probably have to accommodate information that has not been keep in the past.

As you use direct marketing programs to contact your "house" list, be sure you provide a way to keep the list up-to-date. If names, addresses, phone numbers, or contact information change, your database should reflect the most current information. Though a sensitive issue, consider capturing customer e-mail addresses. This process will be discussed fully later in this book.

Your least expensive respondent, lead, or order will be generated from your "house" list of prior respondents and customers. That means this list will represent your most profitable universe for selling products or services. Very often we'll see lists of respondents to direct marketing programs stacked in boxes with nothing being done to further the sales effort. Other than existing customers, those "bad" leads represent your best selling opportunity.

Building a Business Database

Unlike consumer lists where there is one household and, therefore, one target per address, business lists are composed of one address for many people. This one-to-many situation makes list maintenance difficult. In addition, lists are often built as a result of responses received from prospects and customers and often contain abbreviations and user shorthand. The resulting lists tend to be a hodge-podge of data that is difficult to combine into useful information.

In addition to the inaccuracy of information provided by respondents and customers, many house files have been developed from accounting files. As a result, the list doesn't contain the marketing or sales contact.

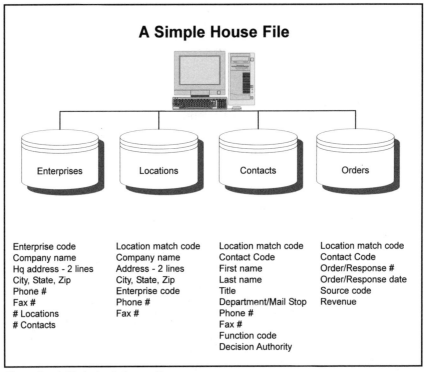

Illustration 4-12: A simple house file.

Business marketing databases (Illustration 4-12) require at least four separate tables or files:

1) Enterprise – allows identification of the parent company.
2) Location – the name and address of the location.
3) People – the names, titles, phone numbers, mail stops, function codes and other pertinent information concerning the contacts at each location.
4) Orders or response – the detail information concerning the activity of the people.

The information in each table can be related to the other appropriate tables using an enterprise number, location number and account number for each contact. Orders should be linked to the people and can therefore be summarized for the location or enterprise.

Business naming conventions, abbreviations and varying addresses make merge, purge and deduplication an imperfect science in business marketing.

To accomplish deduplication of business databases, we have successfully used a match code for each location developed from company name and address information. The code uses the zip code (5 positions), a portion of the company name (the first 4 positions) and a portion of street address (the first 3 positions). The company name and street address portions ignore blanks, special characters and special terms, like P.O. Box. By combining these data elements in a deduplication process, you will only have one address for a corresponding location. Although not fully accurate, this system does eliminate some duplication.

After developing the location match code, you can also consider developing a code for each contact. We typically use the first few characters of the last name along with the first initial. Combining this code with the location match code will allow you to avoid including duplicate people at the same location. If you code their job function as well as decision authority, you can target promotions to the appropriate people. By including the people in a separate file, you have no limit on the number per location.

Orders and responses should be stored in another file and related by match code and contact code. This will allow you to include multiple transactions per person.

Finally, you can use the company name to identify multiple locations for a larger enterprise or company. We will often take the first 4 characters from the first and second words in a company name to develop an enterprise code. You'll be surprised how effective this can be.

This process may sound difficult to complete, but today's technology and software make this pretty easy. We frequently use Boreland's *Paradox* or Microsoft *Access* to build this kind of structure. In a recent program we combined over 500,000 customers to yield 450 enterprises representing 75,000 people. In another situation the total file was almost 80,000 with 250 enterprises representing 13,000 people.

Again, the business-to-business database presents unique problems because of the nature of business; one company with many people; and our inability to control how people respond.

Every company should develop a process to clean and maintain their house file. There simply is no choice. A file that isn't maintained periodically is out of date quickly. If you clean it once and then don't develop a process to ensure it remains up-to-date, it will quickly become inaccurate.

Building the file is only the start. Now you have to determine the accuracy and usability of the names. This isn't a computer issue but a practical usability discussion. Is the company still located at the address? Are the names within the company accurate? Once you determine the accuracy, how will you maintain the file to keep it up to date?

Before you undertake any file building effort, you should decide how you're going to maintain the information. If you're not willing to invest in maintaining the integrity of the database, don't undertake building it because within a relatively short period of time it will be out of date.

Maintaining the accuracy of your house file may require several additional fields. For example, you probably should include the date the record was last updated or verified and also the last date and type of response received. This will enable you to schedule the next appropriate contact to maintain the file.

Most problems associated with adding names to a database center on inconsistent information being entered. In some cases this is caused by inaccurate data entry. In many cases it is caused by respondents providing different versions of the same information. Try to develop standards and procedures to ensure consistent data entry and have someone you trust review the source data for accuracy prior to entry into the system.

Verifying and Maintaining House File Names

Unlike first class mail, which is guaranteed deliverable or is returned to the sender, the postal service discards bulk mailings if they are not deliverable. If you don't constantly maintain the accuracy of your house file, you can be throwing a lot of money right into the trash.

We have often used post cards (they are mailed first class) as an effective method of cleaning and verifying the accuracy of the house file. The double post card allows you to make an offer and still enjoy the benefits of first class.

We suggest you mail every name on your house file at least once each year. Shipments and fulfillment processing can also be the annual activity, because they will verify the accuracy of the name and address.

If you are dealing with larger companies, a first class mailing may not be an effective technique. While the post office will return non-deliverable first class mailings, it will deliver many pieces to mail rooms when the individual is no longer there.

There are several techniques you can use to ensure that the mail reaches your target. You can address the mail to the individual as well as the function or title. Many companies request a piece to be forwarded to the appropriate function if the targeted individual is no longer there.

Another technique is to develop a direct marketing campaign to the mail rooms (Illustration 4-13). You can select companies that have multiple contacts on your house file and target a direct marketing campaign to the mail room manager. Ask the mail room to update your files and remove names that are no longer appropriate.

Your mail package can consist of a short letter requesting updating of your list, a list of names and a business reply envelope. Don't be surprised if you receive over 50% response. Most companies want to remove non-deliverable names and the associated mail that has to be processed each day from their workload.

Dear Mailroom Manager,

QED manufactures ground water sampling, pumping and treatment equipment. As a customer of QED, we send information about our equipment to people in your company who have requested it. We also periodically send out technical and regulatory updates. We want to be sure that the information we're sending is reaching the appropriate people. Inaccurate mail increases your costs and our costs and wastes natural resources.

Please help us by reviewing the names and mailing addresses listed on the attached page and:

- Change any information that is inaccurate
- Cross out any people who are no longer with your company.
- Provide addresses for people who may be at different locations.
- Add names and addresses for individuals who would like to be placed on our mailing list to receive our company newsletter as well as technical and regulatory updates from time to time.
- Check the box below if all the information listed is correct.

Please return this letter in the enclosed self-addressed stamped envelope by July 1st.

Thank you for your help.

Illustration 4-13: A sample mailroom manager letter.

Most mail rooms are happy to remove non-deliverable names from your list because it will ultimately reduce their workload. We have even received unsolicited mail from companies identifying names that have changed. You're actually doing the target company a favor by allowing them to update your list.

You can even attempt a telephone follow-up to the non-respondents to remove still another group of non-deliverable names. Mail rooms are relatively easy to find when you contact the switchboard of most companies. The manager or supervisor is frequently available so the telephone campaign can be relatively inexpensive. There isn't a significant cost associated with not being able to contact your target as in most business-to-business telephone efforts.

Visit your own mail room to determine how they would process a similar request from another company.

Once you determine that a name is no longer valid, don't remove it from your mailing list. Create a suppression file of non-deliverable names. You can do this by flagging the name or moving it to a new file to be used for this purpose. Whenever you acquire a new list for marketing purposes, you can use the suppression file to remove names you already know are invalid.

Maintaining the accuracy of your house file is difficult but extremely worthwhile. You can avoid significant marketing expenses by not mailing names that are invalid and also avoid embarrassing customer situations. After you initially clean the file, develop a process to maintain the accuracy on an on-going basis. As we mentioned earlier, you should attempt to verify every name on your list at least once each year.

Adding Marketing Information to Your House File

Your customer's and prior respondent's file offers you the best source of market intelligence. Unfortunately, most house files do not contain any industry or financial information. Many house files don't even contain appropriate contact information to sustain additional marketing activity.

An investment in your house file to add additional information can make it significantly more usable. Several service bureaus will work with you to add the appropriate information you require. We've worked with several list compiling and information bureaus that have been able to effectively enhance house files with some basic marketing information. You should discuss your needs with your own data service.

These companies append a vendor specific number to a customer or prospect database. With their number system they can also append specific industry, financial and contact information from their files.

The flowchart in Illustration 4-14 identifies a procedure for building a marketing database from a house file in a relatively short period of time. The process would take from one to three months to source the appropriate data.

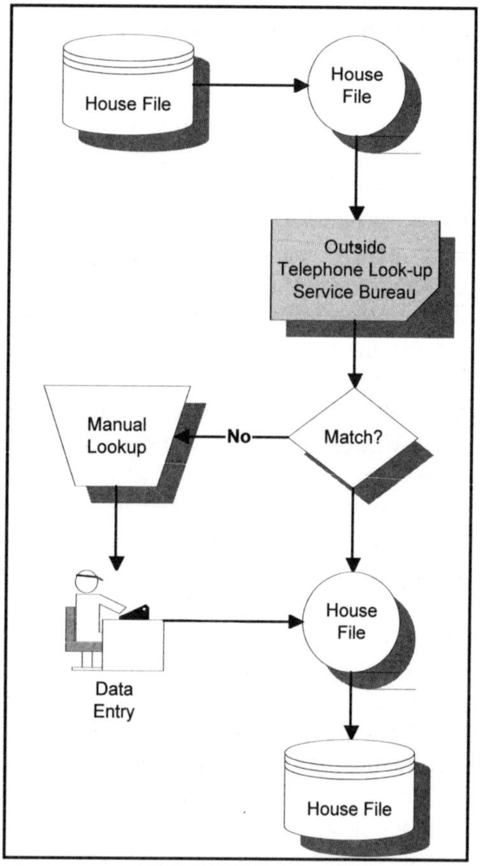

First you will have to build a file of all the customers and prospects on your house file. This file should contain both current and purged names. Any customer that has purchased a product from you is valuable. Any customer, whether current or prior, can help to develop a profile of your best opportunities.

Once the file is created it will be sent to an outside compiling service to have business information appended to the record. Typically between 40% and 60% of the records are matched with existing business information. The number of records found depends on the quality of your house file.

Records that are not found will then be sent through a manual process, which will take longer because of the manual effort. The manual process will identify about the same 40% to 60% quantity. Therefore, with this process you can add information to almost 70% of your house file.

Illustration 4-14: A process for adding information to your house file.

These services maintain extensive financial, industry and contact information about most businesses. You can purchase the information and expand your customer files to contain a great deal of information.

Your house file can now be evaluated to determine which industries are contributing the most customers. Size of business can also be used to determine your best selling opportunity.

This process will allow you to identify other establishments related to your current customers. You can promote other sites and facilities within existing customers and use your existing customer relationship to develop new customer opportunities.

Enhancing your house file with additional marketing information can help you improve your marketing activities to both customers and prospects. You don't have to be a large company to have a valuable marketing house file.

Database Marketing

In the past, computer systems were designed and implemented to solve internal business problems. Most of these systems cannot provide much information concerning the customer relationship.

As we move forward, customers are going to demand that we are more in-tune with their needs. Customers don't think that any contact they have with your company is trivial and will expect everyone who deals with them to be aware of these contacts. The history of the relationship will be available to everyone who is dealing with the customer.

Computer software needs to be chosen for its ability to capture data from a customer's perspective. What data will make it easiest for the customer to do business with you? Financial and operations oriented reports will have to be generated as a by-product of the customer driven contact.

In a customer driven system, the customer's needs and requirements are the primary concern. Every contact with the customer is recorded in an integrated database, which is used to provide information to the customer where and when they want it.

In such a system, when a customer calls customer service to inquire about the status of a current or previous order, the data is readily available to the customer service representative handling the call. In addition, orders can be immediately processed. If the outbound field or phone salespeople have rendered a quote, it is immediately available for updating or processing.

Some of the best contacts companies receive are inbound calls to the help desk or technical support. Many companies are using third-party channels of distribution and don't have the name of the user or purchaser of their products. The inbound support phone call is an excellent opportunity to capture the name and address information of someone who is using or interested in your products.

Once you've captured the inbound customer-initiated contact, you can use the information to sustain or enhance the business relationship. The customer is going to ultimately expect you to have complete knowledge of all contacts they have with you, so they can receive the service they expect.

Unfortunately, systems designed in the past have made no provision for capturing and dealing with customer calls and contacts that do not yield orders. In most cases, the systems don't even deal with the appropriate sales contact.

Customers who call customer service expect you to be able to satisfy their inquiry immediately. As companies begin to design and implement systems that capture every contact, these same customers will expect you to be aware of all of their previous discussions so they don't have to continually bring your company up to speed each time they call. Companies that facilitate this level of service will become dominant and create an expectation level we'll all have to deliver.

Contact management systems have become critical tools to field salespeople. Virtually every salesperson is now using a laptop computer and some form of software to help manage their lives.

Unfortunately, the contact management explosion doesn't often integrate with the other systems within their companies. Salespeople have the information they have created concerning the relationship, but very little information concerning the other relationship between the company and customer.

We immediately focus on providing sales and order information, which is a step in the right direction. But imagine the customer's reaction upon receiving a field sales call from a salesperson shortly after being contacted by the accounts receivable department regarding an overdue invoice. Or a similar field contact shortly after the customer has called several times to technical support concerning a problem they were having with their equipment!

As salespeople, we've dealt with these types of situations and had to spend considerable time dealing with the fall-out or breakage. In the past we could excuse our lack of knowledge of the situation because of the ineffectiveness of our internal communications. But as other companies implement complete customer-driven systems, excuses won't work. Customers will demand the services they've experienced in dealing with other companies.

We continue to hype the internet and the promise of interactive instant communication. To use this new e-commerce channel effectively, we must be able to store, retrieve and disseminate all the information regarding our relationship with our customers.

In the foreseeable future companies will begin to implement complete data warehouses which contain all of the information about the company's relationship with a prospect or customer. This information will come from every contact made within the company.

Database Marketing is the newest marketing concept and the current buzz word that everyone is using to describe their marketing efforts. As you have already seen, a database means different things to different people. This marketing concept presumes that each marketing contact is stored on the computer database. The prior contact history will be used to establish the next logical contact and marketing activity. Because most businesses are still using programs and data files, they are probably unable to implement database marketing today.

To properly implement database marketing, you must be able to change your data requirements as your needs change. It is possible to require a change based on each contact you make to the database. This could mean dedicating a computer programming staff to the direct marketing project. The use of a dynamic database probably requires a database management system.

Your need to capture information about each contact and the results of that contact will require a significant amount of computer storage and the flexibility to change the files each time you introduce a new marketing program. If you have this capability, you will be able to automatically generate contacts to your customers and prospects based on the results of the last contact.

The real question becomes: does database marketing offer you an opportunity to generate a less expensive order and increase your profits? Based on our experience, the answer is yes.

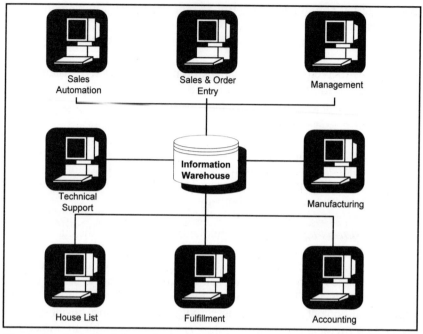

Illustration 4-15: The information warehouse.

Ultimately information will become available from every contact to allow companies to plan and execute customer driven programs. Along with customer contacts from both field and telephone contacts, information from technical support and customer service will also be added to the ultimate data warehouse and available to anyone interfacing a customer or prospect account.

All information will be available to anyone who has contact with a customer or prospect in order to sustain or enhance the relationship. Salespeople will be able to contact customers with full knowledge of inquiries or orders made by the customer. There will even be information concerning accounts receivable collection activity that may have been initiated. Customers will receive great customer service because everyone involved from the company will know about all activity that has occurred in the past.

Marketing will be able to make accurate decisions because complete information about product and customer sales will be available for analysis.

We'll even be able to evaluate the success of direct marketing and lead generation.

Building a Source Code Reporting System

In addition to your customer and prospect information databases, you should also create a series of tables to facilitate evaluating your direct marketing. These tables can be linked to the order and contact tables to facilitate program analysis and evaluation. The following tables will allow you to develop reports to more accurately evaluate your direct marketing. They will also allow you full flexibility:

- Source Code - this table contains information concerning the type of promotion used to acquire the various names on the house file. There are four ingredients in any direct marketing promotion: List, Offer, Format and Copy. The source code table should allow you to assemble results summarized by each of the ingredients.

The source code reporting system contains individual tables for each of the basic elements of the campaigns.

- List Table - identifies the list used in the promotion. If advertising is used, the list would be the circulation of the magazine,

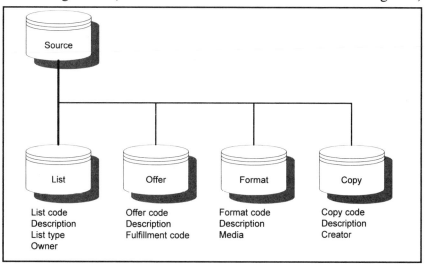

Illustration 4-16: Source reporting system.

Direct Marketing Activity by Source Code

Source Code	Description	Quantity	First Date	Last Date	Responses	%	Leads	%	Orders	%	Rev	Contrib	Ratio
1001	Tri-fold Self Mailer	10,000	6/1/96	8/15/96	356	3.56	125	35.1	25	20.0%	7,350	3,200	8.99
1001	Pers Resp Tri-Fold	10,000	6/1/96	8/15/96	356	3.56	125	35.1	25	20.0%	7,350	3,200	8.99
1001	DPC	10,000	6/1/96	8/15/96	356	3.56	125	35.1	25	20.0%	7,350	3,200	8.99

Illustration 4-17: A sample of a source code report.

trade shows are lists of attendees. The list source should be identified for every promotion.

- Offer Table - shows the offer used and related information such as end-date, fulfillment package contents, response vehicle and the overall reason for the prospect's response.

- Format Table - describes the method used to promote to the prospect or customers, i.e. direct mail, space ad, telephone.

- Copy Table - summarizes the copy and graphics used in the format.

The separate tables will facilitate reporting on the results of direct marketing and lead generation. A report can calculate results and then store the information in a spreadsheet or other electronic format.

This system should calculate the first date and last date of activity. The transaction table provides the inquiry, lead and order information and the report summarizes the data by source code. The source code report will give you the detail information on each specific test cell. By maintaining separate tables of information it will be relatively easy to summarize the data based on the various elements. You can develop summary reports for specific time periods as well as for the various items:

Campaign
List
Offer
Format
Copy

This information will allow you to evaluate the performance of your direct marketing and make informed decisions on how to improve and modify the approach.

By using a database, instead of spreadsheets, you'll be able to store historical information and sort and tabulate results easily. In addition, you only have to maintain the information in source code tables instead of the transaction information in your other data files.

Evaluating and Selecting A Sales Automation System

By Rich Bohn, President
The Denali Group
2815 N.W. Pine Cone Drive
Issaquah, WA 98027
(425)392-3514 FAX: (425)391-7982 Email: richbohn@sellmorenow.com

The one question I hear most often, is "What is the best contact management system?" Let's answer this one right away. There is no "best" contact manager or sales force automation program. The challenge is to find the one that lets you carry out your own marketing objectives and that helps you take better care of your customers. This means first defining your business requirements and only then translating these to computer software requirements. Too often, I see people attacking this problem in reverse, thinking they know their real business needs and plunging right into shopping for software. So that you do not fall into this trap, I will begin with a discussion of some of the key computer issues and how they relate to the business issues. Then I will come back to the business issues by showing you the needs analysis process that I take companies through.

If you have spent any time looking at sales automation software, you have probably already discovered that there are a lot of programs available, in fact my recent book on sales automation software discusses more than 350 available programs. You will also discover that most of these companies don't do a very good job of differentiating their products, making it very difficult to make meaningful comparisons. There are just too many programs making similar claims. Everybody can do everything! When faced with this confusing array of claims, you may be tempted to just give up. Instead, realize the first step is to make sure you are comparing "apples-to-apples."

A New Taxonomy Of Sales Automation Software

Time for a True Confession: At times, I too have been bewildered by the ever increasing array of programs hitting my desk for review! In my quest to help people make meaningful software comparisons, I have been struggling for a new way to categorize all of these different programs. Finally, I realized we needed a new taxonomy of sales automation software.

The solution came to me in a flashback to Sales 101: sell benefits, not features! The software developers are always drowning me with endless lists of new features for their programs. My reply is always, "So what! How does that help people sell more?" Finally I decided the best way to categorize the various sales automation programs is according to the sales or marketing problem they are designed to solve.

The primary job of many sales automation programs is to keep track of the various people you are selling to and the different activities you need to perform with these people. Since these contacts are the lifeblood of your business, I think of these as strategic solutions. Other sales automation programs are designed to solve specific problems like effectively preparing a proposal or quotation for a prospect. I think of these as tactical solutions.

Strategic Solutions

The primary function of those programs I call strategic solutions is to keep track of the many people you deal with and to manage your calendar. Traditionally most of the programs serving these tasks have been lumped into one giant category called contact managers. Software developers who have focused on delivering systems for large sales forces, create software that can consolidate dates, create reports and communicate with legacy computer systems as well. Unfortunately, these software developers seldom did a good job on the basic "contact management" functions. When challenged on this point, the typical reply was, "Our program isn't a contact manager."

This attitude overlooks a basic fact: sales people carry out certain tasks whether they work alone, on a team of twenty, or as a member of a two thousand person sales force. As the size of the group grows, a sales automation program must allow team members to exchange and share information. However, in all cases, the program should provide at least basic contact and calendar management functions. Only after satisfying these basic minimum requirements, should a program branch out to other sales automation functions.

In my view of strategic solutions, I further subdivide the available solutions into the following four categories:

- **Personal Information Managers (PIM)** - As their name implies, these programs are best suited for keeping track of all the little things that help you get through the day. In general, I do not recommend these programs as your primary strategic solution. However, many of these programs can work well in tandem with your main program.

- **Contact Managers** - These programs are best suited for individual sales people working alone. They provide varying contact and calendar management capabilities and may provide a wide array of additional capabilities to increase your sales impact. Most of these programs provide "user defined fields," but they usually aren't very flexible.

- **Sales Team Automation Systems** - These programs work best if you work with more than one person. A team can consist of two people, or two hundred people. These programs should provide the full range of capabilities provided by the better contact managers. In addition, they should provide network versions and database synchronization, so that team members can exchange and share information. These programs should also be flexible enough to adapt to a wide range of selling scenarios.

- **Sales Force Automation Systems** - These programs are also referred to as "enterprise solutions." They should provide all of the capabilities provided by the better contact managers and sales team automation systems as discussed above. In addition, they should provide a client/server version based on a robust database management system (DBMS), such as Oracle, Sybase or Microsoft SQL Server. These systems must be easily customized to support a wide range of complex selling environments. They should also provide the flexible communication capabilities needed to put the right information at the fingertips of whoever needs it to take great care of your customers.

Tactical Solutions

Sales people face many challenges as they continue on their quest of finding new prospects, discovering their requirements, developing quotations or proposals, presenting their products, closing orders, and taking great care of their customers. As the sales automation software category continues to mature, many great programs are emerging to solve specific problems encountered in the sales cycle. These are the programs that I refer to as tactical solutions.

There is no magic formula here. The trick is to look for ways to use technology to leverage your efforts to close more sales and take better care of your customers. I know of many companies that do not even use a strategic program, yet are quite delighted with the added impact they get from some specific tactical program. More commonly, companies are looking for the best program to meet their strategic requirements and haven't even thought about many of the great tactical solutions available. Again, the categories are not absolute and are primarily my judgment. The most common categories you might encounter include:

- Configuration Management
- Database Marketing
- Forecasting
- Lists and Data Sources
- Mapping
- Market Research
- Presentations
- Quotations and Proposals
- Sales Management

As you compare programs, make sure that you consider two or three strategic solutions that are, in fact, comparable. As you define your business requirements, don't feel you have to find one program that meets them all. Most companies find that they are best served by a good strategic solution and whatever additional tactical programs that best help them take better care of their customers.

For information and reviews about many sales automation solutions, visit my Website at www.sellmorenow.com.

Cellular Company Database Case Study

Let's examine a lead generation program that ultimately evolved into a significant database marketing program.

Cellular Company is a major supplier of cellular telephone equipment and was interested in generating sales leads for their independent distributors in several market areas. Broadcast, radio, television, space ads in both newspapers and magazines, and direct mail were used to generate responses. In Illustration 4-18, the responses were handled by an independent telemarketing service bureau. The independent firm was fully automated and handled both mail and phone responses. If the response was via telephone, the inbound communicators were scripted and fully interactive with a computer.

At the onset of the project, Cellular Company recognized that their product was unique and there would be a lot of interest from people who were not qualified. In addition, Cellular Company had a limited geographic area in which they offered services. In order to deal with the unqualified prospect, either through geography or qualification criteria, a less expensive generic fact kit was developed.

The prospect was considered of lower quality if they did not provide a company name. These prospects were sent a less expensive fulfillment package. Cellular Company did not feel that a salesperson could effectively follow-up a responder at their home. Salespeople have a tendency to prejudge the quality of leads. Respondents who only provide their home address are frequently judged to be tire kickers and not buyers.

All respondents were added to a database and each contact was tracked. As new respondents were received, they were checked against the database to ensure that they hadn't already been handled in the last 90 days. Quite often, a prospect who hasn't received a timely follow-up will respond a second time. Cellular Company was selling through outside distributors and there were several distributors in each market. An attempt was made to ensure that the same prospect wasn't sent to two different distributors. We also tried to eliminate prior respondents.

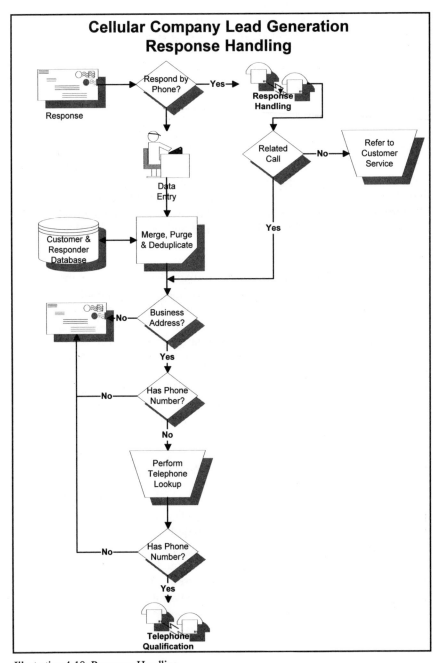

Illustration 4-18: Response Handling.

All respondents were qualified via telephone. If a mail respondent did not provide a telephone number, and the number wasn't available through directory assistance, the record was considered not qualified and sent the less expensive information package.

The qualified prospects, those with business addresses and phone numbers, were contacted via outbound telemarketing. Each prospect was screened for qualification and offered a call by a salesperson. The telephone screening approach is detailed in Illustration 4-20.

The same lead qualification script was used for both inbound and outbound telemarketing. If the prospect wasn't qualified, meaning they didn't meet the criteria for money, authority, need and desire, they were sent the inexpensive mail kit. Qualified prospects were offered the opportunity to be contacted by a salesperson.

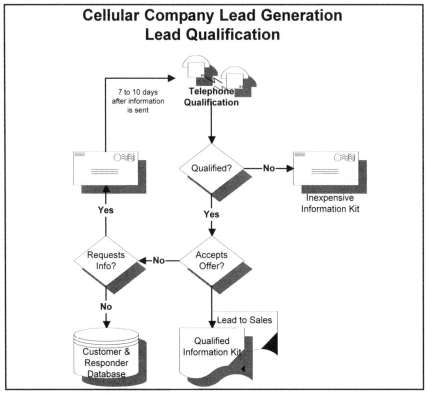

Illustration 4-19: Lead Qualification.

We know that many prospects request literature before they agree to be contacted by a salesperson. We also know that a substantial percentage of prospects who request information can be converted to a lead if they are contacted after they receive the material.

In telemarketing, prospects will frequently request additional information. Some people respond to telephone offers then request information as an easy way to terminate the call. However, people are interested in the offer, but want more information prior to making a commitment. All prospects who request additional information should be considered legitimate prospects. In our experience, about 25% of these literature requesters can be converted into leads.

Keeping track of who requested literature, when the literature was fulfilled, and when the prospect should be re-contacted, will require some form of database. Small volumes will only require a manual database. However as the volumes become larger, the database will require a computerized approach.

Initially, Cellular Company management wasn't concerned about the return of information from the sales force. Management was convinced that the sales force would follow-up on every lead and provide feedback about lead quality. Cellular Company didn't feel that a lead management and control system was necessary.

After several months of lead generation and several thousand leads, only 5% of the leads had been returned with any information. Cellular Company couldn't evaluate the success of the lead program. Senior management received verbal feedback that lead quality was not very good. They were considering shutting down the project.

To evaluate the success of the lead program, a mail questionnaire was sent to all leads to determine their disposition. The respondent database made re-contacting the leads very easy.

The results were startling. Forty percent of the leads had been contacted by the sales force. In our experience, this is a good follow-up rate. We have seen lead follow-up as low as 8% in other campaigns. In this instance the leads proved to be very high quality. Of the leads contacted by a salesperson, over 60% had purchased a product.

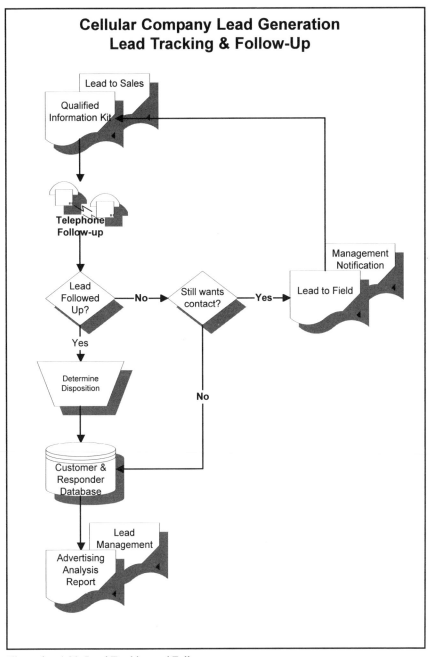

Illustration 4-20: Lead Tracking and Follow-up.

Management was alarmed about the business opportunity that had been lost because the sales force had not followed-up. Several action programs were implemented to ensure that Cellular Company could capitalize on the opportunity within their current and future respondent database.

A complete lead management and tracking system was implemented to ensure that the sales force followed up on all leads. The leads were only given to a distributor salesperson for 30 days. Cellular Company used tele-marketing to re-contact prospects 30 days after the leads were generated to determine their disposition. The follow-up call determined if the prospect had received the information requested and if they had been contacted by a salesperson. If the lead was not contacted, it was regenerated and sent to another distributor salesperson. Illustration 4-20 reflects the flow of activity in the lead tracking and follow-up system.

The results of the project were very rewarding. Follow-up improved to almost 80% of leads generated. More importantly, 30% of all leads generated resulted in orders. The cost per lead and cost per order were substantially less than originally anticipated.

Relationship Marketing

Marketing Activity

Update Database

Extract Records Based on Activity

Illustration 4-21: Relationship Marketing.

The database allowed ongoing contact with the respondent. It also allowed an accurate measurement system to be developed to evaluate the success of the lead generation program.

Additional direct mail followed by outbound telemarketing programs were developed and the database was naturally used as a list source. Prospects on the database were contacted three additional times in the first year to generate more leads. Only those prospects who had already purchased were not included in the continuing direct marketing program. Not surprisingly, the least expensive leads and orders were derived from the database because these database names performed at a higher level of response than other lists.

Each time a contact was made, it was added to the database to track and evaluate the effectiveness of each step of the direct marketing effort. The database also contained all of the information captured during the telemarketing contacts, and this data became valuable market research.

The results of each contact established the next activity for the prospect. The storage, retrieval and updating of the information as a result of each contact developed a dynamic marketing database. As we discussed in Chapter 1, the ongoing database activity is the basis for relationship marketing (Illustration 4-21). The results of each contact had to be evaluated to determine the next step.

> *The use of this information to condition the next selling activity is the essence of database marketing.*

These results and benefits justify the investment to implement a dynamic database. You can experiment with database marketing by handling your literature requesters similarly to the methods we discussed earlier. Send the information to the respondent and then follow-up with a telephone call to attempt to convert the prospect to a lead or an order. We think you'll find the results very encouraging.

Database Summarized

The term database means different things to different people.

Data processing people think about a database in terms of how the computer information is going to be managed and controlled. To them, database means database management systems (DBMS).

The conversion of existing files and programs to a DBMS is a large effort and has substantial impact on data processing. Computer programs are written to deal with data that is formatted in a specific way. Changing the format of the data normally means having to change any computer program that will deal with that data. Even adding a small piece of information to existing systems can mean a massive change to computer programs.

Database management systems separate the data from the computer programs and make changing and adding information relatively easy. DBMS systems allow you to add or change information independently of computer programs. They also move the control of information from the data processing department to the end-user.

The evolution of computer systems and where they have been used in business can have a significant impact on the implementation of your database. Most companies evolved in their use of computers from one of three major areas:

- Accounting - the computer was implemented to solve the accounting, finance and administrative areas of the company. The systems tend to be flat-file derived and have little or no customer information.

- Operations - the purpose of the computer was to improve the internal operations of the company like manufacturing operations, job scheduling and control, or production planning and control. These applications had some database but also had little or no customer information.

- Sales & Marketing - the most current evolution of systems typically focuses on improving customer service and support. Accounting and operations fucntions are by-products of the customer service process. These systems typically require a relational database and contain all information about customers and prospects.

We explained the difference between flat-file processing and relational databases to provide background as you evaluate and implement different solutions to your database problems.

The list industry defines database as an expanded list. Several list companies now offer databases that are the result of combining several lists and then adding demographic, geographic and psychographic data to them. These combined lists are referred to as databases. They are a significant improvement over prior list sources because you can be more effective in selecting and segmenting your target audience.

Other departments within your business can probably give you additional definitions of database. All of the definitions may be correct for their particular application. For the purposes of business-to-business direct marketing, the definition we've been using throughout our discussion is most appropriate.

Direct marketing will develop and maintain a database which:

- Provides names of customers or prospects.

- Is a vehicle to store and measure responses.

- Is a vehicle to store and measure purchases.

- Is a vehicle for ongoing communication with customer and prospects.

Throughout this book, we've continually reviewed each element of the direct marketing database definition. In this chapter, we have explained the five different list types:

- House or Customer lists
- Compiled lists
- Respondent lists
- Subscription or Membership lists
- Combined Databases

We discussed the characteristics of each list type and suggested methods to combine them to create a target universe for your direct marketing promotion. Once you begin direct marketing, your database needs to be able to measure responses and then measure purchases. We discussed the minimum elements needed for both of these functions.

We reviewed a simple database model along with a methodology for implementation which could help you reduce the time it takes to create your own database. Match coding and an algorithm for combining the various files within your company was discussed.

We also discussed a method for verifying your contact names using the mailroom manager and first class mail. Finally, a method for obtaining additional information using outside service providers was discussed.

There are a number of sales automation and contact management systems already available, and more are being enhanced and added every day. Rich Bohn provided an explanation of the various types of sales automation tools along with characteristics and evaluation criteria.

Database marketing offers great promise in reducing costs and increasing results. A complete program was reviewed to demonstrate the elements of database marketing. We discussed how to use the database to condition additional contacts to the prospects and customers.

The explanation of database in this chapter will allow you to effectively communicate with data processing and direct marketing. Database is one of the required elements of direct marketing. If you don't have control of the database, your efforts will probably fail. If you can't automate the database with your data processing department, consider using another alternative that will give you control.

Chapter Five:

Promotion

Promotion Defined

As used in Direct Marketing, promotion can be defined as the activities and materials that develop and encourage prospects and customers to purchase one's products or services without the aid of a sales representative. A promotion can be as simple as a brief letter to a gala event.

Promotion may be viewed as having two aspects:

- Technical
- Creative

The effort and importance placed on these two aspects may be equal, but it is more likely that 60% to 70% is devoted to the technical aspect and 30% to 40% is spent on creativity.

Technical elements are those elements that are a must if you are going to execute successful direct marketing: product information, a reply device, pricing, fulfillment, messaging and media or format. In addition, the approach must conform to legal and trade practices as well as internal product and organizational requirements.

Creative aspects are the big ideas that clothe your information to make it more appealing to its market. Big ideas can be serious, funny, direct, or oblique in product positioning.

Technical Promotion

Let's now focus on how to make you a better technician. Our goal is not to make you a creative director, but to give you the tools to develop the thought processes you need to become a better manager of the direct marketing process.

A promotion has four parts:

      1) List (Market Segment or Segments)
      2) Offer
      3) Format (Delivers Offer to Market)
      4) Copy/Graphics

Lists are discussed in Chapter 4. *Lists* represent those people, from whatever source you select, you have chosen to target. The action you want the prospect to take is motivated by your *offer*. The method you select to deliver the offer to the prospect is the *format*, and the *copy/graphics* is how you say and/or show it. Understanding these parts of promotion will provide you with a basis to evaluate and implement the direct marketing concept.

If you were to weigh the four elements of the direct marketing effort, based on the relative value of each to the ultimate success of the project, they would appear like this:

      List   50%
      Offer   25%
      Format   15%
      Copy/Graphics   10%

These percentages do not reflect what most of us do most of the time. Most of us spend 80% of our effort on copy, 15% on format, 5% on list (generally a last minute detail) and 0% on offer.

Why is there such a wide variance between what we do and what should be done to produce good direct marketing? Simple. We all love our "**It**."

> **It** *(noun) the product or service a company or individual makes available for someone to buy.*

Picture your **It** in front of you. Isn't it the most beautiful **It** in the whole world? Isn't it the most easily understood, most needed, problem solving, cost effective, efficient and user-friendly **It** ever discovered?

Isn't it difficult to understand why people aren't lined up to purchase your **It**? How simple their lives would be if only those people out there would buy and use your **It** .

Before getting too worked up, let's determine how much we know about competitive **It**. A little? Some? We don't have time to learn about their **Its** because we're too busy trying to get them to understand our **It**. We're also trying to fulfill our day-to-day administrative tasks while having some free time for fun. There just isn't enough time to understand and appreciate their **It**.

So the best thing to do is to describe our **It** in eloquent prose. We can never tell people too much, because our **It** is so great. Since everyone needs our **It**, they will take the time to read about our **It**. Then they will surely take action. So, let's spend hours and hours on every verb, noun and adjective. Better still, let's get a committee together to help write the copy -- "the words."

After spending ten weeks getting "the words" just right, we are five weeks behind schedule so let's just blast the copy out into the market. Let's run it up the flagpole and see who salutes. Let's throw it against the wall to see what sticks. What sticks?

Nothing -- or, very little.

Those stupid people don't know what they're missing! We told them about our **It** and they still don't care. They don't know what's good for them.

But it's not their fault, it's ours. We have spent 80% of our allotted time on just 20% of the areas needed in a direct marketing program.

Look through some promotional pieces you've received. How much of each do you read? 10%? 30%? 50%? 100%? And the parts you do read are the headline, graphics, captions, call-outs and subheads -- and maybe 10% to 15% of everything else.

How do you get people to pay attention to your message? Talk with trained successful salespeople and learn what they do to succeed. After conducting a number of interviews, develop a model and approach similar to the one used by a successful salesperson.

Initially the salesperson develops an understanding of the best market to sell to by trying the pitch on anybody who will listen. After a few thousand "nos" the salesperson learns who not to pitch. However, a good salesperson does not limit their sales by assuming that if a need isn't obvious, the prospect doesn't need their product. For example, while screen doors are, seemingly, a little used item in the manufacture of submarines, they may be great inside a submarine. Listen to your instincts, but don't be afraid to test a new market from time to time.

Like the salesperson, spend time seeking out the right market. Define the correct individual to market to within the market. You may have to market to both a decision-maker and an influencer. This is one of the most important aspects of the technical preparation of the direct marketing program. The list work makes the difference between success and failure. If you don't spend the effort to understand and evaluate your list, you'll experience thousands of "nos" in terms of non-response.

You may still believe the best use of your time is in forming the most eloquent description of your **It**. If you do decide that the description of your **It** is most important, go to your sales force to learn how they are selling. The way they describe the features and benefits of your **It** will be strong indicators of how your copy should be written.

Let's again review the four elements of promotion:

List -   The customers or prospects to whom you plan to target your marketing effort.

Offer - The proposition you are making to your customers or prospects in order to get them to respond. It is the motivator for the action you want the prospect to take.

Format - The vehicle for delivering the offer to your market: mail, phone, print, broadcast, trade show, seminar, Internet.

Copy/Graphics - The words and pictures you use to communicate your offer to the market.

For a promotion to be effective, follow the same steps the sales force uses to develop a sale. Use your promotion as a surrogate salesperson.

An easy acronym to help you remember the elements of direct response promotion is *AIDA* -- **A**ttention, **I**nterest, **D**esire, **A**ction. While general advertising has attention and interest as its goal, direct marketing goes further to include desire and action. These last two elements separate unsuccessful sales people and successful sales people, general advertising from direct marketing. Developing desire and moving to action is essential for successful direct marketing.

Just as an experienced salesperson does not bother trying to gain the attention of the wrong people, you should not use the wrong list. Once the salespeople have identified valid prospects, they will try to generate a sale.

The salesperson's presentation will include a complete assessment of the prospect's needs. A good salesperson will find out the prospect's problems. As a surrogate salesperson, your direct marketing promotional material must exhibit knowledge and empathy to gain the prospect's interest.

Once salespeople can identify and understand their prospect's problems, they can begin to relate the features and benefits of their **It** to the specific needs of their prospects. They do so by demonstrating how their **It** will solve the prospects' problems thereby creating a level of desire to make a change. Chapter 1 discusses this concept in detail in its review of the buying decision.

In your direct marketing program, you should perform the same function by proposing to solve problems you already know exist. Format and copy should focus the prospect on their needs and how your **It** will solve their problem. This is the first part of your offer.

Like any good salesperson, you must ask for the order. This is the second part of the offer. Move the prospect to action. Desire and action are easily affected when the offer is compressed by limitations of time, quantities, or pricing for a period of time.

This process can be applied when selling an **It** or when asking for an appointment for selling an **It**. Just like the salesperson, the direct marketing surrogate salesperson can make several contacts with a prospect before asking for an order.

A salesperson may make several contacts within an organization before finding out with whom to speak. Keep this in mind when contacting a company; it is a little presumptuous to believe a single promotional effort will reach the right person in any given company. Depending on the price of the product you are offering, it may even be presumptuous to believe the second effort will get the order.

An initial contact may merely be a probe to discover the name or title of the best person to establish a relationship with in a company. This can be accomplished by contacting a receptionist or mailroom manager and asking that person the name of the most appropriate person to make a decision to buy your **It**. This kind of information can be obtained by mail or phone.

Such an effort could be a waste of time and money if your **It** is easily understood, inexpensive, and generates a strong contribution to overhead and profit. In this case, broad based promotion can be most cost effective; the shotgun approach to many people at each business site that may need what you sell.

If your product is expensive and requires more than one individual to make a buying decision, direct marketing can be an effective enhancement to the selling effort. It may be worthwhile to spend the time and money to make sure you are speaking with the person that will act as a "champion" for your **It** during the review and buy-in cycles.

You can also use direct marketing to sell many individuals within the company on the advantages and benefits of your product. While a salesperson can't talk to more than one person at a time, direct marketing will allow your message to reach as many individuals as needed on the same day in multiple locations.

Whatever approach you select, direct marketing can be used effectively as a lead generator for your sales force after you've established awareness, interest and desire. The action can be the opportunity to be visited by a representative who will provide an analysis at no cost to the prospect.

Before discussing offers, let's explore the major difference between corporate life and entrepreneurial life. Many of the offers received in the business environment are designed to save the prospect time and/or money. This can be expanded into the business school combination: efficiency and effectiveness. In truth, people who work for a corporation don't care much about the company's time and money. They say and act as they do because that is the company line. For corporate employees time and money are not personal needs, so offers based on these do not motivate the employee.

To make an effective offer to employees, appeal to them as people. In general, corporate employees are interested in three things:

1. Getting promoted
2. Reducing hassles
3. Covering their rears

Let's review these interests in terms of life as an employee in a medium to large corporation. Getting promoted means having more status, more money, more power and all the reasons people hang around a corporation. If offered an opportunity to be promoted as a result of making a buying decision, an employee would find a way to make that decision.

Reducing hassle is a game frequently played by the corporate employee. If a promotion is not attainable, then most employees will try to reduce the chaos they experience on the job. If this can be done by making a buying decision, most people will take advantage of hassle reduction, so they can spend more time trying to get promoted.

Covering the rear is the avoidance process most people in corporate environments practice. They get others to share the risk of decisions so that no one can pin the tail on them. It is also the process of making decisions that can be revised in the event things don't work out as planned. Also, making decisions that reflect the industry choice will probably allow one to stay clear of ridicule. As a rear cover, most employees will respond to suggestions from others within the company -- especially from persons ranked above them in the organization. Other reasons to make a decision might be guarantees with a right of return, or offers that are supported by industry belief.

If employees' rears are exposed, they won't have time to reduce hassle and get promoted. If your offer is aimed at the personal motivation of the company employee you're trying to reach, your odds of success are increased.

The *owners* of a business will be interested in how your **It** can save them time and money. Business owners are saving their own money rather than the money of a corporation. The business owner often has better skills at using time. While the corporate employee is willing to delay decisions, the business owner makes decisions fast, especially when there is a way to save time or money. Owners don't need committee support to make a decision.

Lists

The lists you select are clearly the most important part of your direct marketing efforts. Unfortunately, the list is often the item you spend the least amount of time evaluating.

Earlier, during the planning phase, you should have identified the characteristics of your customers and prospects. During the identification phase you should have written a detailed description of the specific individual and types of individuals you intended to reach. We talked about lists in the Database chapter but here are some of the issues again as they relate to promotion development.

Business list selection does not enjoy the luxury of having finite selection information. Business demographics do not exist, even though this concept is frequently discussed. The demographics or profile are those characteristics that are available based on the business itself. The concept of lifestyle would be applicable if we could analyze the corporate culture of all businesses.

Here are some characteristics of businesses that are available. By understanding your market, using at least two of these characteristics, you can improve your ability to be a successful direct marketer:

- Annual sales or revenue

- Number of employees

- Standard Industrial Classification (SIC) or North American Industry Classification System (NAICS)

- Location geography - state, ZIP, SCF (Sectional Center Facility - first three digits of the ZIP code)

- Assets

- Credit rating

- Types of equipment being used

- Expenditures above a certain value in any specific area

- Area of business activity: (regional, national, international)

- Number of locations

- Titles of employees

- Functions of employees

Only by evaluating your customers and prospects and the products you are trying to sell can you arrive at the criteria you should use for list selection. All the characteristics you feel are necessary may not be available on every list you evaluate.

This problem is compounded by the limited size of business lists; you might use an entire list just testing it. You might also find that as your selection criteria becomes more specific, the number of available businesses is too few for you to be successful.

Subscription and membership lists may be a poor selection when you are planning to market in a small geographic area. The publication or organization may not have enough people in the selected area. Tight geographic marketing may necessitate the use of compiled lists.

On the other hand, compiled lists may not have complete contact names so you may be forced to solicit a title or function. This may not be so bad since testing has indicated that there is not a marked difference between title addressing and name addressing. Obviously, it is better to use the name if you have it. However, mailings to the wrong name may never get delivered, while mailing to a title or function may get delivered.

The rate of change in contact name and address in the consumer world runs about 15% to 20% per year. In the business environment, change can run as high as 60%. Compiled lists tend to be about one year old and can have a substantial error rate in the contact name. Responder and subscriber lists may be updated more frequently and the contact name might be more accurate, but remember: you don't have the same number of selection criteria for these lists.

It is often possible to trade customer lists with associates in similar businesses who are not selling competing products. For example, if you sell office supplies and an associate sells cleaning supplies, you can exchange or rent the other list and even use the associate's name in your solicitation. Customer lists always produce a better response than general list sources.

If you're selling a business publication, it is far better to solicit another business publication list than a compiled list. Evaluate your product and target market to identify the best list opportunities. Test all types of lists to determine which ones meet your cost per order or cost per qualified lead criteria. You will always be making compromises in selection criteria, contact name and other characteristics that are important to you.

Business lists are normally much smaller than consumer lists. When you begin testing, be careful not to test too many lists or your results per list might be so small you cannot adequately evaluate any list.

Some final thoughts on lists: Even after you have done a relatively good job of identifying the characteristics of the market segment you want to solicit, the actual list selection is still going to be a gamble. There are many list brokers, direct marketing agencies, and list compilers who can help you select and test list alternatives.

A good list broker can be an important addition to any direct marketing resource team. Most brokers are paid a standard industry commission of 10% to 15% by the list owners, therefore you incur no fee. List brokers have experience with many lists and can recommend specific lists to meet your needs. The Direct Marketing Association can provide the names of list brokers in your area or you can consult the business phone directories.

Offers

The *offer* is the proposition you make to your prospects to motivate them to respond to your promotion. Whether you are selling a notebook or a lifetime of financial counseling, you must get your prospect to take the first step that will achieve your objectives. You need to get the prospects to feel good about your offer so they can overcome fear, uncertainty and doubt (FUD) about your company and its product.

Your offer may include your product, price, payment terms, and any incentive you are willing to include. You might also attach special conditions to the offer. In his book, *Profitable Direct Marketing*, Jim Kobs listed the following 99 direct response offers. This list comprehensively covers consumer and business offers.

BASIC OFFERS

1) **Right Price** - The starting point for any product or service being sold by mail. Consider your market and what's being charged for competitive products. And make sure you have sufficient margin for your offer to be profitable. Most products sold by mail require at least a three-time mark-up.

2) **Free Trial** - If mail order advertisers suddenly had to standardize all their efforts on one offer, this would no doubt be the choice; it's widely used for book and merchandise promotions. Looking at it like a consumer, the free trial relieves the fear that you might get stuck buying by mail because the advertiser is willing to let you try *their* product before they get *your* money. Most free trial periods are 10 or

15 days, but the length of the trial period should fit the type of product or service being offered.

3) **Money-Back Guarantee** - If for some good reason you can't use a free trial offer, this is the next best thing. The main difference is you ask the customer to pay part or all of the purchase price *before* you let them try your product. This puts inertia on your side. The customer is unlikely to take the time and effort to send a product back unless they're really unhappy with it.

4) **Cash With Order** - This is the basic payment option used with a money-back guarantee. It's also offered with a choice of other payment options. Incentives (such as paying the postage and handling charge) are often used to encourage the customer to send their check or money order when they order.

5) **Bill Me Later** - This is the basic payment option used with free trial offers. The bill is usually enclosed with the merchandise or follows a few days later, and it calls for a single payment. Because no front-end payment is required by the customer, the response can be as much as double that of a cash offer.

6) **Installment Terms** - This payment option is similar to the Bill Me Later Option, except that it usually involves a bigger sale price and installment terms are set up to keep the payments around $10 to $20 per month. It is usually necessary to offer installment terms to sell big ticket items by mail to consumers.

7) **Charge Card Privileges** - Offers the same advantages of Bill Me Later and Installment plans, but the seller doesn't have to carry the paper. This option can be used with bank charge cards, travel and entertainment cards, and specialized cards (like those issued by the oil companies).

8) **C.O.D.** - This is the Postal Service acronym for Cash-On-Delivery. The mail carrier collects when they deliver the package. This option is not widely used today because of the added cost and effort required to handle C.O.D. orders.

FREE GIFT OFFERS

9) **Free Gift For An Inquiry** - Provides an incentive to request more information about a product or service. Usually increases inquiries, though they become somewhat less qualified.

10) **Free Gift For A Trial Order** - Commonly called a "keeper" gift - because the customer gets to keep the gift just for agreeing to try the product.

11) **Free Gift For Buying** - Similar to Number 10, except the customer only gets to keep the gift if they buy the product or service. The gift can be given free with any order, tied to a minimum purchase, or used as a self-liquidator.

12) **Multiple Free Gifts With A Single Order** - If one gift pays out for you, consider offering two or more. You may even be able to offer two inexpensive gifts and spend the same as you would on one more expensive item. The biggest user of multiple gifts is Fingerhut Corporation. At last count, they were up to four free gifts for a single order!

13) **Your Choice Of Free Gifts** - Can be a quick way to test the relative appeal of different gift items. But this will seldom work as well as the best gift offered on its own. The choice may lead to indecision on the consumer's part.

14) **Free Gifts Based On Size Of Order** - Often used with catalogs or merchandise that lends itself to a quantity purchase. You can offer an inexpensive gift for orders under $10.00; a better gift for orders totalling between $10.00 and $25.00; and a deluxe gift for orders over $25.00.

15) **Two-Step Gift Offer** - Offers an inexpensive gift if customer takes the first step and a better gift if they take the second step. For example, you might offer a free CD for *trying* a new stereo set, and a deluxe headset if you elect to *buy* it.

16) **Continuing Incentive Gifts** - Used to get customers to keep coming back. Book clubs often give bonus coupons which

can be used to purchase additional books. This option is also suitable for silverware, where you give one place setting per order.

17) **Mystery Gift Offer** - Sometimes works better than offering a specific gift. It helps if you can give some indication of the item's retail value.

OTHER FREE OFFERS

18) **Free Information** - Certainly an inexpensive offer, and a very flexible one. The type of information you provide can range from a simple product catalog sheet to a full-blown series of mailings. Emphasize if the information will *not* be delivered by a salesman.

19) **Free Catalog** - Can be an attractive offer for both the consumer and the business market. In the business field, catalogs are often used as buying guides and are saved for future reference. In the consumer field, you can often attach a nominal charge for postage and handling, or offer a full year's catalog subscription.

20) **Free Booklet** - Helps establish your company's expertise and know-how about the specific problems of your industry. Works especially well if the booklet contains helpful editorial material, not just a commercial for your product or service. The booklet should have an appealing title, like "How to Save Money on Heating Costs" or "29 Ways to Improve the Quality Control System."

21) **Free Fact Kit** - Sometimes called an Idea Kit. It's usually put together in an attractive file folder or presentation cover. You can include a variety of enclosures, from booklets to trade paper articles to ad reprints.

22) **Send Me A Salesman** - This one is included here because the offer is actually a free sales call. The copy includes wording like; have your representative phone me for an appointment. This offer normally produces more qualified inquiries than a free booklet or fact kit. Those who respond are probably ready to order or are seriously considering it.

23) **Free Demonstration** - Important for things like business equipment that has to be demonstrated to be fully appreciated. If the equipment is small enough, it can be brought into the prospect's plant or office. If not, they might be invited to a private showing or group demonstration at the manufacturer's facilities.

24) **Free Survey of Your Needs** - Ideal for some industrial products or services, such as a company that sells chemicals for various water treatment problems. Offering a free survey by a sales representative or technical expert is appealing, and gives you the opportunity to qualify a prospect and see if your product or service really fits their needs.

25) **Free Cost Estimate** - Many large industrial sales are only made after considerable study and cost analysis. The offer of a free estimate can be the first step in triggering such a sale.

26) **Free Dinner** - Like the rest of the offers that follow in this section, this one is particularly suited to certain types of direct marketing companies. It's widely used by real estate and land companies, who offer a free dinner at a nearby restaurant. Those who attend also get a sales presentation on the property.

27) **Free Film Offer** - Many mail order film processing companies have been built with some variation of this offer. Either the customer gets a new roll of film when they send one in for processing, or the first roll is offered free, in hopes that it will be sent back to the same company later for processing.

28) **Free House Organ Subscription** - Many industrial companies publish elaborate house organs for customers and prospects which contain a good deal of helpful editorial material. You can offer a free sample issue, or better yet, a year's subscription.

29) **Free Talent Test** - Popular with home study schools. Especially those that offer a skilled course, such as writing or

painting. Legal restrictions require that any such test actually measures real talent or ability, and is not just a door-opener for the salesman.

30) **Gift Shipment Service** - This is one of the basic appeals of offers used by virtually all mail order cheese and gift food firms. You send them your gift list, and they ship direct to the recipients at no extra cost.

DISCOUNT OFFERS

31) **Cash Discount** - This is the basic type of discount. It's often dramatized by including a discount certificate in the ad or mailing. However, a discount offer will *not* do as well as an attractive free gift with the same value.

32) **Short-Term Introductory Offer** - A popular type of discount used to let somebody try the product for a short period at a reduced price. Offering 10 weeks of the *Wall Street Journal* for only $5.97 or 30 days of accident insurance for only 25¢ are good examples. It's important to be able to convert respondents to long-term subscribers or policyholders.

33) **Refund Certificate** - Technically speaking, this is a delayed discount. You might ask somebody to send $1.00 for your catalog and include a $1.00 refund certificate good on their first order. The certificate is like an un-cashed check -- it's difficult to resist the urge to cash it.

34) **Introductory Order Discount** - A special discount used to bring in new customers. This can sometimes cause complaints from old customers if they're not offered the same discount.

35) **Trade Discount** - Usually extended to certain clubs, institutions, or types of businesses.

36) **Early Bird Discount** - Designed to get customers to stock up before the normal buying season. A great many Christmas cards and gifts have been sold by mail with this offer.

37) **Quantity Discount** - This discount is tied to a certain quantity or order volume. The long-term subscriptions offered by magazines are a type of quantity discount. The cost-per-copy is usually lower on a two-year subscription because it represents a quantity purchase -- 24 issues instead of 12.

38) **Sliding Scale Discount** - In this case, the amount of the discount depends on the date somebody orders or the size of the order. You might offer a 2% discount for orders up to $50, and a 10% discount for orders over $100.

39) **Selected Discounts** - These are often sprinkled throughout a catalog to emphasize certain items the advertiser wants to push or to give the appearance that everything is on sale.

SALE OFFERS

40) **Seasonal Sales** - Such as Pre-Christmas Sale or Summer Vacation Sale. If successful, they are often repeated every year at the same time.

41) **Reason-Why Sales** - This category includes Inventory Reduction and Clearance Sales. These explanatory terms help make the sale more believable to the prospect.

42) **Price Increase Notice** - A special type of offer that's like a limited time sale. Price Increase Notices give customers a chance to order at the old prices before increases become effective.

43) **Auction-By-Mail** - An unusual type of sale that has been used to sell such items as lithographs and electronic calculators, when their quantities were limited. Customers send in a "sealed bid" with merchandise usually going to the highest bidder.

SAMPLE OFFERS

44) **Free Samples** - If your product lends itself to sampling, this is a strong offer. Sometimes you can offer a sample made with

or by your product. For example, a steel company might offer take-apart puzzles made from their steel wire. Or a printer might offer samples of helpful printed material it has produced for other customers.

45) **Nominal Charge Samples** - In many cases making a nominal charge for a sample--like 10¢, 25¢, or $1.00--will pull better than a free sample offer. The charges help establish the value of the item and screen out some of the curiosity seekers.

46) **Sample Offer With Tentative Commitment** - This is also known as the "complimentary copy" offer used by many magazines. In requesting the sample, the prospect is also making a tentative commitment for a subscription. But if they don't like the first issue, they just write "cancel" on the bill and send it back. Legal precautions are advised, your legal counsel should review this offer before you actually make it.

47) **Quantity Sample Offer** - A specialized offer that's worked well for business services and newsletters. One example is a sales training bulletin, where the sales manager is told to "just tell us how many salesmen you have, and we'll send a free sample bulletin for each one."

48) **Free Sample Lesson** - This has been widely used by home study schools, who offer a sample lesson to demonstrate the scope and content of their course.

TIME LIMIT OFFERS

49) **Limited Time Offers** - Any limited time offer tends to force a quick decision and prevents procrastination. It's usually best to mention a specific date--such as "this special offer expires November 20th" rather than "this offer expires in 10 days."

50) **Enrollment Periods** - Have been widely used by mail order insurance companies, who include a specific cutoff date for the enrollment period. It implies there are savings involved by processing an entire group of enrollments at one time.

51) **Pre-Publication Offer** - Long a favorite with publishers who offer a special discount or savings before the official publication date of a new book. The rationale is that it helps them plan their printing quantity more accurately.

52) **Charter Membership (or Subscription) Offer** - Ideal for introducing new clubs, publications, and other subscription services. Usually includes a special price, gift, or other incentive for charter members or subscribers. This appeals to those who like to be among the first to try new things.

53) **Limited Edition Offer** - A relatively new direct response offer that has worked well in selling coins, art prints, and other collectable items.

GUARANTEE OFFERS

54) **Extended Guarantee** - Such as letting the customer return a book up to a year later. Or with a magazine, offering to refund the unexpired portion of a subscription any time before it runs out.

55) **Double-Your-Money-Back Guarantee** - Really dramatizes your confidence in the product...but it better live up to your advertising claims if you make an offer like this.

56) **Guaranteed Buy-Back Agreement** - While it's similar to the extended guarantee, this specialized version is often used with limited edition offers on coins and art objects. To convince the prospect of the product's value, the advertiser offers to buy it back at the full price during a specified period that may last as long as 5 years.

57) **Guaranteed Acceptance Offer** - This specialized offer is used by insurance firms with certain types of policies that require no health questions or underwriting. It's especially appealing to those with health problems who might not otherwise qualify.

BUILD-UP-THE-SALE OFFERS

58) **Multi-Product Offers** - Two or more products or services are featured in the same ad or mailing. Maybe you've never thought about it this way, but the best-known type of multi-product offer is a catalog, which can feature a hundred or more items.

59) **Piggyback Offers** - Similar to a multi-product offer, except that one product is strongly featured. The other items just kind of ride along or "piggyback" in the hope of picking up additional sales.

60) **The Deluxe Offer** - A publisher might offer a book in standard binding at $9.95. The order form gives the customer the option of ordering a deluxe edition for only $2.00 more. It's not unusual for 10% or more of those ordering to select the deluxe alternative.

61) **Good-Better-Best Offer** - This one goes a step further by offering 3 choices. The mail order mints, for example, sometimes offer their medals in a choice of bronze, sterling silver, or 24K gold.

62) **Add-On Offer** - A low-cost item that's related to the featured product can be great for impulse orders. For example, offering a wallet for $7.95, with a matching key case for only $1.00 extra.

63) **Write-Your-Own-Ticket Offer** - Some magazines have used this with good success to build up the sale. Instead of offering 17 weeks for $4.93 - which is 29¢ per issue - they give the subscriber the 29¢ an issue price and let them fill in the number of weeks they want their subscription to run.

64) **Bounce-Back Offer** - This approach tries to build onto the original sale by enclosing an additional offer with the product shipment or invoice.

65) **Increase and Extension Offer** - These are also follow-ups to the original sale. Mail order insurance firms often give policyholders a chance to get increased coverage with a higher-priced version of the same policy. Magazines often use an advance renewal offer to get subscribers to extend their present subscription.

SWEEPSTAKES OFFERS

66) **Drawing Type Sweepstakes** - The majority of sweepstakes contests are set up this way. The prospect gets one or more chances to win, but all winners are selected by a random drawing.

67) **Lucky Number Sweepstakes** - With this type of contest, winning numbers are pre-selected before making the mailing or running the ad. Copy strategy emphasizes "you may have already won." A drawing is held for the unclaimed prizes using all the winning numbers that are actually entered or returned.

68) **"Everybody Wins" Sweepstakes** - No longer widely used, this offer was a real bonanza when it was first introduced. The prize structure is set up so the bottom or low-end prize is a very inexpensive or nominal one. It's awarded to everyone who enters and doesn't win one of the bigger prizes.

69) **Involvement Sweepstakes** - This type requires the prospect to open a mystery envelope, play a game, or match their number against an eligible number list. In doing so, the prospect determines the value of the grand prize they win *if* their entry is drawn as the winner. Some of these involvement devices have been highly effective in boosting results.

70) **Talent Contests** - Not really a sweepstakes, but effective for some types of direct marketing situations. The mail order puzzle clubs and the "draw me" ad which offers a free scholarship from a home study art school are examples.

Note: Chance promotions are locally and agency regulated. Always be sure your offer is within guidelines. Legal review is advised.

CLUB & CONTINUITY OFFERS

71) **Positive Option** - You join a club and are notified monthly of new selections. To order, you must take some positive action, such as sending back an order card.

72) **Negative Option** - Like the Positive Option, you are still notified in advance of new selections. But under the terms you agreed to when you joined, the new selection is shipped *unless* you return a rejection card by a specific date.

73) **Automatic Shipments** - This variation eliminates the advance notice of new selections. When you sign up, you give the publisher permission to ship each selection automatically until you tell him to stop. It's commonly called a "Till Forbid" offer.

74) **Continuity Load-Up Offer** - Usually used for a continuity book series, like a 20-volume encyclopedia. The first book is offered free. But after you receive and pay for the next couple of monthly volumes, the balance of the series is sent in one load-up shipment. However, you can continue to pay at the rate of one volume per month.

75) **Front-End Load-Ups** - Commonly used by record and book clubs, this offer gives you several selections for a nominal charge if you agree to accept a minimum quantity at a higher price during a specified period. CD clubs, for example, may give you 4 CD's for $1.00 if you agree to purchase 4 more CD's during the next year. This is an attractive offer that forces prospects to make a commitment. Most offers do specify a fixed time period during which the remaining selections must be purchased.

76) **Open-Ended Commitment** - Like the Front-End Load-Up, except that there is no time limit during which additional selections must be purchased.

77) **"No Strings Attached" Commitment-** Like offers 75 and 76, except this offer is more generous because you are not

committed to any future purchases. The publisher gambles that you will find future selections interesting enough to make a certain number of purchases.

78) **Lifetime Membership Fee** - You pay a one-time fee to join, usually $5.00 or $10.00, and get a monthly announcement of new selections. There's no minimum commitment, and all ordering is done on a positive option basis.

79) **Annual Membership Fee** - Here you pay an annual fee for club membership. It's often used by travel clubs, where you get a whole range of benefits, including travel insurance. It is also used for fund-raising, where a choice of membership levels is often effective.

80) **The Philanthropic Privilege** - This is the basis of all fund-raising offers. The donor's contribution usually brings nothing tangible in return, but it helps make the world a better place in which to live. This offer is sometimes enhanced by giving gummed stamps, a membership card, or other tokens of appreciation.

81) **Blank Check Offer** - First used in the McGovern fund-raising campaign, supporters could fill out blank, post-dated checks which were cashed one-a-month to provide installment contributions. This offer was later adapted to extend credit to bank charge card customers.

82) **Executive Preview Charge** - An effective offer for such things as sales training films. The executive agrees to pay $25 to screen or preview the film, and if they decide to buy or rent it, the preview price is credited against the full price.

83) **Yes/No Offers** - Asks prospect to let you know their decision either way. In most cases the negative responses have little or no value. But by forcing a decision, you often end up with more "yes" responses.

84) **Self-Qualification Offer** - Uses a choice of options to get the prospect to indicate their degree of interest in your product or service, such as a free booklet or a free demonstration. Those

who request the demonstration qualify themselves as serious prospects and should get more immediate attention.

85) **Exclusive Rights for Your Trading Area** - Ideal for selling some business services to firms who are in a competitive business. An example is a syndicated newsletter that a bank buys and sends to its customers. You give the first bank that responds exclusive rights for their trading area. The percentages that order are such that you seldom have to turn anybody down.

86) **The Super Dramatic Offer** - Sometimes very effective. Such as the offer that challenged, "smoke my new kind of pipe for 30 days. If you don't like it, smash it up with a hammer and send me back the pieces."

87) **Trade-In Offer** - An offer like "we'll give you $10 for your old slide rule when you buy a new electronic calculator" can be very appealing.

88) **Third Party Referral Offer** - Instead of renting somebody's list, you get the list owner to make a mailing for you using his name recommending your product or service. This usually works better than your own promotion because of the rapport a company has with its own customers.

89) **Member-Get-A-Member Offer** - Often used to get customers to send in the names of friends who might be interested. Widely used by book and record clubs, who give their members a free gift if they get new members to sign up.

90) **Name-Getter Offers** - Usually designed for building a prospect list. A firm can offer a low-cost premium at an attractive self-liquidating price.

91) **Purchase-With-Purchase** - Widely used by cosmetic firms and department stores. An attractive gift set is offered at a special price with a regular purchase.

92) **Delayed Billing Offer** - The appeal is: Order now and we won't bill you until next month. Especially effective before the holidays, when people have lots of other expenses.

93) **Reduced Down Payment** - Frequently used as a follow-up in an extended mailing series. If the customer does not respond to the regular offer in previous mailings, you reduce the down payment to make it easier for them to get started.

94) **Stripped-Down Products** - Also used in an extended mailing series. A home study school, for example, that doesn't get the prospect to order the full course might then offer a starter course at a lower price.

95) **Secret Bonus Gift** - Usually used with TV support. The commercial offers an extra bonus gift not mentioned in the corresponding ad or mailing. For example, a record company offers a bonus record if you write the album number in the "secret gold box" on the order form.

96) **Rush Shipping Service** - An appealing offer for things like seasonal gifts and film processing. Sometimes the customer is asked to pay an extra charge for this rush service.

97) **The Competitive Offer** - Can be a strong way to dramatize your selling story, like Diner's Club offering to pay prospects $5.00 to turn in their American Express cards.

98) **The Nominal Reimbursement Offer** - Used for research mailings. A token payment is offered to get somebody to fill out and return a questionnaire.

99) **Establish-the-Value Offer** - If you have an attractive free gift, you can build up its value and establish credibility by offering an extra one for a friend at the regular price.

Excerpted from *Profitable Direct Marketing* by Jim Kobs, published by Crain Books, 740 Rush Street, Chicago, Illinois 60611.

Here's a 100th item to this list: **the perpetual offer**. In business, this is the offer that provides personal benefit to a buyer when spending company money. Examples of the perpetual offer are the airline frequent flyer programs. Similar programs have been implemented by car rental, hotel, and even catalog companies.

The growth of frequent traveler and frequent user programs, sometimes called loyalty programs, has proven that customers can become involved with a supplier on an on-going basis. All the supplier need do is remind customers of their current "use" status and show them when they will receive an award. The only drawback to this type of offer program is in curtailing or eliminating it. The plus of this type of program is the loyal and buying customer database it creates.

Frequent user customers on the database are less expensive to promote because they are known entities. The bonus awards cost less than promoting the market to stimulate an incremental sale. The success and continued growth of these types of programs are proof-positive of how effective marketing to this group of customers has become. In fact, the frequent traveler programs have created substantial joint ventures between airlines, hotels, and car rental companies.

The offer must be in line with program objectives and with the company's operational ability to follow-up on responses. If the objective is lead generation, make an offer that will generate only as many leads as you can effectively handle. Too many leads can be even more destructive to the direct marketing program than not enough leads. Quantity will not be as important as quality.

Whether the offer is for leads or actual orders, make the offer only as enticing as you can afford. It makes no sense to give away profits to generate a response. There are exceptions when you might be willing to not make a profit on an initial order if the potential from future orders, or lifetime value, can make the customer profitable. This is fairly common in the catalog and publishing industries. You will always have to evaluate whether your offer was so lucrative that the quality of the responder was not as good as you had hoped.

When examining the economics of offers you develop, remember that the offers are a variable cost; only respondents are taking advantage of the offer. If a 10,000-piece mailing yields 500 respondents, the cost of the offer is only for the 500 respondents.

When testing a less expensive offer against your control offer, don't assume a lower response rate is less effective. Include the costs for the offer and then review the total direct marketing costs per responder and per order. You may find that the less expensive offer produces a less expensive order. Don't throw out the baby with the bath water because of the difference in response rates.

Lead programs are even more difficult to measure. You have to evaluate not just the responses but the actual orders. Remember, ultimately you're in the sales business. Track your respondents to sales before you decide which offer is best. If sales measurement is impossible, measure your success on the number of qualified leads you develop.

Formats

Format is the method you select to deliver your offer to the market. Many people refer to format as media. This definition may be too restrictive since several of the formats do not fall within a media definition. Telemarketing and the internet are not traditionally defined as media. For the purpose of this discussion, we will define formats as all of the ways to deliver a message to a market.

Once you have researched and determined your market segments, and have developed your offers per market segment, you are ready to select the format to deliver your message to your market. This process is often based on previous

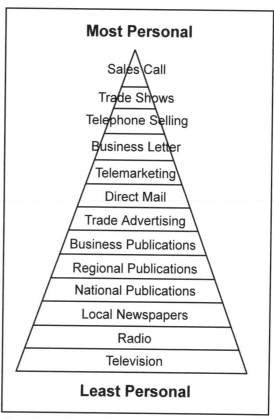

Illustration 5-1: Personalization of the contact.

Most Expensive

Sales Call

Trade Shows

Telephone Selling

Business Letter

Telemarketing

Direct Mail

Trade Advertising

Business Publications

Regional Publications

National Publications

Local Newspapers

Radio

Television

Least Expensive

Illustration 5-2: Cost of the contact.

experience or on recommendations. While it's impossible to provide a fixed formula for selection of formats, it is possible to provide a structure for approaching the format decision.

There are two major selection criteria to consider when selecting formats:

1) The level of personal contact necessary to gain a sale or to generate a lead that can become a sale.

2) The dollars you are willing to spend to gain a sale or to generate a lead that can become a sale.

If we set up a hierarchy of formats (Illustration 5-1) from personal to impersonal contacts, we would see that a sales contact is on the top as the most personal, and broadcast advertising is on the bottom as the least personal. We will discuss each of these later in more detail.

Now if we examine the associated cost per contact of each of these formats, we see that the higher the level of personal contact, the greater the cost (Illustration 5-2).

Overlaying the triangles (Illustration 5-3) provides a quick reference in helping you make general format selections.

Your experience, knowledge of your selling process and the financial proforma are the guides you should use when selecting formats. Most business-to-business applications use more than one format to deliver their messages to their markets. The workhorses of business-to-business direct marketing are telephone, mail, trade publication space advertising and the Internet. These four major formats provide the majority of business-to-business leads and orders.

Most Personal/Most Expensive

Sales Call
Trade Shows
Telephone Selling
Business Letter
Telemarketing
Direct Mail
Trade Advertising
Business Publications
Regional Publications
National Publications
Local Newspapers
Radio
Television

Least Personal/Least Expensive

Personalization ▢ Cost

Illustration 5-3: Cost versus personalization.

Types of Formats

• **Sales calls**. The most common format used in business-to-business selling to deliver an offer to the market. While the sales call is not direct marketing, it is controllable and measurable in its costs and results, although it is the least controllable format. When you send a sales representative as a promotion, you have no ability to control what will be said. The sales call, the most personal contact, is the most expensive sales contact you can make. You can derive your own cost per sales call, as we discussed in Chapter 2, or use published industry costs as a guideline. The face-to-face sales call can cost over $400.

This is not that expensive if you can make a sale on each sales call. Depending on the number of sales calls required per order, you may find that personal selling can cost more than $1,000 per order. The same research that established the average cost per sales call also determined that the average industrial order costs more than $1,100 in sales call expenses. These costs should be part of your marketing plan so you can decide what part of the existing expenses should be displaced by direct marketing.

- **Trade shows**. An alternate format to personal selling where prospects are gathered for the express purpose of reviewing products and services. This is an extension of personal selling with a cost per contact in the $90 to $125 range. This assumes reasonable traffic for the show; otherwise the cost can be thousands of dollars per contact.

  A variation of trade shows are seminars. This technique of group sales situations is becoming more and more popular. It provides an opportunity to spread the sales cost across a group of prospects. Seminars normally require a fair amount of front-end work to drive traffic, but they can be extremely effective in controlling the cost and quality of the sales contact.

- **Telephone selling**. Since this format represents a major opportunity for the business-to-business marketer we have devoted an entire chapter to this subject. For the purposes of evaluating the cost of this format, we will divide telephone into two major segments: telephone selling (telesales) and telemarketing.

  Telephone selling is when you put a qualified salesperson on the telephone to make sales calls as opposed to having the salesperson meet the prospects face-to-face. The use of telesales is fairly expensive per contact. Salespeople will be able to make more calls per day because travel time is eliminated. You probably will not see a rapid increase in sales when you introduce telesales because your sales force is already using telephone as a format. Telephone selling costs $50 to $125 per contact.

  Telephone selling is difficult to measure in terms of both costs and results. In many businesses, telesales is considered a tool and a necessary part of the business. It is often segmented and measured. In many situations, the executive responsible for telesales does not even have control, of or responsibility for, the telephone bill. There is usually not a clear understanding of all the expenses involved in telephone selling.

- **Business Letters**. These are personal letters written, signed, and mailed one at a time. They are used by sales representatives to communicate proposals, offers, contracts and general information to their accounts. This format costs between $7.50 and $25 per contact.

- **Telemarketing**. This telephone format is not dependent on the skill of the communicator but relies on a script, offer, and marketing database to make a contact to the prospect. This format costs between $35 and $65 per hour of activity. Because it is a production activity, it is possible to make a business contact for $7 to $15. The cost per sale will depend on the offer, what is being sold, and the leverage used in the script to increase response (premiums, incentives to the buyer, etc.)

- **Direct Mail**. This is the workhorse of business-to-business direct marketing. We have provided a complete chapter on this important format. Direct mail can be used as part of an unsolicited promotion or as a form of fulfillment when a prospect requests more information about a company and its products. The cost of direct mail can range from a few cents per contact, in the case of card decks, to several dollars per contact for fulfillment or elaborate mail packages. As a general guideline, mail costs per contact range from .50 to $2.

- **Trade Advertising**. Business-to-business marketers are the most comfortable with this format. Trade publications are those publications that have circulation to a specific group. In most cases, subscribers do not pay for the publication; they receive the publication based on their industry, area of responsibility and/or position. To receive the publication, the subscriber completes a qualification card that provides information to the publication.

Advertisers in this type of publication can review subscriber information before placing print ads in the publication. Depending on circulation and area of concentration, cost per contact may vary. We estimate cost per contact to range between 6 cents and 15 cents. Contacts are based on circulation and are referred to as impressions, assuming that one person will see your ad one time. In addition, trade publications tend to have a high degree of pass-along to other readers. A manager will probably pass a publication to all of their subordinates.

Many trade publications offer reader service cards or "bingo" cards, so called because the reader circles numbers on the card based on the numbers the magazine assigns to each ad in the book. The bingo cards are sent back to the magazine or a service bureau where they are processed. The leads are then passed along to the advertisers. Leads generated from this type of service should be carefully screened prior to being given to the sales force.

Additional promotional opportunities are currently being developed and offered by trade publishers utilizing the World Wide Web. In these situations, advertising is placed on web pages through sponsorship and space ads. Success of these efforts is unproven at this time, but may be promising depending on costs involved. Pricing can be included in traditional space packages or on a cost per impression/response model.

- **Business Publications**. These are general interest publications distributed as a result of paid subscriptions. Typically, little is known about their readers except what can be gained from address overlays or subscriber studies. These publications cross industries and are general in nature. If a product crosses many industries and levels of management, these books can work well for it. Like trade publications, business publications normally offer reader service cards to their subscribers. The cost per impression ranges from 3 cents to 10 cents.

- **Regional Business Publications.** When servicing a regional market, regional business publications can be the best print investment. Regional publications are focused on business readers in a circulation area that approximates a given trade area. Regional coverage purchases in national publications may provide greater coverage than regional publications within a trade area, resulting in wasted circulation. While more expensive than national publications, regional publications may be a good alternative. The cost per impression ranges from 9 cents to 20 cents.

- **National Daily/Weekly Newspapers**. There are several newsprint publications written for the business market or that have a business or money section. These newspapers have large circulation intended to cross all types and sizes of businesses. Advertising in these publications can provide large numbers of readers for a relatively low cost. Space ads in these publications can generate a significant number of responders. Leads generated from this type of service should be carefully screened before they are sent to the sales force. The cost per impression can be between 3 cents and 10 cents.

Regional newspapers, like national dailies, can reach large numbers of readers in their business sections. Responders should be carefully screened for qualification. The cost per impression can be the same as in a national daily, however, the circulation contains some people who may not be in the business arena.

- **Local Newspapers**. This is an alternative for the business marketer who is servicing a local area. A national marketer will be concerned about costs, variations of sizes, and submission requirements for ads between all of the local newspapers. Most local papers do not have a business section that will seek out target readers. An ad can be lost in the ROP (Run of Press); the publisher can place the ad anywhere in the publication. Costs range from 10 cents to 25 cents per impression.

- **Radio**. This has not proven to be a successful stand-alone format for business-to-business direct marketing. Radio can support a regional or local marketing effort if the listener is going to receive printed material or additional information at a retail location. Costs per impression vary widely depending on the time of day, frequency of airing, and the length of the ad. When planning to use radio, compare the type of listener the radio station represents to the characteristics of your target.

- **Television**. Television has been used from time to time as a response format by companies that have large budgets and strong mark-ups on their products. More often, television is used as an image and awareness-builder. Direct response ads using 800 numbers can generate large quantities of unqualified responders.

Direct response television has been used successfully in the consumer world where targeting and segmentation are not as critical as in business-to-business. Because there are many people viewing the ad who are not qualified, the cost per *qualified* contact is very high. The cost per contact is very low compared to other formats, but with no way to target the message to a defined group of prospects, the quality of any responder has to be carefully examined. Leads generated from this type of format should be carefully screened before they are sent to the sales force. Most responders will not be qualified. Cost per impression can be from 1/10 to 9/10s of a cent. Although the cost per impression is attractive, there is a high amount of waste in contacting the wrong people.

Internet The internet is developing into the medium of the business marketer for two reasons, it has no variable cost per contact and is global for the same cost as being local. A whole chapter is devoted to the internet.

Direct Marketing Copy Checklist

Before you start to write

1) Develop the action you want the recipient to take.
2) List all your product's features and associated benefits.
   This is done by listing a feature, followed by the words "What this means to you is..." Answering the statement which provides the benefit.
3) Rank benefits in order of importance to the recipient.
4) Identify someone you know who personifies the recipient you are trying to reach, so that you are writing to a person rather than a concept.

Writing copy

1) Write your action step(s).
2) Using the AIDA formula, create several attention-getting headlines and select the best one.
3) As your message unfolds, keep your copy moving. Frequently remind the reader of the benefits your product will deliver and continually call them to action.
4) Ask for the order. Ask for the order. Ask for the order.
5) If your message is to be printed, make sure it is appealing to the eye. Dense copy and long paragraphs produce little white space where the reader can rest.

Illustration 5-4: A direct marketing copy checklist.

Copy/Graphics

This area seems to receive the most attention in the development of the direct marketing promotion. It is clearly an important element within direct marketing, however it will have the least impact on the success of your promotion. At the copy level we spend more time on our **It** than on our **Them** -- the prospects in our market.

Richard S. Hodgson, in his book, *Direct Mail and Mail Order Handbook* (published by Dartnell, Chicago, Illinois 60640) does an excellent job of providing directions on how to prepare and review direct marketing and direct mail copy. Some of his thoughts and recommendations are given below.

Seek an Expert

The best advice on copy which can be given to any direct mail advertiser is to seek an experienced *direct mail* copy expert. Then work with them or have them work with your copywriters to develop the best techniques to meet the specific communications problems involved. With such guidance, the odds are that you or your copywriting personnel will learn many of the techniques that lead to success, and eventually others will be turning to you for direct mail copy help. Copywriters generally can guide you graphically with ideas or recommend designers than can support your creative efforts. Of course, many good designers work with good copywriters, so you can reverse the entire process if you feel graphic representation of your **It** is more important than the words that support the graphics.

In the absence of in-person help from an expert, turn to some of the helpful books on direct mail copywriting that are available.

Because there are so many detailed and helpful volumes available on the subject of direct mail copy, it is our primary purpose to provide some basic guidelines for successful promotion design. This material is presented to assist you in evaluating copy and graphics, rather than trying to teach you to be a creative director.

Checklist for Better Direct Mail Copy

Prepared by Maxwell C. Ross

Copy Technique

1) Does the lead sentence get in step with your reader at once?
2) Is your lead sentence more than two lines long?
3) Do your opening paragraphs promise a benefit to the reader?
4) Have you fired your biggest gun first?
5) Is there a big idea behind your letter?
6) Are your thoughts arranged in logical order?
7) Is what you say believable?
8) Is it clear how the reader is to order - and did you ask for the order?
9) Does the copy tie in with the order form - and have you directed attention to the order form in the letter?

Copy Editing

10) Does the letter have "you" attitude all the way through?
11) Does the letter have a conversational tone?
12) Have you formed a "bucket brigade" through your copy?
13) Does the letter score between 70 and 80 words of one-syllable for every 100 words of copy?
14) Are there any sentences which begin with an article - a, an, or the - where you might have avoided it?
15) Are there any places where you have strung together too many prepositional phrases?
16) Have you kept out "wandering" verbs?
17) Have you used action verbs instead of noun construction?
18) Are there any "thats" you do not need?
19) How does the copy rate on such letter craftsmanship points as (a) using active voice instead of passive, (b) periodic sentences instead of loose, (c) too many participles, (d)splitting infinitives, (e) repeating your company name too many times?
20) Does your letter look the way you want it to? (a) placement of page, (b) no paragraphs over six lines, (c) indentation and numbered paragraphs, (d) underscoring and capitalization used sparingly, (e) punctuation for reading ease.

Illustration 5-5: Checklist for better direct mail copy.

One technical approach to creating effective copy/graphics is to use the AIDA formula (Attention, Interest, Desire, Action). This formula is also used to train sales representatives an approach to selling situations.

Attention - The direct marketing promotion should get the recipient to look at it and focus on its message. This is only accomplished by offering the recipients something of interest to them. Announcing a new product in the opening message does not get anyone's attention unless you relate what the new product is going to do for them. Graphics can also gain the attention of a target.

Interest - Once you have the recipient's attention, you can deliver the benefits and offer of your promotion.

Desire - With the recipient's interest aroused, you can begin to move to close. Restate points of interest in customized terms that are personalized to the recipient's needs. Do not confuse the product's features with the benefits they provide. The classic example is that you are not selling *drill bits,* you are selling *holes*.

It's easy to spend a great deal of time writing about the features of *drill bits*: hardened steel, ground edges, length, weight, etc. What the recipient wants to have is perfect little *holes*. Explain how the *drill bits* will create those perfect little *holes* to satisfy the recipient's needs. If you never make the transition from features to benefits, you will never arouse desire.

Action - This is what it is all about. Many direct marketers never call the prospect to action. You should begin all promotional efforts, including copy, by developing the action you want the recipient to take. Start with the action and weave it through the entire promotion rather than trying to tie it in as an afterthought. Don't be afraid to call the recipient to action frequently throughout the promotion. For example, each time a benefit is mentioned, explain that the recipient can have it now by going to the action step. This is no different than *trial closing* in face-to-face selling.

Illustration 5-4 gives a method to develop direct response copy. AIDA is only one formula you can use to organize the development of direct marketing copy. Hodgson supplies several other formulas that you might find helpful. No matter what approach to copywriting you use, Illustration 5-5, the checklist by Maxwell Ross can be helpful.

Business Personalities

Successful business-to-business direct marketers try to align the personalities of their promotion with the personalities of the people who are going to receive the promotion. This means marketing to individuals -- not to positions within the company. However, sometimes, as we will explore later, personality type and position can be related. When a company's purchasing procedures involve multiple buyers who use a single purchasing agent, this process becomes more difficult. So we must look to the promotion itself -- through its design, copy and graphics -- to project its personality clearly, one that will match that of the business executive we are targeting.

While all people may be created equal, all people do not make buying decisions for the same set of reasons. People are all driven by an almost unexplainable group of forces. Psychology has developed stereotypes to help categorize the many types of people.

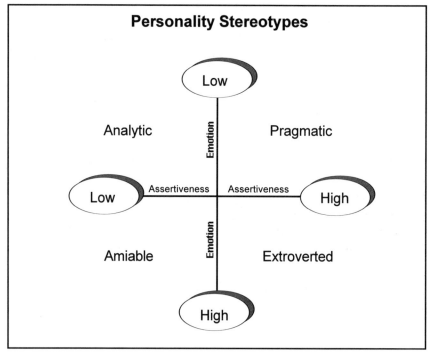

Illustration 5-6: Personality Stereotypes

Business purchasers can be defined using four of the major personality types: pragmatic, extroverted, amiable, and analytic. These four stereotypes are determined by the intersection of a person's assertiveness and emotion, from low to high on a set of axis. (See Illustration 5-6)

Now, let's take a look at each of the personality types:

- **Pragmatic** - These people are businesslike; they don't like to waste time or take vacations, and they make quick decisions based on facts. Pragmatic individuals buy condensed books and use a highlighter to emphasize major points. They judge a seminar on its value, not on its presentation; they would prefer to receive an executive summary of its main points. They don't like spectator sports; they would rather participate (except golf, which wastes too much time). Efficiency is important to them. They are top managers, or striving to reach that position.

- **Extroverted** - Aggressive, impulsive and very friendly, these people make fast decisions based on excitement or enthusiasm. They go to a seminar and are inspired by the presenters; they don't like charts and graphs, and their desks are usually piles of paper.

Pragmatic

Do's	Don'ts
• Be clear, specific, brief.	• Don't ramble with long prose.
• Stick to business.	• Don't try to build a personal
• Provide facts and figures about	relationship.
effectiveness of options.	• Don't speculate or offer
• Call to action by referring to	assurances.
objectives and results.	• Don't try to convince by
• Provide factual alternatives.	personal means
• Make ordering easy.	• Don't dictate or direct.
	• Don't use complicated
	merchandising gimmicks or
	involvement.

Illustration 5-7: Dealing with the Pragmatic Personality.

Motivation is a driving force. This is the type of individual most often found in sales and marketing environments.

- **Amiable** - These individuals like to develop relationships with people and things, and are probably in management positions only in larger companies where the system provides barriers against pressure. They drive older cars because they dislike car salespeople. People who fit this stereotype make decisions slowly, based on what will make everybody happy. Their reason for attending a seminar is simply to be around similar people, and while they are there, they worry about whether or not everyone is having a good time. General traits are openness and friendliness. This type of person is found in personnel, or perhaps as an administrative assistant or staff manager who has protection from dealing with front-line confrontation.

- **Analytic** - A breed apart, these individuals are comfortable with procedures and calculators, and like to be surrounded by gadgets. Because they can't seem to get enough information, they generally make slow decisions. They can attend a 10-day seminar about coaxial cable, for instance, and feel it was a shallow presentation. Analytical people are often engineers or accountants.

It is important to note that these are broad generalizations. Everyone exhibits pieces and parts of each personality style from time to time. If,

---

Extroverted

Do's	Don'ts
• Offer the dream and intentions.	• Don't legislate.
• Talk about people and their goals.	• Don't drive facts and figures.
• Give ideas for implementing action.	• Don't "dream" too much or they will put down the promotion.
• Provide testimonials from people seen as important.	• Don't be dogmatic.
• Offer special immediate extra incentives for willingness to place orders.	• Don't be impersonal or judgmental.

Illustration 5-8: Dealing with the Extroverted Personality.

however, you have identified yourself with two of these personality types, they are most likely adjacent on the graph, and not diagonal to each other. While you can move up and down the emotional scale and back and forth on the assertiveness scale, you will seldom change styles in adjacent quadrants. This is important to remember as you define your promotion's personality.

If you want to shift your promotion's personality or evaluate whom you are selecting as business customers, take a look at some of the do's and don'ts for each personality type. (See Illustrations 5-7 thru 5-10). Then review your (or your competitor's) promotions with these do's and don'ts in mind. To whom are you actually directing your promotion?

The common complaint of business-to-business direct marketers is, "We don't know who is doing the buying." A purchasing agent, for example, may place orders for several people or departments. But, if you allow yourself to express some opinions in your promotion, to stereotype a few titles or functions and relate them to your promotion, you can guess fairly accurately who is doing the buying.

Amiable

Do's	Don'ts
• Use personal comments to lead offers.	• Don't stick coldly to business.
• Present your case softly, non-threateningly.	• Don't be domineering, demanding or threatening about position or power.
• Involve the reader by explaining "how."	• Don't debate facts and figures.
• Be casual and informal.	• Don't patronize or demean.
• Provide personal guarantees to minimize risks and give assurances of benefits.	• Don't offer guarantees or assurances you can't fulfill.

Illustration 5-9: Dealing with the Amiable Personality.

Analytic

Do's	Don'ts
• Be direct; stick to business.	• Don't be circuitous, casual or informal.
• Support your credibility by listing pros and cons.	• Don't be too brief.
• Be accurate and allow for ways to verify reliability.	• Don't use testimonials.
• Provide solid, tangible, practical evidence.	• Don't use gimmicks or clever, quick manipulations.

Illustration 5-10: Dealing with the Analytic Personality.

Creativity

Creativity is probably the one area or endeavor feared the most and understood the least. There seems to be some mystique about it as if there are a few creative people, and then there are the rest of us. The rest of us sit in awe of those few creative types that can turn a phrase, have the big new idea, or draw a pretty picture. In truth, no one has any reason to take a back seat to anyone else deemed creative.

By merely agreeing with the premise that only a few people are creative, you put yourself in a box that keeps you from being creative. Once you have decided that you can't be creative, you are guaranteed not to be.

The people who get the creative labels are the people who are willing to take a chance and let their ideas be revealed to the rest of the world. You may have an idea from time to time but are unwilling to make it public for fear of being ridiculed or laughed at.

Ideas are like water in a brook. Sometimes the brook runs fast. Sometimes there are large pools where the brook doesn't seem to run at all. Sometimes there are falls where the water cascades into space with great force and out of control, free falling to once again join the flow and race to the next larger body of water.

You can and should let your ideas flow freely. Like the brook, you should get into the flow of things. Without sharing your ideas, no matter what brook you are part of, you will become stagnant, uninteresting and boring.

When you were young, no matter where you were or how many toys you had, the strangest things could provide you with hours of enjoyment. You would receive a new bicycle and end up playing with the box it came in instead of the bike. Your mind would fill with so many ideas on what the box could become that there were not enough hours in the day to live out all the fantasies. Who needs reality? Nobody told you it was only a box. You might even have put the box away at night and left the bike out in the rain. Eventually the box would shred, and the bike would become a motorcycle, a chariot, or a rocket.

As we grow older, we become less free with our ideas. Peers tell us we're weird if we don't act like everyone else. Peer pressure stifles creativity. Playing in a box at 8 years old is okay. At 13 it is not. It is amusing to realize that what others think of our actions can inhibit our creative abilities. When that happens, we suppress our creative juices so that we fit into our social environment.

As we've grown older we have moved from one box that encouraged expression of our creative freedom, to an invisible box which curtails our creative expression. We worry about others making fun of our ideas, so we keep them to ourselves. We learn to keep our mouths shut so no one will think we're one of those weird creative people. We would rather be viewed as good managers, in control at all times and supportive of the company line. We let the creative types have all of the fun and take all of the risk. They get to play in the box without fear of criticism. They are *supposed* to do all of the weird stuff. They are supposed to dress funny and they even get to laugh and shout. We are real careful not to be confused as being part of this group. We think, let's be sure we don't do any of the weird things because people may start thinking we're creative.

As consultants, we consistently tell clients that they already have all of the good ideas. Our job is to organize their ideas into marketing programs that will help them achieve their objectives. As soon as this concept is explained, the client begins to look at us strangely. We were hired to bring the creative dust and sprinkle it over the business plan to make magic.

Let's look at the steps you should go through to establish the creative process:

1) State your objectives in a quantifiable form. Even creative people need a destination. If you don't have a destination and you don't know where you're going, any road will get you there. Objectives provide the common denominator for all further discussion.

2) Gather all, or as many people in the company who are involved in the project, into a group. Review with them the objectives and the information available about the market and product or service to be discussed.

3) Set upon the task of developing the *Big Idea* that will strategically position the product or service into the proper market. The *Big Idea* should be developed into the language that will appeal to the market you're trying to reach.

As in Chapter 2, the intensive planning session is an ideal way to run a brainstorming or creative meeting. With all of the involved personnel in a room, start the creative ideas flowing; the energy will grow as the process moves forward.

Start by asking the group members for their thoughts on how to communicate the product or service to the marketplace. What is the first thing you want the prospect to know about the product? What is the headline? In other words, how can you approach someone with your product or service, and what are the first words that you would use to get their attention?

The creative people can develop these original thoughts. The initial concept will give the creative organization a starting point. From this starting point, with all the involved personnel contributing their thoughts, a great deal of time can be saved. All of the people involved in the project have contributed to the project from the germination, which will save a lot of sign off time later on.

Brainstorming Sessions

The real challenge is getting the noncreative people to participate in the creative process of generating the *Big Idea*. The brainstorming session is an organized, structured approach to having everyone actively participate in creating ideas. All of the individuals involved in the project should be asked to participate in the session. The session should be conducted in a conference room, classroom, or office that is large enough to allow everyone to be comfortable.

The following guidelines will help you to run a more successful brainstorming session:

1) No negatives. No one can say anything negative about any idea offered by any member of the group. The session moderator should enforce this rule. A negative can seriously stifle the creative process.

2) No rules of communication. A group member can express himself verbally, in writing, graphically (even if they can't draw well -- nobody cares -- it is the idea that is important), or by acting out an idea. The formal decorum that is normally part of the corporate culture should be suspended. All group members must be able to move about freely. Often, when the energy level is high and people get excited, it is difficult to stay seated.

3) No one is more important than anyone else. No matter what the hierarchy of the organization, in the brainstorming session, all participants are equal.

4) No interruptions. Once convened, the group should not be interrupted for phone calls or any other reason. Interruptions divert energy of the group and often stop the flow of ideas. For this reason, brainstorming should be limited to one to two hours. In less than one hour it is difficult to get the ideas flowing. After more than two hours, individuals begin to get concerned about their work and are no longer thinking of the project at hand. For major efforts, the group may meet off-site or during nonworking hours. This tends to limit interruptions and will help maintain focus.

   The session can be broken into several sessions. This will make continuity of thoughts difficult, and it will take some time to reestablish the energy level of the previous session. We don't suggest multiple sessions, but some business situations will leave no alternative.

5) All of the ideas are written on a board or flip charts by the group leader. Flip charts are ideal because as pages are filled up, they can be removed from the easel and taped to the walls allowing all generated ideas to be in constant view of the group.

As the *Big Idea* is developed and evolves, it should be reviewed in light of the objectives.

Group members are welcome to have note pads, but they are discouraged from taking notes. Note taking forces structure and restricts the freedom you are seeking. Pads can be used to jot down thoughts to be introduced later.

6) All members should state their views once a *Big Idea* is generated. This is a forced communication to allow each member to support, enhance, or challenge the *Big Idea*.

If this step is deleted, disgruntled group members will go back to their responsibilities with the thought of killing the *Big Idea* down the road. If the *Big Idea* cannot stand the test of all of the members of the group, then it needs to be revisited in another brainstorming session.

When planning a brainstorming session, consider the value of the management time it will require. It may be impractical to have the company president involved in a session that pertains to decisions that have not been clearly delegated and identified.

The brainstorming session can be run more effectively by someone from outside of the company. This is the off-the-plane syndrome. For some reason, people who are brought in from the outside, particularly if they travel from out of town, have greater credibility than people from within one's own organization. These outsiders may not have any more knowledge or experience, but they are considered experts and can be helpful in developing the *Big Idea*.

The outside person can be especially effective if they are perceived as a creative type. Employees are often constrained by the formal and informal pecking order within their company. Employees are also interested in their own personal situation within the company. They may have a tendency to control the discussion to their own benefit; this is a natural human reaction. An outsider can keep the session impartial and moving forward.

Once the *Big Idea* is generated, the creative group can explore versions of the idea. They can also put the idea into a form that satisfies the technical requirements of the promotion.

Brainstorming is your chance to be a kid again. You are still just as creative as when you played with the box instead of the toy bicycle. The toy was structured, the box wasn't. Have some fun; let fly with a few wild ideas from time to time, even if they're not part of a brainstorming session. You may be surprised by how many other people might join your brook and journey to the sea. You may find that your little trickle of an idea creates a flow that turns into a river. The energy you create, like a river, can move mountains over time.

Take the *no negative reaction to ideas* rule of brainstorming, and try it in your office for one week. You'll be amazed at how many ideas will be offered up on almost every subject. Creativity is just the free flow of ideas. Everyone has ideas, therefore everyone is creative. The real creative challenge is maintaining an environment that enhances the freeflow of ideas.

Testing

The creative process will often produce more than one *Big Idea*. The problem then becomes determining which concept will produce the best results. Even with a single *Big Idea,* there may be alternative ways to implement the idea. For example, the *Big Idea* may be to send a special offer to the president of prospect companies, and several formats and packages are suggested that will all satisfy the concept. How do you determine which concept will produce the best results? Which *Big Idea* is really the best for the company?

Direct marketing allows you to test many approaches and scientifically determine which is best. To test, you exert one or more marketing efforts to small, representative samples of your market. Then you evaluate the responses to determine which marketing effort yielded the greatest result for the marketing dollar. The representative samples should be statistically significant, and the market conditions should be identical at roll-out as they were during the test period.

The biggest problem in testing is that the forces causing a market to act and react in a certain way are out of your control. In consumer testing, there is a better chance of testing a representative sample because a lot more is known about the people making the decisions.

In consumer testing, you know the following:

1) The person receiving the message is either the president or chairman of the household. Most married men believe they are the president, and know they must report to the chairman of the board who is also the chief executive officer of the relationship.

2) When mail is used to deliver the message, the target reviews it within five minutes after arriving home from work, while standing in the kitchen. The mail is not read at that time, but only reviewed as part of "the kitchen cut," to see if it will be read later or thrown directly in the trash. When phone is used, the target is generally in and available between 5 PM and 9 PM on weekdays and during the day on weekends.

3) Houses buy people, people don't buy houses. The economics of a house select who will live in that house. With census, list, database and all the fancy overlays available in the consumer universe, you can pinpoint which houses meet certain criteria. The demographics and even the psychographics of the occupants of houses can be established prior to attempting a direct marketing contact. When the occupants move, you will want to follow them to their new location, which will be approximately the same demographically as the old location.

   You will also want to contact the new occupants of the first home; they will probably have the same characteristics as the original occupants. They will probably have the same disposable income as your customers. You can create need and desire, you are talking to people with authority, and if they are interested in your offer, money is probably available.

   The biggest flaw in this approach to consumers has been the elderly market, where small retired incomes and houses in less expensive areas have masked people with large cash reserves.

The consumer environment is considerably easier to target than the business universe. Businesses also have some common characteristics:

1) There are a finite number of businesses. While there also are a finite number of households, around 100 million. These are conveniently structured into nine digit zip codes, ZIP +4.

   There are only a few million businesses in the United States. Does it make sense to develop a test program, train your organization and then test 50 companies? If the stakes are high, yes.

   Generally, there isn't time for this kind of luxury, so the test is an effort to the entire market. Also, inherent in the smaller market is the fear of upsetting the apple cart. You are less likely to test a wide selection of offers because you fear that prospects may learn of them through their independent interaction with others. Test variations are seldom a problem for consumer marketers. If a consumer becomes angry and stops buying, there are plenty of other prospects to sell to -- but even this philosophy is changing. In the business arena, losing a customer could represent a significant amount of total business and the risks need to be more carefully evaluated.

2) When promoting to a business, you are never entirely sure who will make the buying decision. You cannot be sure what the process of reviewing your offer may be or to whom you should speak. In today's corporate world, the decision-maker will get the blame if something goes wrong. On the other hand, if the decision proves to be good, at least six people will take credit. Politics are always present in the business world and can have a significant impact on your selling efforts.

3) You must overcome two sets of reviews for each person you reach in the business world. First, you must overcome the emotional, personal bias of the person. Then you must overcome the logical, role-playing process that the same person fulfills as an employee.

4) Response in the consumer world can and usually does mean an order. In the business universe, response is often the first step of

the selling process, particularly when selling capital goods. Response rates are important but should not be the primary measurement vehicle used to determine the success of the direct marketing program. Establish a chain of events or activities that must happen to generate an order. Each link of the chain will probably represent a contact with the prospect or customer. Each will have a cost and a success rate for moving to the next link. When the process is complete, you will be able to measure sales results and compare them to the investment.

A 0.01% response rate could make a lot of money, and a 50% response rate could lose money. The key to measurement and testing is to structure the project so you can measure cost per qualified lead or referral, the actual sales, cost per order, and profitability of the project. Don't fall short by only measuring the initial response rate.

With all of the problems in marketing to the business world, is it worth doing any testing? Yes. You can and should test marketing concepts to determine the best and most profitable approach. Test the big things first: those areas that can have a big impact on costs, results and ultimate profitability of the project. The elements you test should be those changes that have the highest probability of improving final results, not just the initial response rate.

The elements that can have the greatest impact on the success of the program, are exactly the same as the areas discussed earlier:

List
Offer
Format
Copy/Graphics

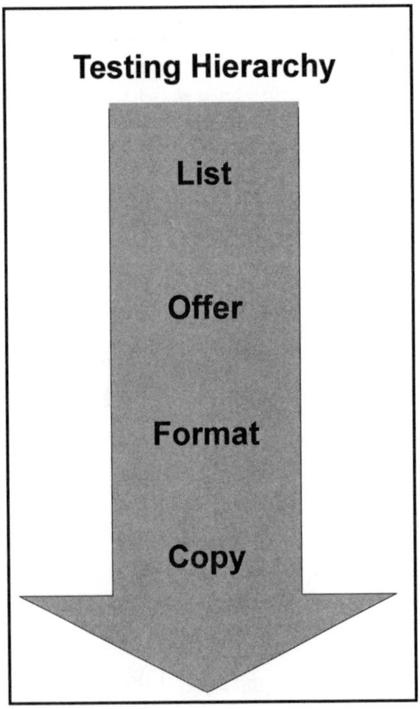

Illustration 5-11: Testing Hierarchy.

The rules for constructing tests are fairly simple. Start at the top of the list and work your way down. Illustration 5-11 shows the hierarchy of the variables.

The corollary is never start at the bottom, with the copy, and work your way up. Never, never test more than one variable at a time. If you do, you will not be able to determine which variable influenced any change in the results. The size of the group you're selling to will limit the amount and types of testing you will be able to do.

If you have a large universe to select from, you can design tests that are fairly complex and complete. If you only have a few thousand names and you're planning to use only direct mail, testing more than one variable may prove impossible. Whenever you construct a test, you should test against a control package that has a proven history of response and sale

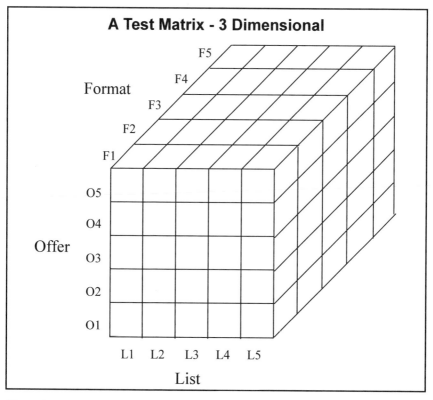

Illustration 5-12: A test matrix - 3 dimensional.

results. This will allow you to measure the success of your new approach at the start and throughout the program.

Let's assume that you have a fairly large universe, and you are going to test five different lists (L1-L5), five offers (O1-O5), and five formats (F1-F5). You will not test copy because, while a four dimensional test can be calculated, it cannot be easily illustrated.

As demonstrated in Illustration 5-12, the intersection of each variable must be filled with a representative group of your market in order to provide reliable results. Each test group or cell will be assigned a code to identify which list, offer, and format were used. This code will be used to measure results and determine the best programs.

Assigning the test cell codes can be an important part of your direct marketing program. If you want your codes to make sense, you can build intelligence directly into the codes. In this example, the first cell could be L1O1F1, next L2O1F1, and so on. Or you can assign codes in sequence from 001 to 125, each number representing the number of test cells (5x5x5=125). It will be a lot easier for analysis and communication if you don't build intelligence directly into the codes. For some reason, intelligent codes tend to become the masters of the program they represent in order not to violate the intelligence they represent. In addition, intelligent codes tend to complicate data entry. Numeric information is much easier to enter into a computer and is less prone to transcription errors.

Unfortunately, the lack of uniformity in company names and abbreviations makes complete and accurate measurement almost impossible. In addition, no matter how diligent you are in coding solicitations, 25% to 50% of responses may not be able to be tracked. This is because some respondents will not use your response format or vehicle. The only consolation in this area is that the lack of measurement is uniform and consistent across the entire program and therefore it is predictable.

The test looks like a box with 125 cells inside. This means you must have 125 separate promotional efforts. If you need five sales per cell to have a large enough sample to evaluate results and you anticipate five sales per 1,000 contacts, you need 125,000 prospects. This may be a reasonable test concept, but it is not necessary if you are willing to evaluate the results and not just the numbers.

You can easily eliminate every second cell in the test and still have enough information to judge the best list, best offer, and best format. If all remaining cells perform equally well, the cell with the lowest cost would be the best direct marketing program.

Very often in business-to-business selling, the sale requires more than one contact and may take a prolonged period of time. If the selling effort is traditionally a four month effort, you will be unable to evaluate results for four to six months. This depends on how long it takes to get a prospect to respond to the direct response effort. This time delay is frequently unacceptable to upper management and becomes a primary reason for not testing. There are some techniques that can be used to still predict the success of a program, but you have to track the results to measure the ultimate success of the test.

If you try to test using the strict rules and evaluation techniques required for statistical accuracy, you may never get anything implemented beyond the test stage. If the sell cycle is long, your odds of statistical measurement will be reduced even further. You can also over-test as demonstrated by the 125-cell test. In many situations you'll have to use your instincts and prior selling history to construct stages of the sale that can be measured as you move through the process.

Your customer file and prior selling experience should help you to determine the best arena for your marketing efforts. Focus on the major items, don't spend time and money majoring in the minors.

If you have a product that can be consumed by many businesses, test lists that will give you a representative result for an industry segment and company size (if this is a key variable). Don't test two similar lists from different suppliers unless you're sure that the industry is good for you.

One test effort should be aimed at the people by name and another group targeted by title. When you rent a list of stapler buyers, Jim Smith, stapler buyer, may have left the company for which they are listed. Your promotional effort does not reach Jim because he is no longer there. If you had aimed your effort at the "person who buys staplers," you would have a better chance of reaching Jim's replacement. You always have to evaluate whether to name or title address your mailings; understand the differences in response and order rates.

Once you know your arena, try different types of lists -- customer, compiled, responder, and subscription -- to discover which type gives the best results. In some consumer promotions, some lists are too small to test because they don't have a large enough universe to roll-out. There is no business list too small if it happens to yield the results you need. If there are a limited number of prospects in your universe, you may have to use a variety of small lists repeatedly. In this case, move to testing offers.

Repetition in the business universe is normally successful. You can and should go back to the same businesses every time you change your offer, format, or copy. If a promotion is successful, you should go back with the same effort as soon as you can. In fact, you should continue to reuse successful lists by varying the offer.

A common mistake is to discontinue a successful program because personnel have become bored with the campaign. Personnel assume that the market is also bored with the promotion. Let the results tell you when the program is no longer effective. When you think a promotion is no longer effective, test a new format or offer against the existing approach. The results will tell you which program to continue. You should always be trying to "*beat the champ.*" Create a program that outperforms your best existing program.

When testing offers, test significant differences. Don't test a free pen against a key chain as a premium for attending a seminar. Test a free pen against a free car. You may have seen an offer to buy 100 pens for only $39.95 and get 400 free. It's more than likely that the selling price for 500 pens is $39.95. It has been determined through testing that this offer motivated the most people to action.

Limiting the time of an offer can build a sense of urgency into the mind of your prospect. Time limits can be effective motivators. Make sure to have the offer expire as indicated by the time limit. Free gifts work better in business offers than discount pricing does. Prospects like to receive something they can enjoy in their personal lives for purchasing things at their place of business. Look at the offers made by airlines and hotels to encourage frequent use; family travel and lodging as a result of company expenditures. Consider these offers as executive green stamps that can be used personally. Powerful, wealthy executives who can afford to pay their own way are taking advantage of these offers. You may want to examine these frequent-user programs and attempt to emulate them to build ongoing relationships with customers.

The offer should promote the next link in the chain that ultimately leads to the sale. If you try to sell the product too soon, you could lose the prospect or the opportunity. Sell the next decision point on the way to selling the product.

The formats most frequently tested and used in the business marketplace are print advertising, direct mail, and telemarketing. Since most businesses generate leads for their sales force, the formats are used in combination with each other as part of the chain of contacts needed to accomplish a sale. The cost comparison of the various media is described in Illustration 5-2. In lead generation there are no rules that dictate which format is the best to use first. Test the point in the process in which you'll need phone, mail or whatever. Integration of the Internet as a response and/or fulfillment medium has greatly enhanced the effectiveness of both print and direct mail.

In testing formats, it is important to know the personality of the people you are trying to reach. You spend a great deal of money training your salespeople to understand the type of individual you're trying to sell. If you're uncertain about who you're trying to reach, test formats that relate to various personalities.

Refer to the earlier discussion on business-to-business personalities. Each general type of personality can be found in each person at any time at work or home. People are, however, generally constant in one quadrant and tend to move only to adjacent quadrants. People seldom move to non-adjacent areas.

Format and copy will reach out to the people that identify most with its approach. You will probably have to create different formats to reach different parts of your market. Let's use the stapler example. Since the pragmatic person only wants to know product, its price, and guarantee, the promotion could be a picture of the stapler, price, and a little copy explaining the guarantee. It would be printed on inexpensive, uncoated stock. The promotion doesn't have to be personalized.

On the other hand, extroverts wants to know the benefit of using the stapler and how it relates to them personally. You want to convince these prospects that your stapler is of unique design and will make them look better. Rich photography on quality coated stock enrich the image of the product.

The amiable prospect will want to know that everybody that uses the stapler will be happy and content. Graphics showing happy people printed on rich stock will support this sale.

The analytical person will want to know the specifications of the stapler: metal content, mean time between breakdowns, weight, staples per minute potential, etc. Inexpensive paper with massive copy and small photographs will get this message across.

Which approach will work best can only be determined through testing and evaluating the results. You can take the exact same layout for a space ad, web site, mail effort, or phone script and revisit the four main personality stereotypes. Your copy can be tailored to target different personalities and then you can test the results.

Format Selection

Now you have enough information to get yourself into real trouble. The big question after you digest all the previous material is: What is the right format and medium for your needs?

Format selection is directly related to your total budget and how much you can spend to acquire an order. For example, if you can afford to spend $100 per order, and you need 25 orders, your total budget is $2,500. You can't afford national TV on this budget, even if it could produce a cost per order of less than $100.

The other consideration is how many leads or sales you can handle. This will lead you to analyze the quality of the inquiries and not just the quantity. Too many leads is worse than not enough.

Timing is another consideration. You can generate telephone and local media placements much more quickly than a direct mail program or national publication advertising.

Chain Analysis

Assumptions: Historical performance data is available

Existing customers will contribute $3 million in sales

Product is sold by face-to-face sales representatives

Sales Goal	$6,500,000	
	- 3,000,000	(Sales to existing customers)
Net Goal	3,500,000	
	÷ 15,000	(Average order from new customers)
New Customers	= 233	(# new customers required)
	÷ 20%	(Sales rep closes 1:5 proposals)
	= 1,165	(# of proposals required)
	÷ 30%	(3:10 appointments end in proposal)
	=3,883	(# of appointments required)
	÷ 60%	(6:10 leads secure appointments)
	= 6,472	(# of leads required)

Leads from Advertising

Leads	3,000	
	x $80.00	(Average cost/lead, space ads)
	=$240,000	(Space ad budget)

Leads from Direct Marketing

Leads	3,480	(Remaining required leads)
	÷ 3%	(3% response rate)
	= 116,000	(# of direct mail pieces required)
	x $900/m	(Direct mail cost)
	= $104,400	(Direct mail budget)

Lead Generation Budget

Space	$240,000	
Direct mail	+ 104,400	
Total budget	=$ 344,400	

Illustration 5-13: Chain Analysis - determining volumes and budgets required prior to testing.

The major factor in determining the format you'll use is the target audience. If you're trying to sell office supplies to purchasing agents, it probably doesn't make sense to use broadcast media to reach them. Direct mail catalogs have proved effective in this arena.

Illustration 5-13 demonstrates one approach for setting up a model to evaluate the available funds for your promotion efforts. The model should review the entire process from initial contact to the ultimate order. This approach can be helpful in determining where to spend money in order to have the greatest result.

Evaluate the prospects you're trying to reach and the ability of certain formats to contact that particular group of people. For example, the cost-per-contact in a specific magazine may be attractive, but only a small percentage of the readership is a part of your prospect group. The cost-per-contact of your prospect group in this scenario could be higher than having a salesperson call directly on the prospect.

The more expensive the cost-per-contact, the more directed and targeted it can be. You'll always be trading off costs and the ability to reach a specific market segment. The smaller a group of specific prospects, the harder they will be to reach. Direct mail and telemarketing are ideal vehicles to contact precisely targeted audiences.

Unfortunately, there is no magic formula or easy method of selecting the appropriate format or media to reach a specific target. It is easier to eliminate certain approaches because of expense and result considerations. The planning and creative brainstorming sessions are critical in the selection of format and media.

Even after you have identified an approach, you should identify at least two alternatives and test both to see which is best. A direct marketing agency can help you evaluate and create different approaches to fulfill your requirements. After you discover a format and media that works and produces an acceptable cost per order, don't rest on your laurels. Look for other approaches that may improve on your existing successful effort.

The old adage, "We've always done it this way," can cost you a lot of money. Looking for efficiencies in the relationships you have with your customers and your potential customers can be fruitful and exciting. Being completely sales force oriented or channel of distribution oriented is myopic.

The high technology industries are faced with an unusual problem: the prices of the products they sell are coming down while the cost of selling is going up. Companies in these industries which are not continually looking for better ways to sell and market their products will not survive.

Formats obviously lend themselves to a given media. For example, catalogs are most often used in direct mail, however they can be inserted in newspapers or delivered by salespeople, used as a handout and displayed on the internet. An advertisement that was used in a print format can also be used as a reprint and sent as direct mail. However, using a format that was designed for a different medium with a different objective can be far more expensive than creating the format for the medium. Effective direct marketing demands that you continually use specialized promotional materials to produce a lead or an order.

We recently worked with a client interested in reaching the senior underwriting executive in the largest insurance companies.

The company is one of the largest and oldest providers of reconstruction estimating data to the insurance industry. If you have a fire or suffer damage to your home, the odds are likely that the company's data will be used to estimate your damage claim. The reconstruction information is made available to users in many printed and electronic formats.

Historically claims experiences have demonstrated that many homes are not adequately insured to cover losses. Unfortunately, both the insurance company and the property owner don't realize the mistake until a claim is filed and it is really too late. These under insurance problems cost insurance companies in lost premiums and property owners when they suffer a loss.

The best source of accurate information about a property and its value is the homeowner. They understand the size and materials used in the home. Unfortunately, most homes are appraised for insurance purposes by an agent with little involvement by the property owner.

The company created a new service, tele-estimating, using telemarketing and their database to contact a homeowner by telephone to verify the characteristics of the home prior to policy renewal.

The service proved extremely successful finding about 15% of the homes to be under-insured. To expand this portion of their business, a direct marketing campaign was initiated to offer the largest insurance companies an opportunity to try the tele-estimating service. Each company was offered an opportunity to try 100 tele-estimating calls to policy holders just prior to renewal.

A two-page letter, response form, and business reply envelope were designed to make the offer to the senior underwriting executive in the top 100 property and casualty insurance companies. The letter was personalized.

Breakthrough to the executive was thought to be a major problem, even with an exciting offer. The small list made it impossible to test different creative approaches. We decided to mail half the list via 1st class and half via overnight letter.

The program experienced terrific results with 37 respondents requesting contact to discuss how to take advantage of the free trial. A 37% response in any direct marketing program is almost unbelievable -- clearly not something that would be planned in advance. Expectations were wildly optimistic at about 5%.

The results from the two delivery approaches was considerably different. Nine respondents came from the group that had been mailed via first class mail. The mail cell produced an 18% response (9 out of 50) -- still an unbelievable response rate.

The overnight letter produced 28 respondents -- 56% response! The response from the express delivery out-produced the mail by over 3 times. It was clear that express delivery made an enormous difference. The additional cost was only about $10 for each name mailed.

Express delivery tends to be handled differently by many companies. The mail room expedites delivery to the addressee and many times the package is delivered unopened by a receptionist or secretary. Delivery, and therefore response, is better.

We have been searching for an outer envelope that is similar in appearance and composition to an express delivery outer envelope. A package mailed via first class but that looks like express delivery may be handled and delivered similarly to express mail. Express mail imitations have been attempted many times but the package is frequently obvious and never bypasses the standard mail delivery process in most companies.

Express mail can help breakthrough and produce significantly higher results. If you're contemplating a limited mailing, with a solid offer, consider testing express delivery to determine how it may help you.

In direct marketing, everyone can have a good idea. Evaluate the format and media alternatives in light of the financial implications. *If the effort looks like it can meet your cost-per-sale requirements, find a way to test it.*

Multimedia Synergy

Combining one or more formats or media can dramatically affect your results. Using a combination of media can be planned or accidental. For example, participating in a trade show at the same time you are using direct mail in a particular market can boost direct mail results by three or four times. In addition, the traffic at the trade show booth can be increased. This response is most likely to occur when large companies have separate groups responsible for direct marketing, sales, and trade shows.

It has been proven time and time again that there is a dramatic synergy in combining direct marketing promotions to substantially increase results. If planned properly, the combination of mail and telephone produces three to five times the results of either program individually.

If you are executing telemarketing lead-generation or sales programs, you should also use direct mail. This may not be immediately apparent, however telemarketing prospects will ask for more information as often as they accept the offer. The direct mail material used to fulfill this request for information will force you into a combined phone and direct mail program. Similarly, you should use direct mail with space advertising, unless you are selling a product directly from the space ad. In all cases, the internet should be used as one response option and for immediate fulfillment of information.

These synergistic approaches may not be planned but will be required when you begin to implement any direct marketing promotion. View your prospects who request additional information as people who are beginning to close, not just rejections. Often, particularly in telemarketing, prospects will request information simply to end the dialogue. Prospects don't want to be rude, so they request additional information as a put-off. However, about 25% of this group of people can be converted to orders and sales if they are handled properly.

You may not consider this a synergistic promotion; you may look at it as simply linear common sense. Don't be misled; if you're using multiple formats and multiple media, there is a synergy in the promotions. Without proper planning and execution of the *Big Idea*, synergy can be reduced and sales opportunities lost.

These are the types of questions that are most often asked concerning multimedia:

- What happens when you use mail prior to telemarketing?
- What happens when you use direct response print advertising in a market at the same time you are doing a direct mail promotion?
- Does awareness advertising have any affect on the success of your direct mail or telemarketing programs?
- How important is the timing of direct mail followed by telemarketing?
- Does the internet improve the results of other media?

There is a significant increase in response rates when mail is used prior to telemarketing. In Chapter 6, we will discuss several specific programs that combined the use of mail and phone. There is a definite correlation between the time the mail is dropped and the time the phone call is made. When you examine the results of mail and phone together, use the combined totals for the promotion as compared to the individual results of either medium alone.

An example: A direct mail program by itself might produce a 2% response rate. Telemarketing of the same product without direct mail might produce a 6% response rate. While you might think that using mail followed by telemarketing would produce a response rate of 8%, we have seen the combined program produce results as high as 20% and 30%!

Timing is one of the major issues of the synergy of media. You may not be able to wait for all the responses from one medium before you implement another medium within the same program. Since telephone calls are placed about two weeks after bulk mail is dropped, you may have to start the telemarketing program before you are able to receive all of the mail responses.

We have conducted direct marketing campaigns for cellular telephone companies and high-technology companies while they were also using awareness ads in the same markets. We have also performed the same direct marketing campaigns in different markets with no advertising support. There was an increase in response rate in the markets with the advertising, but it was difficult to determine if the increase in results justified the cost of the advertising. The fact that the campaigns were in different markets tended to distort the results.

We have frequently tested mail followed by telemarketing and found there is a definite correlation between the time the mail is dropped and the time the prospects were called. Telemarketing response rates seem to be at their highest between 11 and 16 days after the mail is dropped. We have also had occasion to execute telemarketing effectively even though the mail was not dropped by the mail house. Perhaps caller attitude or a really strong offer carried the program.

Media synergy does not always have to be a major program. An example is using two 30-second TV spots on the three network morning programs in the same market while participating in a trade show. The day this was done, the traffic in the booth was three times as high as it was on any other day. The total cost for the advertising was under $3,000.

We have now examined a full cycle. The media selection and synergy flow from format and media selection. These issues flow from your *Big Idea*. Your *Big Idea* came from your brainstorming session. We cannot say enough about the planning phase and brainstorming phase of the development of your direct marketing program. Don't be afraid to go back and have additional brainstorming sessions if you are working too hard to make the *Big Idea* a reality.

Time

Today we have many sources of information to make decisions. These decisions will hopefully lead to action. Unfortunately, we must often convert data into information hamstrung by partial information from data processing and/or accounting where cycle times are measured in months, quarters and even years.

We do not have the luxury of time. Many of us have learned that immediate response and rapid cycles of contact improve our chances of gaining and maintaining a customer. Time is an asset that is constant to all competitors and it is fixed and inflexible. Winners in the game will have many contact cycles, while the loser will have a few in the same time frame. The winner will act quickly when requested; the loser will act slowly. The winner will drive the activity of marketing while the loser will be driven.

Many of us spend more time at work than with our families trying to survive in ever more competitive markets. You constantly gather data and try to make decisions that will maintain your market share and profits. Growth has become more an expectation than a reality. You probably struggle with company structures that got their origin from the cycle times of the 50's when the military model moved to business. These antiquated structures are power-based and have grown inflexible. These structures treat time as if it were of no value in the present or for the future. Many of these organizations have fallen in love with their products and their structure instead of their customers. The internet has re-defined time and is re-defining the organization.

What is your cycle time for customers to make a decision about acquiring products or services (not what you think, but what you can make happen)? Is it 2 days? 90 days? 120 days? 180 days? This cycle time for action by a customer or prospect is your window of opportunity before a competitor may eclipse your last innovation or beat your last price cut. The only way you can stay in the game is by embracing time as your competitive asset. Reduce your cycle time for decisions, action, and order generation. You cannot become so involved in the process of generating promotional programs that you forget the stakes of the game.

As time is compressed, the costs of delivering a product or a service decrease because the allowable fixed costs per unit can be less. As time is compressed, you can increase the price you charge by being the first in the market with a product or service. As time is compressed, your risks are reduced because you are less exposed to obsolescence and your revenue can go up. As time is compressed, your market-share increases because you are gaining and maintaining customers more rapidly than your competitors.

You can take full advantage of time by including offers in ALL marketing programs so you can begin taking action on initial and subsequent contacts. *Get out of the education business with your promotional materials. Gain involvement and ask for action with every element of your program.*

The Direct Marketing Creative Product You Buy -- It Looks Good -- It Sounds Good... So How Good Is It?

To gain some additional insight on the issues involved with outside creative services we turn to Mark Mancini, President of Mancini Creative (mancini@voicenet.com). He presents the following:

As a purchaser of creative services, you surely know by now that direct marketing AE's, like most any advertising executives, will sell you good creative or bad creative. As long as you'll buy it, it's all good to the guy who is selling it. So, what criteria should you use to establish the value of the creative you buy?

"Ad men" and "ad women" often say: "all we have to sell is our time." I'm not sure that's a flattering evaluation of our business. It's one more in a long line of cliches (a' la *apples vs. oranges, carts before horses, balls in the air* and the ever popular -- *enough on the plate*) we've all, hopefully unconsciously, used to build personal credibility in the client meeting. But, somehow, I like to think expertise is more what you, the client, has in mind when they develop the program advertising budgets.

So what's good creative? Any creative director who has risen through the copywriting ranks will tell you it's a clever phrase that grabs attention and furthers the positioning of the concept in the prospect's mind. Any graphics-driven creative director will assure you it's the visual stopping power and impact that really influences your final results. Either can be right or wrong. Here are a few of the things you can look for and use to force them both to give you more than just the "time" they're so willing to sell you.

First and foremost, make sure you know what you want from your prospect. This one issue could be, and *is* for that matter, the subject of many books full of explanation. This isn't the time or place. But just make sure you've got a clear objective that will provide you with quantifiable results. And, make sure your offer is tangible, basic, and easy to understand. Otherwise, just save the money and use it to order a few hundred pizzas; it will be much better spent.

The second thing you have to remember is that you, your people, and probably your ad representative are the only ones in the world who really care even the tiniest bit about your product or your company's success. And understanding this simple fact will help you determine the content of your basic communication. <u>Do not tell your market all the things you'd like them to know about you, your product or your company.</u> <u>Unfortunately, nobody cares</u>.

1. Your creative must communicate only what your prospect needs to know to take the action you want that individual to take, not one thing more. Generally speaking, this will mean your communication should constantly be saying, "you'll get this, you'll get that" not "we've got this and we're doing that". When you've run out of things to say centering around satisfying the needs and desires of your prospect your creative job is done, put a fork in it.

    The next thing you can throw in the face of your pet ad representative is this copy vs. graphics thing. Remember, your advertising material is a communication and that's all it is. Most agency's creative product ranges between mediocre and just plain rotten for the simple reason that their creative director is either copy-driven or graphics-driven. This means the concept is not necessarily developed using the best method of communication for the task at hand. Rather, it is being processed as a copy problem or a graphics problem based on the background of the individual creative director.

2. Base your evaluation of the creative product solely on its ability to communicate. The efficiency with which it delivers the benefit to your prospect, whether visually, verbally (or ideally both), will bring you a much higher return than a clever but ambiguous phrase or a "neat" but irrelevant graphic image. Don't forget you're spending *your* money to do this stuff and the object is to

make more money than you're spending. It can be a very expensive mistake to fall in love with clever creative that doesn't accomplish your goals (although this kind of mistake will frame up very nicely for your wall where you can look at it forever -- just something to consider).

3. Make sure the message is presented in logical order relative to your eye flow across the material. Logical order relative to the prospect's interests. For example, the most appealing benefit would logically be the first thing your prospect should notice. Make sure it is. Your eye should then logically walk through the components of the material, picking up the information you, as the prospect, need to understand the message, the offer, the urgency, and the modes for response.

And finally:

4. Tell your prospect exactly what to do! Your potential customer, which will be you in the review process, must exit the material with the response message -- the call to action. The last thing your prospect sees must be the "how to" of your offer. Whenever fulfillment constraints will allow, both phone and mail response options, and sometimes fax response as well, should be offered. Don't worry about one form of response stealing from another. Certain individuals will be predisposed to responding via one vehicle or the other and most will not deviate from their pattern. If you use a mail-back coupon, it's wise to display the phone response number prominently on the coupon. Individuals predisposed to ordering by mail won't even notice it. Individuals predisposed to ordering by phone will. And start offering Internet response vehicles including e-mail and the Web.

Never, never, never ever listen to yourself say: "we'll just put our phone number down here, y'know, small. If they like what we're selling, they'll find us." Remember, your prospect doesn't care about you. They will not go out of their way to find you and make you rich.

While these points may seem somewhat general, you'll find them useful in helping you establish a mind-set. A frame of reference you can use in a world where baloney is king. Wipe any measure of schmooze away from your agency's creative offerings. Replace it with some specific objectives, and you'll be elevating the effectiveness of the creative product you're buying. You won't have as many of those pretty ads and kits to frame for your office, but then you might just generate enough extra revenue to buy a couple of nice paintings to fill the space.

Reaching Outside Control by Editing Copy

Mancini goes on to demonstrate how a final editing technique can give you the edge against a stubborn control audience:

Here is the scene. I'll be the ad-person from your agency, sitting with my staff in a client meeting... you know... looking for something profound to say so you, the client, actually think you're getting something for all the money you're spending.

OK, you're the client – you've been in this seat before, and you know how frightening this exact moment can be. You're just sitting there waiting for that one pearl of wisdom to hatch like a two-pound kidney stone from deep within your ad-person's coconut. Wait! The lights just flickered. Whoa, there's something moving in there behind those restless eyes!

I drop my hand from my chin to the table top, and you watch as the intense stare I've been sporting turns to that smug look you know so well. Look out, here it comes:

"Well Bill, (remember, you're Bill), you've got to keep one thing in mind with a program like this. What you want to do is direct your message to your target market (and here's the emphatic part), to the exclusion of all others!"

There it is folks – this month's entry into the ad-person's "the faster you say it, the better it sounds" cliche hall of fame. Just one more of those sweeping statements, tricks of the trade if you will, that instantly renews faith and credibility in the hearts of clients everywhere.

OK, so this one's a little bit right. Unquestionably, this is decent advice for many newcomers to direct marketing. This statement can put them in the right frame of mind to view any given program analytically, which in itself is probably good superficial advice. But, if you do this stuff for a living, whether from the client side or the agency side, it's the kind of thinking that will help you lose a close fight with a stubborn control program.

If you're going up against a good control, the deliberate exclusion of peripheral market groups can mean the difference between winning by a few points and losing. Developing your initial message to the exclusion of all outlying market groups is fine. It's only a mistake if you think you're finished.

Like any good marketing communication, yours should be initially developed from the standpoint of your principal target's characteristics, wants, needs, biases, beliefs, etc. But once that message has been perfected, the communication should be viewed in reverse against the secondary and tertiary markets that lie at the periphery of your principle target.

By looking at each of these outlying groups the same way as you looked at your main target market, you can review your creative message from their unique perspective as well. What you will generally find is a number of opportunities to include outlying markets without damaging the message directed toward your principle target. For example, a headline for an ad selling field glasses in a bird watching magazine could be written:

"Spot even the most elusive species! Get the lightest, most powerful field glasses in the world —just $79.95!"

In many cases, the actual words chosen can be adjusted to include peripheral groups, but to keep the example as clear as possible, we'll just leave the emphasis alone.

By simply increasing the size of the first six words and positioning it as a pre-head, the initial communication casts a much broader net. While the appeal to the principal target hasn't been diminished, the incidental reader, who may not be an actual practicing bird watcher, is approached by the general feature statement. This peripheral group may have other interests that would put them in the market for the field glasses. There may be opera or sports lovers who can take their own message from the ad.

Even though the pre-head, (and the subsequent sub-head as well) will direct the specific benefit to the target market, the first message encountered is still general enough so that it does not necessarily and immediately exclude secondary and tertiary markets.

Copy applications can be reviewed in the same way. By using a different word here or there, or maybe adjusting a photo or visual, you can still carry at the same impact to your principle market while not specifically excluding one or more peripheral market segments. Adjust to achieve at least the same impact. Never settle for less impact on your principle market for any reason. This kind of reverse editing will bring you the incidental added response that can mean the difference between winning and losing.

This method of editing is especially effective in print, free standing inserts (FSI) and broadcast, where it can be difficult to define your target as clearly from the outset, as compared with direct mail for example. But the same basic approach can also help you win in a mail test. Even in mail, where you have an improved degree of control over the characteristics of your target segment, there's no such thing as a homogeneous market group. Only the level of detail at which you examine your group changes, not the conceptual approach.

The name of the game in direct marketing is competition – it's winning and losing, and when you do it for a living, a couple of extra edits is a small price to pay for success. Use this kind of analytical approach to your editing and you won't need a new cliche in your next marketing meeting. You can just show them the numbers.

Promotion Summarized

Promotion is defined as the further development and encouragement of prospects to purchase one's products or services. It has two aspects: creative and technical.

The creative elements are the *Big Ideas* that are used to present a product or service to the marketplace. Technical promotion has four parts:

> **List -**   The customers or prospects to whom
>   you plan to target your marketing
>   effort.

Offer - The proposition you are making to your customers or prospects in order to get them to respond.

Format - The vehicle for delivering the offer to your market: mail, phone, print or broadcast.

Copy/Graphics - The words and pictures you use to communicate your offer to the market.

The four parts of technical promotion were explained and the relative importance of each part to the ultimate success of a direct marketing program was discussed. List is 50%, offer is 25%, format is 15% and copy/graphics is 10%.

List selection is the most critical element in the process of developing a direct marketing program. Determining the elements that can be used for better target identification is more difficult in business marketing. List selection and testing are critical and should not become an afterthought in direct marketing program development.

Offers were discussed in detail and 100 offer techniques were described. Business offers can appeal to the individual as a business person or a consumer. As a business person, you have to appeal to your prospect's professional motivations. As a consumer, the appeal can be on how the offer will yield the individual personal gratification. Both approaches should be tested to determine the best alternative for your company.

We discussed formats and reviewed how to select the most appropriate for your needs. The cost per contact and personalization of each type of contact were contrasted to help you evaluate the best approach to reach your prospect or customer. A detailed description, along with the advantages and average cost per contact, of many types of formats was discussed.

Direct marketing copywriting was discussed. Several formulas were reviewed to help you develop a hard-hitting explanation of your product and offer. One formula, AIDA was examined in detail. Several approaches to reviewing copy to insure that you are taking your best shot at success were also considered. These approaches also focus on the AIDA formula for copy development.

Targeting the correct individual in business marketing is probably the most difficult challenge you will face. A complete review of the types of personalities involved in the business world was discussed. There are four personality stereotypes: analytic, pragmatic, amiable, and extroverted. Each personality stereotype has different likes and dislikes and should be approached separately. You should determine the personality type that is most closely aligned with the environment to which you're trying to sell and develop the direct marketing program around that personality. We discussed the do's and don'ts in marketing to each of the personality stereotypes to make creating the direct marketing program easier.

Creating the ideas behind the direct marketing program can be the most fun and most difficult aspect of the entire effort. Everyone has a certain amount of creativity and can help in the creative process. There are several approaches that have proved successful in creating the *Big Idea* behind any direct marketing effort. Brainstorming sessions that are designed to foster ideas and get the creative process started, are an excellent method for creating the *Big Idea*. Regardless of the creative approach used, a simple rule of no negative reaction to ideas is required to allow a free exchange of information.

The creative process will normally result in more than one approach. Direct marketing testing allows you to determine the most effective approach. Developing tests and measuring the results are critical to the ultimate success of your efforts. We discussed how to test and measure different concepts for your programs. Business-to-business direct marketing often involves longer selling cycles and multiple contacts. The testing and evaluation techniques must also address interim measurements to evaluate the program as it progresses. When testing different concepts, focus on testing the big things: those areas that can have a big impact on costs, results, and the ultimate profitability of the project. Create a program that outperforms your best existing program.

Selecting the best format for your direct marketing program is difficult. Illustration 5-13 demonstrated a technique and formula that might be used. An example was used to demonstrate how to establish the minimum required results for a format to be effective. Some of the variables you will need to consider were also discussed: timing, target audience, costs, and available budgets. It is easier to eliminate certain approaches because of expense and result considerations than to determine which format will be best for you.

What happens when you use more than one format in the same direct marketing program? Will multiple contacts improve results? Is there synergy in using multiple formats at the same time? Does one format require the use of another format? These questions and their answers were reviewed in some detail.

The question of how to best reach the prospect with the offer is never going to have an easy answer. As time changes so does the best approach to promotion. What is effective today may not be effective tomorrow. You will have to continually evaluate the success of your programs and seek new and better ways to promote your products and services. One of the beautiful things about direct marketing is its testability. This chapter gave you a foundation to build upon.

If you're already using direct marketing, try a brainstorming session to see if you can create a better way to approach your market. Use the testing techniques to determine if you can "beat the champ".

If you're trying direct marketing for the first time, test multiple approaches to determine the best promotion techniques for your company. Don't rest on your laurels; continue to look for better techniques to improve your results.

Embrace time as part of your promotional materials -- always have an offer that will call for action. Rapid cycles of action will put you in the winners circle more often than having the most well-informed prospects in your markets.

Chapter Six:
Telephone Selling

While the database concept discussed earlier is too new for its definition to be found in every dictionary, telemarketing is so new, as a word, that to date it does not even have a dictionary definition. In this chapter we will establish a definition for the concept of telemarketing.

Many companies believe that they are using telemarketing, when in fact they are performing telephone selling or telesales. A substantial difference exists between the two.

The Elements of Telephone Selling

The increasing cost of making a sales call in person has created a need for less expensive methods for:

    a)   Handling smaller customers
    b)   Setting up appointments for the salesperson

Many companies take some of their outside salespeople and convert them into telephone salespeople, sometimes called TSR's or telephone sales representatives. They're paid commissions and make sales calls using the telephone.

This ***Telesales*** concept can be worthwhile, but it is not telemarketing. Telesales or telephone selling does not conform to our definition of direct marketing because its cost and results may or may not be measurable.

As you may recall from our discussions in Chapter 1, we believe that direct marketing:

Explores, tests, and substantiates methods of :

- *Prospecting*
- *Qualifying*
- *Closing*

exclusive of a face-to-face contact by a salesperson.

Although the salesperson is using the phone, they are actually still making a face-to-face sales call via the telephone. The key to direct marketing is its measurability and predictability. As you perform an activity and determine its success, you can expect similar results when you duplicate the activity.

Using Illustration 6-1, let's review telesales in light of the definition of direct marketing.

The Definition of Direct Marketing

- **An organized and planned system of contacts**

- **Using a variety of media -- seeking to produce a lead or an order**

- **Developing and maintaining a database**

- **Measurable in costs and results**

- **Effective in all methods of selling**

- **Expandable with confidence**

Illustration 6-2:   A simplified definition of Direct marketing.

Telephone selling is not an organized and planned system of contacts using a variety of media. In most cases, the salesperson is allowed to schedule and execute the telephone selling on their own. The average salesperson will make about 25 telephone calls per day in the telesales environment.

We're never quite certain of the objective or results of telesales. The salesperson is not scripted and may or may not record the results from the sales call. Performing telesales is like sending a different letter to each customer. It may be a good idea and have very positive results, but it is not measurable direct marketing. Because each contact is personalized and specific to that customer, there is no common standard that is necessary to measure or predict performance.

Some companies have become fairly sophisticated and will allow the telesalesperson to interact with a computerized database. The database may or may not schedule the telephone selling activity, record respondents, or record purchases. In essence, it is probably not a direct marketing database. It is a sales automation tool instead.

Measurement of costs and results of the telesales operation is problematic. We can probably establish the costs (in most cases they are substantially understated); but measuring the results can be difficult. Since the offer and actions of the salesperson are not controlled, a true measure of results is hard to determine.

The telesales activity may not work in all methods of selling. And the ability to predict similar results and expand the project is impossible. Telesales is based on the effectiveness of the individual salesperson. There will be a wide disparity between good and bad salespeople. Results are based on the competence of the individual, not on the list, offer, promotion, or activity.

We are not discouraging the use of telesales, but it is not telemarketing as part of the direct marketing effort. We have developed lead generation programs where true telemarketing has been used to generate sales leads which are followed up by a telesales call. You have probably received calls from brokerage and insurance companies, where telemarketing is being used to screen the list for a qualified salesperson who will execute a sales call and attempt to close you on the phone. This approach can be a

cost effective way to sell products and services, but only the first screening
call is true direct marketing.

Telemarketing Defined

If telephone selling isn't telemarketing, what is the definition of this
powerful concept?

Telemarketing is a medium used to perform direct marketing.

- It is controllable, measurable, and not dependent on the
  individual for its success.
- It can be used to support direct mail or advertising, or as a
  stand-alone campaign.
- It is a planned series of contacts, using a constant message,
  seeking to produce a lead or an order.
- It yields information to build and maintain a database and is
  completely measurable in its costs and results.
- It can be outbound or inbound telephone calling.
- It can be used to sell to consumers or to other businesses.

Telemarketing uses a scripted or message-controlled communicator to
deliver a direct marketing message over the telephone.

Telemarketing incorporates two different approaches:

- Inbound Telemarketing
- Outbound Telemarketing

Inbound telemarketing involves the systematic handling of a call from a
prospect or customer, resulting from a message seen in another medium.
The person initiating the call has taken the first step in the sales cycle.

Inbound telemarketing is not controllable since the volume of telephone
calls is determined by the prospects or customers. Planning and
controlling the inbound telephone effort is difficult because you never
know when the calls will occur.

When an inbound call is accepted, you're usually not certain what caused
the call. In order to measure the effect of specific direct marketing

programs, you'll want to determine the specific source of the call. However, a prospect or customer often will indicate an advertisement from a medium that never had an ad. The source of the inbound call is not always accurate, but it can still help evaluate advertising effectiveness.

Because inbound telemarketing can occur at any time, manning and facility requirements are difficult to determine. Prior response history can be valuable in anticipating activity as a result of new ads or mailing programs.

Frequently, advertising people will forget to tell the people responsible for handling inbound telephone calls that a new ad has been placed. Unfortunately, it is not unusual for the inbound telemarketing people to handle calls with no prior warning. It can be most embarrassing and damaging to a company to have prospects and customers call in reference to a direct marketing offer and realize the communicators know nothing about the program.

Outbound telemarketing is more controllable. You can plan and execute the telemarketing effort at your leisure. You will know who to call, when to call, and you can plan to deal with almost every selling situation. *Outbound telemarketing* is a direct mail message being delivered over the telephone.

The outbound call can be timed to take advantage of the synergy that occurs between various media. If direct mail produces a 1% response rate, and telemarketing produces a 5% response rate, the use of both media together will produce more than 6% response. In fact, it is not unusual for the total to be twice the combined results. There is a critical time frame of about 10 days between the mail drop and follow-up telephone call. This varies by program and should be tested for your environment. There is also synergy possible when print ads and other media are used in conjunction with mail and telemarketing. Testing is the only way to determine your best balance of various media.

Within each area of telemarketing, there are two sub-categories of targets that you can reach:

- The *consumer* -- a person who will be contacted at their residence, usually during evening and weekend hours.

- The *business person* -- a person who will be contacted at their office or place of business, usually during the business day.

The time of day and day of week that you attempt to place or receive calls has a major impact on your telemarketing efforts.

Inbound Telemarketing

To effectively coordinate and control inbound telemarketing, a number of steps must be taken. Inbound telemarketing can never be used by itself. It is the response vehicle used for some other direct response media. Develop a detailed media plan that projects the number of respondents you anticipate. If you use direct mail or an advertisement with a coupon, project both the total response and the response via telephone.

Every program is different, but in most cases, a company's valuable respondents will come through inbound telephone calls. This makes a lot of sense if you consider that the prospects went out of their way to take immediate action and call the number you provided. Therefore, you want to ensure that your response to these people is of the highest quality, anticipates their needs, and is complete in fulfilling the promise of your offer.

The use of a toll-free number will make it easier and more attractive for your customers and prospects to overcome their resistance to call you. Several companies are against using toll-free numbers because they feel it makes it too easy for people to call and gripe or comparison shop. Evaluate the reason you want people to respond to your company. The toll-free number can be an effective tool to help prospects overcome their fear of responding.

Think of how you react when you see an offer to call to respond to an ad or promotion that you've received. You probably conjure up an image of someone who is waiting for you to respond and is prepared to take your order or answer your inquiry. The marketing challenge is to fulfill this mental picture.

When direct mail offers an inbound telephone response as an option, between 5% and 20% of the total response will come via inbound telephone. This is not a hard and fast rule; your product or service may produce different results. However, prospects are frequently reluctant to call because they don't want to be aggressively sold at that particular time. They may only want to receive information to evaluate at their leisure and then make a decision to purchase or see a salesperson. The group that does respond via telephone represents the cream of the crop and should be handled accordingly.

Knowing that your best responses will probably come through inbound telephone activity, you must ensure that they are handled in a timely and professional way. If you don't plan, the worst will happen: the prospect will be ignored, handled discourteously, or not handled at all. You must plan how you'll deal with respondents during peak and off-peak hours; how you'll ensure that the telemarketing communicator is prepared for the calls; and how you'll deal with the responder in a timely and professional manner.

Whatever media you've used, you should plan for about 15% of the total response to come via the telephone. This may be more than you'll actually receive, but planning for a higher response rate will ensure that the calls are handled professionally.

A broadcast medium (TV, cable, or radio) with only a telephone response option, will usually cause almost all the response to occur within 15 to 30 minutes of when the ad was run. This naturally requires that you have a larger number of communicators available to handle the volume of calls for a very short period of time. In consumer advertising, thousands of calls can be received in 10 or 15 minutes when a national direct response ad is run on television. This normally doesn't apply to business-to-business direct marketing, but with the increase of successful national cable business programs, it might be a consideration.

A number of considerations are in motion when your prospects call your phone number. If it is a toll-free number, they may have to decide whether to respond to an interstate or an intrastate number. The phone companies have made it much easier and less expensive to have one number for both intrastate and interstate activity. You will have to evaluate your needs and decide on the best approach for your company.

Some companies prefer to have their local offices handle the inbound telephone respondents. They feel that the local number makes the responder more comfortable. They're responding to someone who is local, as opposed to an unknown person at the end of a toll-free number in 'never-never' land.

Bear in mind that you will have no control over the quality of the response that will be provided at these remote local locations. In addition, it will be difficult to communicate advertising schedules to everyone involved. You also will have a great deal of difficulty measuring the response and the success of your direct marketing program. We have tested both scenarios and found no difference in the level of response between local numbers or centralized toll-free facilities. But the centralized facility gave us a lot more control and information about the program.

When the prospect responds, they will either hear the phone ring or get a busy signal. The result is directly tied to the number of phone trunks you have available to handle the incoming calls. A *trunk* is the line connecting your business to the phone company. A *telephone line* is the extension or instrument connected to the telephone system within your business. Normally, a company will have 8 to 10 times more lines than trunks. Most phones are not in use all day long, so they do not have to be connected to the external telephone network at all times. Many companies install a telephone switch to handle the switching of the network or trunks to the appropriate line.

Telephone capacity planning is more difficult when evaluating inbound telemarketing. You must plan for the high volume peak. If you do not have enough inbound trunks assigned to the toll-free or other inbound numbers, your prospects will receive a busy signal. Hopefully, they'll attempt to call back. But about half never bother according to a recent AT&T study on inbound calling patterns. Your phone bill for the phone service will confirm how many calls were attempted to your toll-free number but ended in a busy signal.

Toll-free telephone usage is charged similarly to other WATS (Wide Area Telephone Service) type coverage. The heavier the usage on each line, the less you pay per minute of usage. If you put in excess trunkage to handle the highest volumes you anticipate, you will pay substantially more per minute of actual usage. You'll also pay a monthly access charge per line. Your phone company representative can be of great help in evaluating and recommending the appropriate number of lines. Always compare additional costs against the need for customer service.

Since the phone company will take about one month to install additional trunks, anticipate your volume requirements as accurately as possible. Initially, consider putting in more trunks than you really need and then evaluate the usage. There is an added cost to this safe approach since the phone company will charge to install and remove the trunks.

Busy signals may not achieve the results you want, but at least the prospect may call you back and probably will get the impression that your offer must be pretty good if others are also calling. Not having the phone answered at all can never be perceived positively. There are three primary situations that can cause the phone to ring but not be answered.

1) The prospect is calling when your office is not open for business. As we indicated earlier, you can't control the volume or timing of inbound phone activity. You should anticipate that there will be activity beyond your normal business hours and establish some form of coverage.

   One option is to use a message machine to announce that you're closed, give your normal business hours, and ask prospects to call back. Better yet, also ask them to leave a message and then have them recontacted through an outbound telephone call.

   Another option is to have the number automatically switched to an answering service. This will give you coverage, but may not ensure the consistency you desire.

2) You have more trunks than people to handle the activity. When the prospect calls there is no one available to handle the inquiry. The same result can occur if you're using a telephone switch and have not programmed the system to handle overflow traffic.

   If your inbound lines terminate individually at a unique telephone, take the empty phone off the hook to send a busy signal to that number. A busy signal is better received than no answer at all.

   If it is outside your normal business hours, consider using the tape machine mentioned earlier.

If you're using a telephone switch, ensure that it is programmed to overflow to a tape recording when all lines are busy. If you anticipate higher inbound volumes, consider adding some form of automatic call director to ensure the calls are handled in a professional way.

3) You have a trunk that is not working properly and is not ringing through to your company. Test your inbound lines frequently and have the phone company check them as well. If your phone bill indicates lines with no usage activity, investigate to determine if the line is operating properly. As an aside, if a line is working properly and it has no usage, you have too many inbound trunks and should cut back.

Now that the call is properly coming into your inbound telemarketing operation, make sure that each call is handled in a professional manner. Publish a letter to all employees that tells them of your activity and that inbound calls are expected. Make sure to also inform all of your remote locations.

As we mentioned earlier, in order to conduct true direct marketing your telemarketing program must operate independently of the personalities of the personnel and be measurable in its costs and results. To ensure that each call is handled similarly, you must script or provide a call outline for each communicator.

In the business-to-business selling environment, you must identify the individual calling, their company, title, and business phone number. No matter what the reason for the call, always try to capture this basic information before answering any questions.

When a prospect calls any inbound number, including yours, they expect to be asked for some information. Prospects tend to be fairly tolerant during an inbound call and normally will answer most reasonable questions. Use the prospect's tolerance to your advantage. Unlike outbound telemarketing, the call has not interrupted the prospect and they normally have more patience.

Prepare a form for your communicator to fill out to give you the following basic information:

> Contact Name
> Contact Title
> Company Name
> Company Address (2 lines)
> Company City
> Company State
> Company Zip
> Contact Phone Number (during the day at their business)

Also try to source the media and specific ad or mail piece that caused the prospect to call, even though this can often be difficult. Never lose sight of your primary objective: to sell something, not to generate information. If the prospect is uncertain or can't answer the question, quickly move into your sales presentation.

Once you establish a uniform front-end for handling an inbound call, it will be easier to train people. In addition, if a problem occurs during the call, you'll have all the information to recontact the prospect. Getting all of the name and address information at the beginning of the call makes a lot of sense. It isn't difficult to ask a series of non-threatening questions, and doing so often relaxes the responder. Even if the prospect or customer is

---

Good AFTERNOON/MORNING -- Thanks for calling ABC Company. My name is _____ (use your full name).

May I have your name and your company name please?

And your company address?

And the zip code?

Mr(s) _____ (use full name from above) may I have your title, please?

And the phone number at which you can be contacted during the day?

And finally, can you tell me what prompted your call today?

Illustration 6-2: An opening for an inbound telephone script.

```
Date __/__/__   Time __:__   Communicator _____

   Contact name      _____
   Title             _____
   Company           _____
   Address           _____
                     _____
   City          _____ State _____ Zip _____
   Telephone No. (___) ___-_____

   Reason for response _____
```

Illustration 6-3: A sample form for handling inbound responders.

calling to complain, it is easy to explain that you're capturing this information in case you're cut off and need to recontact them.

Design a form that follows the script so your communicators have a call guide that is easy to follow. Keep this form the same, regardless of the type of response, so it will be easy to train your people. By forcing a uniform approach to handling every inbound call, you are fostering good call quality and professionalism. You will also have a basis to build a database for the future.

Prospects who do not give a company name or phone number are usually of lower quality. They may be good leads or referrals, but your company probably doesn't operate during the hours that these prospects are available. If you're sending a responder to your sales force without a company name, the odds are pretty good that the salesperson will not even attempt to contact the prospect.

We have seen situations where prospects will respond either by mail or phone and give their name and company address but no company name or phone number. There is no way to establish the phone number for these prospects and contact them in the future. In the business-to-business arena, if respondents don't give you a company name, just send them literature (as inexpensively as possible) and consider them suspects.

Because the prospect has taken the initiative to call you, they will be more tolerant of your questions. They also expect you to be able to handle his queries in a professional manner. If your communicators cannot answer every question, they should admit that to the prospect. Establish procedures for more qualified personnel to return calls to prospects who asked difficult questions. If varying levels of prospect qualification will prompt different kinds of fulfillment, ask qualification questions during the phone call. These calls should be scripted and the answers entered on the form used to record the call information.

Don't forget our discussion in Chapter three concerning lead qualification - - establish money, authority, need and desire. Don't get trapped by asking market research type questions. These respondents are of the highest quality; don't run the risk of turning them off. They may be more tolerant of questions, but don't lose sight of your objective to generate a sale or a lead. Only get the information necessary to establish the best way to handle the prospect.

Keep a copy of the information gathered from inbound respondents to develop a database. These tend to be your best qualified respondents; they called because they wanted to be handled quickly. Try to fulfill their requests within 48 hours of their call. Consider sending each respondent a letter thanking them for their response and describing how their inquiry will be handled. If you've ever been treated this way, you know how powerful a letter like this can be. One note of caution: Keep the promise delivered in the letter or it can create a terribly negative situation.

Inbound telemarketing is a powerful response tool. However, whenever you offer a phone response option, you should always also offer the opportunity to respond through the mail. Some people feel threatened, inhibited, or incapable of using the phone, and will not respond if only a phone option is offered. Internet response via e-mail and websites are other options that may be substituted for mail or replace mail entirely.

If you anticipate a very high volume of responses to your program, consider using an outside telemarketing service bureau that specializes in inbound telemarketing. Another reason to consider an outside service could be your company hours of operation. If you're doing business across the country and only operating eight hours a day, three hours of your non-business hours are business hours for your customers in other time zones.

The decision to use an outside telemarketing service bureau, or to handle calls in-house is complex:

1) Your company management may be nervous about the quality and customer service issues in sending the inbound activity to a service bureau. In fact, these fears can force management to decide to handle the activity in-house, when a service bureau may be a better alternative.

2) Unless you're selling commodity type products, the service bureau will probably not be able to handle detailed questions. The inbound responder is your best and hottest responder. You may want to strike while the iron is hot. This is a strong argument for keeping the inbound activity in-house.

3) The volume of activity may require a large staff to handle inbound activity only for short periods of time during the day. Even with part-time personnel, this staffing problem can be difficult to address.

4) Non-business hour activity could require you to operate your telemarketing operation at odd hours. This can create management and staffing problems.

5) Scripting and call control tend to be more difficult with in-house staffs.

6) Trunk availability is difficult to plan. If you're not in the telemarketing business, you probably have never planned or evaluated facilities required for handling inbound calls. An outside service has the experience and expertise to guide you through the planning process.

Inbound telemarketing is very complex and planning for it is difficult. It becomes even more complicated if you are targeting the consumer universe as well as the business-to-business arena. The best advice we can give you is to try to provide the same kind of response you would want to receive if you were calling another company.

Establishing the Costs of Telemarketing

Whether you're planning inbound or outbound telemarketing, you must be able to evaluate the true costs and results of your efforts. The costs for telemarketing are more than just the communicator costs. If you're evaluating whether to keep the function in-house or go to a service bureau, you must know your cost per hour of telemarketing.

Three broad areas should be considered when evaluating the total expenses associated with telemarketing.

    1) The cost of operations - telephone
    2) The cost of operations - clerical support
    3) General and administrative expenses

Within the cost area defined as *cost of operations - telephone*, are all the labor expenses. Include the cost of phone center management. If this function will only occupy a percentage of time for an individual, include the total cost and then apply the appropriate percentage. Supervision and communicator costs are obviously an important part of the labor costs.

Use the Telemarketing Expense Worksheet (Illustration 6-4) to help you establish your cost per telemarketing hour. Before you get started, try to determine the amount of telemarketing you're planning to perform. This quantity will be critical in all of your planning and evaluation. We have provided areas to establish both the annual and monthly costs. In many cases you'll find it easier to get either the monthly or annual expense. You can convert either to suit your needs by dividing or multiplying by 12. This will give you a methodology to evaluate all of your costs.

Illustration 6-5 summarizes typical selling expenses. Additional detailed cost worksheets that can further help you identify typical selling expenses can be found in *How to Manage and Execute Telephone Selling*, by Bernie Goldberg, Direct Marketing Publishers.

	Annual	**Monthly**
Hours of Telemarketing	_____	_____
Cost of Operations - Telephone		
Labor - Mgmt $_____/yr		
% of Mgmt needed ___%	_____	_____
Labor - Supv $_____/yr	_____	_____
% of Supv needed ___%	_____	_____
Labor - communicators	_____	_____
Payroll taxes	_____	_____
Fringe benefits	_____	_____
Temporary - outside labor	_____	_____
Telephone equipment	_____	_____
Telephone network - inbound	_____	_____
Telephone network - outbound	_____	_____
Telephone network - local usage	_____	_____
Telephone installation	_____	_____
Total cost of operations - phone	_____	_____
Cost of Operations - Clerical		
Labor - Mgmt $_____/yr		
% of Mgmt needed ___%	_____	_____
Labor - Supv $_____/yr		
% of Supv needed ___%	_____	_____
Labor - Clerks		
Look-up	_____	_____
Maintenance	_____	_____
Tabulating	_____	_____
Sorting	_____	_____
Payroll taxes	_____	_____
Fringe benefits	_____	_____
Copy machine rental/depreciation	_____	_____
Copy machine supplies	_____	_____
Telephone equipment	_____	_____
Total cost of operations - clerical	_____	_____

Illustration 6-4: Telemarketing Expense Worksheet

	Annual	**Monthly**
General & Administrative		
Rent	_____	_____
Heat & electricity	_____	_____
Insurance	_____	_____
Equipment depreciation	_____	_____
Furniture & fixtures depreciation	_____	_____
Telephone equipment	_____	_____
Telephone network	_____	_____
Receptionist/secretarial support	_____	_____
Data processing	_____	_____
Data processing supplies	_____	_____
Repairs & maintenance	_____	_____
General office supplies	_____	_____
Travel & entertainment	_____	_____
Dues & subscriptions	_____	_____
Training & seminars	_____	_____
Advertising & public relations	_____	_____
Bad debt/bad pay/returns	_____	_____
Total cost of operations - G & A	_____	_____
Total Costs	_____	_____
Cost per hour of telemarketing	_____	_____

Illustration 6-4 (continued): A Telemarketing Expense Worksheet.

Outbound Telemarketing

Outbound telemarketing can be used by itself or in conjunction with other methods of direct marketing. It is a medium to deliver a message over the telephone. Unlike direct mail, telemarketing is interactive and allows you to quickly alter one or more variables while you're still conducting your campaign. You can plan and control outbound telemarketing better than you can control direct mail.

The first element in planning and executing outbound telemarketing is similar to any other direct marketing effort...the **List.** When selecting a universe to use for telemarketing, you will need to establish the availability of telephone numbers.

Typical Telephone Selling Expenses

Type of telephone selling	Cost per hour	Cost per contact
Inbound	$35.00 - $65.00	$5.00 - $15.00
Outbound Telemarketing		
Consumer	$18.00 - $35.00	$1.80 - $ 5.00
Business-to-Business	$35.00 - $60.00	$6.00 - $10.00
Outbound Telesales	$50.00 +	$10.00 +

Illustration 6-5: Typical telephone selling expenses from *How to Manage and*

Businesses are in a constant state of change. People are constantly changing jobs and responsibilities. The larger the company, the more likely it is that the mailing list contact will have changed. You can anticipate about a 30% change in contact and other information each year. Depending on the age of your list, the odds are pretty good that you'll be reaching a different target than you initially pursued.

When you use direct mail to contact businesses, if no contact name is available, you can use title and function addressing. This type of mailing will normally prove successful and not substantially alter the results. When you consider the relatively high degree of turn- over, title addressing can be almost as effective as personalized, name-directed mailings. Each company is different and the only sure way for you to establish the difference between title addressing and name addressing, is to test both and evaluate the results.

Many compiled and response lists have phone numbers, however, most lists do not. If you plan to use outbound telemarketing as a stand-alone medium, or in support of direct mail, you'll need to make sure that you can use the list for telemarketing. Many list owners are reluctant to allow their lists to be used for telemarketing because:

1)   They have a negative attitude about telephone selling. Many have received unprofessional and poorly executed calls at home and in their offices. They don't want to have the people on their lists subjected to this kind of activity.

2) List ownership is a major concern. Many list owners have heard of telemarketing response rates of 20% to 40%, and are concerned about losing their list to the telemarketer.

If the original list doesn't contain phone numbers, typically you'll only be able to secure about 60% of the numbers through most phone number appending services. Then through the telemarketing effort, you'll be able to reach about 65% of the phone numbered list to make your offer. If even 40% accept your offer, a great response rate, the net acceptance against the list you started with is only 15.6%. Yes, this is still a high response rate, but it is not so overwhelming as to worry the list owner that they will lose their list. We must educate the list sellers regarding the true nature of telemarketing and its impact on their lists. It will take time.

As you are probably aware, you normally rent lists for a single usage. Any responder who accepts your offer, or asks for additional information, becomes yours for future activity and action. In direct mail you're only allowed to retain the names of your actual acceptances. In addition, you may have an opportunity to learn about the quality of the list if you elect to have the non-deliverable (nixie) mail returned to you. The acceptances and nixies are all you ever receive back from any mailing.

In telemarketing you'll receive information not only from the acceptances and nixies, but also from other segments of the list. If someone refuses your offer, you can still learn a great deal about their business. You clearly will own the data captured, which is valuable market research information. However, in most cases, you can't keep and re-contact any name that doesn't accept your telemarketing offer. Review this situation with the list owner prior to starting your campaign.

Many list owners are now renting their lists for annual or unlimited usage, to enable you to make multiple contacts via mail and phone. Some contracts allow you to use the list for both a mail and phone contact. If you rent a list for a single contact, and plan to use mail followed by a telephone call, that is two contacts. Make sure you review your plans with the list owner.

Outbound telemarketing creates many segments to the original list that must be dealt with independently. The most familiar and obvious segment

---

List Usage in Telephone Selling

1,000	Names on original list with no phone numbers
60%	Obtain phone numbers
600	Net names for telemarketing
65%	Are reachable on the phone
390	Net offers made
40%	Accept the offer
156	Net acceptances
15.6%	Response rate of original list

Illustration 6-6: An example of telemarketing response rates.

consists of those who you were able to contact and who made a decision concerning your offer.

Let's look at all of the ways a record can be used:

1) The record is on the original list, but an outside service cannot obtain a corresponding phone number. This record is never used for telemarketing.

2) The phone number is obtained and you attempt to contact the prospect.

   A) It is a wrong number. You reach a company, but it isn't the correct one. Your prospect may have moved on to a different company. If you attempt to contact their successor, then this record would not be consumed as a wrong number.

   B) The call results in a tape-recorded message which states that the number has been disconnected. This is consumed as a technical difficulty.

   C) The company is moving or going out of business and can't make a decision about your offer.

D) Completed Call

1. Prospect refuses to talk and aborts call in the middle of the conversation. In fact, this prospect made a decision concerning your offer; they rejected it.

2. Prospect accepts offer. There are a number of possible ways to accept an offer. These can include a request for literature or a later contact.

3. Prospect rejects offer. A prospect who is unsure about your offer will either reject it or accept it. You should have a plan to handle rejections.

E) The prospect is not reachable after a pre-established number of attempts.

F) The prospect reached is not at a decision-making location. This happens from time to time in the business world. You can consume the record, or attempt to get the phone number and appropriate contact at the decision-making location, and then call that location.

When measuring telemarketing you should evaluate the number of dialings made in a specific time frame, normally an hour. In addition, you should also measure the number of completed calls, and the number of acceptances of your offer in that same time frame. When people discuss outbound telemarketing performance standards, many confuse apples and oranges. A constant set of definitions needs to be established that will allow everyone to compare the same thing. Business-to-business calling complicates the situation because additional dispositions are added by the nature of the calling.

In the consumer universe, you normally get through to the prospect or spouse. There is typically no one screening calls and no switchboard to get past. The prospect is normally the decision maker, and most lists used for telemarketing are name-directed.

The business universe is totally different. In most cases, the phone is answered by a receptionist or switchboard operator. The list may not be name-directed, or the name may be wrong. In either case, you'll have to establish your individual prospect's name and title through the switchboard. This prospect probably has an assistant, whose whole mission in life is to prevent calls like yours from reaching the boss. When you finally get to your prospect, there is a good chance that they will not be the person responsible for making the decision and you'll be referred to someone else within the company.

If this scenario occurs in only one call you'll be very lucky. Normally it takes several calls to reach the original prospect and perhaps just as many to contact a referred name. Obviously, the calls tend to be longer due to the multiple contacts required to reach your prospect. In addition, many dialings will have to be rescheduled in order to ultimately consume the record.

Bobby Barrier, the assistant assigned to the mission of screening your calls from their bosses, complicates business-to-business telemarketing even further. You must get past them to make your presentation to your prospect. They also perform the same function when they screen face-to-face salespeople and direct mail; they can't be ignored.

In the consumer world, it is fairly common to attempt to reach each record four times before considering the record not reachable. The timing and the way you make these attempts can change, but four attempts seems fairly common. Because of multi-contact problems, the business universe requires a higher attempt threshold. Six attempts is average and it isn't unusual to see as many as eight attempts.

Every program and list differs on anticipated results. In our experience about 25% to 35% of dialings made to the business universe will end in a completed call. This is substantially less than the 50% to 65% completion rate of dialings in the consumer world.

Depending on the type of product and the list being used, whether the list is name-directed, and the length of the script, the number of completed calls per hour ranges from 5 to 13. Dialings range from 20 to 35 per hour. These are not hard and fast standards, but production results that most business-to-business programs seem to operate within.

As part of your business planning process, establish goals that enable you to measure the program at all times. Set dialing, completion, and acceptance objectives for each hour of telemarketing. Once you've

Telemarketing Plan

Total records	1,000
% of records contactable	65%
Total records contactable	650
% of dialings that are able to be contacted	30%
Dialings per hour	25
Contacts per hour	7.5
Planned response rate	10%
Acceptances per hour	.75
Total telemarketing hours for project	86.7
Total acceptances	65

Illustration 6-7: A Typical Telemarketing Plan.

established your cost per telemarketing hour, it will be easy to evaluate your cost per lead or cost per order.

Illustration 6-7 shows how a typical outbound telemarketing plan might appear. This plan assumes that we are starting with 1,000 records. Only 65% of the records will be contactable, because many records will either have wrong numbers, not be decision-making locations, be going out of business, or be records that reach the re-call limit after a predetermined number of attempts.

About 30% of dialings will result in a completed call or contact. This plan assumes that we will dial the phone 25 times per hour of telemarketing, with 30% or 7.5 completed calls per hour. The plan also assumes that 10% of the completed calls will accept the offer, or .75 acceptances per hour.

The number of hours required for this project is 86.7 hours. This was derived by dividing the total number of records that were contactable by the number of completed calls per hour. The total number of acceptances was established by multiplying the number of hours by the planned acceptances per hour.

With the cost per telemarketing hour we established earlier, we can develop the cost per responder and the cost per order.

This type of planning gives you measurable objectives to evaluate the success of your outbound telemarketing project each hour of the project. The model can also be used to measure the success of different lists, offers, and products being sold over the telephone.

Each communicator should make the same presentation to each member of the list to whom you're marketing. This is one of the basic criteria to telemarketing as opposed to telesales. We recommend the use of scripts that control the complete flow of the telephone call. The communicator is even provided pre-scripted answers to questions and objections.

There are a number of script techniques that you can use.

1) A script outline. This approach uses an outline of the structure that you want the communicator to follow. Every word is not scripted and the communicator has a great deal of flexibility in what is said. Normally a record or form is provided to record the responses from the phone call. The form should be the outline for the call.

    The script outline approach is easy to use, and not cumbersome during the phone call. It has a stronger dependence on the individual communicator and you're never absolutely certain of what was said on the phone. The communicators have to be well trained to handle questions and objections.

2) A script on pages. This is a typed version of the complete script. This approach scripts virtually every word that you want the communicator to use. It is an easy and quick way to introduce short, easy to learn scripts, into the phone operation. It also uses a record or form to record the responses from the phone call.

    The script on pages approach is easy to introduce and change in the phone operation. Typically the communicator will memorize the script and then never use it during the phone call. After a period of time, the script becomes personalized to the individual and really isn't a script at all. As in the outline approach, the record ultimately becomes a call guide and directs the call.

3) A script on flip cards. This script has one or two statements on a flip card. Based on the interaction during the phone call, the communicator is instructed to proceed to an appropriate card. In Chapter 3, we used an example of this type of scripting during the example program. The communicator says the same thing all of the time. It also uses a record or form to record the responses from the phone call.

The script on flip cards approach is a little more difficult to create and introduce into the phone operation. It takes more time and effort to produce. You might consider using a photo album with flip windows that are staggered so you can see the base of the next window. This type of scripting is dynamic and can change by simply changing one or two of the cards. Your communicator will still memorize the script and eventually use it less and less, but the script on cards approach makes handling questions and objections fairly easy.

4) Computerized scripting. This approach uses a computer terminal in front of each communicator. As the call progresses, the reactions to various questions are entered into the computer and these answers determine the next part of the script that should be read by the communicator. No paper record is used in this approach as the information is entered directly into the computer system.

The computerized approach is great but expensive to implement and difficult to change. The communicator may memorize the script but really has no alternative but to read and view the computer terminal during the phone call. This is probably the most reliable approach to ensuring that the same message is delivered to every person on the list.

Telemarketing is an effective and proven media to ask for an order or commitment from a prospect or customer. However, it is very difficult to sell unfamiliar products or services via telemarketing. The products sold on the telephone almost always must be commodities or well-known items.

A telephone call is disruptive. Think about the calls you've received either at home or in your office. The call probably interrupted something you were doing. You may have been tolerant or even interested, but your patience probably wore pretty thin in a relatively short period of time. This reaction is fairly typical and is the challenge you face when using telemarketing.

Most people will not allow you to sell a product to them over the phone. If they already are familiar with the product or a similar product, they may agree to try yours. You only have between 25 and 45 seconds to generate interest and get your prospect involved in the phone call. The key to the phone call is the offer you make up front to interest the prospect in allowing the call to continue.

This means that you must make your offer easy to understand, risk-free and easy for your prospect to decide on. Multiple offers and choices are difficult to sell over the phone. However, you can make a single offer and then an additional offer after the initial offer has been evaluated and accepted or rejected by the prospect.

If you're selling a product directly, consider offering a trial or money-back guarantee. Remember that, you're asking a prospect to purchase something without seeing, feeling, touching, smelling, or tasting the product. The prospect has to evaluate your offer with no sensory support. If the product is a known commodity, depending on the offer, the prospect is more likely to be able to make a buying decision. The less-known the product is, the more difficult, and less likely, the buying decision.

When using direct mail or direct response advertising, you can write longer copy to describe and inform the prospect. If they're interested, prospects can read the material provided and then evaluate and research the information to reach a buying decision. Although you are still asking prospects to make a decision without actually seeing the product, they have more time to consider it.

Telemarketing asks the prospect to make a decision immediately. Because you don't have a lot of time to explain your product or offer, your scripted copy must be short and to the point. On the phone, people do not have time to internalize the words presented. They may not envision what the speaker is trying to convey. Decisions are threatening to most people and they look for reasons to avoid uncomfortable situations. As you are making an offer on the phone, your prospect will be searching for reasons to reject or object to your proposition. They probably will not hear a lot of what you might want to present.

Does this mean that you can't sell over the telephone? Absolutely not. But we have found that you really won't have a lot of time to convey your message. If you're trying to sell a more complicated product or service, a combination of direct mail and telephone will probably be more appropriate.

If you're using the telephone to qualify leads and offer the prospect an opportunity to see a sales representative, similar rules on the offer and length of the message apply. Explain to the prospect why seeing a salesperson will be good for them or their company. This message also must be delivered in a very short and direct presentation. Again, words and copy that work well in other media may not perform as well on the phone.

When designing a telemarketing script, try reading something out loud for 30 to 45 seconds. You'll be surprised how long a period it is. Your prospect will have to be hooked very quickly to allow the call to continue. If you're asking for information to evaluate qualification, you still must get the prospect interested in continuing with the call.

In many cases, the prospects will ask that additional information be sent to them so they can make a decision. Many telemarketers view prospects who request literature as disinterested people simply looking for an easy way to get off of the telephone. Most people do not like to be rude. By asking for additional information, they are deferring the decision and they don't have to be rude to the communicator. A good percentage of these people in fact are simply doing it to get off the phone. However, some of these prospects are legitimately interested in the offer. You must deal with the interested group in a very professional and effective way.

When conducting lead qualification telemarketing programs, we tend to see more prospects requesting additional information than agreeing to seeing a salesperson. And depending on the offer being made in the direct selling programs, they also can have a large number of literature requesters.

As you may recall, promotional material must be designed with prospects who ask for additional information in mind. It must be designed with the specific mission of creating a lead or an order. You can't expect a promotional piece that was designed to be left behind by the salesperson after their sales call to perform the direct marketing mission. Trade show literature won't work any better. What should become obvious is that when you start your telemarketing campaign, you will also need to create some direct mail follow-up material.

You might think that it is easier to treat literature requesters as rejections of your offer who will not care about the material, if any, that you send them. If you're generating enough activity from the prospects accepting your telemarketing offer, this might be a good decision, particularly if your universe is large enough to support your sales and lead requirements for the foreseeable future without dealing with prospects who want additional information.

We have found, however, that when literature requesters are re-contacted by telephone about ten days after the material was sent to them, approximately 25% will convert into a solid lead or an order. The fulfillment material used was specifically designed to move the prospect further along in the buying process.

Evaluate the financial impact to create, produce and fulfill literature. The cost of the second phone call also must be evaluated against the anticipated results to ensure that the program is profitable. If you decide to re-contact the literature requesters, you will be starting down the road towards database marketing.

We are obviously recommending the use of direct mail to support your telemarketing efforts. Telemarketing works best when it is used in conjunction with direct mail. Direct mail followed by telemarketing will normally yield better results as a combined effort, than when either media is used separately.

We have tested the use of mail and phone separately, and then tested mail followed by phone and the results were very different. The mail produced a 2% response rate and the phone produced at 7.5%. You would therefore expect the combined results to be about 9.5%. The actual result of the combination of the two was almost 13%.

We also tested to determine the best time to follow the mail with telemarketing. We began telemarketing about five days prior to the mail. The first scripted question asked was, Do you recall seeing the information we sent you? Even before the mail was dropped, about 30% of those asked indicated that they could recall receiving the mail. This may sound amusing, but some people will respond positively so as not to appear ignorant. After the mail was dropped, we continued to track the answer to this question. The favorable response peaked at almost 70% from day 11 after the mail was dropped and remained there through day 17. The response rate then began to drop. Within 30 days after the mail drop, the favorable response rate dropped to 40% and stayed there for the next 15 days. It ultimately went back to the 30% range.

Answer rates to this question by itself were interesting, but the front-end results were even more informative. The response rate followed the awareness of the mail fairly closely. There was an increase of almost 25% in response rate when the awareness of the mail was at its peak.

Mail and phone work exceedingly well together. To maximize the combined effect of the two media, the phone call should be timed to follow the mail from between 10 to 15 days after the mail is dropped. We have been involved in programs that delayed the phone call to allow for all of the mail responses to be returned. This may make sense, but the results should be carefully evaluated. Test both approaches to determine the best results for your company. If your mail response rate is anticipated at about 2%, you'll only be calling and contacting a very small group who would have already responded by mail. Remember, you will achieve only about a 65% contact rate of all of the records that have phone numbers. Therefore, given a 2% mail response rate, you will only duplicate about 1.35% of the list. The only way to find out the impact of phone and mail together is to test... test... test.

Managing the Outbound Telephone Selling Process

It is difficult to manage a person on the telephone to perform exactly as you want. Scripts can go a long way to getting the message delivered exactly as you want it stated. If you're using telesales, you have no control over the message. Training and call monitoring are some of the tools you have available to improve call quality, but unless you listen to every call, you really can't guarantee each specific presentation.

However, you can take complete control of the calling process by managing the flow of records as they pass through the phone operation. The concept of managing the calling records is referred to as managing the process of telephone selling. Process management is appropriate in either telemarketing or telesales. Unfortunately, many telesales operations have not focused on managing the process, and they are at the mercy of the salespeople in both quality and quantity of telephone calling.

Management should control which customers or prospects get called, the frequency of calling, the scheduling of the call, and the recording of the ultimate disposition of the record after the call is made. This process is a way of life in most telemarketing environments. It is relatively new to the inexperienced telesales manager.

Typically, the salespeople manage the calling process similarly to field salespeople. The telesales representative schedules calls based on their feelings concerning their customers and what they perceive is their next opportunity to sell. This is particularly true if no telephone offers have been created to make the calling process easier and more productive. Many customers are never contacted, and a few select customers receive calls almost weekly.

Telephone selling, particularly business-to-business, works most effectively with current customers. Additional contacts can be made to enhance the company/customer relationship and allow additional products or services to be sold. The customer is familiar with the company and products, so it is not unusual to get a yes or no buying decision during the phone call.

Once you've decided which customers you want to call, these records should be given to the telephone selling operation. As these records are consumed, have them returned and then provide additional records. Provide the calling information for each customer on a card or form, a **unit record** for each call. This approach will allow the communicators to schedule and annotate the record as they are on the phone.

Illustration 6-8 shows the process of telephone selling. Records are extracted from the database, printed on a unit record, and forwarded to the telephone selling operation. The calls are scheduled and attempted by the communicators. Each dialing attempt is annotated on the unit record and a

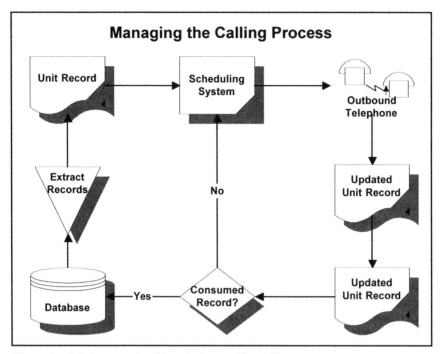

Illustration 6-8: An example of the telephone selling calling process.

daily tally sheet. If the call is completed or the record is consumed, the unit record is returned to management for disposition. Records that need rescheduling are handled appropriately. The system is a closed loop with management in control of the calling process.

Outbound Telemarketing Results

Every direct marketing and telemarketing program is different and it is dangerous to apply hard and fast rules to all programs. However, we will try to give you some guidelines to help you do a reasonable job in estimating results. We have found that after about 100 hours of business-to-business telemarketing with a list and script, the results will not deviate substantially (more than 10%) for the balance of the program. This assumes that the list, script, and offer remain the same. Consumer calling results also will level off, but after about 250 hours of calling.

If the list is sent to a computer service bureau, normally about 50% of the list will have phone numbers added. This can vary depending on the quality, age and techniques used to compile the list. You can establish additional phone numbers (about 15%) by sending the remaining unmatched names to a manual telephone look-up service. This tends to be more expensive and take substantially longer. Evaluate the complete information you require on your list prior to sending it to the service bureau. It is possible to have S.I.C. and other sizing information added to your list at the same time as the phone number.

Now that you have the list ready for telemarketing, what kind of results can be expected? Our experience says -- it depends. Not a comforting answer but a truthful one. When you're calling different industry groups or different sized companies the results will vary greatly. It is fairly difficult to get a doctor on the phone, but fairly easy to reach office managers and purchasing agents. The single biggest factor in altering the calling results will be whether the list is name-directed or not. If you don't have the contact's name, then you must make multiple calls to the same company to first establish the contact, and then to make your presentation.

Long scripts with lots of market research questions can also alter the results significantly. The more questions and the more prospects or customers have to think about their answers, the longer the call will take.

The number of phone attempts made to a particular name on the list can also affect the results significantly. We suggest that the average business-to-business contact be attempted six to eight times and then considered not reachable.

With six attempts, the average list will yield about 65% of the records as able to be contacted. In addition, assuming cross industry calling, about 20% of dialings will result in a contact during the first three attempts, 15% will result in a contact in the next two attempts and then 10% or less will result in a contact after six attempts. About 10 to 15% of the list will not be contactable because of wrong number and out of business situations. These will normally be found during the first dialing attempt. Let's examine 1,000 records and identify what happens on six attempts.

1000	Records to start
15%	Not contactable due to wrong numbers and out of business
150	Records not contactable
850	Records contactable

20%	Contacted on 1st attempt
200	Records contacted on 1st attempt
650	Records remaining to contact (200 contacted + 150 not contactable)

20%	Contacted on 2nd attempt
130	Records contacted on 2nd attempt
520	Records remaining to contact

20%	Contacted on 3rd attempt
104	Records contacted on 3rd attempt
416	Records remaining to contact

15%	Contacted on 4th attempt
62	Records contacted on 4th attempt
354	Records remaining to contact

15%	Records contacted on 5th attempt
53	Records contacted on 5th attempt
301	Records remaining to contact

15%	Records contacted on 6th attempt
45	Records contacted on 6th attempt
256	Records remaining to contact and will be treated as not contactable.

As you can see, we will contact 599 records of the original 1,000 or about 60% of the records we started with. Eight attempts will bring the total to about 65%. It gets very expensive to contact records as more attempts are made. A certain percentage of the records will never be reached and they will make up a larger portion of the remaining records after each attempt. You must evaluate the number of attempts you'll make and the results you anticipate.

The dialings and contacts per hour will vary depending on each program. Business-to-business programs average about 20 to 30 dialings per hour and about 20% to 30% as completed contacts. Therefore the average business program will result in about 5 to 8 completed calls per hour. A good planning number for most business programs is about 7 to 7.5

completed calls per hour. If your list is not name-directed, you will lose about 1 completed call per hour.

When executing lead generation programs, we have found for every person that accepts our offer to see a salesperson, about the same number of people request additional information. This group of literature requesters, when followed up with a phone call after the information was sent, converted into a lead about 25% of the time. This seemed to occur in almost every lead program we executed using phone follow-up to the literature requests.

When planning a follow-up call, within 90 days of an earlier phone contact, you can expect to contact 90% of the list in four to six attempts. This is true when the list is name-directed, and we have established a correct phone number and a prior relationship of some sort with the prospect. In fact, you can use this prior relationship as a method to overcome Bobby Barrier. You can start your call by telling Bobby that you're calling about some information that Mr. Contact requested.

Your response rates will vary significantly based on your offer and script. As you establish your business plan, the required response rates will be established to determine whether your program is successful.

The Telemarketing Plan

Like any other direct marketing program, outbound telemarketing has to have a detailed plan prepared prior to the start of the program. After you develop the business background and the strategy for your direct marketing program, you should review the use of telemarketing. If outbound telemarketing is an appropriate medium, then you'll have to develop a detailed flowchart and business plan for the use of outbound telemarketing.

As you'll note from Illustration 6-9, the flow chart will start with the tape of records that are being used for the direct marketing effort. We assume the tape was deduplicated against the existing customer file and within itself to ensure that there are no duplicate records.

Frequently, you'll acquire lists that contain several names of people within the same company. Although these can be correct and appropriate names,

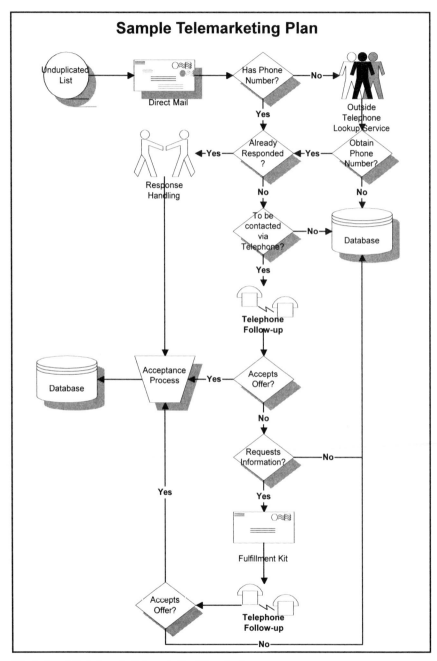

Illustration 6-9: A Sample Telemarketing Flowchart.

you may find that all of the records must go through the same switchboard. We have found that when you call the same switchboard with a production telemarketing approach, you may overwhelm the attendant. After a number of calls, the attendant may be reluctant to switch the call to the appropriate person. If your list contains duplicate phone numbers, evaluate mixing the records throughout the calling period, or only selecting one record to contact.

Now that you've established the list that you'll use for telemarketing, you may want to eliminate the respondents from direct mail prior to starting the telemarketing. As we mentioned earlier, the number of respondents will be a very small part of the total list. You should evaluate the cost of eliminating the respondents and the additional time it will take before you can start telemarketing.

As the telephone calls are made, you will determine if the prospect accepts your offer. Acceptances will be processed similarly to other acceptances from direct mail and inbound telephone. With the telephone program, we will generate another group of prospects who will request additional information. This is because outbound telemarketing forces prospects to make an immediate decision.

Don't lose those prospects who request additional information. Although most are asking for information simply to get off the phone, in our experience about 25% can be converted into a lead or an order if they are recontacted after the material is sent. You should test this concept with your product in order to determine the number of prospects that can be converted to an order or lead.

This sample flow chart, as illustrated in 6-9, is a simplified approach to a telemarketing program. However, it introduces some interesting concepts in using telemarketing and will give us a practical example to develop a business plan and measurement plan.

The Sample Telemarketing Business Plan

Product Information

Total Revenue per Acceptance	$750.00
% Allowable Expense per Order	10.00%
Allowable Cost per Order	$75.00
Total Records in Test	2,000

List Costs

Direct Mail @ $85 per 1000	$85.00
Telemarketing @ $85 per 1000	$85.00
Total List Costs	$170.00

Direct Mail Costs

Cost per 1000 Pieces of Mail	$1,500.00

Phone Number Look-up

% of Records that Find Number	1,000
Cost per Record for Look-up	$150.00

Telemarketing Costs

Total Telemarketing Hours	92.3
Cost per Telemarketing Hour	$38.00
Total Telemarketing Costs	$3,507.00

Direct Mail Results

Total Direct Mail Costs	$1,585.00
Total Acceptances Required	21
Required Acceptance Rate	1.10%

Telemarketing Results

% of Total Records Contactable	65.00%
Total Records Contactable	650
Dialings per Hour	25
% of Dialings that Are Contacted	30.00%
Contacts per hour	7.5
Total Initial Call Telemarketing Hours	86.7

Total Telemarketing Costs	$3,530.00
Total Acceptances Required	47.07
Required Acceptance Rate	7.20%
Required Acceptances per Hour	0.54
Planned Request Literature Rate	7.20%
Literature Requests per Hour	0.54
Total Hours	86.7
Total Acceptances	47
Total Literature Requests	47

Send Literature Follow-up Call

% of List Contactable	90.00%
Total List Contactable	42
Contacts per Hour	7.5
Total Hours	5.6
Follow-up Telemarketing Costs	$212.80
Literature Request Fulfillment Costs	$70.50
Total Literature Request Costs	$283.30
Required Acceptances	3.8
Required % of Follow-up Calls that Accept	8.1%

Total Direct Marketing Costs

Direct Mail	$1,585.00
Initial Telemarketing	$3,530.00
Request Lit Fulfillment @ $1.50 each	$70.50
Request Literature Telemktg Follow-up	$213.00
Total Direct Marketing Costs	**$5,398.50**

Acceptances

Direct Mail	21
Initial Telemarketing	47
Request Lit Fulfillment @ $1.50 each	4
Total Acceptances	**72**
Required Response Rate of 2000 Records	**3.6%**
Cost per Acceptance	**$74.98**

Like most business plans or proformas, the revenue and expense that will be allowed for direct marketing needs to be established. In our example, the average order is $750 and the allowable sales expense is 10% or $75 per order.

For the telemarketing test, we will acquire a list of 2,000 records. This list will be sent to a service bureau for phone number look-up and we anticipate that 50% of the original names will be returned with phone numbers. The list is being rented for two contacts, a mail and a phone contact. Therefore, we will have to pay the list owner for using their list two times. The cost for the list is $85 per 1,000 records, therefore our total list costs are $170. Many list owners have minimum charges and small quantities may not meet the minimum charge requirement. You will have to discuss your unique list requirements with your list vendor.

The cost of direct mail is completely variable and will depend on the quantity of material printed, quality, the type of postage and a number of variables that can only be established as you develop your own requirements. Obviously, the more expensive the mailing piece, the higher the results have to be to cover the additional expense. For our example we used $750 per 1,000 pieces mailed as our direct mail costs. We are planning to mail all 2,000 names on the list, even though we will not be able to call all of the names. The mail costs are $1,500. We assumed that the fulfillment kit for people requesting additional information would be more expensive and estimated them at $1.50 per package.

The telephone phone number look-up service will only charge you for those records that match and for which they can provide a telephone number. The telephone look-up services also have minimum charges. The price per phone number look-up record will vary depending on the quantity and turn-around time you require. The smaller the quantity of records sent to the service, the higher the cost per look-up. For the small quantities we used for this test, we estimated the look-up charges at $.15 per record. This probably will not meet the minimum charges at most service bureaus. We estimated, in our example, that only 50% of the records would be found during the phone number search. Therefore, the total expenses are $150.

The cost per telemarketing hour will vary significantly for each company. You can purchase a telemarketing service bureau calling hour for between

$35.00 and $60.00 depending on volume and the level of support you require. We have used $38.00 as the cost per hour in our example. As an aside, we have rarely seen the average business conduct in-house outbound telemarketing at $38.00 per hour if all of the costs are reviewed. You should find the telemarketing cost worksheet discussed earlier very helpful in establishing your cost per hour. As you'll see, the total hours required to make the initial calls and perform follow-up calling to the literature requesters amounts to 92.3 hours at $38.00 per hour for a total telemarketing cost of $3,507.00

People use many techniques to estimate the results they expect from direct marketing programs. Most of the time the expectations are unreasonable or are just guesses as to what people would like to have happen. As the first step in our business plan, we established the revenue per order and the allowable sales expense per order. With these "tools" you can establish the required response rate to have a successful program. By establishing required response rates for each step of your program, you'll be able to measure results as the program is being executed.

If you take the mail and list expenses and divide them by the allowable cost per order, you'll establish the number of orders required for the program to be successful. The total required orders divided by the quantity mailed will give you the required acceptance rate.

Establishing telemarketing results is probably a new experience for you. Remember, we only anticipated that 50% of the records would come back from the service bureau with a phone number. Therefore we'll only be starting with 1000 records for telemarketing. As you may recall from our discussion earlier, the number of attempts you plan to make to each record, the composition of the list, and the length of the script can all significantly affect the results you'll experience in telemarketing.

For this business plan we have assumed 8 attempts per record, and anticipate 25 dialings per hour with 30% of the dialings concluding with a completed call. We have assumed that 65% of the records are contactable. This means that we will complete 7.5 completed calls per hour of calling. This is arrived at by multiplying the initial number of records on the telemarketing list by 65%. In this case we started with 1000 records in telemarketing and 65% of this list equals 650 records. We then divided the 650 records by 7.5 completed calls per hour and arrived at 86.7 hours required for the initial calls to the prospects.

Now that we have established the number of calling hours, the costs for telemarketing are derived by multiplying the hours by the cost per hour. In our example, 86.7 hours x $38.00 per hour = $3,530.00. As you know we have allowed $75.00 per order in sales expense. We divide the total costs by the allowable sales expense per order and establish the number of orders required in order for this program to be successful. It will take 47.07 orders to have a successful program.

Establishing the required response rates seems pretty easy at first. However, how many records did you really start with? If you assume the 2,000 records that were on the original list we acquired, the required response rate is 2.35% (47.07 ÷ 2,000). The percentage of the 1,000 records available to telemarketing is 4.7% (47.07 ÷ 1,000). The percentage of the 650 records able to be contacted is 7.2% (47.07 ÷ 650).

We suggest you do your planning using both the records available to telemarketing and the records that are contactable. The original list that included names without phone numbers doesn't help measure the program. Our plan reflects the percentage of completed calls. This allows us to focus on the per hour results and measure the program while it is in progress.

We established the acceptance rate per hour by dividing the number of acceptances required by the number of hours. In our example this was .54 acceptances per hour (47.07 ÷ 86.7).

We have assumed that for each acceptance we will also generate another person who will request additional information. Therefore, we will have .54 literature requesters per hour in addition to the .54 acceptances of our offer. Literature requesters are important because we plan to fulfill their requests with information and then make an additional phone call to follow-up and attempt to convert them into a lead. It will cost $70.50 to mail fulfillment kits to the literature requesters (47 x $1.50 fulfillment kit expense).

The additional phone call will be made 10 to 15 days after the mail is sent. We have planned a 90% contact of these prospects at the same rate of 7.5 completed calls per hour. Therefore we anticipate 5.6 hours of telemarketing (47 x 90% = 42.3 completed calls) (42.3 ÷ 7.5 = 5.6 hours). The total cost for the literature fulfillment and follow-up calling is $283.30

($70.50 mail costs + $212.80 phone costs). For this part of the program to be successful, we need 3.8 acceptances ($283.30 ÷ $75.00 allowable sales expense). This is a required response rate of 8.1%. We could have actually planned this segment of the program at a 25% response rate based on our prior experiences. Either approach would be acceptable; if you have no prior experience, the 8.1% planning number is more conservative.

The total direct marketing costs are now easy to establish. We summarize the total direct mail, initial telemarketing, literature request fulfillment, and literature request follow-up telemarketing to establish the total direct marketing costs.

The total acceptances are also summarized. The total costs are then divided by the total acceptances to establish the cost per acceptance for the program. If we had used the required 3.8 acceptances for the follow-up calling, we would have only had 72 acceptances for the project. This means that we need a total response rate of 3.6% of the initial 2,000 records. It may seem contradictory to go back to the 2,000 original records, but this allows you to examine the entire program. We have included all of the costs and if this program performs as planned, we will have a successful direct marketing program.

Mail and Phone Synergy

Mail and phone together can create powerful results. Like any other direct marketing program, the results will depend on your approach, product, and list. We had an opportunity to actually see and measure a program that proved how effective the two media can be together because it allowed us to breakthrough and reach our target contact.

Our example is a small software company that sold an innovative product to personal computer users. The product established a common interface to several of the most popular software products operating on the PC. The company was in deep financial trouble and looking for a way to contact the major users of PC's in larger businesses.

A direct marketing program was designed to use direct mail and follow-up with a telemarketing call. The telephone call was to follow the mail by 10 days to maximize the synergy of the mail and phone. A special offer was created which allowed the prospect to receive 5 copies of the software product for 30 days absolutely free. At the end of the 30 day trial, the prospect could keep all the copies and pay our invoice, which was substantially discounted, or return the software and owe nothing. In addition, the prospect could keep one copy of the software as an incentive for trying the product.

We acquired a list of 2,000 known large users of PC's. These were mostly larger companies and all had at least 50 PC's in use in their business. Our contact was the PC coordinator or the director of data processing. The list was name-directed and fairly current -- no older than one year.

A mail-gram format was used to make the offer and explain the product to the prospect prior to any telemarketing contact. A response vehicle was included to allow the prospect to accept the offer in the mail. The free trial and free copy premium were highlighted in bold headlines in the mail-gram format. In addition a small brochure was included to give some limited details about the product. The response in the mail was under 1%.

The phone program started 10 days after the mail was dropped. The telemarketing service bureau actually performed the mail creation, production, and letter-shop services, so we were able to ensure the proper timing of the phone behind the mail.

The results were not very gratifying. The phone produced at about 4% of completed calls and the results were not considered successful. We began to examine the phone results and found that the prospect did not recall our mailing and could not understand the benefit in trying the product. Our problem was breaking through to the decision makers and making them understand the offer. As we mentioned earlier, it is almost impossible to sell a new concept over the phone. The prospect has to have an understanding of the products for the phone effort to be successful.

We decided to send the prospect a premium that we thought would help our total effort. An inexpensive tee-shirt was designed and created. We again included a personalized computer generated letter and mailed the tee-shirt, first class, to the prospect. Our offer remained the same. There was almost a 30-day delay in the program while the shirts were developed. Due to timing problems, we only offered inbound phone as the response vehicle in this mailing. The outbound telemarketing program remained virtually the same.

The combined mail and phone results on this second approach were over 45%. Almost all the executives we talked to recalled our mailing and were very interested in trying the product.

This program clearly demonstrates the powerful effect of mail and phone. It also proves that we can only get through to our targeted contacts if we create an appropriate mail and phone approach. The data processing executive is overwhelmed by mail from many sources. For your program to succeed in this environment, the offer will have to "break through" the clutter on their desk. We found that a premium (amusing and personalized) could be very effective. The mail and phone combined approach allowed the prospect to have a prior understanding of the product and accept the offer with less reluctance and fear. We had informed the prospect in the second mailing that we intended to call and ask for their acceptance of our offer.

Integrating Field and Telephone Sales

Combining field and telephone selling is difficult but something that virtually every business must look to accomplish if they are going to survive in the foreseeable future. The cost of a face-to-face sales call is about $400. If a company's allowable selling costs are 20% of revenue, for each $400 sales call there must be $2,000 in revenue. All too often, the revenue requirement is only considered in selling new products and services and customer support is overlooked.

Considering the impact of the expensive sales call when servicing customers, every company has to add direct marketing and telephone selling to support smaller customers. In order to justify even one sales call, a customer must spend at least $2,000 with your company. Every company has customers that aren't spending this minimum amount. How do you service these smaller accounts? Many companies abandon the smaller customer because they're too expensive to support. Direct marketing, especially telephone selling, is the ideal vehicle to deal with smaller customers.

The objective in implementing a telephone sales organization is to make it complement any other distribution channel you're using or plan to use. There are some things you can do that will help make the phone operation complementary.

Don't call it *Tele*-anything. The term telemarketing or teleselling or tele-anything is often negatively perceived. Many people receive so much telemarketing at home that they are turned off by any word that conjures up those images. Many executives and managers are aware of this negative perception created at home and are concerned that a phone program will also discourage their business customers.

The telephone center is often the lowest rung on the ladder within the organization and a job that most people want to passionately avoid.

Give the phone operation a name consistent with the function it is going to perform, for example, "customer service" or "sales support." The people operating on the phone then become Customer Service Representatives (CSR) or Sales Support Representatives (SSR).

Create a team environment. Team one SSR with one or more field salespeople. Let your customers know that they have another resource available to support them.

We have even gone so far as to implement voice mail systems and required the SSR to leave a voice mail message for the field salesperson after each contact. This is quickly discarded but it is a great way to overcome the natural fear of the field salesperson when you first introduce the phone operation.

It will create difficulties if you team two extroverted personalities together. One of the most common mistakes made by sales management in introducing telephone selling is to separate field selling and telephone selling. Often accounts are taken from the field sales force and turned over to the telephone sales department. Typically telephone selling is being considered because sales costs have become too expensive to certain segments of the market.

Field salespeople are extremely protective of their territories. Taking a portion of their territory away and reassigning it to another channel of distribution (telephone selling) is never received positively. The field is often threatened and hostile to the telephone selling department when this is done.

We often advise potential users of telephone selling not to cut territories or eliminate commissions when introducing telephone selling. It is important to develop a complementary environment. Field sales and telephone sales will work best if they can work together.

Consider teaming telephone sales and field sales in a way that they work together. Rather then removing territory from a salesperson's control, why not allow the smaller customers to be covered by both the field sales and the telephone selling representative?

Don't cut commissions or territories. This will be the biggest fear that your existing sales channels will have.

Instead of removing accounts from a salesperson's territory, change your compensation programs to motivate the salesperson to sell to larger accounts. Don't eliminate commissions completely in the smaller accounts, but make them significantly smaller. Implement a sliding scale commission program that pays significantly more for sales to larger and more profitable customers.

By offering smaller commissions to the field representative for smaller accounts, and comparatively larger commissions for those larger customers, you'll force the field rep to serve larger companies. Introduce telephone selling as a way to help the field salesperson better manage his territory. Make the field salesperson and telesales person a team. One telesales representative can probably support more than one field sales representative.

Because you'll be paying smaller commissions to the field representative for smaller accounts, you'll be able to afford a commission plan for the telesales people. Their compensation should be designed to motivate them to turn over larger accounts to the field representative. Leads should be rewarded at a fixed bonus amount if one converts to a larger customer.

The telesales representative can be introduced to customers as a way to improve their support. The field salesperson is still available to assist and work with the customer.

As customers are scheduled for periodic calling, the telesales person can generate orders and sales opportunities. Those orders sold by telesales are credited for commissions for both field sales and telesales. If a situation requires face-to-face contact, the field salesperson can be scheduled to make the call.

Because the field sales person will want to spend time on larger accounts and will still be receiving compensation for telephone sales, they will automatically begin to turn accounts over to the telephone selling department. Everybody wins!

Even if the telephone selling department generates orders and new accounts that do not involve field sales, pay the appropriate field sales representative commissions. Make the field salespeople feel that they still own their territories. Motivate a team environment and eliminate any fear on the part of the field salesperson. Don't spend a lot of time trying to arbitrate whether the field or telephone selling departments should get credit and be compensated for a sale. Motivate both to work together. Your field salespeople can make or break a telephone selling program.

The team approach provides an excellent vehicle to improve customer service, generate additional sales and improve employee morale.

Staffing Telephone Selling

Telephone selling is hard work. It can become extremely monotonous and communicators tend to burn out in a relatively short period of time. It requires dedicated people, measurable objectives and strong management.

The type of people used in this kind of an environment can have a significant impact on your ability to succeed. The best personality for telephone selling is a person who wants to work on the phone. Salespeople who strive for face-to-face selling will find the phone limiting. Very often, managers will use a telephone sales program as an opportunity to train junior salespeople. These people will ultimately be moved to a field territory. In my experience, this type of situation will not provide optimum telephone selling results. A field sales personality tends be more extroverted and doesn't perform very well in a planned telephone selling environment. The best personality for telephone selling is an amiable person. Customer service oriented people tend to make the best telephone selling representatives. They like talking on the phone and don't object to management controlling and planning their calling patterns.

Results of Staffing Alternatives

		Salespeople	Full Time Amiable	3rd Party Supplemental	Perm Part Time
A)	Hours per day			6	6
B)	Hourly $			$12.00	$6.00
C)	Daily $ (B * C)			72	36
D)	Weekly $ (C * 5)			$360	$180
E)	Monthly $ (D * 4.22)			$1,560	$780
F)	Annual earnings (E *12)	$40,000	$22,000	$18,720	$9,360
G)	Multiplier	3	3	2	2
H)	Cost per Year (F * G)	$120,000	$66,000	$37,440	$18,720
I)	Calls per hour	3	5	5	5
J)	Hours per day	5	5	5	5
K)	Calls per day (I * J)	15.00	25.00	25.00	25.00
L)	Days per year	235	235	250	250
M)	Calls per year (K * L)	3,525	5,875	6,250	6,250
N)	Cost per call (H ÷ M)	$34.04	$11.23	$5.99	$3.00
O)	Allowable selling expense %	15.00%	15.00%	15.00%	15.00%
P)	Required Revenue per call (N ÷ O)	$226.93	$74.87	$39.93	$20.00

Illustration 6-10: Staffing alternatives.

By using an extroverted personality the program never has the best resource applied to the problem. If the telephone selling function is used as a training ground for new people, it will quickly be perceived as not as important and lose appeal to strong people.

Amiable personalities enjoy working in an office and get satisfaction from the group around them. Administrative personnel and former customer service people tend to be amiable personalities and will probably be well suited for a telephone environment.

Most business-to-business telephone selling is telesales. The communicator is not scripted but rather allowed to have open dialogue with customers and prospects. The conversation will dictate the direction and tone of the call. On the other hand, telemarketing uses a scripted communicator in a heads-down production calling environment. Most telephone service bureaus sell telemarketing.

There are a number of techniques that have been developed in telemarketing that can be employed in a telesales environment to improve productivity.

In a managed telesales operation, you should be able to achieve about 5 completed calls per hour. You should only require a communicator to spend 4 to 6 hours per day on the telephone. With this in mind, you may want to consider using a totally different group of part-time employees to make telephone calls. Part-time workers and physically challenged personnel make ideal telephone workers.

- They may only want to work a few hours per day.
- They may have knowledge about your company and your products and can have open dialogue type calls with your customers and prospects.
- They aren't doing the function as a method to get another job. They want to make phone calls.

You have several options in the types of people you can use on the phone. Besides hiring full-time employees, you can go to permanent part-time supplemental. They can be hired directly or through an agency. Illustration 6-10 depicts the costs and capacities of using full-time salespeople compared to full time amiable personnel, supplemental part-time from an agency or using permanent part-time personnel.

When you examine using salespeople, assume they will make about 15 calls per day. Allowing for all the non-selling days, they can complete about 3,525 calls per year. Assuming an allowable selling expense for this function of 15% (all of the other sales functions are still present) each representative will have to generate $227 for each telephone call.

Changing the type of person on the phone dramatically changes the results. The big difference between the approaches lies in the nature of the individual. Full time personnel are paid for vacations, holidays and personal time off. In addition, their burden rate is higher due to the larger fringe benefits and general and administrative costs. Supplemental employees still have additional expense in management time, telephone expense, general and administrative costs and other miscellaneous expenses. But their burden factor is somewhat lower.

With a managed telephone selling environment and the right personality on the phone, productivity will increase sharply and the number of accounts supported can also increase. The results per customer are lower and it is easier to justify supporting even smaller accounts. As you'll notice part-time communicators only need about $20 per call and can make over 6,000 calls per year.

Telephone Selling Summarized

In this chapter we established a definition of telemarketing that clearly distinguishes telephone selling or telesales from direct marketing, telemarketing. If you are using telesales there are some elements of direct marketing that can significantly improve your results. The database and timely follow-up of information requests can substantially assist the salesperson who is selling on the telephone. However, it will remain very difficult to measure costs and results in the telesales environment.

Telemarketing removes dependency on any individual's personality for results in the marketing program. It uses a script and is controllable in both its costs and results. Let's again look at the definition of telemarketing we established earlier:

Telemarketing is a medium used to perform direct marketing.

- It is controllable, measurable, and not dependent on the individual for its success.
- It can be used to support direct mail or advertising, or as a stand-alone campaign.
- It is a planned series of contacts, using a constant message, seeking to produce a lead or an order.
- It yields information to build and maintain a database and is completely measurable in its costs and results.
- It can be outbound or inbound telephone calling.
- It can be used to market to consumers or to other businesses.

Telemarketing uses a scripted or message-controlled communicator to deliver a direct marketing message over the telephone.

You will have to evaluate both your inbound and outbound requirements for the effective use of telemarketing. If you're using inbound, make sure that the communicator staff is aware of your advertising and direct mail plan. In addition, plan your efforts to deal with respondents who may call your phone number during your non-business hours.

As you evaluate your inbound requirements, examine your costs to provide the service yourself and then price outside vendors. You may find that an outside service is more economical and efficient.

Outbound telemarketing is a strong promotional format but is dependent on the offer you make. You really can't sell anything new during an outbound call and, after list selection, the strength of the promotion will be your offer. Remember, you will only have about 30 seconds to convince your prospect to listen to the rest of your proposition. Good script writing includes making a compelling offer very early in the phone call.

We examined a number of script approaches including outlines and flip cards. Evaluate and decide on the best script approach for your program.

We also reviewed how to manage the process of telephone selling in a telesales environment. The key to measuring and managing telephone selling is controlling the records and their ultimate disposition.

Telephone Selling Productivity

Type of Calling	Dialings /Hour	Records Consumed /Hour	% Dials Completed	Completed Calls /Hour
Inbound	12-18	12-18	90%	10-16
Outbound Telemarketing				
Consumer	25-35	15-18	40-60%	10-15
Business-to-Business	20-30	8-12	25-35%	5-10
Outbound Telesales-Unmanaged	3-5	2-3	30-40%	1-2
Outbound Telesales-Managed	12-18	5-8	25-35%	4-7

Illustration 6-11: Typical telephone selling productivity.

Illustration 6-11 identifies typical productivity expectations in various types of telemarketing. This table can be very helpful in planning telephone selling programs.

Like any direct marketing program, outbound telemarketing is controllable and measurable. You can plan and evaluate your results in a fairly short period of time. The key to measurement is the plan you develop prior to the telemarketing program.

Mail and phone are the ideal combined direct marketing program. In fact, once you commit to telemarketing you will need direct mail to answer requests for additional information. The combination of the two formats typically produces greater results than the sum of each format run independently.

Telemarketing is a powerful weapon in your marketing arsenal. It is one of the fastest growing promotional formats being used by business today. If you haven't tried telemarketing, you're missing a tremendous opportunity.

Chapter Seven:
Direct Mail

Direct Mail Defined

Direct mail is the primary format businesses use to execute direct marketing. The direct mail format allows the business-to-business marketer to select from a large variety of creative options for soliciting prospects and customers. With direct mail, you can select whatever environment and voice you feel is appropriate. Direct mail allows you to lead the reader through the offer and to the response vehicle using your own tempo and rhythm.

There are other media and formats that may allow similar creative flexibility (such as space advertising and the internet), however, none are as targeted as the direct mail format. Direct mail allows you to involve the reader as no other medium can. A mailing has the unique opportunity of receiving 100% of its reader's attention. A name-directed mailing can be targeted and personalized more than any other medium.

Direct mail (and e-mail to customers and qualified leads) is the most testable of media; you can vary each mailing piece. Readers can receive personalized mailings suited to their individual needs, tastes and desires. You can test the positioning of your product and provide research on how to proceed within the entire market. The same flexibility exists with telemarketing, but it is not available in print or broadcast promotion.

Illustration 7-1: Cost versus personalization.

The advantages of personalizing, targeting, and changing your copy, cause direct mail to be somewhat expensive on a cost-per-contact basis while e-mail is one of the least expensive. Direct mail is just ahead of telemarketing in the cost-per-contact matrix. Illustration 7-1 reemphasizes the personalization and cost-per-contact comparison. The cost per contact of e-mail is unmeasureably low.

The additional costs mean that the response rates and closing rates for inquiries generated through direct mail have to be higher than similar inquiries generated in print or broadcast promotions. E-mail is covered in the internet chapter ten.

Direct mail responders tend to be of high quality because the message they receive in the mail is clear and concise. The prospects understand the offer and are responding to something they are interested in. When evaluating the success of the direct response marketing program, the cost per order or cost per qualified lead will normally prove that direct mail and direct e-mail to known individuals are the most economical direct marketing media available.

Creating a Direct Mail Piece

The varieties of direct mail pieces range from simple postcards to full color catalogs. Anything mailed to potential customers can be classified as direct mail, even a price list.

By definition, direct marketing is designed to produce a lead or an order. An ad run in a magazine to create awareness and a brochure used as a "leave behind" aren't designed to produce leads or orders. Don't start a direct mail program by taking inventory of existing printed material and deciding what will fit in an envelope.

Many a business manager has mailed a reprint of an ad and decided "direct mail doesn't work!" These managers did not execute a direct marketing program; they simply mailed an advertisement. Mailing an existing brochure designed as sales collateral can prove just as unsuccessful. Saving pennies in the cost of producing a mailing can cause the loss of dollars in terms of results.

The design of a direct mail package begins with the business plan you have created and the objectives you want to achieve. In the promotion chapter, we discussed the four elements of a direct marketing program:

- List
- Offer
- Format
- Copy

In your business plan, you defined the target universe you want to reach, focusing on their personalities and buying motivations. As with any direct marketing promotion, these personality issues will govern the format and copy. A brochure designed to be left with the president of a company should not be delivered to a specifying engineer.

The list and offer account for 75% of your success. If your existing materials do not contain your direct response offer, they should not be used. If you use existing matcrials in a mailing, your list may be correct but your results may not achieve your objectives.

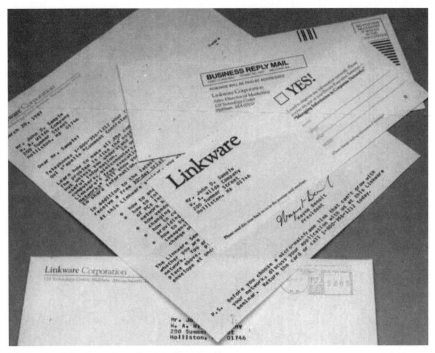

Illustration 7-2: A standard direct mail package.

To produce a lead or an order, make your target market an offer that will ask them to take the desired action. Making the offer a second thought will prevent the package from achieving its objectives.

Create the direct mail package as if you are writing a single letter to a well-defined individual. The goal of the creative effort is to move the target to take the action you want. During the planning process you defined an offer that, if accepted, would achieve your objectives. In addition, you identified the personality of the target people in your market. Your creative effort should use a custom format and direct mail copy to reach your targets.

A direct mail piece created to reach an analytical individual will not be as effective when mailed to an extrovert. Such a mailing may generate results because the list is correct. However, the results may not be enough to constitute a successful program.

The standard direct mail package contains:

- an outer envelope
- a letter
- a brochure (optional)
- a response device
- a prepaid reply envelope (optional)
  (see Illustration 7-2 for a standard direct mail piece)

Except for the outer envelope and the reply envelope, each element of the direct mail package should be able to stand alone. Each element should contain the product benefits, the offer, and instructions for responding by mail, Internet and/or phone. A mailing may arrive disassembled in its target's office; the prospect may receive or save only a portion of the mailing. The letter, the brochure, and the response device should all be stand-alone elements creating their own AIDA (Attention, Interest, Desire, Action). This is why existing materials may not fit your direct mail needs.

Copy and Graphics

There are two major areas of consideration within the creative process:

- Copy: The words you use to explain your offer and product.

- Graphic: The visual elements you use to explain your offer and product.

It is unrealistic to try to explain all of the rules of style that pertain to copywriting in this book. For more information about complete texts on copywriting for direct mail, request a bibliography from the Direct Marketing Association, 1120 Avenue of the Americas, New York, NY 10036-6700.

The point we want to make here is that copy should be written with the target in mind. The length of the copy depends on the needs of the target. When writing copy to a person working in a stand-up industry (hair stylist, gas station manager, independent retailer) copy must be short and to the point. This type of individual is not oriented to heavy reading while sitting at a desk. The stand-up manager will probably review a mailing package in the same manner as a consumer standing over a trash can.

If you are writing to a lawyer who is accustomed to reading while sitting, long copy can be successful. In this environment there is a bigger problem: Getting your mailing passed a secretary and to the reader. Remember Bobby Barrier! This problem is independent of the length of copy and must be addressed in the overall strategy of the direct marketing plan.

The length of the copy can be tested. There is a perpetual battle between those who advocate long copy and those who advocate short copy. There is only one rule that applies in either case: copy that interests the reader will be read.

We have all heard and used the term "junk mail." Mail that addresses products of interest to the reader is not junk; mail that addresses products that are of no interest to the reader is junk. If the reader is interested in the copy, its length is insignificant.

Headlines are copy set apart from text by position and size. Headlines and sub-heads are copy used as word graphics. Being set apart and in larger type, headlines pull the eye toward them. Headlines should reach out to the reader with the strongest benefit available. Many people do not read past headlines unless their interest is aroused. Headlines are, therefore, the magnet that will draw people into your offer.

When there are too many headlines and sub-heads on a page, the overall visual effect may put off the reader. Too many headlines mean no headlines, no visual magnet that stands out to draw the reader's eye in.

Using headlines in letters reduces the similarity between promotion and a true business letter. Few people use headlines in business correspondence. Headlines create more of a promotional impression than a business correspondence impression. Headlines are fine in brochures and on reply devices, which are normally viewed with promotional eyes by the reader. If you're trying to convey the image of a standard business letter, headlines may not be effective.

In the research for this book, we found that we could not improve on Bob Stone's formula for letter writing. As found in his book, *Successful Direct Marketing Methods*, (Crain Books, an imprint of National Textbook Company, Lincolnwood, Illinois), here is Bob Stone's letter writing formula:

Promise a benefit in your headline or first paragraph - your most important benefit. You simply can't go wrong by leading off with the most important benefit to the reader. Some writers believe in the slow buildup. But most experienced writers I know favor making the important point first.

Immediately enlarge on your most important benefit. This step is crucial. Many writers come up with a great lead, then fail to follow through. Or they catch attention with their heading, but then take two or three paragraphs to warm up to their subject. The reader's attention is gone! Try hard to elaborate on your most important benefit right away, and you'll build up interest fast.

Tell the reader specifically what they are going to get. It's amazing how many letters lack details on such basic product features as size, color, weight, and sales terms. Perhaps the writer is so close to their proposition they assume the reader knows all about it. A dangerous assumption! And when you tell the reader what they're going to get, don't overlook the intangibles that go along with your product or service. For example, they're getting smart appearance in addition to a pair of slacks, knowledge in addition to a 340-page book.

Back up your statements with proof and endorsements. Most prospects are somewhat skeptical about advertising. They know it sometimes gets a little over-enthusiastic about a product. So they accept it only with a grain of salt. If you can back up your own statements with third-party testimonials or a list of satisfied users, everything you say becomes more believable.

Tell the reader what she might lose if she doesn't act. As noted, people respond affirmatively either to gain something they do not possess or to avoid losing something they already have. Here's a good spot in your letter to overcome human inertia -- imply what may be lost if action is postponed. People don't like to be left out. A skillful writer can use this human trait as a powerful influence in his or her message.

Rephrase your prominent benefits in your closing offer. As a good salesperson does, sum up the benefits to the prospect in your closing offer. This is the proper prelude to asking for action. This is where you can intensify the prospect's desire to have the product. The stronger the benefits you can persuade the reader to recall, the easier it will be for him or her to justify an affirmative decision.

Incite Action, Now. This is the spot where you win or lose the battle with inertia. Experienced advertisers know, once a letter is put aside or tossed into that file, they're out of luck. So wind up with a call for action and a logical reason for acting now. Too many letters close with a statement like "supplies are limited." That argument lacks credibility. Today's consumer knows you probably have a warehouse full of merchandise. So make your reason a believable one. For example, "It may be many months before we go back to press on this book." Or "Orders are shipped on a first-come basis. The sooner yours is received, the sooner you can be enjoying your new widget."

The old adage "a picture is worth a thousand words" is applicable in direct mail. Graphics can be in two forms: photography and illustration.

Photography is just that: pictures of the product and its use. Use either color or black-and-white depending on the overall design and budget of your package. Color can be a powerful tool to support or defeat your offer. When offering a budget priced product, color can defeat the offer. When offering color-coordinated work clothes, black-and-white can defeat the offer by not showing the benefits color coordination will bring to the buyer.

Graphics should show the reader the benefits of the product. Just showing pictures of the product, without showing a benefit, will not help the selling effort. Using photography because it already exists can do as much damage as using brochures that already exist.

Another decision you make will be whether to use photography, illustrations, or both. This simple concept can help you decide which approach to use:

- photography depicts reality
- illustrations depict illusion or fantasy; the dream of what can be

We can use a combination of photography and illustrations in the same piece to generate both of these impressions in the mind of the reader.

The overall layout of any direct mail component is also a graphic. A brochure that is copy from top to bottom and from side to side is visually oppressive. Most people will not bother to read such a piece. Because the overall look of the piece is visually unappealing, the copy will never be read.

Graphics can also take the form of small design elements that are used as visual breaks between copy points. Such graphics, like *, give the mind a chance to pause ^ before continuing to read.

An illustrated graphic can be used to present a product and its application. The mailing in Illustration 7-3, shows how a piece of capital equipment solved confusion in a manufacturing environment.

Illustration 7-3: An illustrated graphic.

Many field salespeople found this illustration posted on prospects' bulletin boards with names of employees written on the illustrated people. The illustration from the mailing lived on long after the mailing was complete. The company name, product, solution and, offer were continually selling the prospect.

The Components of a Direct Mail Package

The differences in direct mail packages are as varied as the individuals who create them. A package can include many different pieces. Many companies even include multiple types of components in the same mailing.

Outer Envelope

The outer envelope is the passport that will get the message to the reader, just as a salesperson's appearance is the passport that allows them to make a presentation. You never get a second chance to make a first impression, so do not underestimate the outer envelope.

The most acceptable outer envelope appears as a professional business letter to someone with whom you have a relationship. The envelope has a preprinted *cornercard* (the return address information printed in the upper left-hand corner) with company name and logo, a personal address and first class postage. This type of outer envelope is the most expensive since the contents, (the letter and the reply device) should also be personalized where appropriate. Prospects receiving this kind of expensive looking mailing usually open the envelope. Creating this type of personalized mailing is a tedious task for the lettershop and will increase the cost.

If you decide against the business letter format, you can try a variety of creative approaches with the outer envelope. Keep in mind that your goal is to have the prospect open the envelope and read the message.

If you decide to use window envelopes to cut costs, there is no point in maintaining the professional letter appearance. No one uses window envelopes for business letters on a day-to-day basis. With a window envelope, you can use bulk postage, oversized envelopes, graphics and/or copy on the outer envelope. You can test these variables to see which outer envelope yields the greatest results. In essence, if you are not going to use the professional letter format, you have no limit on what you can do with the outer envelope so you should experiment.

Quite often, the outer envelope is stripped from the contents by an administrator before the prospect sees it. Unlike consumer mail, Bobby Barrier may strip the contents from the outer envelope as a service to the boss. You therefore have a two-step creative challenge:

- To get the mailing reviewed and accepted by the administrator before it is passed along.

- If the mailing reaches the prospect unopened, to have it opened and reviewed.

It is probably better to use more professional envelopes when mailing to larger businesses that typically have administrators. When mailing to small businesses that do not have such a screen, a more graphic attention-getting outer envelope may improve results.

Letter

The best responding letter appears as though you were sending a one-of-a-kind letter to each individual, just as though you were mailing a personalized business letter. This process is expensive and may not prove cost effective.

Write your direct mail letters to someone you know, assuming they know nothing about your product or service. Follow the AIDA formula we discussed earlier in Chapter 5.

The elements of the direct mail letter are the same as a normal business letter:

- Printed letterhead
- Date, month and year are sufficient
- Addressee information - name of contact, title, address. It is appropriate to title- or function-address letters when you don't have a contact name.
- Salutation
- Letter body
- Complimentary close

- Signature
- Administrative code
- Postscript

Like most written works, your letter must be readable and attractive to your prospect. If a page is packed with prose, the odds are pretty good that it will not get read. Examine the letters you read and enjoy. They are probably written with short paragraphs and contain lots of white space around the copy or prose. Use yourself as a guide and don't mail anything that you wouldn't read.

The reader's interest and eye movement will travel first to the letterhead and addressee information, next to the salutation (those parts that contain the reader's name and title), to the signature block (to see who the letter is from), and then to the P.S. (unfortunately an uncommon occurrence in a business letter, but when used a real eye-catcher). The P.S. should contain the primary benefit and a call to action since it will probably be read before the body of the letter.

Direct mail letters can contain headlines and sub-heads to get the reader involved with your sales presentation. Be careful not to sell features, but to focus on the benefits the prospect will receive from your product or service. The use of headlines and other eye-catching techniques, such as boldface type, italics and different sizes and styles of type fonts, set direct mail apart from the standard business letter. Unfortunately, these techniques can be overdone to a point that they become a turnoff to the prospect. The best approach will move prospects completely though the presentation and have them feel as though the letter was written to them personally.

Brochure

The brochure may or may not be necessary. We have tested direct mail using 50% with and 50% without a brochure on several occasions. Our findings are that the brochure depresses results by 15%. If needed support information cannot be put into the letter, a brochure may be required particularly if you are selling something that needs to be seen, like a business calendar with a color cover.

The brochure can cover all of the information readers may need to satisfy their technical questions prior to making a purchase decision. However, if you are selling the next step to purchase a piece of capital equipment, rather than a product, a product brochure does not enhance the next step.

A brochure can be multi-color, multi-page with beautiful (and expensive) art and pictures, or it can be a single page of information about a specific product or service.

If you do require a brochure, make sure that it is consistent with the objective of the direct mail program. Excess brochures from a trade show, or sales force collateral material, may not be effective as a direct mail brochure. The brochure must contain all of the information about the offer and a call to action. Remember, it may be used separately by your prospect.

The brochure is also a place to sample your product or service. Prospects can see (using art and photographs) the product and receive a detailed explanation of how the product can meet their needs. Citing testimonials and case histories can help prospects overcome FUD (fear, uncertainty and doubt); and the offer can be reinforced and explained. The brochure can be much more explicit than the letter. In fact, you can even reference the brochure in the letter.

A brochure is not always required or advisable. A brochure that gives an overview of the product or service, may provide insufficient information to make the sale, but enough for the readers to determine that the product or service is not for them. If you are selling a seminar that will give detailed information on a specific product or service, enclosing a brochure in the mailing will depress response.

Lead generation programs are designed to have a salesperson visit the prospect and review the product offering. You may not want to give prospects enough information to determine that they don't need your offering. A detailed brochure could do more damage than good in this situation. On the other hand, you may want only a few good leads and offer a brochure as a fulfillment device with detailed information on your products or services. You may want to offer the brochure as an information kit if the prospect fills out the response vehicle and returns it for fulfillment. An internet brochure can involve prospects immediately in your fulfillment and response acquisition.

Whether or not your mailing requires a brochure is directly related to the objective you've set for the program. If your objective is the direct sale of your product, the mailing should probably include a brochure explaining the details of your product or service. If you're trying to generate leads, the use of a brochure may be excess baggage in the mailing package.

If you determine that a brochure is appropriate in your mailing package, it may be worthwhile to test a group of prospects who receive no brochure to determine the affect the brochure is having on your program.

Reply Envelope

The prepaid business reply envelope (BRE) has become a standard if you are requesting confidential information. If not, the BRE can be an unnecessary expense now that the fax machine is the most popular response option. Your local post office can supply you with BRE layouts. The preprinted portion of the reply envelope is strictly regulated by the United States Postal Service.

Since this element of the mailing is more of an administrative piece, it is probably not worth the time to overlay your creative efforts in either design or paper selection to enhance it. Black printing on white envelopes will fill the bill if you use a BRE. In fact, you may choose not to include a BRE as a part of your mailing package.

It is not unusual to use a Business Reply Card (BRC) or to request inbound telephone or internet as the response vehicle. Reply envelopes or cards may go largely unused when you provide a telephone/fax number or online contact for prospects to use for their responses. Test using a BRE in your mailing package.

If you are an infrequent mailer, you may not want to go through the process of getting a reply mail number from your servicing post office. You could instead provide prospects with a self-addressed envelope that they could stamp and return. This could save expense, and there is no evidence that prepaid postage in business mailings is as critical as it is in consumer marketing.

The easier you make it for your prospects to respond, the better the odds are that they will take the desired action. If you only offer a telephone response vehicle, the prospects may feel uncomfortable with the pressure of being sold on the phone. A BRC-only response vehicle may make prospects uncomfortable with having the information able to be read by all. A BRE without postage may turn prospects off because of their financial doubts about your company. Evaluate your market and the prospect you're trying to reach to determine the requirement for response options.

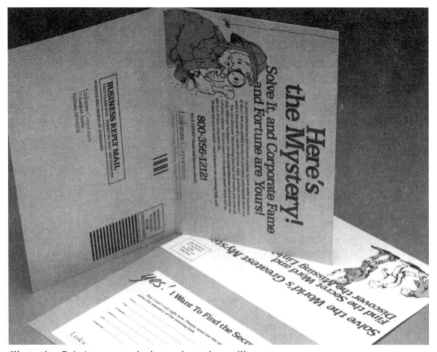

Illustration 7-4: A response device as the entire mailing.

Response Device

The most critical element of a direct mail package is the response device. In fact, you would be well advised to begin your creative process by creating the response device. By creating the response device, you finalize the action you want the prospect to take as a result of the direct mail program.

With the response device designed, you can create the letter and brochure around the action you want the reader to take. This sounds simple enough, but direct mail is not always implemented in this way. More often than not, people spend weeks on the letter copy and put together a response device as an afterthought. The situation is often compounded by a lot of time pressure, as mailings often run behind schedule and have to be finished immediately.

The response device should be easy to understand. People in business are generally careful about what they respond to since they are representing their company when they act. The response device should not be a legal looking document that may frighten the reader. If you are looking for a legal, binding commitment, your response will probably be small.

The flow of the response device should be the same as the flow of the letter and brochure. Do not introduce anything on the response device that has not been covered elsewhere in the mailing. Remember, each piece of the mailing should be able to stand alone.

The concept of no surprises as you ask for the order or next step is not new to the art of selling. Good salespeople know that once you've built your proposition with the prospect, ask for the order and shut up. The next person to talk loses. Never introduce a new idea or concept at the close that gives the prospect something to question or creates FUD. This basic approach to selling holds true in direct mail. The response device asks for the action. You may want to reestablish the benefits -- but ask for the action and shut up.

The response device should contain your phone number in several places. If prospects completing the reply form and your fax and phone number are conspicuous, they may decide to pick up the phone and call or drop the completed document on the fax machine and send it. The impulse decision can be important, and you want to make it easy to reach you.

If the prospect does decide to call, you can begin selling and cross-selling during the phone conversation. The phone moves you more quickly into a personal relationship with the prospect reducing time-to-next-step. The prospect took the effort to call you; this is a great time to move your relationship forward.

Many readers of direct mail breeze through the letter and the brochure and go directly to the response device. They want to determine how much money, if any, the offer will cost if they choose to take advantage of it. They look at the response device as a summary, an outline of the mailing. Many people read the response device to determine whether it's worth their time to read the entire mailing.

If you're asking your prospects to spend $2,000 for your proposition and their buying authority is only $100, you have probably lost the buyer. If they perceived a benefit and value from your proposition and response device, they may read the mailing and refer it to someone who has authority. In either case, you are not going to make an immediate sale, but the response device sure played an important role in the direction they took.

It could be fun to test mail your response device as a stand-alone mailing package. It may work as well as the entire package at a much lower cost. In this type of mailing, your offer is for a simple response only - - no money enclosed. You can offer a "Bill Me" or trial samples or free issues of a magazine. Illustration 7-4 shows an entire mailing. This is an example of a response device without a package.

Since the fax is a common response option, provide a Business Reply Form (BRF) using full letterhead second page. The prospects can put the BRF easily on the fax for immediate transmission. When mailing packages are computer generated, take advantage of the personalization possibilities and pre-complete the BRF with the prospect's complete information and list codes. Prospects that respond will make corrections to any incorrect information.

Postage

One of the most frequently overlooked components of the direct mail format is postage. There are three methods of applying postage to a mailing:

- Preprinted -- where the type of postage is printed on the mailing pieces as part of the printing process.

- Metered -- where a postage meter applies postage directly to the piece.

- Stamped -- where actual stamps are affixed to the mailing.

The preprinted form is fine for promotional mail but may kill the personalized image when using the business letter format.

In the business letter format, use metered postage since most businesses use postage meters in their day-to-day operations. Stamps can be an attention-getting device on a business mailing, since stamps are seldom seen on business letters. Test stamps: we have found a 12% lift in some markets.

Your target may never see the outer envelope, so in a lot of cases the postage decision may be moot. However, some businesses have instructed their mailrooms not to deliver third class or bulk mail. The mailroom personnel do not look at the postage actually paid, but at the mailing's nature and approach. If mail looks too promotional, it may be discarded by the mailroom staff even if it carries first class postage.

There are two basic postage rates for direct mail:

- First class - cost fixed for the first ounce, and restricted in size to no larger than 6-1/8 by 11-1/2 inches and no smaller than 3-1/2 by 5 inches. Additional weight costs extra per ounce up to 12 ounces maximum.

- Standard mail which used to be called third class or bulk - cost fixed for a few ounces with no size constraints. Additional weight costs extra per ounce up to 16 ounces maximum. A minimum number of pieces is required for a third class mailing.

Each of these two classes of postage also has reduced rates for pre-sort, tie and bag preparation before entering the mail stream. Check with your local post office for the regulations that will affect your mailing. A lettershop that prepares mailings will also be able to provide current postal information.

Postage can be a major cost element for direct mail efforts. Almost every conceivable approach to affixing postage and postage rates has been tested. There typically is little difference in response between first or third class rates. Metered mail usually pulls better than stamps, and a well-designed, preprinted permit will pull as well as metered mail.

The decision to use either first or third class postage will be governed by the speed at which you want the mail delivered. First-class mail is normally delivered within three to five days. Standard class mail is delivered at the leisure of the post office but can stay in any single facility for a maximum of 48 hours. For a national mailing, it could take as long as 15 work days for standard class mail to be delivered.

First class delivery costs almost twice as much, therefore you should evaluate the speed at which you need the mailing delivered in making the postage decision.

There are no rules or known formulas that can govern the best method to affix postage to your mail or determine the best postage rate to use. The way to determine which will be best for you is to test different techniques. However, this is not a major point. After establishing the best lists, offer, and major formats, it may be worthwhile to test postage approaches.

Breaking Through

The biggest challenge in direct mail is breaking through the clutter of mail that a prospect receives each day. As mailers use more standard creative direct mail packages that are sold by various production facilities around the country, the clutter will increase. As you economize more and more, you'll run the risk of becoming part of the clutter rather than beating it.

You can test to determine if frequency will be more important to your direct mail program than creative approaches. Most business publishers and sem-

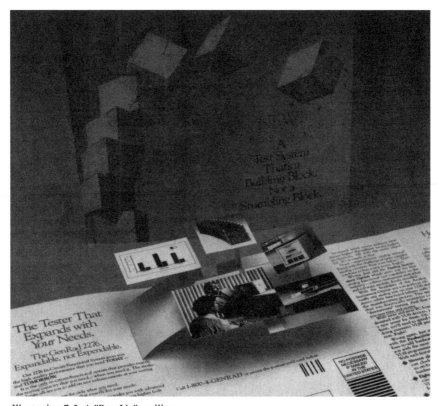

Illustration 7-5: A "Pop-Up" mailing.

Illustration 7-6: Popcorn Breakthrough Mailing

inar companies have decided that frequency, and not creativity is the key to results. If you are on any business lists you have received the 8-1/2 by 11 inch three-fold, self-mailing brochure from at least one seminar company. This format seems to be a standard.

Breakthrough creative is the development of some type of package that yields the best results for the investment. In some cases, breakthrough can mean just getting a mailing read. This can be a real challenge in markets where there are a few buyers and many sellers. For example, trying to reach MIS managers for the Fortune 1,000 companies.

To reach a difficult and highly mail-cluttered prospect, it may be necessary to develop packages that get attention because of their size and shape. These are called *dimensional mailings*.

Dimensional mailings are generally large in a three-dimensional sense; they are packages or fat letters that have a tendency to get put on top of the prospect's mail pile. Once delivered, a dimensional mailing should follow the AIDA rules.

The use of a dimensional mailing can be effective in breaking through to a prospect you have been trying to reach. The dimensional can be directly related to the offer or just a cute approach to getting the prospect's attention. Illustration 7-6 shows a dimensional mailing to presidents of industrial companies in the metal grinding industry. A six gallon can of popcorn labeled with a fake OSHA placard was used to breakthrough. The purpose of the mailing was to generate leads for a $40,000 filtration system. Sales were 14% of those mailed. Even when sales representatives followed-up non-respondents (up to a year later) the popcorn mailing was recalled.

Formats

Business Mail

As discussed earlier in this chapter, business letters are the format generally used for direct communication in business today. The business letter is a closed-faced envelope addressed from one individual to another. It has no promotional copy on the outer envelope. The letter inside is signed by the individual. A brochure may or may not accompany the letter. There is seldom, if ever, a response device. The response device is the difference between a general business communication and a direct response promotion.

Laser printers have created personalized letters as the standard for business mail. Laser printers even allow for an imaged signature. You might want to test a pre-position signature in blue, smearable ink to provide a more personal appearance.

We don't believe there are such things as junk mail and junk telephone. There are poorly implemented uses of the media that get classified as junk. We hope you will think about how your promotion will be classified by your targets. Don't mail anything you wouldn't want to receive. Here are some things to consider:

NO LABELS. Business mail is never sent with an address label. If you must use labels, do not waste your energy on a personalized letter. The label will probably be a different color than the envelope and will probably be affixed to the envelope a little askew. The labeled envelope does not demonstrate the same care given in the preparation of a business letter. If you are going to use labels, spend your money on other elements of the mailing. It will be clear to the target that it is not a business letter, and you will have to use other techniques to ensure that it is read.

NO TEASER. Teaser copy or teaser graphics on the outer envelope are designed to get the reader into the envelope. Teasers are not normally used on business letters, so do not use them when you are trying to make an envelope look like business mail (as demonstrated in Illustration 7-2).

Illustration 7-7: Typical seminar invitations.

Making your promotion appear like a business letter increases its chances of being read but also increases the cost.

Letter Packages

A *letter package* is a direct mail promotion that uses the same general size envelope used for business letters. This can range from an invitation size to a number 10, regular business size envelope. The envelope can be closed faced or have a window. A great deal of business direct mail uses the window envelope since it is less expensive to address and mail. Illustration 7-8 shows a letter package in a regular business-size envelope.

A mailing in a window envelope costs less because the target address appears only one time and shows through the window. The address often appears on the response device. Addressing on the response device allows

Illustration 7-8: Letter Package - Number 10 envelope.

you to capture accurate information about the responder. It also makes it easier for the target to respond because they do not have to complete a response device.

We suggest that you personalize the response device. Business promotions are often passed on to other people, so you may receive responses from people you originally did not target. Personalizing the response device ensures that you will be able to establish the coding and source information even if the responder is different from the target.

Letter packages generally only carry personalization on one piece within the package. The balance of the mailing includes:
- the letter, which is generically addressed to Dear Executive, or Dear Associate
- a brochure
- a response device
- a business reply envelope (if the response device is not a BRC)

This type of mailing can often prove to be the most productive because of its relatively low cost compared with a business letter format. The cost savings are primarily in the addressing and matching of addresses. The components of the mailing are often the same as the business letter. The personalization, high-quality printing, and matching of multiple elements in the business letter format tend to be expensive.

The letter package can carry a teaser on the outer envelope. The teaser can be in the form of copy or graphics intended to get the reader into the package and into the offer.

Oversize Packages

The United States Postal Service defines any mailing package that is larger than a number 10 business envelope as an oversized mailing. Fulfillment literature sent in a 9 by 12 inch envelope is an oversized mailing. The advantage of oversized packages is that they receive special handling because everyone thinks there is extra postage involved.

This is true in mailing first class. It is not true in the bulk mail rates where the 9 by 12 requires the same postage as the number 10 envelope. This means you can use the 9 by 12 mailing to gain extra attention in a direct mail promotion. You can go larger or smaller than the 9 by 12 depending

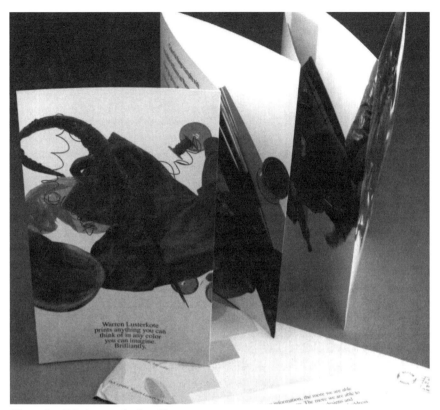

Illustration 7-9: An oversized mailing.

on the production techniques being used. Keep postal regulations in mind when producing an oversized package.

Check with your local post office to determine the appropriate regulations that govern the relationship of your package's height to its length. Regulations govern the ratio of height to length because of postal machines and handling. If your package does not meet the requirements of the postal service, you will be subject to additional postage even for a bulk mailing.

Teasers can be used on oversized mailings when you determine a promotional look is best. If you're not going to use teasers on the envelope, you may want to consider a business-looking label, similar to the concept of the business letter. The more a promotion looks like general business correspondence, the better the chances are that it will be opened and read by your target.

Illustration 7-10: A Self-Mailer.

Self-Mailers

You can choose not to use an envelope at all. The elements of your promotion can be printed on a single sheet and folded to a size that can be mailed. Self-mailers can also be brochures or catalogs consisting of multiple sheets bound together and mailed.

The advantages of self-mailers are that they:
- are generally inexpensive to produce
- are easily readable
- get the target involved without opening an envelope
- allow you to quickly state your offer

The main disadvantage of a self-mailer is that the response device is printed on the same weight paper as the entire mailing, unless a heavier weight paper is bound or attached for the response device. This means you must print the entire piece on a seven point paper stock, the minimum the post office allows for a return postcard.

Your choices are:

1) Use seven point stock so the reply device can be mailed back as a card.

2) Use 3.5 point stock so a response device can be made of a sheet folded in two to yield the seven point necessary for mailing. This requires a glue strip or some other form of closure. The post office is getting touchy about staple mail because it hangs in their machines. You could get hit with extra postage if you ask the recipient to use a stapler.

3) Request the prospects to insert the reply form in their envelopes. One of the basic rules of direct marketing is to make it easy for your prospect to respond. If you ask prospects to use their own envelopes, you've made it more difficult for them to respond. Most targets will not have an envelope handy and may not make an effort to get one.

4) Ask for telephone response only. Even though you will get a lot of response by phone, some people will not call in order to avoid talking to a salesperson. If you choose this option, we suggest you provide an address for those interested in responding by mail.

5) Require recipients to use their own envelopes and letterheads to respond. This is certainly a qualifier, since you are making it as tough as possible to respond. You will get much fewer responses because of the additional work involved. This is generally not a good idea.

6) Use the internet as a response option.

Most self-mailers are designed so the response device does not carry the original address and coding information. The prospect is asked to complete a response device and provide all the pertinent information. Illustration 7-10 shows this approach. One format that works provides personal addressing and coding on the face of the mailing and the same on the response

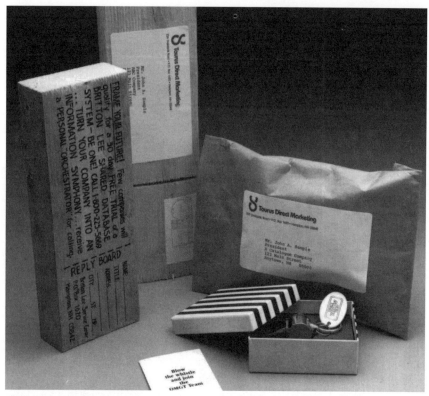

Illustration 7-11: Dimensionals.

device. This format is generally printed on seven point paper stock. Illustration 7-3 is an example of this format.

Dimensionals

The easiest explanation of a dimensional format is any mailing that has more than two dimensions (height and width). A dimensional mailing also has depth. While a regular letter package has the depth of a few layers of paper, a dimensional's depth is noticeable to sight and touch. A box, a tube, or even an envelope containing something fat is considered a dimensional mailing.

The advantages of dimensional mailings are that they generally are not opened during the screening process and that they often are put on the top of the mail pile when it is delivered to the recipient.

A dimensional mailing appeals to two strong motivations of your prospect:

- Ego. We all feel good when we receive a gift.
- Curiosity. We all want to know what's inside.

These two motivations are the overriding advantages that justify the cost of using the dimensional format. Everyone loves to receive packages they can open and be surprised by. So it is with a dimensional. It will get opened and reviewed and has the highest opening rate of any mailing package. The dimensional will not ensure results; it only ensures that it will be opened. Results will be determined by the list and offer.

Card Decks

In the last few years, the card deck has evolved as a popular form of mailing. The card deck mailing began as a cooperative form of mailing with

Illustration 7-12: A card deck.

several marketers sharing the cost of production and mailing. It is still a cost-effective promotional format. Today, many multiple-product companies use card decks as a form of catalog and preclude other companies from participating in their mailing.

A card deck is a collection of 3 x 5 cards gathered in a wrap, bound together or placed in an envelope. Each card is a stand-alone sales-and-response device offering to sell or provide information about a product or service. Each participant in the card deck pays a fixed fee for each card in the deck. This form of mailing has proven to be very effective for several types of business mailers when evaluated on a cost-per-inquiry or cost-per-sale basis.

The marketer supplies either camera-ready art in the sizes specified by the printer/mailer, an electronic file of the same material, or printed pieces in sizes specified by the mailer.

Co-Ops

A card deck is a type of co-operative mailing organized by a printer/mailer to generate a profit. Another form of co-operative marketing is when two or more marketers get together to share expenses and lower the cost of marketing to a common market.

This approach has become common in the travel and entertainment markets. Airlines, hotels, and car rental companies will often get together and promote their individual products in a joint mailing. They may even share offers or the mailing piece with the creative effort unified to improve the overall impression of the mailing package.

The reduced cost and improved results of this type of marketing is being repeated in other markets. Companies dealing in the same vertical markets are beginning to work together to improve their promotional position. For example, service contractors, equipment suppliers, and finance companies will all promote in the same package.

Inserts

Inserts are more a process than a format. The process is when one business uses another business publication or product fulfillment vehicle to carry its promotion. This process delivers the first company's offer to recipients of the host's product. Inserts are most frequently used in the consumer application in which a promotional flyer is inserted in the newspaper. Another application is placing promotions in invoices for your credit cards and utility services. A fundamental difference between a co-op mailing and an insert is that the inserter will pay a fee to the mailer. This fee will be in addition to mail costs and preparation of the mailing material.

This same approach is being used in selling to other businesses. Insurance companies will allow non-competing companies to insert flyers in their mailing packages. The frequent-flyer program mailings from the airlines are often filled with inserts.

The insert process can generate cost-effective leads and sales. However, it can also be uncontrollable and unreliable. For example, if you're paying to have your product promotion inserted in another company's product packages, you are relying on the inserter's shipping department. The insert program in this case is an additional duty for which the shipper's production people are not normally compensated.

Insert programs can be limited in scope. The customer list of most businesses is limited in size. This type of a program may not achieve the contacts you want.

Letter "Grams"

The now unfamiliar yellow format of the Western Union Telegram has high delivery and readership for markets over 50 years of age because telegrams were the original important or urgent format for delivering information. This format has been copied, expanded, and used by many mailers to achieve a variety of objectives. All of the objectives capitalized on the opening and reading rate of this format.

Inserting a brochure decreases its effectiveness because it makes it more of a letter package. Copy is generally computer generated on continuous form colored stock.

Copy for this format is written in an abrupt form in order to simulate the by-the-word cost of a telegram.

This format, which once ensured high readership, is now experiencing a reduction in readership due to the age of those that recognize the format.

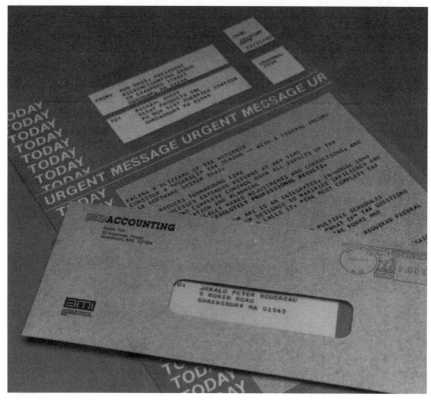

Illustration 7-13: A Letter "Gram".

Catalogs

Since catalogs are a unique way to sell products, this form of direct mail is covered in-depth in Chapter 8.

Frequency

Successful salespeople will tell you one of the keys to their success is that they never let go of a qualified prospect. They constantly stay in contact with known qualified prospects through personal contact, telephone selling, and the mail. The salesperson believes that over time the prospect will understand their product or service and will ultimately agree to investigate further. The concept of repetitive contact is also highly effective in direct marketing techniques.

Frequently in business-to-business selling, products can be sold only when the customer or prospect has an immediate need. A demand cannot be created in all cases. For example, if you are selling light bulbs and the prospect has just purchased a three month supply, you want to position your company and products to be the alternative the prospect considers the *next* time they are acquiring light bulbs.

Consumable products will often only be acquired when there is a need within the company. Sustain your marketing effort so you will be on the prospect's mind when the purchase decision is being made. Being thought of at the time of the purchase decision does not guarantee an order, but not being thought of guarantees no order! In fact, the selling of consumable products is a major area of business-to-business direct marketing today. Consumables generally carry margins and volumes too low to support the use of a field sales force. The challenge is to be in front of the prospects when they are making a buying decision.

If you are selling a capital product which is acquired infrequently, the decision process is prolonged. Successful salespeople of capital products use frequency techniques to move the prospect through the decision process. They *condition* the prospect to move closer to their product. People cannot grasp many concepts at one time. A frequency or conditioning program will allow the salesperson to gradually move the prospect through the selling process.

The lessons the salesperson has learned through experience about multiple contacts and frequency should be applied in direct marketing. The promotional approach you use may vary depending on what you are selling. However, the concept of frequency and multiple contacts will improve results.

To gauge frequency, evaluate cost versus the results achieved. In face-to-face selling, you can't measure the effect of multiple contacts. Because every salesperson does their own thing, you may never know the detail of the contacts. You do know they occurred, but you don't know when, how, or the ultimate results of each contact.

Direct marketing allows you to control the contact, content, method used, and measurability of each contact made. With this in mind, you can continue to contact a customer or prospect until the frequency does not provide a return on the investment.

There are several different issues related to frequency:

- The number of times you contact a prospect

- The length of time between contacts

- The format of the contact

There is no magic formula to determine how frequently to contact a customer or prospect, or how much time to allow between contacts. Each situation is unique. During the planning phase, determine the level of investment you can make in acquiring a lead and/or a sale. Your algorithm, how you measure your program for required response, will dictate the success you require for each contact.

The format of your contact will vary. However, we suggest you continually test your most successful promotion against any new format. In capital goods selling, it may be worthwhile to develop three different formats delivered over a three-month period. On the other hand, catalogers have found that they can mail the same catalog with a new cover to the same group 14 times per year and still get acceptable results on the last mailing.

The key to determining the effect of frequency is to test. You can perform multiple, small tests fairly inexpensively when you combine mail and telemarketing follow-up. You can gain readable results in small samples. To effectively measure the results of frequency you will probably require the use of a marketing database.

Each contact you make will condition the prospect to have a better understanding of your company and its products. The conditioning process can be particularly helpful if the prospect is part of a decision-making team. You may even consider mailing to a number of contacts within a single company to help sell your products.

The sales force has learned that people cannot absorb a lot of different points at one time. Salespeople will frequently focus on a key point in each of their contacts. Hopefully, they are relating the features of their products to the benefits that the prospect will enjoy.

Direct Mail Formats

Package	Components	Cost/Piece
Business Letter - 1st Class	POE, PLTR, BRE, PRD, #, BR	$1.50
Promotional Letter - Bulk	WOE, LTR, PBRC, #, BR	$1.00
9 x 12	WOE, LTR, PBRC, #, BR	$1.50
Self-mailer	BR, PBRC, #	$.90
Invitation	POE, INV, RD, #, BRE	$.95
Double Postcard	BR, PBRC, #	$.50
Postcard	BR, #	$.50
Newsletter	BR, #	$.75
Catalog	BR, RD, #	$.80

The listed formats are estimates and can vary substantially based on your approach. The cost-per-piece estimates, which are delivered prices and include, package, list, production and postage can be helpful in planning and estimating direct mail programs.

BR=Brochure	**BRC=Business Reply Card**
BRE=Business Reply Envelope	**INV=Invitation**
LTR=Non-personalized Letter	**PBRC=Personalized Business Reply Card**
PLTR=Personalized Letter	**POE=Personalized Outer Envelope**
PRD=Personalized Response Device	**RD=Response Device**
WOE=Window Outer Envelope	**#=Phone Number**

Illustration 7-14: Direct mail formats.

Your multiple contacts should also stress a limited series of points. Don't try to take a prospect completely through a complex product and all of its benefits in one mailing. Focus on the primary benefit that will help the prospect relate to your product. Don't lose sight of your objective: to create a lead or an order. If you awaken desire and convince the prospect there is a need, you don't have to fully explain all of the features and run the risk of confusion. Use frequency to help educate, but don't forget to continually ask for the order.

There are some promotions that, by their very nature, are frequency programs. These programs use the formats discussed earlier but require more than one contact.

- **Continuity programs**: As the name implies, these programs use continual or ongoing contacts to a group of customers or prospects. Book or tape clubs and magazine subscriptions are examples of this type of program. The definition of this type of program requires that the marketer continually contact the prospect or customer; the frequency and type of contact may vary.

- **Catalogs**: The economics of catalogs demonstrate that their profits come from the follow-up of catalog sales. A catalog marketer will frequently break-even or lose money on the first catalog sale, in order to acquire that customer for future programs.

- **Newsletters**: These can be sent to prospects or customers but are not often used for direct marketing. If you are using a newsletter or periodic contact to your marketplace, it should be used to help sell products and services. Newsletters are an excellent opportunity to use frequency to your advantage.

- **Frequent-user programs**: These are the loyalty programs. To be effective, you will want to frequently tell your prospects about their accrued benefits and the opportunities available for additional usage.

- **Showmanship mailings or super-premiums**: This form of dimensional mailing is so expensive you are compelled to follow-up the original mailing with additional, less costly contacts.

Schedule

There are a number of factors that have to be considered when planning and scheduling a direct mail program. The most obvious is the time necessary to execute a program. Illustration 7-14 shows a schedule of rough time estimates needed to move through a mailing project. This 14-week schedule shows the steps to implement a program. Your actual time frames will depend on your own program and the capabilities of the vendors you select.

Campaign planning and development is covered in Chapter Two. It is critical that you spend enough time developing a written plan. If you move directly to the creative step without planning, you may exclude proper list and offer development. Without these two elements, the creative execution will probably not achieve your objectives.

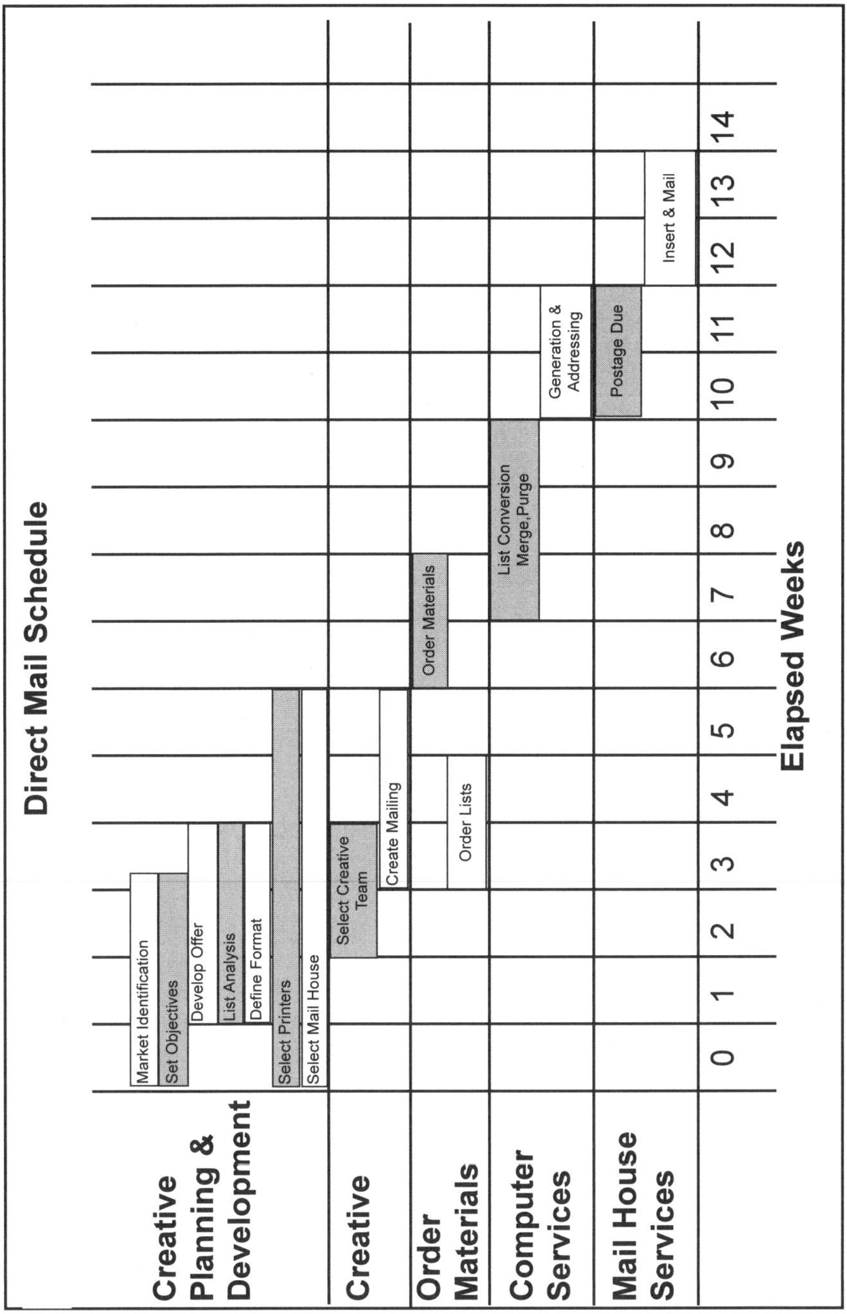

Illustration 7-15: Direct Mail Schedule.

Creative execution is covered indepth in Chapter Five. Your creative staff or outside creative vendor should have a working knowledge of the capabilities of your computer service and your mail house. It is quite possible to create direct mail packages that cannot be assembled by the mail house's machines. This means that the mailing may have to be assembled by hand, causing time delays and substantial increases in mail house charges.

You should do a complete list analysis prior to ordering your lists. Since 50% of the success of the direct mail program depends on the list, you should be comfortable with the available lists before finalizing your target audience. When you are ready to order lists, be sure to provide written instructions to the list vendors including the specifications on list variables plus the technical requirements of your computer service company. There are far too many variables in list ordering not to document your instructions.

Printed materials may be ordered from several printers. There are three major types of printers:

- Continuous form printers. Check with your computer service to see whether they use continuous forms or sheet fed materials.

- Commercial printers that print from one color to full color materials. These printers will print brochures and other non-continuous form materials to insert in the mailing.

- Envelope printers that provide the specialized printing necessary for creating envelopes. Typically, this printer will have the longest lead time for delivery, especially if you order custom envelopes. Beware of envelope lead times.

Computer-generation and mail house service may be offered by a single vendor. More and more mail houses are providing computer-generation services. If you are planning to do a merge/purge, query your mail house to see if they have this capability.

After the mail has dropped, request a Postal Form 3602 if you mailed standard class or a Form 3606 if you mailed first class. These forms, prepared by the mail house and then verified by the post office, are your receipt and proof of the mail quantity. Verify that the actual quantity mailed is consistent with the materials and names you provided and the postage you paid.

The Lead Generation Letter—Six Steps for Better Results

By Mark Mancini, President
Mancini Creative
64 South Main Street
Medford, NJ 08055
(609)654-7700 FAX: (609)657-7709 Email: mmancini@voicenet.com

A good direct marketing letter is a good direct marketing letter, right? Well...not really. Treating a lead generation letter in the same way as a direct sell (1-step) letter is a common mistake made by both inexperienced and experienced marketers alike. While there are certainly many similarities between the two relating to the most basic rules of good direct marketing copy, there are some striking differences you'll need to understand to get the most from your lead generation mailings

Use the following six-point outline while writing your next lead generation letter, or use it as a checklist to rate and edit letters you've already written.

1) What Are You Offering?

This can be a fundamental pitfall, and it will destroy any chance at success unless you deal with this question properly. Remember, you are not just out delivering information, you're trying to get qualified response leads. That means you want prospects to write, call or fax you their names and addresses, etc. They won't do it for the heck of it—you'll have to give them a good reason!

Most often, inexperienced direct marketers will offer "more information." This is usually a weak offer, (although, it should be noted, your response will be highly qualified). In essence, you're asking your prospect to raise their hand and ask you to sell him something. Most people are not going to go out of their way to help you sell them something. You will lose some measure of qualified response with an information offer. There are better ways to get your message into your prospects' hands and still maintain the maximum response.

The best offers promise some intrinsic usefulness or value to the prospect, independent of the information you want to convey. As an offer for a computer hardware company several years ago, we created an inexpensive piece specifically designed to help our prospect determine the best computer configuration for their needs. The resulting piece had a fundamental, objective measure of value for anyone considering the purchase of a new PC. (And more importantly, it held no value for anyone not considering the purchase of a new PC—making it an excellent offer from the standpoint of 'qualifying' our response.) The prospect, whether they decided to purchase our product or not, saw value in better understanding the available options. For our part, we received three benefits: first, we now knew any respondent was almost certainly considering a new PC purchase, or the piece would have had no value to them; second, we now had at least a measure of relationship with this individual for further marketing efforts; third, we were able to select the parameters and considerations on which that prospect based their purchase decision. (We also shipped a new product catalog and sales letter along with the 'objective' planning guide!)

As you can see, we were still able to get our information into the prospect's hands. The prospects were still highly qualified. And, because of the perceived independent value of the offer, we didn't sacrifice any valuable gross response!

2) What Do You Want Your Prospect to Do Immediately After Reading Your Letter?

If you don't know what you want your prospect to do, then they won't know either. Figure out exactly what you want the prospect to do—and come right out and tell them to do it! "Send or call 1-800-xxx-xxxx right now to receive your..." If your call-to-action is confusing or weak, your response will be weak as well!

3) Write in a 1-to-1 Personal Style.
Use "You, Your, You'll, You're" often—Use "We, We'll, Us, Our" as little as possible.

This is a letter—a personal communication between you and one other person—don't make it sound like an ad! Direct mail is an expensive form of advertising (per impression), don't defeat the purpose by sounding like a radio announcer. Remember, the object is to use personal influence to convince one person at a time. View your communication this way. Don't write to impress, write to communicate. Save the big words, long sentences and complex concepts for your next job interview!

4) Don't Tell Them What You Want Them to Know!

Tell them only what they need to know to do what you want them to do! There are tons of great things you know about your company and its products and services, and you'd probably like to tell them all to anyone who will listen. The fact is, nobody cares, (I know I don't). They only care about the stuff they can use. If you bury "the stuff they can use" in the middle of all "the stuff you want them to know" they won't find "the stuff they can use." They'll simply throw the whole stinking mess into the trash. Don't give them more than they need to know to do what you want them to do. Remember your prospects don't like you, your company—or the horse you rode in on. (Well, maybe they do—but don't bet your response on it!)

5) Don't Tell Your Prospects the Whole Story!

Remember, the object is to get your most qualified prospects to respond and identify themselves. The best way to do this is to raise questions that only your best buyers will find compelling, and then tactfully tell them that they can find answers to these and other related questions when they respond, (again, telling them what they need to know to do what you want them to do).

For example: if your assignment was to generate new leads for a consumer gardening catalog, you might raise questions in your letter like this one: "There are more than 20 varieties of tomatoes in our new 1999 catalog, and four are brand new this year! See these and more than 700 other varieties of fruits, bulbs, vegetables and trees when you send for your FREE 1999 (Brand name here) catalog!"

You'll notice, we never had to actually 'ask' a formal question, we simply raised one in our prospect's mind. More importantly, the question we've raised is of no importance to a non-gardener. Only an avid gardener, and therefore a qualified lead for our catalog, would find this missing information worth responding for!

6) The 'Long Copy' vs. 'Short Copy' Rules Do Not Apply, (Whatever they Are)!

This is lead generation—you aren't asking for a buying decision—you just want potential prospects to raise their hands and tell you they're interested in your message. If you've considered the point explained in item #4 of this section carefully, you are not likely to require a lot of words to effectively do the job. Long copy...short copy...at this point in today's over saturated markets, the rules don't hold up particularly well anyway. When you've said what you need to say, your letter is long enough.

Where To Start Developing Your Direct Mail Promotion

The biggest problem we have when designing a direct mail package is where to begin. Your instincts often tell you to begin with the letter since that is the element of the package you are going to sign.

If you are the product manager you have a tendency to begin with the support brochure since that is where you demonstrate how your product will be used.

The designers want to begin with the layout. And the direct marketing production manager wants to begin with the dimensions of the piece.

You first need to develop an offer and select the list you want to promote. These will be the most important ingredients in your direct marketing effort. As we have often said, there are four elements in a direct marketing promotion. The percentages indicate the relative importance each of these will play on the ultimate success of the effort.

- List   50%
- Offer   25%
- Format 15%
- Copy   10%

Once we have identified the list and offer, we have found that the best place to actually begin creating the direct mail piece is with the reply device or response form.

Write down what action you want your targets to take when they have decided to respond. Don't worry about the copy at this point. Make sure you understand what action you want taken and how you plan to deal with the response. You might want a direct order by mail, phone, or web site. You might want the target to answer several questions that aid your qualification process. You may be interested in referral generation.

Whatever you expect to happen, you must be clear *before* you begin to create the mailer. With a clear understanding of the action you want the responder to take, your creative effort will be more effective. If you are communicating the concept for a direct marketing program to other creative people, it is even more important that you are very clear about what you expect to have happen. If you are not clear to your creative staff, they may develop a promotion that doesn't meet your expectations and requirements. Sometimes the creative staff may develop terrific ideas that don't necessarily drive the response you expect.

Each element of your package should carry your offer and tell the reader how to respond. The response form can often be the most important element of the mailing package because the prospect will be using it independently of the rest of the package. Many times the response form may be all that the prospect retains hoping to complete it at a later time or referring it to someone else for action.

Many companies often forget the importance of the response device and spend most creative effort and dollars on the brochure or letter. In many programs there is more creative time spent on the outer envelope than on the response device.

As you create your direct marketing plan, spend some time documenting your offer. As the creative process is moving along, keep the offer close at hand and make sure you are accomplishing what you set out to do.

Review the response form first and be sure it tells you to respond to your offer. If it is unclear, don't go any further until the response form meets the objectives you set for the promotion. You can avoid a lot of costly rewrites and creative effort if you ensure the response form calls the prospect to the action you want. The rest of the mailing will follow the response form.

A web-based response form must also fit this criteria, providing a clear process for responding to a specific offer while referring to the program or mail piece that drove the response.

Direct Mail Summarized

Direct mail is the primary tool in business-to-business direct marketing. Direct mail is used as a fulfillment vehicle for other media and formats in direct marketing promotional efforts. It can't be overlooked and should be an important part of your campaign strategy.

Once you have established the list and offer you plan to use, you should begin to consider the format and copy to deliver the message. Direct mail is flexible and the most testable of all media. It is easy to control and to evaluate.

You must have a well-defined set of objectives before you create your direct mail package. The personality of the individual you're trying to reach can substantially alter the creative strategy you choose. Although using existing materials may save money, the objective and target of the direct mail program will probably preclude their use.

The offer and format you use with your audience, will dictate the copy and graphics you use in your direct mail package. A photograph depicts reality, and an illustration depicts a dream. The combination can be an exciting visual experience for the reader and an effective support vehicle for the package.

Whatever components the direct mail package contains, each should be able to stand alone. If the package components become separated, you don't want to lose the selling opportunity. The flow of the mail package should continually ask for the order. The old sales adage "close early and close often" applies to direct mail.

The target audience and offer may dictate the use of a special direct mail format, such as a dimensional. These promotions are more expensive, typically take longer to implement, and have greater success in breaking through to the target. Carefully control and test each element of your direct mail program. When working with a small universe, direct mail coupled with telemarketing can be an effective combination to test and evaluate the success of different direct mail formats.

Multiple contacts and the use of a frequency program can significantly increase the effectiveness of your direct mail efforts. Evaluate the techniques being used by the salespeople in your industry. Frequent contact will probably be the key to the success of the better salespeople. Direct marketing results also improve when used in a sustained program. Evaluate, test, and measure the effectiveness of multiple contacts.

The Achilles' heel of direct mail is the time it takes to execute a program. It is not unusual for a program to take 10 to 14 weeks to develop and implement. Trying to short-cut the time frame can negatively affect a program's quality and increase its cost.

Direct mail is an important and dynamic direct marketing promotional format. You will use direct mail whether you intend to or not. If you plan your direct mail program, it will be more successful.

Chapter Eight:
Business-to-Business Catalogs

Business Catalogs Defined

The business-to-business catalog is probably one of the most widely used and least understood options of the many business-to-business media. While there are approximately 6,000 consumer catalogs in the United States, there is no definitive source for how many business-to-business catalogs exist.

Let's establish a definition of a catalog:

> *A catalog is any device that offers a potential buyer (customer or prospect) the choice of more than one product or service at one time in the same promotion.*

This definition differentiates catalogs from solo direct mail, where only a single product or service is offered. One example of the difference between a catalog promotion and a direct mail effort is the multi-magazine sweepstakes offered by several subscription agency companies. This promotion offers the purchaser the opportunity to acquire a number of magazine subscriptions in one promotion. While the magazine publisher uses direct mail to solicit a potential purchaser to subscribe or renew their subscription, the catalog mailing offers a number of product alternatives to the purchaser.

A catalog does not always have to look like a fancy, full color magazine. Card decks are a form of catalog marketing. Card Decks are a form of catalog marketing. This is where many dissimilar offerings are printed on separate cards and gathered together in an envelope or cellophane wrapper and mailed to a potential purchaser. The mailing provides ease of response because each card carries its own business reply device.

A catalog is a shopping vehicle while direct mail is a targeted sales call. Any time you gather several products together in any format, you should call it a catalog. Most companies prepare some type of sales literature. It may be in the form of product fact sheets for each item offered by the company. If the company provides a vehicle to gather these product fact sheets together, such as a binder, they have in essence created a catalog. If the company doesn't provide the vehicle to gather the material together, the field sales people are probably performing the function themselves just to organize their presentations. Many companies are in the catalog business and don't even know it.

You may not be mailing your catalog, but instead have it delivered by your salespeople. This is the most expensive delivery system for your catalog, so you may want to re-examine your catalog effort.

We worked with a company that was generating sales through a catalog and didn't even know they were in the catalog business. The company sold office furniture designed for computers. The company used a field sales force that called on end users and sold the potential purchaser on the benefits of their products. The salesperson carried an extensive set of promotional materials, including a series of product fact sheets on each of the company's products.

A fairly industrious member of the company's advertising staff thought it would be helpful to send out product sheets to the company's customers and prospects who had inquired about its products as a result of trade advertising. Over a period of six years, 1976 to 1982, the sales from this direct mail (catalog) effort grew from $0 to over $45 million. This direct response sales growth greatly contributed to the success of the company since it experienced overall growth in sales to over $80 million.

Since the company's accounting systems assigned all sales to a specific sales territory and field representative, the sales people were making great commissions. This accounting system masked the effectiveness of the catalog operation; it appeared that all of the sales were coming from the salespeople because the company didn't even know it had a catalog operation.

In fact, the sales force wasn't very effective when you isolated the sales made directly. We suggested that the company reexamine its approach to catalog sales and establish a reasonable measurement and control system. The company now has an established catalog group with a mission and budget. The catalog now carries the company's normal merchandise as well as items purchased outside when it proves profitable.

The acquisition of additional products to sell through your catalog can increase the profitability of the catalog operation. Once you make the decision to have a catalog as a profit center, you may want to consider allowing it to grow by selling any product that makes sense because it is profitable. But first a basic question has to be resolved: Should the catalog exist as a profit center or as a support vehicle for other sales activities?

The answer to this question lies in the mission of the department that is handling the catalog. Historically, printed materials are within the domain of the advertising department. Because the budget for the catalog is controlled by advertising, a cost center, the catalog is typically viewed as a cost item.

Two things happen when you send out a catalog:

1) You affect your current customers. We are assuming that you will mail the catalog to your existing customers, which we strongly recommend -- this should be your most profitable available list.

2) You will generate orders and sales. If you do not intend to sell products, you're doing direct mail advertising or public relations and not direct marketing.

These two activities traditionally have been the province of the sales force. Customer contact and sales are the activities we expect from our field sales force. Based on the functions being performed by the catalog, it seems more appropriate to align the catalog operation with the sales activity than with advertising. Because the catalog operation is also producing revenue, it makes good business sense to convert it to a profit center from its current cost center role. You may even want to consider moving the catalog operation to the sales organization.

Catalog budgeting is very different than traditional sales budgeting. Annual budgets usually allow for a fixed amount of money to be consumed. The consumption of the budget will normally coincide with the end of the fiscal year. If the money is spent sooner, or if more money is spent than the budget allows, the manager responsible is usually penalized. The catalog activity should be budgeted as dynamic activity, similar to a cost of goods accounting concept. If the sales are higher than anticipated, additional dollars should be allowed to increase the promotion of the catalog. The catalog should be allowed to flow with the dynamics of the market.

If the catalog is not successful, the budget should be reduced and moved to other, more successful channels of distribution. Good catalog budgeting should be based on the percentage of sales allowed for promotion through the catalog. If the catalog is very successful and ahead of the plan, additional dollars should be allowed for catalog efforts. If the catalog is less successful, less dollars should be allotted for catalog efforts.

Catalog Missions

In order to properly measure your business catalog, you must understand and develop your catalog's mission.

    1)   The most basic mission a catalog will perform is that of a sales aid; the visual documentation a salesperson uses during a face-to-face sales situation. This documentation can take the form of printed material, audiovisual aids or even videotape. If the sales representative is giving the prospect the opportunity to purchase more than one product through the material, consider it a catalog. This form of catalog

activity doesn't require any change to your existing organization. If your company has not created a sales catalog directly, you can be sure that the sales people have. Each sales person has probably created some type of presentation book as a leave behind after making a face-to-face sales call.

2) Another mission of the catalog is to support a telephone contact with the ultimate objective of spurring a face-to-face contact by a sales representative. This type of catalog is frequently used to help qualify responders from other trade advertising.

Before a prospect or responder becomes a referral, some type of information is normally provided. Generally, more than one product or service is offered in the material sent to the prospect. This means that the material is actually a catalog. This can be counter productive, because the catalog is a shopping vehicle and too much information can actually confuse the prospect. It is similar to the proverbial kid in a candy store with only limited time and money. There are so many options that the kid can't decide what to do. Ultimately, the kid will run out of time and may buy nothing or something just out of desperation to make a decision.

If you confuse your prospect with too much information, you run the risk of the candy store syndrome. Review the information being sent to your prospects. We have seen situations where so many different product sheets and brochures were being mailed, they were actually packed in a box. This volume of material is so overwhelming that the prospect may not read any of the information.

3) The catalog may have the mission to replace the field sales representative in situations where the product sale is relatively small. In other words, the sales potential is too small to warrant wasting a salesperson's time to make a face-to-face sales call or even a telephone contact. These catalogs are most often used in the role of customer support. The most common use for this catalog is to offer purchase of periodic consumable support products to a customer who has made a large capital expenditure.

Computer supplies are a classic example of this type of catalog effort. The sales representative is interested in selling the computer but really doesn't want to spend the time to sell the customer each $20 consumable item needed in the future. This doesn't mean that sales representatives aren't interested in supporting their customers, but rather that selling low-priced consumable items may not be a good use of their time.

This type of selling really works well through a catalog. The catalog frees the time of the salesperson to work on bigger opportunities and allows the vendor company to still generate the revenue from the consumable items. This same approach can work for repair parts, add-on products and even new additional major capital equipment items. This type of catalog is well-suited to provide customers with products and services that enhance your product, even if you don't normally offer these enhancements through your sales force. You can realize additional sales and revenue because:

- Your customers already have credit with you.

- They have a relationship of trust and confidence with you as a vendor.

4) The catalog is used to replace the field or telephone sales representative. This type of catalog is often introduced with the sales force's support, because the company will continue to pay commissions to the sales force even if the sale is consummated via the catalog. When the catalog has become firmly established, the company may decide to reduce or eliminate the commission structure.

The elimination of the sales force channel of product distribution by a catalog must be carefully planned and executed. Customers have to be weaned from their dependence on the field organization for ordering. Plus, the sales force must be convinced that they can still earn at least the same amount or more once commissions are reduced or eliminated for these products.

In short, the field sales force can make or break the catalog effort.

These are the basic missions catalogs can be designed to fulfill. A catalog may be used to perform more than one mission at a time.

Another group of catalogs have a different set of mission statements. These missions are not related to the true mission of the catalogs described earlier, but focus on management's desire to use the catalog to perform other functions. Let's look at these peculiar and generally unsuccessful missions:

1) ***Catalogus Junkus***. This is when management decides to take all of the great products the company has made over the last several years, in spite of the fact that they were never sold successfully by the sales force, and put them in a catalog. This mission will cause you to dust off your resume the quickest. Unless you can identify and correct the major reasons why the products didn't sell in the first place, you are guaranteed a disaster. Not only will you need a new position, but your customers will receive a lot of wrong signals about your company being in the "dog product" business.

2) ***Catalogus Maximus***. As the name implies, this catalog will do it all. It will attempt to satisfy certain specific needs of your customers while also being the showcase for everything you make from your largest product to your smallest replacement washer.

You will have created the tome of your company. Properly indexed, this type of catalog can be valuable to you and your customers. You will, however, produce very few of these type catalogs.

First, it seldom will get into print because there is always something new to add to the book, or something that needs to be dropped or changed. Creating new photographs and prices will also cause constant delays in printing this catalog. This tome involves every product manager's sign off and quickly becomes the nemesis of your department.

Second, the tome catalog is very expensive. When management reviews the cost of producing this type of catalog, you will have a great deal of trouble justifying the investment. This catalog will serve as an advertising vehicle to help the sales force sell products. It will be difficult to track sales specifically to the tome catalog. Return on investment will be very difficult to evaluate.

3) ***Catalogus Mistakus***. This catalog is generated without any support from the organization. It has no budget or management commitment. You can generally squeeze a few bucks from various sources. Even if the catalog is produced, it will rarely succeed. If management doesn't provide financial support to the catalog effort, moral support is probably also lacking. As you generate orders, there will probably be difficulties with shipping and billing.

It is very difficult to develop a catalog and have it succeed by trying to squeeze resources from other areas of the company. Each person who is asked to contribute to the catalog effort will be asked to participate by sacrificing something from their own primary areas of responsibility. It is possible to succeed and become a hero, but the odds are against it.

Consumer and Business Catalogs

Business-to-business catalogs have increased tremendously in the last few years. Many catalogs are being established completely independent of the sales force. The field sales force is intentionally left out of the development process. The mission of this catalog is to create customers that will only be serviced by phone or mail. These types of catalogs have proliferated as the cost of selling face-to-face has increased.

The growth of the consumer catalog arena has helped to increase interest and activity in using catalogs in the business arena. This propensity to order products through the mail based on a picture and a brief description has flowed over into business.

The business catalog is proliferating because it may be the only place to get information on certain products and services. For consumers, the retail store employee traditionally has been helpful in explaining and demonstrating the products you want to buy. With the increasing use of technology in business and the lower costs of high technology products, business people typically have no one to explain products. There are not enough salespeople to satisfy the questions being asked by all levels of business.

Business oriented retail stores, like computer stores or office supply stores, are frequently staffed by little more than cash takers. Typically there are not enough information givers available to satisfy every question, simply because the number of products available in the business oriented store is so large that no one person can know every product.

As in the consumer catalog, the business catalog must provide plenty of clearly written information about the products. The payment and return policy offered by the business catalog should be as powerful as any consumer catalog. One of the primary reasons attributed to the initial and sustained growth of the Sears and Roebuck catalog was its unwavering policy of a no questions asked money-back guarantee. It allowed the customer to purchase products with little concern about quality or applicability. The same kinds of techniques will help the business catalog become effective.

In both realms, the customer must perceive that the products offered are not readily available elsewhere in order for the catalog to succeed. They must at least perceive that the product is a good value and that it will be easier to purchase through the mail than other methods. Buying toothpaste by mail is not normally a cost-effective way to distribute the product, unless you can sell it in quantity. Most people won't buy and store large quantities of toothpaste when it is easily available at a reasonable price. In business, we may only need one printer ribbon at a time, but we are not uncomfortable buying 12 or more at a time. Businesses are fairly comfortable carrying an inventory of consumable products while consumers are not.

As we discussed in Chapter one, consumers are spending their own money and are very concerned about quality and price. The business person is spending company funds, and although price and quality are issues, time and availability can be even more important.

The major difference between consumer and business catalogs is the basic design. The consumer catalog is designed as a shopping vehicle. The design is developed to interest the reader to make several trips through this paper and picture store. The business catalog is designed to be a reference document. It should be well-indexed so that the purchaser does not have to shop through the book in order to find the item they are looking for. The difference between the two types of catalogs is beginning to change, but it will take time.

Consumer catalogs must develop a style that is attractive, in the graphic and order-generating sense. The catalog is competing with retail stores that offer many similar, if not the same, products. As business catalogs grow more numerous and competitive, they too must develop an attractiveness that is enticing to the potential buyer.

Probably the best way to present your business is with an editor's eye. Don't look at yourself as a supplier of widgets requiring an inventory of 1,200 units. Consider yourself a publisher of a special interest magazine that your readers will enjoy reviewing. You want your magazine to be a book that will deliver some enjoyment to your readers.

The editorial approach uses both copy and graphics to give information that is helpful and interesting. Your reader can move through the book quickly to get an overview of the contents through headlines and graphics. They can go deeper into the book for more details on the products being offered when time allows or the need arises.

Consumer catalogs have a shelf life dictated by the consumer's interest in the products and the attractiveness of the book. Business catalogs often enjoy a much longer shelf life if the buyer has perceived the need for the products being offered and is attracted by the presentation of the book. Research has revealed that most business catalog buyers keep a primary and secondary catalog by type of products the catalog offers. If your catalog can attract the attention of the buyer, it may become the first or second catalog retained by the potential buyer.

The high and long retention rates of business catalogs provide powerful reasons to try to offer complete product lines in the catalog. If your customer wants an obscure item you dropped from your catalog, that customer could go to a competitor's catalog and it will replace your catalog as their primary or secondary catalog. However, the full-line concept can take a company down a dead-end street if unprofitable items are maintained in lieu of current, more popular items.

Consumer catalogs add and drop products all the time. This keeps their books fresh and new to their customers. Consumer products have a high and fast fatigue rate because they tend to become oversold and therefore must be replaced by new items that will cause the inventory to turn. On the other hand, business books should not drop a product just because it is not pulling its space right now. Only customer research into sales patterns for each product will tell you if a product is turning into a dog or if it is just in a sales valley.

Editorial Techniques

In order to keep the same products interesting, here are some editorial techniques you might experiment with:

1) <u>Personalize the content</u>. Present the products and their descriptions like you are a salesperson talking to a buyer. Don't be afraid to include pictures and information about the people that are supporting your catalog. We are all comforted when we feel we can pick up the phone and call someone if we need help.

2) <u>Repeat the name of the company on every spread.</u> This will enable the reader to identify the source of the products. This is a standard technique used in the publishing industry. People who requisition an item through their purchasing department often attach a copy of a picture of the item they want. If your company name is not included in the copy, the purchasing agent may not turn to you as a supplier. (Note: Even if your name is visible, it may not guarantee you will get the order, but it helps get you on the bid list.)

3) <u>Include sidebar stories</u>. General information that might pertain to a product or group of products or a company philosophy can be highlighted. A sidebar story is then used to emphasize the point and develop a theme just as this technique is used in magazines.

4) <u>Feature products</u>. Feature certain products on a two-page spread to draw attention to that product and to provide a variety of rhythm throughout the book.

5) <u>Group products by theme</u>. Grouping the products by theme like a newspaper does in its various sections will add continuity to the thoughts of your reader.

6) <u>Use headlines</u>. Use headlines to call attention to the product groups or new products.

The Business Catalog Process

There is no easy track to follow when putting the catalog together. There are, however, some steps which follow others on a linear basis. That is, you cannot go to the next step until you finish the previous one. But there are some steps that can be accomplished simultaneously. We will discuss all of these steps so that you will understand what needs to be done to get a catalog in the mail.

The first step in the creation of a catalog is the most important. It is the conceptual step which provides the foundation for the future development of the entire catalog. So that a great deal of time is not wasted later, convene a meeting of all the managers that will be involved with and responsible for the catalog. This group should agree on the theme and image that the catalog should project as well as the objective statement of the catalog.

This first step is important because as the development of the catalog progresses, it is increasingly difficult to make changes. Changes to the catalog are much more expensive than the execution of original ideas since they are generally executed on rush schedules. If all of the key players are not involved at the outset, changes become the norm rather than the exception as each manager not present at the conception stage tries to redirect the objectives of the catalog.

This group should understand the budget for the creation of the catalog as well as its profit and loss objectives. The conceptual committee sets the strategy for the catalog so that the organization cannot play its normal games of redirection for the benefit of different self-interest groups within the company. Here are some examples of strategic statements this group might prepare:

- Catalog Z is being developed on a modest budget of $50,000 in order to provide support to the field sales force, in the sales of products that cannot justify a personal face-to-face call. This catalog will be developed primarily from existing product information and photography. All sales from Catalog Z will be credited to the individual sales representative's area.

  Sales for Catalog Z are forecast at $3,000,000 with a contribution to marketing and profit of $1,000,000 based on our dealer wholesale pricing of 66.6%.

- Catalog M is being developed as a direct sales catalog with a budget of $200,000. This catalog will represent our state-of-the-art products in order to generate sales from current and new customers. New product photography will be taken whenever existing photography is not in keeping with the overall design concept of the catalog.

  Sales representatives will receive commissions on sales they make as a result of leads rather than sales generated by the catalog. Direct sales will not be commissionable.

  Sales for Catalog M are forecast at $10,000,000 over the 12 months following mailing with a contribution to marketing, and a profit of $5,000,000 based on dealer wholesale pricing.

These are highly abbreviated statements and financial projections. They are intended to provide a basis for the preparation of a more detailed business plan. These abbreviated definitions are excellent tools to communicate the mission and plan of the catalog to others within the company and senior management. The preparation of a mission statement is also politically important; its existence makes it more difficult to have the strategy or budget changed.

The next step is determining the space allocation for the catalog. Each product manager is sure their product line is the most important to the company.

There are several ways to set parameters for the usage of space within the catalog:

1) <u>Profitability</u>. Feature those products which provide you the greatest profit per unit of sale.

2) <u>Visibility</u>. Feature those products which generate the highest number of units sold per year.

3) <u>Importance</u>. Feature products which are the hub of all other sales. That is if you sell the hub products, you will sell the spoke and wheel products.

4) <u>Appeal</u>. Feature products that will keep readers interested so they will shop the catalog and see other products.

5) <u>Dogs</u>. *Do not* feature products that are losers. Products that do not sell currently will probably not sell when offered in a catalog. This argument does not apply to products that have not had visibility.

6) <u>Overstock</u>. *Do not* feature products that you happen to have a lot of unless you are offering them as a loss leader. Manufacturing may have overproduced an item because they were easy to produce. If an overstocked item is a dog, do not feature it, even if you are going to reduce the price.

7) <u>New</u>. Feature products that are new to your markets, not just new to you. Your markets do not really care if you have a new product that everyone else has had for a year, unless you can offer a benefit that differentiates your new product from the competition's.

8) <u>Weighting</u>. This process incorporates all of the above based on whatever qualitative and/or quantitative information is available. Each product is given a weight on a scale of 1 to 10, or 1 to 100 (you decide the measurement system). Each product's rating will influence the position and size of display it has in the catalog. This approach gives your designers the greatest level of information when they are laying out the catalog.

A similar technique, used frequently by book publishers, is to assign every product a "tier" designation. Except for features, a product will fall within the "A," "B," or "C" tier. Each tier represents a specific amount of space. This method gives precise guidelines for both copywriters and designers.

The term feature, as it is used above, refers to giving a product more room on a page or on a spread than the other products. It is boring to a reader to shop a catalog where everything pictured is the same size. Give the reader some graphic variety in your presentation. If you do not select the weighting approach for all the products of your catalog, use a modified version of this approach to give your designers the relative graphic value of each item you have selected to feature.

9) <u>Mission.</u> If the purpose of the catalog is to sell lower priced items to customers, don't feature the key products and mention the lower priced items. Show what you want to sell.

When you are allocating space, it is easier to identify your featured products first. Once these are identified and specified, the remainder of the catalog can be designed.

Creative Process

The most frustrating and time-consuming part of creating a catalog is dealing with the general lack of understanding by non-creative management regarding the processes that must take place. This lack of understanding causes most tardy catalogs.

Once the strategy of a catalog is established and agreed to by everyone, catalog creation becomes largely mechanical. Designers and artists are technical crafts people that engineer the desired theme and image into a catalog. While the artists normally prefer to put one item per page, they can design in whatever format they are instructed. You will direct them to achieve your objectives within a specific number of pages and budget.

If you are not specific with the designer and artist, you will actually hurt the end product, your catalog. With complete information, the artists can create your book within your guidelines. Any lack of up-front information and direction from you will generally result in a catalog that is late and over budget. Initial vagueness will lead you to be continually revising or changing the creative concepts delivered by the crafts people. Write complete instructions to your designer and artists and include your concept and objectives for the catalog. Also include the budget and size limitations you have established for the catalog.

At the same time, you must also manage the product managers to ensure that they supply product information and camera-ready samples according to the catalog production schedule. When this is not done, the artists and designers cannot do their work. They can design leaving empty spaces for products not yet specified only to find out when these products are finally specified, they cannot be shown in the space provided.

When the catalog 'evolves' as the creative process is being performed, as opposed to following a pre-established plan, inevitably a page, a spread, or an entire section of the catalog must be redesigned. If photography has already begun on the known products, it could be necessary to re-shoot entire sections, because a product that was originally shot is wrong for the revised catalog. This normally causes time delays and cost overruns.

Incomplete catalog definition is a simple example of only one area that irritates the creative staff. The following list will give you an idea of some other pitfalls you might be able to avoid when you manage the overall catalog process:

1) *Product managers are allowed to write copy.* Product managers should be good at their job of evaluating and selecting products. They may even have a good understanding of the market and marketing requirements. However, they are typically feature-oriented or specification-oriented and are not benefit/sales-oriented. As we discussed earlier, people respond to benefits, not features. In addition, product managers typically have no professional experience in writing or selling. They should not be allowed to control the copy or creative concept in the catalog.

2) *Products are not selected and made available to the creative staff on schedule.* You can't be too specific or too early in providing information to your creative staff. **Put it in writing**.

3) *Samples provided are different than the actual product.* Sometimes buyers and product managers will provide samples that are similar to the product being offered, but are not the actual item. When the item does arrive it can be significantly different than the sample. This can cause a major revision of that product's page or even the entire section.

4) *Only one sample is made available for photography.* If the sample contains a blemish it may have to be photographed in a way that is not consistent with the design of the section. You should supply more than one sample for photography.

5) *Copywriters are not given type size and typeface specifications.* This can frequently cause the copy to be too long or short for the space available for all products throughout the catalog. Make your type decisions before you begin the creative process.

6) *Several photographers are used to expedite the work.* This will cause different lighting presentations or lighting values throughout the catalog. Different lighting values can be disconcerting for your readers, and project less than a high-quality or professional image. Try to limit your photography to one shop.

7) *Manufacturer's supplied photography is used in lieu of original photography.* As we just mentioned, this will yield many varied values of photography. Although you may save on photography expense, the overall quality of your catalog can suffer. We suggest you limit the use of manufacturer's supplied photography.

8) *Blow-ups of 35mm photographs are made larger than 1/4 page.* If you do enlarge a 35mm photo, it may become grainy and fuzzy (two very exacting words). How large you can enlarge a shot depends on the quality of the original photo.

Don't try to use a poor quality enlargement. Re-shoot the item to produce the quality you desire.

9)   *Final color and type are not proofed before you go to press.* This means that you may have to correct your color on the press, the most expensive place to do anything. And, where you have the least control. See a color proof before your catalog goes to press.

10) *The order form is not the first image file completed.* Generally, your catalog printer is not the printer of your order form. Since the order form is the most complicated image to complete, it is often avoided until the 'pretty pictures' are complete. This is a mistake. The order form carries all of the ordering information your customers will need to buy from you. If you complete the order form first, your copywriters will have a chance to use the order form information when they are writing product copy.

Producing the order form also forces you to solve all of your business questions early:

*   credit cards
*   toll-free numbers
*   Internet contact information
*   customer service information
*   shipping and handling charges
*   guarantees
*   taxes

This will improve overall understanding of the catalog for everyone involved.

11) *Customer service is excluded from the creative process.* When you do not include the people that frequently talk to your customers, you are not taking advantage of the visceral feel these people have for your market place. For example, the product manager may feel that an item's color is its most important feature. Your customer service people, however, have learned that your customers are more interested in how this item is packed or the number of units per box. If you

listened to the product manager alone, you would not have shown the key feature your customers are truly concerned about but rather the color array.

12) *Shipping is excluded from the creative process.* This is only a problem if your product managers are not required to provide shipping information as part of their product specifications. If shipping information is not provided, someone from shipping should be involved early in the creative process.

13) *The pre-press vendor and printer are not included early in the process.* If you wait until the catalog is completed before you include your pre-press firm and printer, you are making two mistakes:

1. Their experience and wisdom can save you both time and money.
2. Their involvement creates a cleaner transition between the steps.

Never, never restrict your output vendor from talking to your printer. These professionals will communicate at a level that you may not understand but that is necessary to get the job done right.

When using desktop publishing, make sure you have a team approach that includes the designers, the pre-press and the printer. Technology promises are little consolation when you must become a problem solver between the design and publishing outputs and the printer requirements.

14) *You delegate your responsibility to produce the catalog.* This is the kiss of death. If you do not stay actively involved in the process you will not get a satisfactory result. You may delegate the responsibility to a manager who may not have the authority to keep the process rolling on schedule. This is not to say that you must oversee every detail. You must, however, let the organization know that the catalog has your attention and you expect everyone to give it their full support to meet your schedule.

The creative process includes many aspects of your business and is coupled with a variety of external suppliers. For this reason, it is impossible to outline everything you need to be aware of throughout the ordeal of creating a catalog. The best advice we can give is to encourage you to familiarize yourself with the nuances of every step you will take.

Ask questions and try to anticipate any potential problems in order to prevent them from occurring. Meet with the managers and suppliers that will be involved so you will understand their needs. Be particularly aware of how each participant in the process wants to receive materials. To use a football cliche, you need a "clean hand-off" at each step in the process. If hand-offs are not clean, the down-line manager or supplier will point the finger at the previous step. When the catalog doesn't come out as planned, it is difficult to establish where the problem occurred. In addition, you will not get the catalog in the time frame or quality you anticipated. Don't focus on blame, focus on getting good hand-offs.

Scheduling

There is no magic in any fixed schedule; you can always shorten a time-line with money. A wise man once said that in any creative or production process there are three variables:

- Price
- Speed
- Quality

Pick two of the above. If you buy speed your price goes up and your quality suffers. This is not a mathematical formula; however, it seems to be a heuristic model.

Let's look at the steps you must go through in order to create and print your catalog.

- <u>Product Selection</u> - This step is self explanatory. If you do not have the products you want to sell you cannot begin. The product selection should be complete, or as complete as possible, before you begin the next step.

- List Selection - You cannot begin too early to select your lists.The list you use for direct marketing is the most critical variable in the process. If you haven't selected your list, which identifies the target and market you're selling to, it is impossible to create an effective catalog.

  If you are only mailing to your customer files it is wise to schedule your requirements early with your computer service. If you are renting lists and plan to do a merge/purge, starting early will facilitate your mailing.

  You can order too far in advance due to the rapid aging of rented lists. To avoid getting stuck with an old list, check the update schedule of the lists you want to rent and compare them to your schedule to see which lists you can order and still get the most current update. The earlier you can order a list, the easier it will be to meet your schedule dates.

  Another intrinsic problem to catalog scheduling is that you are always waiting to get more definitive results from the last catalog before you order lists for the next catalog. Do not wait too long. Having your catalog sitting on skids with no one to send it to will not sit well with your boss.

- Printer Selection - When selecting your printer you will become aware of the different catalog sizes you can print, at what price, and with what trade-offs. When you have made your selection, immediately provide your creative staff with the exact specifications of what they must provide to the printer in writing. This fundamental step will prevent many future headaches.

- Layouts - This next step occurs when the copy and graphic teams collaborate to generate rough sketches using pencil or rough graphic design on computer. General outlines of the products, headlines, and blocks of copy will begin to appear. Often this step is created in miniature (approximately 1/8 scale) and is called a *Thumbnail*.

  Desktop technology has greatly reduced the necessity to work in the smaller thumbnail scale. The speed offered by using thumbnails has been eclipsed by the use of desktop publishing.

The greatest challenge to the use of desktop publishing is the creative team. If they are computer and application literate, you will never find them using the pencil approach again. If they are not computer literate, you are starting the process hamstrung by traditional, less flexible processes.

When used, thumbnail versions of the catalog are done quickly in order to communicate various approaches to an entire layout concept. Thumbnails can be done by page or by spread (two facing pages) depending on whether you use pages or spreads as the creative unit. This first step shows the interdependence of the products as they will appear in final printed form.

The approved thumbnails are then expanded to full size. This is why you should know how large your finished page size is going to be before you begin the creative process. A 1/2-inch difference in page size on the printing press can turn a well-executed creative product into a mess.

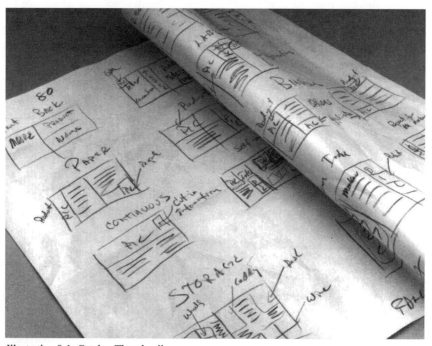

Illustration 8-1: Catalog Thumbnail.

The full size layout will show the products expanded to relative size and position on the page. Headlines will be in place and copy blocks will be aligned to show relative copy size.

Layouts are the blueprints for the construction of the catalog. At this point, your product managers have the greatest flexibility and least painful opportunity to make inexpensive changes. The problem is that most non-creative managers do not take the layouts seriously because they appear so basic. Instruct your product managers on the timing of the creative process so they will understand what they are looking at when they see layouts.

Color can be added using the computer system or by scanning art into the layout. Electronic layouts move you to the final phases of the catalog in one-third the time necessary for old methods.

- Copy and Photography - These are simultaneous activities and are not mutually exclusive. It might prove helpful to your copywriters to touch base with your photographer. The preparations for a photo might yield some feature of the product that the writer missed. The writer can also share the highlighted benefits of the product with the photographer, so that a shot could be enhanced with a prop to illustrate that benefit.

Both copy and photography should be reviewed and approved on a dynamic basis. That is, do not wait until the catalog copy and photography are complete before you circulate them for approval by product managers. If you send the entire catalog's copy and photography at one time, you will overload your product managers and their attention to detail will decline. The approval process should include a copy of the layout, the copy, and photo to establish the complete presentation of the product in that section of the catalog.

Another reason not to obtain approvals and reviews until the entire catalog is complete, is the inevitable time delay. The catalog will not move forward while you are waiting for approvals from different managers. Some managers will not move as quickly as you would like and the catalog will be further delayed. To keep the catalog moving you should insist that a linear review process is unacceptable. As an alternative, you

Illustration 8-2: A catalog tracing.

could allow a single block of time where all of the product managers could review everything in one place when the catalog is complete.

- Tracings - This step is a creative option. If you are working with outside suppliers, you should provide them with an exact layout of the catalog. This tracing will show the exact position of type and photographs.

The steps after tracings are production-oriented and they generally do not require your constant feedback. Tracings allow multiple copies of the catalog to be made and distributed to various suppliers in order to control the technical steps.

Desktop output makes this process unnecessary. With desktop output, multiple copies can be provided without distortion and with minimal effort.

- Assembly/Stripping - This technical stage is where all of the photography is electronically assembled so that color can be separated for the printing process.

- Separations - This is the process that prepares your photography and other color backgrounds. The color is separated into four primary colors: black, red, blue, yellow. The colors are represented by dots, so that the primary color inks can print the respective dots and recreate the color. If you use a magnifying glass to view any color printed piece, you will see the pattern of dots used to create the color. Black type can be mounted on the black plate of the press without being separated.

  Desktop publishing will provide separated films (assuming stripping is not required) that move directly to the printer for plate making. However the separations are supplied to the printer, color proofs should be generated as a last check for color accuracy.

  There are two ways you can review your color separations:

  - Some color separators have a proofing press. This allows you to actually receive printed samples of your catalog.

  - Several manufacturers provide equipment that uses color powders in lieu of ink to photo-electrically create color proofs.

  When you review the color proofs, it is your last opportunity to make any changes. Changes from this point on are very expensive and time-consuming.

- Printing and mailing - Many printers provide both of these steps and some provide in-line addressing. This means that you can address the catalog while it is being produced. This allows you to address your catalog and order form at the same time and bind them together.

  In-line addressing allows you to establish codes that will be returned with the order form that will make your response analysis much easier. Determining the cost justification of this process depends on how many orders you receive by mail as

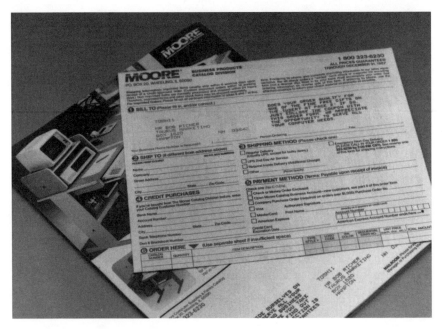

Illustration 8-3: In-line addressed catalog and order form.

opposed to telephone. It is fairly difficult to capture the coding information from telephone orders.

At this point, any prior sins of list selection and/or order form neglect will become apparent. Without your list and order form at your printer/mailer, you are not ready to mail your catalog.

- Timing - The amount of time you allow for each step in the process depends on:

    - how many products you are introducing into your catalog
    - the timeliness of your merchandise (seasonal or non-seasonal)

    Calendars, for example, must be sold prior to the year in which they will be used.

For discussion purposes (Illustration 8-4), we will review a catalog production schedule that takes over one quarter (16+ weeks). You can compress, expand, realign or do whatever you want to this schedule depending on your situation.

Our schedule is based on work days. Keep this in mind when you set-up your own schedule. Weekends and holidays are very expensive days to have work done by suppliers. Your people will not be happy if you regularly make up time using week-end and holidays, but it is a management choice.

The starting point for the process begins when the products are selected and the samples are received. The more you stray from this policy, the more confusion you will have in later stages of the catalog's development.

Back-End Fulfillment

We have just spent a great deal of time on the front-end of the catalog. The strategic and creative decisions that get your catalog to the printer comprise the fun and glorious end of the business. However, the real key to your catalog's success is how well you deliver your products to your customers. People will not remember all of the little creative details you put into your catalog. Yet, they will never forget if your product arrives damaged, if you have substituted products, voided products, or if you mess up the billing charges.

The major areas of fulfillment you should be aware of are:

- Order receipt - This can be by mail or phone. Review returned mail order forms to see if order forms are easy to complete. You can determine how difficult the order form was to complete by how many marginal notes the customer made. A purchase order with your order form attached will still allow you to capture your coding information if you performed in-line addressing. If you just receive a purchase order without your addressed order form, it will be difficult to trace your ordering information and it should be treated like a telephone order. Don't get too hung up on coding; take the order.

  Hopefully, your phone orders will outnumber your mail orders. The phone provides you the opportunity to upgrade and cross-sell the customer. We have already mentioned that it will be difficult to source your telephone orders. Spending time sourcing orders on purchase orders or telephone is not worthwhile because you must remember that your objective is to sell, not source.

However, telephone orders are good occasions to do a little research by asking one or two questions. For example, you may be able to find out information like number of employees or industry type. This information might help

Catalog Schedule*

Activity	Work Days to Complete
Layouts/Pagination	13
Copy/Photography	12
Desktop Publishing	15
Changes/Approvals/Revisions	6
Pre-Press/Separations	12
Printing	15
Bindery	4
Address & Mail	5
Total Work Days	82
(16+ work weeks)	

* Schedule depends on number of pages and quantity being printed.

Illustration 8-4: A typical catalog schedule.

you determine your future list rentals. But do this *after* you have taken the order. We keep stressing that your objective is to get an order. Why risk irritating your customer for the sake of market research?

After you get the order, ask the customer if they would mind reading the code on the address label, assuming the customer has the catalog handy. It is easy to add an afterthought question like,"Would you mind helping us understand" or "By the way, would you mind telling me..." Limit the questions you ask and always be sure not to lose sight of your objective, taking an order.

Test whether a toll-free number is cost-justified. Unlike a consumer who pays for their own home phone bill, a business manager generally has access to lines to make long distance calls without even seeing the charges. Several business catalogers have determined that a toll-free call is not cost-justified. We believe you should make it as easy as possible to order. A toll-free number overcomes the obstacle of cost, whether it is in fact a deterrent or not.

- Credit checking - If you are extending house credit or taking credit cards, you should use a credit service that can support your needs. The major business catalogers have as much as a 15% credit rejection rate and still have 2% bad debt.

You must decide your acceptable credit risk--the cost of the services--and weigh them against your cost per order. Offering credit in some form is definitely to your advantage. Remember, the easier you make the ordering process the more orders you will receive. If you require cash with an order, or even a purchase order, you will receive fewer orders. The problem of getting a check or P.O. from the prospect's accounting department can easily stop someone from doing business with you.

- Order Processing - The temptation is to use low-paid clerical people for this function. It is not the best place to economize. This will probably be the highest volume area of customer contact within your company. The customer will perceive good customer service or customer apathy from your order processors. Information incorrectly handled at this point will probably have the most far reaching and expensive repercussions later.

It is easy to make mistakes. How well you deal with errors and satisfy your customers' concerns could be the key to the success of your catalog. Errors fall into any one of three categories:

	Right Product	Wrong Product
Right person		X
Wrong person	X	
Wrong person		X

This matrix demonstrates that you can send the wrong product to the right person; the right product to the wrong person; or the wrong product to the wrong person. There are other administrative errors related to pricing, quantity, and customer service that complicate the matrix and increase the opportunity for error.

Review your mail or phone orders with skilled, talented, and committed people. Establish some form of meaningful quality control measures to evaluate how well you deal with customer service calls. Publicly recognize and reward outstanding employee performance. Quietly remove chronic under-performers.

- Inventory - You cannot ship what you do not have. Whenever you back-order an item you increase your cost through increased handling and shipping. This also will affect your cash flow. Be frugal in your inventory management but not at the expense of customer satisfaction. The opportunity cost of a lost customer who does not get the products ordered can be higher than all of the cost savings combined and multiplied by ten.

- Order filling and shipping - This is the true nuts and bolts of the catalog operation. The warehouse people are responsible for receiving products, keeping track of them, and picking, packing, and shipping them when orders are processed.

  Someone must also make hundreds of decisions a day regarding the shipping carton to be used for a given order. This person is your last link with your customer. If a carton is selected that is not strong enough to protect the customer's order, and it arrives damaged, you have probably lost a customer.

  Take a little walk around the shipping area without a supervisor present. Let the shipping staff know how important they are to the success of the business. Tell them not to skimp on shipping materials. The difference between bad and good shipping amounts to pennies per order in costs, but dollars in customer satisfaction.

- Billing - Always include your bill with the shipment. If you cannot, bill as quickly as possible after you ship the order. This will help your cash flow. It is easier for customers to get an invoice approved when the memory of the product is still fresh in their mind.

You should not bill prior to the product being shipped. This can cause irritation and a dissatisfied customer. The only exception to this rule is if you told the customer that this is part of your terms for the order.

- <u>Problems</u> - No matter how hard you try, you will have some complaints and returned goods. Your customer service department can expect contact with 2-8% of your customers. Problems should be handled as quickly as possible. Refunds or credits should also be processed quickly. If you are responsive, you will keep your customers. If you hold a refund for an extended period of time, you will lose a customer.

Controls

In order to monitor your fulfillment operation and ensure competent service in all areas, a few simple "red flags" should be established. Some examples are:

- <u>Inventory in-stock conditions</u> - Monitor your inventory by keeping a percentage calculation of your back-ordered items. Track this calculation by product manager or category, by vendor, and overall. You should also know the total number of orders with a back-order, and the percentage of total orders that have a back-order.

- <u>Order turn-around time</u> - Monitor the number of days from receipt to shipment of all orders received. Slow order fulfillment could indicate too many items due-in; inadequate staffing in the warehouse; a back-log in order processing; or some combination of all of the above. Set a target of x days to fulfill an order. All orders falling outside the target should be reviewed to correct the cause of the hold-up.

  Many catalogers have tested order fulfillment times to determine the effect it has on customer re-orders. The faster the order is fulfilled the higher the customer re-order rate. You should attempt to fulfill your orders in one or two days after receipt.

- <u>Response time of complaints</u> - This is also a time-critical situation. It does not matter as much whether you actually solve the problem, but rather that you try to resolve the situation quickly. Even if you do not resolve the situation totally, you will be more apt to keep these customers for future orders if they know you are paying attention to their concerns. If you do not respond and show interest, you will not have the customer in the future.

- <u>Returns</u> - A daily log and a period-to-date log of returns will tell you a great deal about your products and promotion. Numerous returns for any item can indicate that you over-presented the product in your catalog. It may also tell you that a product is below your normal level of quality. If the items are being returned because they were damaged, perhaps the packaging is inadequate for delivering the item.

- <u>Confusion rate</u> - This is a comparison measure of the number of times you communicate with a customer about an order or item. You should be tracking the number of customer contacts you have per order. If the number increases beyond your norm, for a specific product or customer support person, you have a problem. You could have a product problem or a customer service personnel problem.

The late Stanley J. Fenvessy, wrote in a publication for the Direct Marketing Association (Release: 500.1), ten suggestions on *How to Avoid Fulfillment Problems*. Even though this was written primarily for consumer products in all areas of direct marketing (not just catalogs), the points certainly apply to business-to-business catalogs and mail order.

The ten points as they appear in the DMA publication are:

1. *Clarify your promotion and offerings.* Be sure the customer understands what you are offering. Do not oversell. Explain the customer's obligations and the nature of your continuation program. Explain clearly return and refund privileges and who pays the postage. Provide a simple order form or coupon. Design the form with the customer in mind -- not your own fulfillment operations. Be sure it is of workable size with plenty of white space. Help the customer through

the form by numbering the steps that must be followed. Ask for a telephone number so that they might be contacted if there is a question.

2. *Don't promise service you can't deliver.* Measure service from the customer's standpoint -- from the time they telephone until they actually receive the merchandise. It is misleading to advertise that orders are *handled* within 48 hours, when it may take days longer for the customer to actually receive the merchandise.

3. *Date and control all incoming customer orders and correspondence.* In the case of orders this is done by batching orders or payments in groups of 50 to 100 as soon as they are received. These batches are frequently identified by different colors for each day of the week and are controlled throughout their processing. The original orders are eventually filed in their original batch envelope.

   When correspondence is received, a color-coded date tag is stapled to the top of the letter. The indicator shows the day of the month the letter was received. With this system an administrative person can quickly arrange an accumulation of mail into sequence, either for processing or an aged inventory count.

4. *Exercise care in billing and collection.* Do not bill merchandise before it is shipped. If possible send the bill with the merchandise. Structure your dunning cycle so that payments and bills will not cross in the mail. Be judicious in employing outside collection agencies.

5. *Do not abuse the back order privilege.* If you must back order, cancel back orders after four weeks unless the customer specifically requests you to hold the order. Acknowledge the status of back orders every four weeks.

6. *Instruct your customers on how to complain and how to return merchandise.* Years ago it was considered contrary to sound sales policy to mention complaints or returns in any sales material or order papers. Today, well-run direct

marketers include instructions on how to return merchandise on the back of the packing list enclosed with each shipment. The result: no added returns or complaints and those that are received can be processed easier and quicker because the customer has instructions to follow.

7. *Use the telephone.* With the high cost of the three R's of correspondence handling -- Reading, Researching and Responding, telephone communications prove less costly in the long run. Further, the goodwill generated is simply amazing, and the company saves money -- even after paying the telephone bill.

8. *Follow the maxim "the customer is always right."* That retail maxim applies to direct marketing as well. Too many firms waste time and money and aggravate the customer by requiring additional information, particularly cancelled checks or order acknowledgments before making an adjustment. If the amount is small -- $10 to $25 depending on the merchandise offered -- make the adjustment immediately.

9. *Test your own service* (and that of your competitors). This involves two approaches. First, install effective quality control procedures *within* your own fulfillment operation. Quality control inspections should be conducted at all key points in the fulfillment cycle and should include the opening of a meaningful sample of both packages and correspondence ready for mailing to the customer. As a result, individual workers should be evaluated by applying a quality control rating to the work sampled.

   Secondly, a regular and continuing program of test ordering should be undertaken. The results of these tests will give you valuable information about delivery, conditions of merchandise on arrival, and the accuracy of the actual order fulfillment.

10. *Accumulate data concerning the nature of customer calls and correspondence.* Management should regularly review the nature, volume and disposition of consumer complaints. This review should specifically include samples of actual

complaints and some personal contact with consumers and grievances.

Changes of pattern in customer contacts and complaints provide valuable hints on weakness in deliveries, deteriorating merchandise quality, confusing sales offerings, poor packaging, computer errors and other areas which obviously need improving.

Measuring Profits

It is relatively easy to measure the profitability of a stand-alone catalog. Either you are making it or you are not.

The mail order catalog that is only one part of a business that has multiple channels of distribution may make it more difficult to determine if the catalog is profitable. This often happens because the catalog is considered a cost center within the company and existing staff develop and operate the catalog. The profitability of a catalog embedded among several departments within a company is difficult to measure. This confusion can be solved by setting up the catalog as an operating subsidiary.

It is not difficult to measure direct sales that result from the catalog. Establishing who is responsible for creating the order, however, is an area of confusion. There will always be a conflict between the catalog and other sales approaches as to who should get the credit for sales. The sales force will claim that there would be no direct sales if it were not for their efforts. The catalog managers will always claim that the catalog is stimulating the customers to buy from their assigned sales representatives. This is a never ending dilemma, which you cannot solve. There is no easy answer. Your control stops when you decide whether to pay the assigned salesperson commissions on orders generated by the catalog.

One point to consider about commissions: If you pay commissions to salespeople for catalog sales in their territories, your catalog has an additional expense and may not appear to make money. You will be subsidizing your sales force with additional unearned income. You can reduce the salesperson's commissions to improve the catalog's apparent profitability. Or, you can eliminate commissions on direct sales from the catalog. The action you take depends on your catalog strategy. If you want the catalog to be a stand-alone activity, you must separate it from field sales control.

If you are just starting a catalog and already have a sales force responsible for the customers, you must also evaluate how you will introduce the catalog. All sales currently made to the customer are done by the sales people. They are paid commissions and depend on these orders for their income. Eliminating this source of income can prove to be a serious mistake in launching the catalog. We suggest you implement a strategy that compensates the salespeople at a rate that reduces over time. In addition, management must determine how the sales force will recover the lost income opportunity the catalog can create. The fastest way to fail with a catalog launch in the business-to-business area is to disregard its impact on other existing sales channels.

In addition to the sales force, a larger issue is how you allocate the company's general support overhead to your catalog. You will have a difficult time measuring profitability if you have company-wide services supporting your catalog operation. Accounting departments tend to load unfair overhead onto the catalog which seriously impacts its profitability.

The following are some identifiable expense and overhead items:

- Phone line charges (if they are separate from company lines).
- Square footage utilization for warehouse and other identifiable activities that are only used for the catalog. (If the same inventory is used for all activities, it is impossible to separate square footage utilization and other shared activities).
- Promotion costs are easily identified because the catalog costs are normally separate.
- Creative costs, when purchased from outside suppliers. Creative costs transferred from inside tend not to be accurate. If you are uncertain about creative costs, get an outside quote.
- Postage is measurable and assignable.
- Direct labor expenses for catalog creation, operation and management should be easy to identify. Any allocations of personnel expenses other than those reporting directly to the catalog manager will probably be inaccurate.

Keep in mind that a catalog operation can be very profitable. Higher margins draw the attention of top management. As a result, your finance department and other managers may attempt to allocate additional expenses onto your operation.

One approach to managing the overhead problem is to sell items to your catalog operation at your regular wholesale price. Using your wholesale price of goods assumes that overhead is fully covered in the selling price. It is far easier to charge your catalog operation at the same cost of goods as charged in other parts of your business than it is to try to allocate expenses that are not directly related to the catalog operation.

An important point to consider is that your company cannot show the profit on wholesaling an item until it is actually sold and billed to an external customer. Just transferring goods on paper will not make a profit for your company.

Another way to handle the confusion of allocating your overhead costs is to work on a contribution to overhead and profit basis. No matter how many operating divisions you have, you can compare each division's ability to make a contribution to the overall company. By using the contribution measurement, you can compare activities and design compensation packages that do not include any arbitrary assignment of costs. The method is easy to understand and implement. For example:

> NET SALES (Gross less returns and allowances)
>
> less Cost of Sales
>
> less Direct Costs
>
> = Contribution to Overhead and Profit

As you can see, once you have deducted the direct associated costs and expenses, the remaining revenue is a contribution to overhead and profit. This type of measurement system eliminates one department trying to allocate its overhead expenses to another. Politics don't become as important. After you set profit objectives, the balance of the contribution of all the divisions must equal overhead. If your overhead expenses are higher, you only have two options: reduce profit expectations or reduce overhead.

A point of caution: Don't look at a division's contribution, decide it is not enough and eliminate the division. Add back the profit and see if it is now making a contribution that is acceptable. If you close the division, you will not have any contribution to absorb company overhead. Think before you cut.

If a division is not making any contribution to overhead and profit, it may be time to take some aggressive action to eliminate that division.

Customer Acquisition Costs

A prudent way to calculate how much you should spend to acquire a customer is to look at the life cycle of a customer. Over the life of a customer, you can anticipate or forecast some revenue stream. To be prudent, you should factor the gross contribution using present value techniques to establish the lifetime value of that customer in today's dollars.

Year	Customers	Rev.@$600	Cont %	Contrib $	P.V. 10%	Total
1	100	60,000	35%	$21,000	.909	$19,089
2	65	39,000	35%	15,650	.826	12,927
3	49	29,400	32%	9,408	.751	7,065
4	39	23,400	30%	7,020	.683	4,795
5	31	18,600	30%	5,580	.621	3,465

Thus, total present value contribution of 100 customers discounted using 10% cost of capital..$47,341

The amount of investment to make in present dollars to acquire a customer is calculated by dividing the total present value dollars by the original number of customers:

$$\$47,341 \div 100 = \$473.41$$

This model makes assumptions on the contribution, average sale per customer, and the rate of customer loss. You have the freedom to do everything you can to change any of these variables as they affect your business. Our point is that you can't look at a customer's one year history and determine what you are willing to spend to acquire that customer. Lifetime value of a customer, discounted by the present value method, is a reasonable way to set the maximum investment you should make to acquire a customer.

Some things you can do to change the results are:

- You can keep customers alive longer through various regeneration programs.
- You can add new products and upgrade customers to increase your average order.
- You can work with your costs to drive up your contribution percentage.

You must make some assumptions based on your situation in order to arrive at the amount you should spend on customer acquisition. In the example above, you can spend $473.41 to acquire a new customer without making any profit on the customer. Anything less than this customer acquisition target number should mean a profit over the next five years.

In the example above, we did not include as a separate expense, the cost to service and promote the customer on an ongoing basis. We have assumed these costs to be a part of the overhead expense when calculating the net contribution.

If you spend more than the $473.41 to acquire a customer, you will lose money unless you can find other ways to generate additional revenue to offset the acquisition expenses. Perhaps you can borrow money at no cost; streamline operation costs to increase contribution; or create some other form of income (like list rental) to offset the higher acquisition cost. These are all nice ideas that may or may not work. The most prudent course of action is not to spend more than your customer acquisition cost target.

Acquisition costs are dynamic and should be reevaluated on a sustained and ongoing basis.

Critical Mass

Whether you are just starting your catalog operation or have been in business for years, you should evaluate how large your catalog operation should be. As in all business, growth may resemble an upward sloping curve, but overhead growth occurs in plateaus. To evaluate how large your business can be, you must be realistic in estimating the size of the market opportunity.

Once you have determined the size of the available market, you must determine the resources you are willing to invest to acquire your desired market share. In the case of catalogs, market share is not some abstract number computed by an external research company. Your market share is the number of customers you have.

As we discussed earlier, you should set a target acquisition cost for each new customer. Then, applying the most prudent cost accounting system you can, you should begin the process of new customer acquisition.

The dynamic model you enlist should constantly measure the price you are paying to acquire each new customer. The method we demonstrated earlier is one approach to evaluate acquisition costs.

When you have tested and mailed all of the available lists that you can identify and have not exceeded the acquisition cost objective, you then should examine your operating costs. In this environment, growth consists of reducing costs thereby increasing the catalog's contribution.

If you are dissatisfied with the size of your catalog operation, it may be time to look at alternatives. Keep in mind that you must evaluate the contribution of a customer over some period to determine the total value of that customer. Earlier we discussed one method of determining the value of a customer. If you are uncomfortable with the size of your catalog operation, there are two things you can do:

1. Develop additional product lines and/or catalogs to sell to your existing customers. These new lines could also give you new growth as well as a new customer base for your existing catalog.

2. Restructure your catalog operation to allocate all overhead to your existing customers. Using this approach you could acquire additional customers using only the variable costs of list, production, and postage. This would lower your acquisition cost and allow you to spend more to acquire new customers.

These two approaches are not mutually exclusive. You should undertake both of these courses of action once you reach your critical mass and are profitable without new customers.

Be very careful of the never ending growth syndrome. Business catalogs have grown at incredible rates for the last 15 years. Growth is currently slowing for many business catalogers due to competition. Do not be afraid to call a halt to geometric circulation growth. It is very easy for costs to increase faster than sales. In direct mail, your costs are sunk in promotion before you realize the sales are not going to be there. Be willing to stick with known productive lists that can give you the new customers you need to maintain your critical mass.

Direct Mail Assets

All good businesses are becoming more sensitive to the needs of customers. Peter Drucker said "that the goal of business is to gain and keep customers." This philosophy is even more important in the catalog business. The way to determine the value of anything is to sell it.

Assets of any business are represented on its balance sheet and are normally fairly easy to identify. The most important asset of the direct mail catalog is not an asset that normally appears on its financial statement. To financial analysts unfamiliar with mail order marketing methods, the catalog's customer file may appear as a goodwill item. Traditionally they have found it hard to quantify.

In the catalog business, always remember that your main asset is your customer file. Different customers will buy from you at different volumes and different levels of frequency. The recency, frequency, and monetary concepts used by consumer catalog marketers also apply in the business world.

Consumer catalog marketers long ago identified that the customer that purchased from you most recently has a high tendency to purchase again. Customers that buy from you on a sustained and frequent basis will continue to buy from you as long as you meet their expectations And the more money a customer has spent with you, the better the chances that they will buy from you again.

As you develop your customer database, you should 'score' or categorize all of your customers using some algorithm that identifies customer levels. For example, one of our clients used the following algorithm:

- A Customer -- any customer who has purchased $1,500 or more in last 12 months.

- B Customer -- any customer who has purchased between $1,000 and $1,499 in the last 12 months.

- C Customer -- any customer who has purchased between $500 and $1,000 in the last 12 months.

- D Customer -- any customer who has purchased less than $500 in the last 12 months.

- E Customer -- any customer who has not been coded by the previous criteria but has purchased in the last 24 months.

Different categories of customers should receive different levels of marketing activity. For example, an A customer may warrant a telemarketing or even a face-to-face contact at least once a quarter or once a year. On the other hand, you can probably only afford to contact the D customers every quarter by mail.

Too frequent contact is sometimes thought to be a problem. The reality is that you cannot contact your customers too frequently. Business catalog marketers that used to mail once a quarter are now mailing as frequently as once a month to a portion of their customer base. Your customers will tell you by their purchasing levels what your schedule should be. Your A customers have bought at a level that generates enough contribution to allow you to contact them as frequently as you desire. On the other hand, your E customers only generate enough contribution to justify one or two mailings per year.

The scoring system above is very basic. You might use a different algorithm that is more comprehensive. We have seen systems that identify each of the elements of RFM; that include product categories in their algorithm; information characters in the code; or combinations of all of these. If you have not already created a scoring algorithm, select something simple to start with. Follow the age old KISS adage: keep it simple, stupid.

The scoring system you select must be dynamic. Don't code a customer an A and never rescore that customer. Some suggestions can prove to be very helpful as time goes on. All require that you completely document your actions:

- Identify the scoring algorithm and review it with everybody involved in the catalog effort.

- Identify how, and how frequently, you will reevaluate the customer file and rescore customers.

- Don't force the scoring issue. If you have been too stringent in your category selection you may have no A customers. On the other hand, if you have no A customers, it may be because your catalog performance is slipping.

All of the other assets within a business can change; they can be purchased, sold, and exchanged. All except your customer file. You establish the relationship with your customers. Even if you sell your company, the customers will still continue to think they are doing business with you.

If you are careful in maintaining and utilizing your customer file, it will be your most valuable asset. This customer file can allow you to grow and expand in other product areas and even other markets. The classic example is Sears. Initially only a catalog marketer, they have expanded into retail, insurance, and other financial services. It all starts with the customer base.

Financial Planning

In the chapter on business planning we explained how to develop objectives for lead generation and for selling a single product. The catalog process complicates the issue because, by definition, you are selling more than one product. Your financial controls are therefore based on a different system and cover more than just the marketing issues.

The catalog, or even face-to-face sales, will create a group of prospects who respond to your offer and want to do business with you that you will decline for various reasons. You may have prior experience with the customer and decide that it is not in your best interest to reestablish the relationship. For example:

- Customers who did not pay their bills.
- Customers who continually take advantage of your return policies. They are, in effect, continually trying products but never purchasing.
- Customers who return the products incomplete.
- Customers who constantly generate service problems. This group includes customers who are always complaining in an effort to negotiate better terms and conditions.
- Customers with insufficient credit.

In the catalog environment, other catalog marketers have declined about 20% of their orders for credit and other reasons. From a financial review and planning perspective, these orders should not appear as gross sales. Since they did not accept the order, they never sold to the customer.

You must handle your financial reporting in a method that is acceptable to your management. In the model outlined below, we illustrate gross orders received and then allow for returned goods and allowances to arrive at the net sales.   Note that we include the gross demand, which includes customers who want to purchase from you that have been rejected.

Item	Description	% of Gross Demand
1	Gross Demand	100%
2	Gross Sales	80%
3	Net Sales	70%

In the above model, the gross demand (1) is the total amount of products that the market would like to buy from you. As we have discussed, you will not want to ship a part of the demand. The gross sales (2) represents the total amount of sales that you have accepted and for which products have been shipped. As you can see, there is about a 20% shrinkage from gross demand to gross sales. This shrinkage may be different in your business, but other business-to-business catalog marketers are experiencing about 20%. The net sales (3) are the actual revenues you collect for product sales. The difference between the gross and net sales are those orders that are returned.

We use the net sales figure as the basis for our financial model calculations. You may choose to use gross sales for your percentage calculation in your financial model. Either way, consistency is the key. The purpose of the financial model is to give you a management indicator if your catalog operation is running as expected.

In our model, Illustration 8-6, net sales equal 100% of the production of the catalog being measured. This model uses all costs and expenses applied as a percentage of the net sale or total revenue of the operation. The percentages in this model are used for illustration only. You must develop your own model using your own conditions. While these numbers are not absolute, they are indicative of the order of magnitude of the various costs and expenses as they relate to net sales.

When you subtract your cost of goods (2) from net sales (1) you arrive at your gross margin (3).

Gross margin (3) less the costs you incur as a direct result of being in the catalog business, catalog production and mailing (4), establishes the net margin (5). Catalog production and mailing expenses are the total cost of creating, printing, list rental, addressing and postage required to mail your catalog. If you are using in-house creative services, and can specifically identify the actual expenses, you can include the costs in this figure. If you are charged an overhead number for the creative services, the costs are really overhead and should not be included as a variable expense.

Net Margin (5) less the variable expenses related to the actual catalog operations (6) will establish the net contribution (7) from catalog operations. We have identified several broad categories of variable expenses. You should work with your accounting department to establish the variable expense items for your operation. The following identifies the items we have included:

6a Wages and benefits are the employee expenses that are directly related to the operation of the catalog.

6b Toll-free telephone is your cost to provide free inbound telephone service to your customers.

6c Credit card fees are the cost for your credit card suppliers as a result of customers using charge cards to pay for their purchases.

6d Freight out is your shipping expense to get your products to your customers.

Catalog Planning Model

Item	Description		% of Net Sales
1	Net Sales		100%
2	Cost of Goods		60%
3	Gross Margin		40%
4	Catalog Production and Mailing		19%
5	Net Margin		21%
6	Variable Expenses		
	6a Salary/Benefits	4.5%	
	6b Toll-free Phone	1.3%	
	6c Credit Card Fees	2.2%	
	6d Freight Out	3.0%	
	6e Shipping Income	-5.0%	
	6f Packaging Supplies	.9%	
	6g Miscellaneous Postage	.3%	
	6h Bad Debt	2.0%	
	Total Variable Expenses		9.2%
7	Net Contribution		11.8%
8	Fixed Expenses		
	8a Exec Salary/Benefits	4.0%	
	8b Travel/Entertainment	0.3%	
	8c Office Supplies	0.4%	
	8d Professional Fees	0.5%	
	8e Rent	0.5%	
	8f Utilities	0.2%	
	8g Repair/Maintenance	0.1%	
	8h Insurance	0.2%	
	8i Equip Lease/Maintenance	0.8%	
	8j Telephone	0.5%	
	Total Fixed Expenses		7.5%
9	Net Profit Before Taxes		4.3%

Illustration 8-6: A catalog planning model.

6e Shipping income is what you charge your customers per order or per item for you to handle and ship your products to them. Shipping income is a contra-expense or an income item. We have chosen to list this income item under your variable expenses so that the net sales number is not inflated. This allows you to keep an exact accounting of your costs as a percentage of the true net sales.

6f Packaging supplies are the cartons and packing materials you use to ship your products.

6g Miscellaneous postage covers items too small to ship economically by other means and also your postage to support customer service.

6h Bad debt is the expense you incur when customers that keep your products do not pay their bills.

Net contribution (7) less the fixed expenses (8) will establish the net profit before taxes (9) from the catalog operations. The fixed expenses are the costs you incur no matter what business you are in. Our example does not include:

- interest expense or income
- business taxes
- depreciation

We are trying to provide a guideline and not a complete financial proforma. Fixed overhead is different in almost every business. It needs to be monitored and evaluated on a regular basis. Since individual fixed expenses are often very small as a percentage of sales, they sometimes are allowed to get out of control. Even though they are small, overhead can quickly destroy the profit from your operation. The overhead items we have included are:

8a Executive salaries and benefits are the costs of the management team and supervisory team not already included as a variable expense. It is not unusual to include only percentages of some people's salaries as they have other functions not related to the catalog effort.

8b Travel and entertainment are the expenses incurred by the personnel identified in 8a above.

8c Office supplies.

8d Professional fees are the charges you receive from your lawyer, accountant, and outside consultants you might engage.

8e Rent.

8f Utilities include your heat, electricity, water or other services.

8g Repairs and Maintenance are the expenses you incur to keep your facility in good operating condition.

8h Insurance are costs for the coverage you need to carry by law and as a prudent manager.

8i Equipment lease and maintenance is what you pay to lease the machines and equipment necessary to operate your business.

8j Telephone are the costs you incur to operate the business telephones exclusive of the cost for inbound telephone service already identified as a variable expense.

In our example, the pre-tax profit for this company is 4.3%. Decide what your profit objectives are before you begin, and again as you grow your catalog operation. Review pricing, quantities mailed, variable costs, and fixed costs to increase the net profit from your catalog.

One additional income item was not covered in our model: list rental. Some business catalogers rent their lists in order to generate additional income. The income from list rentals can be 6% to 8% of net sales, a very substantial revenue source. Most businesses that are operating a catalog imbedded within their overall operations do not rent lists to others.

If you do not rent your list, you will not enjoy this income opportunity. If you do rent your list, we suggest you account for your list rental income as another income item. This would be done after you have accounted for your income from operations. By not including the list income in the net revenue figure from operations, you will have a clearer picture of operating expenses compared to operating income.

Break-Even Analysis

You have to make a lot of significant business decisions to create the model of your overall catalog operation. Once this is done you can use the information to make some very practical applications. You can use the percentages to calculate the level of sales you will need to operate your catalog business at a break-even level.

The following break-even calculation is one method to establish some measurement objectives that can prove invaluable in evaluating the success of your efforts. You can also use this calculation to determine if a given catalog test or venture looks feasible. This formula establishes the break-even sales revenue required from each catalog mailed.

$$BE = \frac{CC \div (GM\% - OE\%)}{(1.00 - R/C\%)}$$

BE = Break-even *gross* sales per catalog stated in cents per catalog

CC = Catalog cost stated in cents/catalog

GM = Gross margin stated as a percentage of net sales

OE = Operating expenses (fixed + variable) as a percentage of net sales

R/C = Refunds/cancellations as a percentage of *gross* sales

Using the figures from our model above, assuming a catalog cost of $ .40; the break-even would be:

$$BE = \frac{.40 \div (40\% - 16.7\%)}{(1.00 - 11\%)}$$

$$= \frac{.4 \div (.4 - .167)}{1.00 - .11}$$

$$= \frac{1.72}{.89}$$

= $1.93 gross sales per catalog mailed to break-even

If you do rent your list, the break-even formula would be:

$$BE = \frac{CC \div (GM\% - OE\% + LR\%)}{(1.00 - R/C\%)}$$

LR = List rental income as a percentage of net sales

In this calculation (using a 6% list rental figure), the income from list rental lowers the break-even of the necessary gross sales. The gross sales per catalog would become $1.54 to reach break-even.

You could use the gross revenue per catalog figure to determine when your gross sales reach your break-even point. For example, let's say you calculate a gross sales per catalog break-even of $1.75. If you mail 500,000 catalogs, the gross sales you need in order to reach break-even is:

500,000 x $1.75 = $875,000.00

You can also use the break-even calculation to determine the sales you need per page, per spread, and per item on a per catalog basis. If you use the $1.75 figure for the gross sales per book, you can divide the pages and products into this number to arrive at some interesting objectives.

- Sales per page (assume a 40 page catalog) =

  $1.75 ÷ 40 = $0.044 sales/page per catalog

- Doubling the sales per page will give the per spread (you may not be selling off your cover which will change the numbers slightly). The sales per spread per catalog would be $0.088.

- Sales per item (assume 100 items) =

$1.75 ÷ 100 = $0.0175 sales per item per catalog

These calculations are only intended to provide you with a way to evaluate and analyze the dynamic performance of your catalog. As you change any part of the formula it is fairly easy to recalculate the gross sales needed for you to reach break-even.

If you are accustomed to working on a cost per thousand basis, multiply the results by 1,000 to arrive at your objectives. If you calculate that you need $1.75 gross sales per catalog to break-even, you will need $1,750.00 per thousand catalogs mailed.

However you do your calculations, establish some type of easy to use objectives. You will continually be measuring the overall financial performance of the catalog operation. The break-even analysis gives you a method to review the progress of your catalog on a more dynamic basis. It also allows you to focus on the strength and weakness of each catalog.

Catalogs Summarized

We have covered a lot of ground in this chapter and tried to give you a foundation that you could build on. Virtually every business is in the catalog business in some way. Even if you are only publishing a price list for various manufactured items, you are really preparing a catalog. Whenever you offer your market more than one product choice at a time, you have created a catalog.

The method you choose to deliver your catalog can range from direct mail to sales representatives delivering them personally. Whatever the method used, your ability to calculate your catalog's profitability does not change.

The performance and sales of catalogs are as varied as there are types of businesses. A manufacturing company making higher priced products can generate hundreds of thousands of dollars of sales per page of the catalog. In fact, in these kinds of situations, the companies use catalogs as a tool for the sales force. On the other hand, an office supply company might only generate $0.10 sales per page, and the catalog may be their only channel of distribution.

Whatever your strategy, catalog as a sales tool or catalog as a mail order vehicle, your catalog is your sales representative. When you are not present, the catalog will present your products to your prospects and customers. You should review your catalog and ensure that it is representative of you, your company, and your products. Don't just reprint your catalog and assume that the market will find it interesting. As we have stressed in other parts of this book, never mail or deliver anything that you wouldn't want to receive yourself.

Chapter Nine:

Using Direct Marketing Space Advertising More Effectively

By Mark Mancini, President
Mancini Creative
64 South Main Street
Medford, NJ 08055
(609)654-7700 FAX: (609)657-7709 Email: mmancini@voicenet.com

When Do You Use It?

Your first major question regarding direct response space advertising should be: When should you use it?

In the business to business arena, it is generally difficult to justify using space on a strict cost-per-lead or a cost-per-sale basis. Whether you're generating leads for a two-step program or selling directly off-page, you are likely to get more response per dollar using direct mail.

Recently, we constructed a lead generation ad for a new pollution control software product designed for industrial use. The ad was done well, the offer was good, and we ran in a trade publication that was perfect for the prospect we wanted (as we were to prove later).

But in the final analysis, we acquired just three leads and two were would-be competitors. Refusing to believe the obvious, that the pathetic response was indicating that we had the wrong product, or the wrong publication, or that the product solved a problem that nobody cared about. We rented the list from this same publication and sent a double postcard with exactly the same offer. This was anything but a clean test, but to give it some semblance of objectivity, we kept essentially the same copy as we had used in the space ad. We even kept the same basic copy as we had used in the ad, right down to the type faces.

More than three percent of the list responded to the offer. No kidding! We received 176 responses, with more than 110 of the inquiries turning out to be highly qualified. I'm not sure whether this speaks more about space advertising in general, or to the readership of trade publications, but it certainly was saying something--and loud!

As with just about anything, there are exceptions--times when you can get value from direct response space. But, you've really got to stay focused on your objectives and use your head. Space can be an attractive medium, and it's easy to lose sight of precisely what you hope to gain by using it. Most advertisers, even good direct marketers, can easily find themselves drawn into the trap of spewing facts about their company (that nobody cares about), or exercising their newly discovered artistic talent to create fine art that doesn't produce response.

That said, when is it a good time for space advertising? Most obviously, when an appropriate list is not available or, when you want to establish a new market by allowing it to "select itself" (actually define itself) out of an untested universe or, when you want to build awareness, or communicate some new information to your market, and finance the effort by generating new revenue or leads.

I recommend, however, that the best time to use space is more appropriately determined by the shape of your market and the margin in your product.

For example, a bad product to sell in space ads would be a very specialized assortment of valves. While you could target your space ad's exposure using a trade publication for example, you'd probably be far more effective (on a response per dollar spent basis), by renting the publication's list and sending a well constructed, inexpensive double postcard or letter package.

While you can certainly run an ad in the trade publication itself, you have no way to know if anyone actually opens the thing. You also have no real reason to expect that they will actually look at the ads in that trade publication, and worse yet, you have no real way to measure either factor outside of a few inferential methods that are probably questionable anyway. (Of course, the media kit provides irreproachable batteries of proof that 99.9% of the circulation reads the pub cover to cover and remembers about 97.6% of the ads run. You can believe that ad sales pitch if you want to, but I don't--and I don't know too many direct marketers who do.)

A good example of a situation where space would pay off might involve a product that is more horizontal, like a high-quality travel bag. Anyone might be a prospect for reasons you can't possibly anticipate. (This is not entirely true of course, but certain significant segments of this market would be impossible to select out. For this example, they are the segments being discussed.) It would be difficult and expensive to find and mail potential prospects for such a horizontally oriented product. A space ad, placed in an airline magazine for example, would allow you to deliver your communication to a very broad, non-industry-specific group, that might find your offer attractive.

Another factor that makes this example interesting involves the relatively low margin, in real dollars, per order. When you don't have a great deal of profit in a one-time sale, like the travel bag, you can't afford to use a medium like mail. The cost per impression is simply too high. Only with a well targeted niche, and significant margin dollars, can you afford to sell in the mail, unless the lifetime value of the respondent provides an additional variable for the equation. The space ad can get you a high number of impressions for a relatively low cost, which, with a product offering broad horizontal appeal, can make the final effort profitable.

We're going to look at specific examples where space has performed well in many of the applications listed above. We'll even examine the differences between creative approach in direct mail and the more aggressive approach necessary for space. We'll explore offers that have worked well for us, and the copy and design approaches that will work best for you.

When you get to the dregs of the issue, direct response space advertising can work for you, but it's a dangerous and expensive place to make mistakes. Space is sexy...and colorful...and vice presidents love to hang 4-color match prints on the walls of their offices. Many of these VP's have been trained for years by general advertising agency executives who have passed along their time honored tradition of defending abysmal ad performance with the classic insanity defense: "...sure, it looks like it didn't work...but you'd better believe we bought some awareness, people know who we are, and that's going to pay off in the future...blah, blah, blah."

A Different Medium Requires a Different Approach

When you consider using space advertising as a component in your overall marketing plan, don't take the decision lightly. Creating an effective direct marketing space advertisement can be a formidable challenge even for a seasoned direct marketing creative professional.

The fact is, creating an effective direct marketing ad is just plain tough, and cost-justifying it can be even tougher. Do it well, and you could get a good cost-per-response, and some general awareness advertising for free-awareness that can help boost the effect and results of your other media! (Oh no, not the S-word. Yes...Synergy! There, I've said it.)

So what's the problem? It's the *do it well* part.

Obviously, direct mail has been the principal training ground for most D.M. creative pros. Space ads, as a constituent part of a mixed media promotion, are usually turned over to the general advertising folks, even when they're supposed to produce response. Upper management, as a rule, is more concerned about the "look" than anything else, and those general ad guys are real artists! The problem is, these artists rarely understand the global principles of creating direct marketing work.

Either way, you lose. The general ad guys are feverishly building your new wall art, and the direct marketing guys are trying to shoe-horn a mail kit onto a 7" x 10" page.

Here's why it's tough. To produce an effective cost-per-response, you have to address all the issues of any good mail kit plus a lot more. You have to deliver the benefits succinctly and powerfully. You have to support the benefits and make them credible. You have to develop a self-qualifying offer and make sure it appeals to your principle target. You have to execute an effective call-to-action, and design all this pabulum in such a way that you control every eye-movement, and thereby, the attention of your prospect. But because this is a space ad and you're going to have to do a lot more than that if you're going to succeed!

First off, with the exception of a couple of key placement options, you're starting with your puny little message buried in a bound stack of paper somewhere between a quarter of an inch and an inch thick. Nobody knows you're even there, so you can say good-bye to the 7 to 11 seconds of undivided attention you'll get using a mail kit. Assuming some prospect does stumble upon your page (or fraction of a page), you still will not have their undivided attention unless you've purchased the full spread. Realistically, you've probably got someone else in the seat next to you trying their best to steal your thunder: instant competition--automatically. Worse yet, you don't even know who or what that competition is going to be! One popular movie star on the facing page, and you've just wasted 14 grand or more!

No, that's not all! You don't get anything for free here--your best prospect doesn't owe you even one full second of his or her attention. This is a toll road, and your prospect is cruising by at about 140 mph. They're not stopping unless you stop them (and, by the way, you're the one paying the toll). Experts say that you get one or two seconds to grab the readers attention. I don't think the actual time matters at all. What matters is, it isn't very long, and the harder you can hit the better off you're going to be.

Finally, you have to keep in mind that the majority of the space ads in your publication are general ads in nature. They don't ask for response at all. That means your prospects are not pre-conditioned to expect to be asked to actually do anything, (another bonus for mail).

This is the down side! Now let's look at the up side. (Could there even be an upside?)

Making All the Right Moves (You're Going To Have To!)

If you're going to take on direct response space and make it work for you, you're going to have to do everything right! And, I do mean, everything!

The first and most widely made mistake comes when you assume too much. This goes for space as well as mail, (and just about every other medium). Assume that your prospect knows nothing about you, your product or your offer. The first question your prospect is asking is, what are these people talking about?. You have to answer that question first, and you have to answer it in the first glance. You can use a short headline, an obvious graphic device, or a combination of the two, but you have to get this message across instantly if you're going to stand a chance.

The biggest mistake you can make is to fall in love with a "concept". By using some clever play on words or obscure graphic imagery, you're almost sure to put a bullet squarely into your own foot. Don't do it! Say what you mean. Say it as clearly as possible. And say it loud! Being understated and tasteful makes great art, and it's good for the ego, but it's a huge waste of cash in space advertising.

This point seems clear enough, right? Right. Now let's make it difficult. Since you've decided on space advertising, you have to add another element to the mix. Remember, you no longer have the luxury of your prospect's undivided attention, (like you often have in mail advertising). Now you have to get your message across clearly, and with impact...but if you haven't stopped the reader in the process, your message is nowhere.

Adjust Your Thinking.

So what do you do? First: don't let your no-account creative guys, (I'm allowed to say this because I am one), start anything until you have the media kit for your publication and as many samples of the publication as possible. Second: look at the publication(s) carefully. See what the editorial layout looks like. See what the advertising looks like. Does the pub seem 'white', 'gray' or 'dark' as you flip through it? Which ads stand out, and why do they stand out? Third: think of what you need to do to stand away from everything else in the book. Fourth: If anyone says, "let's do what all these other ads are doing...it must work or they wouldn't be doing it!," tell them to shut up.

The Offer--Again It Rears Its Ugly Head!

Nowhere will your offer be more critical than in a direct response space ad. If it isn't straight forward, easy for your prospect to grasp, and of substantial perceived value (again-high perceived value to your prospect...not to you!), don't waste your money on the space.

The mechanics of your space ad must be this simple. Your messages must address your prospects concerns: "What is this about? What can I get? Hey, that's worth something to me! What do I need to do to get it?" End of story. If you can't make it this simple, get away from space. It won't work.

Your offer must contain something of real practical and objective value to your prospect. Also make it a self-qualifying offer. Your offer should have value only to individuals that would be viable prospects for your product or service. A very good example of a self-qualifying offer involved a self-evaluation and planning guide we developed for a computer hardware company. The guide helped prospects determine the best PC configuration as it related to their usage. Because the guide only held value for people actively considering a computer purchase, it was the perfect self-qualifying offer.

Consider Your Format

Anything you can do to cut down on the competition is well worth the effort. This is a double edged sword however, and in print advertising, it's a sword that swings on the issue of budget. Certainly, it should help your response to go with a full page color ad, as opposed to a quarter-page black and white. But, you always have to consider how much additional response the format will net you, and relate it to the new break-even associated with the increased cost.

If you think your offer can cost justify it, you can eliminate competition by purchasing a full spread. When you own both sides of the page, you will at least gain an instant of your prospect's undivided attention.

As usual, your best option for maximizing response with regard to format is also the most expensive--the bind-in full page ad. Again, you'll have to look at the cost/reward side of testing this format.

In my experience, this format is likely to be your absolute best bet. Some publications will not offer this option, but a great many will. A full-page insert (printed on 7 point stock and bound into the publication) offers two key benefits. Because the stock is thicker than the surrounding text, the publication will fall open to your space ad instantly, helping you skate the problem of being lost in the vast pile of pages. The second key benefit also lies in the thickness of the stock. As long as your insert is printed on a minimum 7 point stock, you can construct your coupon as a self-mail reply card that perforates out of the ad itself. (Coupon...did somebody say coupon? We're coming to that!)

I can't say enough about this format (when properly used) as it relates to direct response space advertising. It's user-friendly and very powerful. In a clean test it has never failed to bring us our highest gross results.

The Coupon--Don't Leave the Drawing Board Without It!

Use a coupon in every direct response ad you do. (I know it looks like hell-but trust me!) This is a free message from me to you. As soon as your prospect sees a coupon they know they're supposed to do something to get something. These are two powerful messages, and you didn't have to spend a word to get them across.

Here it is in a nut shell: Get yourself a right hand page when you purchase your space, (if you're not using an insert, in which case you automatically have a right-hand page...and a left for that matter). You can generally get one if you ask. Stick your coupon in the lower right corner of the ad. If you hate coupons, that 's OK. Just test against your tasteful ad and see what happens. The coupon will pull better response.

Also, get your placement as close to the front of the publication as possible, as a general rule. Obviously, there are exceptions. If there's an editorial subject running that sings the praises of your product or service, for example, you may want to try to locate your ad nearby.

Here's the rest of it: Put a great big 24 point phone number on the coupon along with an Internet response option. Stick a smaller fax reply number under it, when it's appropriate. Again, don't try to be dignified. Believe me, nobody's looking at you that closely. Your prospects are creatures of habit and, as unlikely as it seems, they will not deviate from their response behavior. Some folks will respond by phone...they always respond by phone, and you're not going to change them by only providing them with a mail-back response vehicle. I've tested this many times, always getting the same message loud and clear. No mail-back response option = no mail-back respondents. No phone number = no phone respondents. (Incidentally, it goes even further. We've done some tests that have suggested that the smaller the phone number appears on the coupon, the fewer phone responses. Scary, huh?)

Editorial and Design Tips

Writing copy for direct response is an art in itself, and it's going to be impossible to adequately cover this issue as a function of space advertising only. But here are a few common mistakes you'll want to avoid.

Don't give everything away. Suggest a lot of neat stuff, (stuff that matters to your prospect), then tell them how they can get the rest of the message. "Want to know about something that can cure cancer and keep that nasty road tar from sticking to your tires? Send back the coupon, call or fax and I'll tell you all about it." It works...and as long as you deliver what you promise, it's certainly fair enough. By the way, you still need a fundamentally compelling offer. The answers should come as a function of your offer. For example: "Here are all these interesting questions...and you can answer them all by writing or calling for you free self-evaluation guide."

Don't forget the basics of any good direct marketing communication. Sometimes in the crunch for space, even the pros start to forget the basic components. Give yourself room for a solid 'call to action'. If you don't come right out and tell 'em what to do and how to do it, they ain't doin' it! It's basic, but you don't want to miss it.

Design: It's Nothing More Than a Vehicle for Your Editorial Content

Your prospect must be driven through the ad in an orderly fashion. They must get the messages in the order that you intend. Your designer's job is to make sure that you direct the attention of your prospects as they move through the ad-from the upper left, (where they will enter your ad), down to the lower right (where coupon calls for action). Along the way they need to get the following messages through headlines and subheads--even if they never read the body copy:

1.   Here's what we're talking about and here's why you should care.

2.   Here's what you're going to get and why you should care.

3.   Here's what you have to do to get it!

The Long and Short of It

Obviously, we can't cover all the subjects and their numerous exceptions. And, there are a thousand exceptions to the precepts and advice given above. In terms of "best bets" however, you should find some very solid and valuable suggestions here that will bring you better results should you venture into the twilight zone of direct marketing space advertising.

I should also say something one last time. I still believe that 9 out of 10 times I'll get more from my advertising dollar by renting the publication's list (using mail), and staying out of their space.

An Example of a Successful Direct Marketing Space Ad

Now that we've explored do's and don'ts in creating effective space advertising, it's about time we examined a successful case study.

The ad we're about to evaluate (Illustration 9-1) was developed for W. Atlee Burpee and Company, a seed company located in Warminster, Pennsylvania. The company sells using both catalog and retail distribution. This promotion was designed to generate qualified leads for the catalog division.

The ad produced nearly four times the response necessary to achieve a break-even compared to the costs associated with running the ad. In fact, more than 5% of the entire circulation responded to this ad. The level of qualification (as determined by the conversion rate to sales and the average order amount, compared to the average acquired lead) ranked above average.

One of the first things that this project had going for it, as is characteristic of any successful ad, is a clarity of mission. The objective was developed to provide a clear focus that made measuring success or failure cut and dried (that's a little "herb" humor).

A Successful Direct Marketing Space Advertisement

Media Description
Herb Companion Magazine
- Full Circulation: Approx. 40,000
- Distribution: National
- Subscribers: Approx. 20,000
- Demo: Approx. 70% Female

Offer
Free Trial Packet of Dill Seed and New Burpee Seed Catalogue
- Newly developed variety of specific interest to herb gardeners

Strategy
- Design ad to resemble editorial matter reviewing a new herb variety. The assumption was, only an herb enthusiast would be interested enough to read a piece with a large amount of copy relating to a new herb variety. A secondary assumption was that the seed offer would only appeal to avid gardeners. Thus the offer was "self-qualifying" in nature.

Illustration 9-1: A successful direct marketing ad.

Our objective was to add qualified names to the catalog subscribers database. The plan was to appeal directly to herb growers. As you might expect, the publication, Herb Companion, gave us an identifiable vertical slice that made it easy to tailor the message accurately.

As you'll see in the following bulleted section, we used all the elements described above, and then some, to produce a very successful promotion.

Headline and General Positioning

- Both pre-head and Main Head attract targeted prospects by identifying the subject and promising independent editorial value. Again, only a gardening enthusiast would find the issue of a "New Dill" variety worth reading about. The same enthusiast will be our best performing catalog sales lead.

Coupon

- The coupon, Illustration 9-3, is a necessity. It visually alerts the prospect that there is some action required.

- This coupon restates and visually exhibits the offer.

- The coupon (in the lower right, the last place your prospect will focus upon before leaving your ad) shows the mail response option. The phone response option is shown just above the

Illustration 9-2: Use of the headline.

coupon. The answer to the "how do I get it?" question is contained in the lower right corner loud and clear.

Copy Considerations

- Notice that the text (Illustration 9-4) begins in the third person as though it represents the opinion of an objective party. This was done to establish immediate credibility.

- The copy first sells the Free Seed offer, not the catalog. Only viable, qualified catalog leads would be interested in the seed offer, making it unnecessary to sell the catalog as a name acquisition offer.

- Notice that after the first subhead, the copy changes to classic first person direct marketing sell copy. Now we're selling the offer and telling the prospect exactly what they will get and how to get it.

- Also notice that you can get all the important messages by scanning just the heads and subheads.

Illustration 9-3: The coupon.

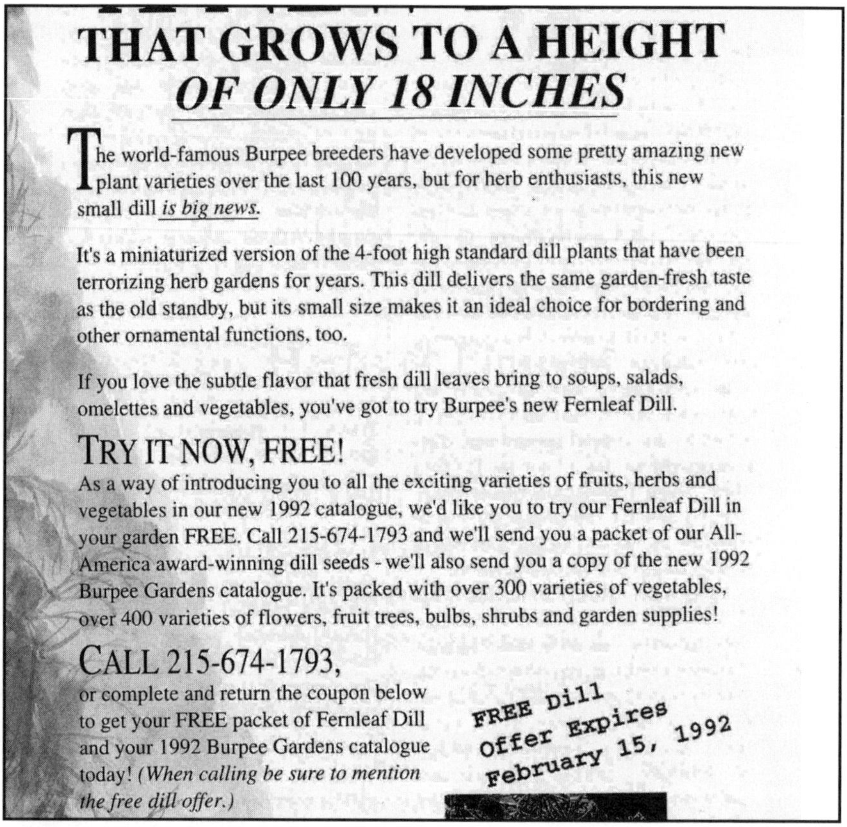

Illustration 9-4: Advertising copy.

Graphic

- Illustration 9-5 was designed to mirror the editorial style of the magazine.

- Note that the art is positioned on the left-hand side of the ad. This location made it possible to control the eye-flow of the reader, assuring the messages are received in the proper order.

- Also notice that the art and copy in this ad is backed by white. This has been shown to improve reader comprehension and response.

Illustration 9-5: A Graphic.

Aside from performing very well, this ad spawned a continuity series that continued to produce fine results. The Burpee Dill Ad was recognized as a finalist in the International Echo Awards.

Lead Generation—The Trick to Better Response

Space advertising for lead generation requires a highly specialized approach. While the key to creating a successful promotion in any direct response ad will hinge on the offer you create, how you create that offer, and the way you present it can vary substantially.

The Offer

To get the greatest and most valuable response to a lead generation ad, you're going to have to focus on the offer you make. This sounds obvious, but how often have you seen the phrase, "call for more information" at the bottom of an ad? Bad offer!

The idea is to create an offer that automatically selects the individuals, (or more accurately, invites them to select themselves) that you want your sales force to focus on--a self-qualifying offer. And, that means offering something that only a qualified prospect (someone with a legitimate need for your product or service) will see as having objective value.

An example of a bad offer for a mail-order computer seller might be a sweepstakes entry where the prospect could win a new PC just for responding. Almost anyone will take a new PC if you want to give it away for free. You'll be pulling all sorts of unqualified respondents. (Your uncle Louie will respond to this kind of offer, and you know how likely he is to shell out $1,900 for a new PC!)

An example of a good offer for the same company might be a PC configuration planning guide. This offer has independent value only to prospects actively considering a computer purchase (with some minor exceptions of course). If you're not considering a PC purchase, a guide to plan and configure a computer based on your needs is useless. For this reason, anyone who responds is likely to be a highly qualified prospect. That's a self-qualifying offer. (Uncle Lou will flip right past.)

Stopping power. This is the one you hear all the time. This is a legitimate handicap inherent in direct response space advertising that you don't have to deal with in direct mail, (at least not as much). Personally, I'll take six big powerful words (in the form of a command if possible), addressing a specific benefit of my offer to all the fancy graphics in the world. Again, there are exceptions, but I haven't seen many.

Use a coupon--in the lower right if you can.

Sell the offer. Don't sell your product. Don't sell your service. You should have designed your offer so that the only prospects who respond should ultimately have a need for your product anyway. It's a linear logic thing at this point. You don't need to sell "it" to them here. This is lead generation. Besides, if you could make a one-step sale of your product in a space ad, this would be a direct off-page sell ad. Just sell the offer, your salespeople will close the sale.

The Real Trick to an Effective Lead Generation Ad

When you create the copy for a lead generation ad, you'll be selling your offer. That's great, but don't say too much. Instead create a lot of questions about the offer. Refer to a number of benefits and hint at some very valuable information or some other benefit, but don't fully explain it. You don't want to give too much away.

Then slam the door. Tell them, in your call to action, to get the answers: "Find out...send for (offer)." Make them do what you want them to do to get the answers to the questions you've raised. If you can do this as a function of benefits they will receive by taking you up on your offer, you're going to succeed at the mailbox.

Using our PC company as an example again, you might say:

> "The fastest processor may not give you the fastest performance.
> You'll find out why when you send for your FREE configuration
> planner."

Notice we're not telling them we're the best or any of that...we're not even
telling them what we're selling. But if they're interested in answering the
question we've raised, they're probably shopping for a new PC. Now,
you've got the offer and the trick for exploiting it.

The challenge of creating the perfect self-qualifying offer, positioning it by
building the prospect's interest with a series of baiting questions, can be
interesting and even fun.

Two useful thoughts you should keep in mind when you're writing your
lead-generation ads:

1.   Don't tell them what you want them to know. Tell them what they
     need to know to do what you want them to do.

2.   If you can read any of your copy, (putting yourself in the prospec-
     t's shoes), and reply, so what?, you're not writing benefit oriented
     copy.

The Role Of The "Big Idea"

For years, both general advertising and direct response agencies alike have
sold the value of the "big idea" to their clients. Often this big idea boils
down to a recurring graphic image or a clever play on words. So, what's
wrong with that?

Plenty--particularly these days, with the ocean of promotional noise we all
swim through every day, and with the resulting cynicism that has become
a major dynamic of the mass market. The years of stopping a prospect
with some cryptic headline, designed to "make them wonder what we're
talking about" are all but gone.

And, if that's not enough for you to watch out for, there's also the fundamentally bad "big idea"...the kind that starts with some cliché like, "don't

paint yourself into a corner," (usually accompanied by the obligatory photo of an exhausted painter sitting in a corner).

So what should you be looking for in a big idea?

First: If the idea, or theme doesn't work to further the message of the ad, dump it. Don't convince yourself of the clever value, or of how well it fits your company's image or, (worst of all) that it's a one in a million idea that's just too cool to pass up. If your prospect can't look at your headline and know what you're talking about, what you're selling, and why they should care, it's costing you.

That brings us to the clever headline again. Assume you're talking to an extremely cynical audience at all times, because when it comes to the dynamics of a mass market, this outlook will usually help you and rarely hurt you. These people are not going to work to get your message. Put something cryptic in front of them and they'll tell you to "go scratch."

They don't know you, (even when you think your corporate name makes the earth move). If they don't see something in it for them, they're gone--or at least some percentage of the market you're trying to reach will be gone. And, forcibly excluding any percentage of viable prospects right out of the box, leaves you a smaller universe from which to succeed later.

Be clear. If your big idea works to alert the prospect of what you're going to talk about, and why the prospect should care-and at the same time provides some handy hook to carve out a corner of their mental awareness...use it! That's what you're looking for.

But, be aware, it's not always there. Sometimes every big, cool idea you get works as a distraction in relation to the goal you've set for your space ad. If so, just bag it--forget the "big idea." Write a clear, concise, benefit-oriented head that alludes to, or just unceremoniously states the offer. You're going to do better response numbers without the distractions. Clarity is king, the rest of the "big idea" is great if you can get it--but never trade clarity for a clever play on words.

That brings us to the basic function of any big idea. What should your big idea buy you? Without going into a lengthy discussion, your theme should try to provide a mental frame of reference for all the individual features and benefits associated with your company, product and/or service.

Ideally, when a prospect thinks of the allegorical, or visual nature of your concept, all the reasons why they should care, (the "what's-in-it-for-me") will come rushing to mind.

There is one other thing to watch out for, and that's becoming too broad with your concept...even if it fits well otherwise. If you can pull your company name out of the concept and drop in someone else's with the same level of effectiveness, don't use it. "Don't paint yourself into a corner" for example, could apply to an insurance offer, or some deal on flexible advanced airline fares. Use this type of line and the only thing you'll be carving out will be percentage points from your response numbers.

The bottom line is, be clear first. Make sure that your prospects can see what you're talking about and what's in it for them in as few words as possible. Then if you can accomplish that within a theme that adds value-without taking away from your message at all--you've got a "big idea." The best way to "stop" a prospect on your space ad is still by offering a good old-fashioned benefit!

Does Format Really Matter?
Case Study: Successful Business-to-Business Direct Marketing Space Ad Insert

The example we've just examined might seem strange for a book like this one. Considering the fact that it is a consumer ad, I suppose it is. The general precepts covered in the point-by-point 'how to' that preceded it however, were more obvious in this example than in any other I know of.

In this next example, we will move from a consumer ad to an example of a more business oriented space ad. You'll notice that the core tactics however er are essentially very similar.

The ads we will now review (Illustrations 9-6 and 9-7) were developed for Swan Technology, a manufacturer and direct seller of PC's. This example examines a clean A/B split test between two creative approaches, and a not-quite-as-clean test between formats (the two-page spread vs. the insert). You'll notice the separate 800 numbers used to keep the phone response measurable.

As with the previous example, you'll see that the ad shown in figure 9-6A contains all the basic elements we've already covered: begging self-qualifying questions from the first four words (headline), the response coupon in the lower right to provide visual notification of an offer, etc.

More interesting however, is the fact that this is one ugly ad! It's dark and weird-looking to say the least. This was not a mistake. In examining the publication which, by the way, was about three-quarters of an inch thick, we noticed that virtually all of the ads were 'white', tastefully designed, wall art.

Illustration 9-6A: DM Front of insert for PC Guide.

Needless to say, this one is not. Blending in was never the objective, and as you'll see, this ad did not.

You'll also want to take note of the fact that the offer in this ad is flashy, and colorful and promises independent value. In actuality, it was an inexpensive diskette with trial software mounted inside a CD jewel case to promise maximum value.

The competing ad in the A/B split test (figure 9-7) was certainly more tastefu and clever. But, it smacks of general advertising in its tactics--and its results.

Not only were most pertinent questions begged in weak fashion (when addressed at all), but the few questions that were framed, were actually

Illustration 9-6B: DM Rear of insert for PC Guide.

answered on the opposing page (or side in the case of the insert). The prospect had no motivation to respond for the trial to get their questions answered. They could simply scan page two of the ad and then go on looking at other articles or ads. They may have been interested enough to want the answers, which would indicate a potential interest in purchasing a new PC, but they were able to satisfy any curiosity on limited information listed in the ad. We never got the opportunity to know them or sell them.

This obvious error in strategy is a minor detail when you consider some of the other key issues discussed in this chapter that profoundly influence response:

Stopping power: Lets put a 'white' ad in a thick book full of white ads...that should jump out (or not!)

Headline: Let's come up with something clever that doesn't mean a thing.

Offer: Can we make the piece we're offering look like a generic pornographic video or something? I don't want it to appear to have any independent value.

Call-to-action: I will not come right out and tell the prospect what I want them to do...it isn't dignified.

Phone number: Look, if they want to reach us they'll find the phone number no matter how small it is.

This ad makes Mount Saint Helen look like a hiccup. It's the kind of disaster that could only be engineered by a general advertising agency pretending to know direct response.

When the final numbers came in, the 'ugly' direct response ad outpulled the 'sophisticated' general ad by more than two to one. Considering the fact that the client spent more than $180,000 per month in placement costs, you have to consider the implications. This client could have obtained

INSTEAD OF GOING AFTER OTHER COMPUTERS HEAD TO HEAD, WE'RE CHALLENGING THEM FACE TO FACE.

YOURS: OURS:

Illustration 9-7A: Front of insert for PC Guide.

twice as many qualified leads per month for the money they were spending, or they could have maintained their current lead flow while leaving an extra $90,000 per month at the bottom line! These are some pretty far reaching implications to result from the tactical aspects of creative execution alone!

That brings us to the two-page spread vs. insert test. Each of the creative tests was run as both a 2-page spread, and as a stand alone, front/back insert in its respective split of the publication. This gave us a fairly clean read of the relative difference in response determined by the format alone. To make an ugly story short, the insert delivered slightly more than twice the response of the two-page spread (in both A and B creative splits, incidentally). The spread was more expensive to produce, but the increase in performance was able to justify the expense.

IN CASE YOU HAVE TROUBLE WITH THIS TEST, THE ANSWERS ARE BELOW.

If our Free Time Trial shows that your computer's video performance isn't as fast as you'd like, perhaps you should switch to a super-quick Swan Direct Bus 486.

Beginning last spring with the ground-breaking Swan 486/33DB—the *Swan 486SX/25DB* system that shattered every video speed record for an Intel-based PC—we've moved even further ahead by building the first complete line of high-performance modular Swan 486 Direct Bus computers.

Each Swan 486DB system is engineered with true local bus architecture, the advanced dedicated bus technique that connects the video controller directly to the CPU, bypassing the relatively slow ISA bus.

Instead of sharing a 16-bit/8MHz data path with other peripheral instructions, the Swan 486DB provides video instructions with their own dedicated 32-bit path running at the same speed as the CPU. You won't get that in other local bus systems. So you can't possibly get the same startling results.

But that's not all. Our Direct Bus 486s are also powered by the latest version of the super-fast S3 video accelerator chip, optimized to off-load video routines so your CPU can work more efficiently.

This results in screen refresh rates that are *up to 20 times* faster. Which means you can run both Windows and DOS applications at astonishing speeds. Like re-draws in DTP and CAD. Page scrolls in word processing. Switching from one window to another is virtually instantaneous every time.

And when your CPU works faster, so can you.

THE FASTEST VIDEO, THE LONGEST WARRANTY
From high-end file servers to high-performance workstations, Swan has a 486DB system to fit every need and budget.

And when you buy from Swan, you also get our commitment to quality. Which means brand name components from Intel, Sony, Hewlett Packard and others. A system that's hand-built and signed by a single skilled craftsman, and tested for two days before it ships. Service and support that consistently earn high marks in customer satisfaction surveys.

And the only free 2-year, on-site warranty offered by a major direct marketer.

So now that you have the facts, it's time to call or send for the test. Of course, if you want the answers first, we'll be happy to provide them.

Swan

CIRCLE 104 ON READER SERVICE CARD

BUSINESS REPLY MAIL
FIRST CLASS MAIL PERMIT NO. 140 STATE COLLEGE PA

POSTAGE WILL BE PAID BY ADDRESSEE

SWAN TECHNOLOGIES
PO BOX 1006
STATE COLLEGE PA 16804-9959

NO POSTAGE NECESSARY IF MAILED IN THE UNITED STATES

When you look at this test, you begin to realize how important precepts of creative execution can actually be. Between the creative issues and the format, the execution accounted for a swing of about $135,000 per month in this case. (The difference between the performance of the poorly conceived two-page spread and the well-conceived insert accounted for an increase of roughly 75%!) Now, you can begin to see why we describe direct response space as a "dangerous and expensive place to make mistakes."

Illustration 9-7B: Rear of insert for PC Guide.

Selling Directly From the Space Ad

Using direct response space advertising to sell your product directly off-page can be a tough undertaking. While the fundamental elements of direct response apply in much the same manner as they do in lead generation, the ultimate goal is considerably more difficult. This time we're asking, in one way or another, for a monetary commitment and a decision on the spot.

That means the pressure will be on for you to make your offer even more compelling, your choice of messages more precise, and your creative execution, in both copy and design, flawless. With the right product or service and the right offer, this approach can be very rewarding. With the wrong product or service and the wrong offer, it can be a disaster, no matter how perfect the execution.

Your first problem is, you're working without a net. When you sell in the mail, it's easier to test the water to get a feel for your response without committing a large investment right off the bat. Then you can gauge your program around your initial results with some degree of confidence.

In space advertising, particularly in business to business applications, the circulation is often small or has a limited number of segmenting options available for you to limit your test. As a result you can find yourself stepping onto the wire with no idea of what you can expect.

One way you can at least get a feel for your response is to drop a very small mail test to a small portion of the circulation. The list will usually be available to you for the usual fee, particularly if you're going to be buying space from the same publication. Use an inexpensive format, like a double postcard, making the same offer with much the same creative treatment and see what happens. At least you'll get a sense of what to expect.

The next issue you'll want to address is the product or service you want to sell off page and the offer you construct to sell that product or service. The first question you may want to ask yourself is: What advantage will my prospect gain by ordering this sight-unseen, right now?

If the prospect can get an equivalent product through other less risky channels, they will probably do so unless you provide a darn good reason why that prospect should go with you. You have to do two things to overcome these concerns immediately.

First you need to eliminate the risk factor. That means you'll need some type of satisfaction guarantee. A free trial works well, (We won't bill you unless you decide to keep the product). Making this a time-sensitive, negative-option offer will probably benefit you best. (In other words, return it within x days and pay nothing. After x days, your credit card will be billed $xx). You can also offer a straight money-back guarantee if you can't administer a negative option.

Second, you need to provide a differentiating factor that makes your product more appealing than any other competing products. The most frequently used option here is price. It's not necessarily the best option. Obviously, you're far better off if you can build value in your product, rather than reduce the price of it. If you don't have a bona fide competitive advantage, you may be forced to offer a price concession to make your offer compelling. Always build in a time limit for the reduced price. Aside from protecting your margin in other channels, it will add the urgency factor.

If you can't do these two things, rethink selling off-page in direct response space advertising. Your product may not be suited to this channel. While direct mail can give you the "real estate" you need to build a convincing argument that can help you overcome these problems, space won't give you that much room or time.

Another concern you should be aware of is the packaging of your offer. Can you build a simple and concise message that describes your product and offer with the immediacy required to be successful in space? If you can't grab your prospect with your message, your product may not work in this medium.

Position the product or service you're selling. You'll want your offering to feel as tangible and self-contained as possible. In many cases, this is not an issue. For example, if you're selling a camera, it is what it's called. But if you're selling a collection of warranty services you could have a mess on your hands unless you position the group correctly. Give it a name. Label your group of products or services so your prospect perceives your offering as a single item that can be stored in their head as a single unit. This cleans up the decision-making process for the prospect, reducing it to a single "yes or no" choice. For example: the warranty group could be called The Productivity Assurance Pack. Now you've positioned your product in such a way that the prospect perceives your product as a single solution, not a group of associated products, each weighed on its own. As a result, your prospect has a single yes/no decision to make.

This will be one of the most important fundamentals in making your direct selling off-page successful. As in any direct marketing, the fewer choices your prospect is forced to make, the more successful you will be. Assuming that your prospects will work to understand how your product or service can help them is a pipe dream--they won't. And, in direct marketing space advertising the situation is even more extreme. If any part of your communication isn't perfectly clear, they'll demonstrate their protest by simply turning the page. The bottom line is boil your product or service offering down to a single decision in all facets of your communication--starting with the positioning of the product itself.

Next, you'll want to turn your attention to the headline, where the same fundamental issue of condensed clarity will apply, but with some added challenges.

There is no concept more overstated than the "Grabber" headline. If I had a nickel for all the times I heard a client ask for a real grabber, I'd have a bunch of nickels. The point is this: Forget about coming up with a grabber. Instead, focus on the customer's end benefit. What will the prospect have that they don't have now? Then make the line as short, concise and impact-oriented as possible. You'll have your grabber.

Going back to our warranty services package, a properly focused headline and subhead might read, Downtime A Problem? Your Machines May Fail...But Now Your Business Won't!

The moral to the story is: people are grabbed by what's in it for them-not by your cleverness. From their perspective, there's only one question, Why do I care?

In writing the copy for your ad, your focus should remain the same. Obviously, you need to tell them about the features of your product or service if you're going to ask them to make a decision on the spot. One formula you can use to communicate your features is as follows: start with a benefit, "Keep your productivity at 100% even when your machinery goes down." Then follow with your feature to make the benefit credible, "You'll receive a free loaner machine within 1 hour from one of more than 10 service trucks on the road in your area." Finally, if possible bring the offer into the story, "and, there's no better time to assure your productivity than now...order The Productivity Assurance Pack before June 21st, and your first month is free!" This is a simplified formula you can use to keep your prospects following a very linear path to the ultimate action you want them to take.

You're bound to do better in your direct off-page selling if you force yourself to answer these questions in this order: Why do I, the prospect, care?, What am I going to get that will make your claim hold water?, and What do I have to do to get this benefit/Why should I do it now instead of later?

As always, your offer construction will be critical. First, you need to eliminate the risk factor. Second, you need to provide a differentiating factor that makes your product more appealing than any other competing products.

Urgency is extremely important in selling directly off-page. You have very little time to convert your prospect. As a result, you want to force the decision process into your time frame, which is as close to immediate as possible. If your offer is attractive, a time limit will overcome the natural inertia of inaction. You're basically using the hardball technique: Get this now, or the deal's off!"

Finally, make sure you tell the prospect what action you want them to take. Use a coupon so the prospect knows, at a glance, that you want them to do something. Then, tell the prospect, in large enough letters that they can see them, exactly what you want them to do in order to take you up on your offer.

Make both responding, and options for payment as streamlined and simple as possible. Provide a toll-free number, and include the option of mail ordering your product. Make payment options as simple and clear as possible, reducing shipping and handling where applicable to a single cost with no computation required on the part of the prospect. Here again, make ordering as close to a single yes/no issue as you can.

In the general sense, the trick to direct-selling off-page successfully is the same trick you'll use in all your direct marketing: Get out of your own shoes and into those of your prospect. Look at things from their perspective. Communicate the messages that are important to them. Make ordering an easy decision for them. You just might make direct off-page space selling work for you.

Start talking about your company history...how you've spent years developing your reputation. Convince yourself that everybody knows you and wants your product, and that they just need to know how to get it--and you're finished.

Space Advertising Summarized

If you've been keeping up with this chapter, you've already had your fill of "the long of it." So, let's take the next few paragraphs and summarize "the short of it."

When to use Direct Response Space Advertising:

1) Lead Generation-If you have a product or service that appeals to a broad horizontal audience, direct response space is a great vehicle for locating qualified prospects and prompting them to separate themselves from the non-qualified prospects.

    -or-

    Lead Generation-If you have a narrow market niche and you can gain access to tightly targeted publications that go exclusively to your prospect group, space can be made to work as well.

2) Selling Directly Off-Page-You can make this work if your product or service has broad horizontal appeal, has a strong enough price point and margin to support the selling cost, and can be wrapped up tightly enough, (via your offer), to be perceived as a single "yes/no" decision for the customer. But remember, you're asking for money and that's the ultimate qualifier. You will need some form of guarantee to eliminate the risk for your prospects.

How to use Direct Response Space Advertising:

1) Remember to sell your group one step at a time. If you're selling a $20,000 technical product, don't try to sell directly off-page in a single step. First use a self-qualifying offer to get viable prospects to identify themselves. That means promoting a lead generation offer that will have an appeal only to those who would ultimately want or need your product. Then forget about your product. Sell only the next step. Sell only your immediate offer. You'll have plenty of time to sell them your product after you know who they are!

    There is an extremely valuable axiom I try to keep in mind whenever I work on a Direct Response Ad: Don't tell your prospect what you want them to know...instead, tell them what they need to know to do what you want them to do.

    That brings us to the construction of the self-qualifying offer. Remember that a self-qualifying offer should have appeal only to your ultimate sales prospect. Don't use sweepstakes. Everybody wants to

win something for free--even prospects that would never want your product or service. On the other hand, if you're selling computers and you offer a Computer Configuration Planning Guide, you can rest assured that the only prospects requesting that type of offer, are people that have an interest in configuring a new system. Those prospects will by definition fit your ideal sales prospect profile. As you can see, the offer itself selects only qualified leads-hence the term "self-qualifying."

2) Clarity is King-Don't try to use clever plays on words or cryptic photos and graphics. Make your communication as clear and impact-oriented as possible. Remember, the object is to convey what you're going to talk about, why your prospect should care (benefit), what they're going to get by doing what you want them to do (offer), and what action you want them to take to get it. Anything else you add will dilute these messages. Stay focused on selling the single step you want the prospect to take.

3) Use a coupon in the bottom right-hand corner of your ad. It's ugly, but it works.

4) Specify the right-hand page whenever you can and get as close to the front of your publication as possible.

That's it. These are a few of the most important elements in determining how well your direct response space advertisement will work.

There is just one more thing. After you've driven yourself crazy trying to make direct response space pay off for your business, rent 5,000 names from your best publication and mail a double postcard that makes the same offer as your space ad. Odds are, you'll make a lot more money and spend less doing it.

About Mark Mancini:

Mark Mancini, is Founder of Mancini Creative, a direct response agency specializing in creative development for business-to-business advertising. He has authored a two-year series of articles on the subject of direct response space advertising for The Business Marketing Notepad, a bi-monthly industry newsletter. He has also written and co-illustrated (with project partner Michael McVey) The Aaronville Midnight Parade, a children's book slated to be published and distributed nationally in summer 1999 by Pelican Press. After personally directing more than 2,500 business-to-business and consumer promotions over the past 14 years, Mark works with clients nationwide who have already committed themselves to the expensive and widely misused medium of direct response space advertising, helping them achieve successful, quantifiable returns.

Mark Mancini
President
Mancini Creative
64 South Main Street
Medford, NJ 08055
Phone: (609)654-7700
FAX: (609)657-7709
Email: mmancini@voicenet.com

Chapter 10
The Internet

No other communication medium has evolved as quickly and dynamically as the internet. The format has been in wide commercial use for less than five years and is growing exponentially with each passing year. Where will it go? When will the rate of growth slow down? No one knows the answer to these and other pressing questions. As we complete this chapter, the internet has probably expanded from when we started. One thing is for sure, it is changing the way business does business.

We think that the internet will eventually become the primary means of communication between businesses and their customers. As you read this chapter, the internet is moving from the pre-historic era to the cave-dweller era; internet communications are beginning to dramatically affect traditional direct marketing systems and procedures. By now, the internet's affect has caused realignment of channels, companies, customer communications and customer relationships.

The explosive growth in the past few years in the commercial use of the internet is an indication of what we can expect in the future. In the past four years the easy-to-use World Wide Web (WWW) has fostered:

- Companies traditionally associated with face-to-face selling are specializing in selling products directly over the internet. One company is selling $500 million a month in automobiles. Two companies are selling PCs on-line at the rate of millions of dollars a day.

- Yellow pages and telephone books are becoming obsolete and sliding into the archives along with road maps and travel agents.

- Overnight delivery companies 'hiring' their customers to do their own package tracking thus reducing their own overhead by millions of dollars each month.

- A paradigm change shifting one-third of business communication to e-mail.

The applications of the internet for the business direct marketer are exciting and challenging. Your deployment of this communications medium is largely up to your imagination and vision coupled with the abilities and capabilities of your support systems.

Internet Defined

The following is the definition of the internet from the marketing perspective. This definition is an attempt to establish a common understanding for business marketers.

> *The internet is an interactive communications medium capable of supporting human/business interaction directly (synchronous), indirectly (asynchronous) and surreptitiously (artificial intelligence) through the transfer of digital information from and to text or database formats.*

It can be used for advertising, promoting, enhancing and selling ideas, goods and services through reactive and proactive contact to qualify, reply and close.

It can be employed locally, regionally, nationally and internationally at the same cost.

It is not bound by traditional media or by artificial constraints of borders, territories, regulations and controls.

It provides increased satisfaction to users/buyers due to on-demand immediacy.

It provides improved results to sellers due to decreased costs, content flexibility, expanded markets, enhanced customer relationships and increased market reach and feedback.

The Internet in Business

The progression to full use of the internet in business typically follows six steps:

- Advertisement
- Promotion
- Interaction
- Transaction
- Transformation
- Community

Most companies seem to go through these steps, so a brief explanation will help you understand where your company is in this progression.

- **Level I - Advertisement**. This entry level is the use of the World Wide Web to display a home page and a few associated or linked pages. Most companies putting up the initial page for WWW presence have overly enthusiastic dreams of being overwhelmed by new business inquiries. The truth is that having a home page on the WWW is like putting a billboard in your basement. You probably feel very good about the home page, but no one using the WWW knows where to look for your company. The typical home page is usually linked to very exciting information like pictures of the company's building, and a message from the president complete with their picture. We like to refer to this level of internet use as the ego phase. Companies rush to have their home page so the owners and/or senior management will be included in social circles as a company that has a presence on the WWW.

- **Level II - Promotion**. The ease of programming basic web pages encouraged many companies to convert existing brochures and promotional materials from desktop publishing applications (electronic format) to WWW electronic pages. This caused an explosion in the number of pages on a website from a few to several hundred. It also caused the number of pages on the WWW to expand exponentially to millions of pages with tremendous growth continuing with every passing day. Often called brochureware, this expansion of the number of pages in the company site added to the personal pleasure of owners and managers but, like the home page, did nothing to generate additional business inquiries. While promoting the company was the intent of this phase, it can more aptly be called the 'bit-barfing' phase. Millions of data bits regurgitated into cyberspace.

- **Level III - Interaction.** This phase of internet use is the first time a prospect or customer can benefit from your company's web presence. Visitors to the website can receive information about something that is of concern to them and not your company. Once the prospect or customer has located your website, they can learn about your products, capture information about a reseller and even determine how to purchase a specific solution to their problem. A customer can access the company site to download a specification sheet, manual or material safety data sheet (MSDS); services previously only provided by customer service. The interactive level allows a prospect or customer to gain desired information when they want it with no delay or hassle. The interactive level satisfies customer needs and lowers costs by reducing demands on customer service. One example allows a customer to access the website and determine the status of an overnight delivery. The customer, using their air bill number provided by an overnight delivery company, can access the location of the package, status, and even the person who signed the delivery receipt. In essence, the overnight delivery company has hired its customers to perform their own customer service. Research demonstrates that customers are more satisfied with this new relationship even though they are doing more work and incurring the cost of internet access.

- **Level IV - Transaction.** At this level the prospect or customer can initiate action from your company. The prospect can request a sample or accept another offer you may have made. In some cases, the customer can even order a product or request a technical support visit from your company. If you are selling products or services on the website, a customer or a prospect may be able to order on-line using some form of credit billing. Some customers may have pre-established credit and receive a bill for their purchase, while others would have to provide a credit card number. At the transaction level, the company can significantly reduce selling costs of its sales people and customer service while increasing revenue and acquiring new customers. The effect on ROI can be substantial with decreased costs and increased revenue.

- **Level V - Transformation.** At this level the relationship between your company and its markets has moved from traditional to electronic. The internet is not used occasionally, but has become the accepted and preferred form of communication between you and your customers. In the early days of the internet you might have to call someone to tell them you had sent them an email. Most of us have now transformed far enough that we no longer call to make email notification. We send the email in lieu of calling or any other form of contact. The transformation is powerful because internal office communication is more efficient and effective since many people can be contacted with the same email. In addition, communication can be timely and available whenever needed locally or internationally. Transformation can have a disruptive effect. It can cause the re-alignment or re-structuring of the relationship between a distribution channel and its markets. For example, a manufacturer can eliminate one or more channel levels, opting to use the internet to sell directly to an end user or OEM. Transformation of this nature will become common if channel partners do not use the internet to increase their added value in the relationship between themselves and the customers. The less involved a business-partner is in dealing directly with their customers, the easier it will be for them to be abandoned by the manufacturer. The manufacturer will instead interact with customers directly via the internet.

- **Level VI - Community.** At this highest level of internet progression, a group of people with common interests are bound together by emotional involvement. The emotional connection can range from personal commitment to a subject, like a health issue, to a professional group supporting each other through information transfer. The community is a group of people with common interests in a topic or issue who may not otherwise come together. Communities can be mailing lists (email subscription or opt in, not mailing lists as it applies elsewhere in this book), collaboration forums, bulletin boards, chat rooms, IRC (internet Relay Chat) or any combination of these. A company cannot set up a community and expect it to flourish. The energy of the community comes from the participants. It can be fostered or supported by a sponsoring company, but it will only be successful if it is of emotional value to the members. Many web sites have some type of forum or bulletin board, 99% of which are unused. The motivation for a community is user based and emotional. A community will thrive only when emotion is satisfied.

As we mentioned earlier, many companies evolve in their use of the internet and seem to follow the progression described above. Evaluate expansion on the internet within your company. Consider where you are today and where you would like to go in the future in view of the flexibility and opportunities the internet can provide.

Internet ROI

In non-catalog business direct marketing, communications return-on-investment is difficult to determine. As a communications medium, the internet is no exception. Determining the specific ROI of direct mail, advertising, telemarketing, trade shows and internet when used as multimedia is impossible to determine for each medium. Revenue cannot be assigned to the medium that generated the sale. If an order is placed online, the sale is assigned to the internet. However, if an order is placed via phone for a product only available on the internet, the revenue is assigned to the phone center. This debate will continue as long as sales people and managers are compensated based on the sales generated by them and their departments. However, there are ways to determine general ROI for the internet.

The internet creates a ROI in three ways:

- Reduced costs
- Increased revenue
- Increased lifetime value

One of the most obvious areas experiencing reduced costs is customer service. The internet can allow customers to provide their own customer service. Order status, product availability, pricing, and service tracking can all be done by the customers using their own computer. As mentioned earlier, overnight delivery companies experienced dramatic and immediate reductions in customer service staffing levels and reduced phone charges by allowing their customers to check their packages via the internet directly from the company's database. These cost reductions were due to a decrease in inbound customer service calls. Based on the amount of reduced call volume, it is obvious that customers are satisfied with the flexibility and convenience of on-line interaction.

Similar savings can result if you make your customer support data available for review and inquiry to specific accounts. Some companies are allowing customers to place their own orders, inquire about product availability and track shipment status. In the future the more access you provide to customers directly, the better your opportunity to increase loyalty and lifetime value. Finally, allowing customers direct access to your database via the internet can eliminate the need for expanded customer service departments in traditional off-hours. If you're an east coast company providing service throughout the country, you can maintain high service levels and improve customer service by making information available via the internet.

Another opportunity to reduce costs can be achieved by providing international service via the internet without having to add special bi-lingual personnel or expand the hours of your customer service center. Electronic customer service is not the end-all solution to all problems, but combined with a well conceived customer service strategy, you can reduce costs and improve customer service worldwide.

Increased revenue is the second opportunity for ROI from your internet expansion. Many companies have products and services that are bought but seldom sold. These are the core products and services that are your market staple. For example, replacement parts and contract-service extensions are often purchased by customers, but never sold by a salesperson or promotion. Both of these types of products or services generate increases in sales without increased marketing and selling expenses. These are ideal products that can be offered and sold via the internet with little or no disruption to your existing sales approach.

You can control the quality of the sales presentation as well as provide a strong unique selling proposition on the internet. Your customer has made the decision, breaking the inertia, to visit and shop at your website. If you provide complete product descriptions and benefits, many customers will purchase immediately. In addition, you can cross-sell and up-sell 100% of the time by designing additional products for the specific customer based on that individual's purchase history.

Experience has demonstrated that the average on-line purchase is higher than the average value through catalog or direct mail purchase. We surmise that customers are more relaxed and can make decisions without intervention by a sales or customer service person. Many are willing to take more time evaluating and studying alternatives as well as solving their entire problem instead of just purchasing a single product. Available data on on-line average orders indicates that the more control customers have in a buying situation, the more likely they are to buy even larger quantities. Think about how defensive you become when it feels like someone is trying to sell you something. During an interactive session on the internet, the customer is always in 'control.

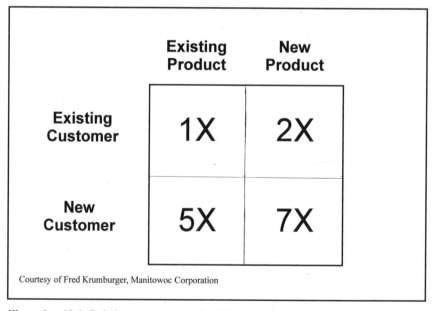

	Existing Product	New Product
Existing Customer	1X	2X
New Customer	5X	7X

Courtesy of Fred Krumburger, Manitowoc Corporation

Illustration 10-1: Relative resources required for marketing current and new products to current and new customers.

Increased revenue on the internet will take six to eighteen months to gain momentum. Even with millions of people on-line, sales grow at a slow but increasing rate. You may experience some immediate uplift in sales by offering product sales on the internet, but the real payoff will come in the future as your website gains acceptance.

Increased customer lifetime value is the third opportunity for ROI available from the expansion of your use of the internet. The business marketer has long known that it is five to seven times more expensive to acquire a new customer than to increase sales to existing accounts (Illustration 10-1). The internet offers you an opportunity to create more loyal and satisfied customers because they can control their relationship with you. Your responsibility is to make available what they want on-line.

Reducing customer loss by as little by as 5% can double a company's profits. As mentioned earlier, you can allow customers access to their sales history with your company as well as your product and order processing files. Instead of having to inquire via the customer service department, the customer can have access to their complete history with your company directly on their desktop. Customers will often review other products and services while visiting your website. In addition, you can provide information about other related products or services. Although we will often train customer service personnel to cross-sell and up-sell, they will often resist actually selling the customer because they may feel too 'pushy'. The total control and anonymity of the internet experienced by the customer allows them to navigate into other areas of your company without fear or pressure. This feeling of control goes a long way to enhancing the positive experience the customer has in dealing with your company.

Most people are nervous and threatened when dealing with salespeople and the internet eliminates this insecurity. By allowing customers complete access whenever they need it, you can develop a level of loyalty that will increase the length of time a customer does business with your company as well as their level of purchase activity. Customer service is perceived by customers and is often based on their last experience with you. The internet can allow you to ensure a 100% satisfaction level all of the time. One word of caution, although we firmly believe that you can and should make as much of your customer relationship information available to your customers as possible, you will still need a customer service department. As time goes on and technology expands, it will be possible to automatically connect an internet transaction to a live operator when the need arises.

Internet Options

The internet can be used as a synchronous and/or asynchronous communications medium. Like so many other technological terms, these two have come to mean different things to technology and communications personnel. For our discussions the following definitions will be used.

- *Synchronous communication requires that all people be involved at the same time.* For example, when talking on the telephone with one or more people, everyone needs to be on the phone at the same time.

- *Asynchronous is when communication occurs at different times.* When you leave a voice message for someone to listen to later, or when many people call in at different times to hear a message, you have communicated asynchronously.

There is a popularity among many internet community people to use synchronous text communications known as Chat Rooms. In a Chat Room

	Synchronous	**Asynchronous**
Text	**Chat Rooms**	**Email**
Graphics	**IRC**	**GIF, JPEG, HTML, JAVA, On Demand Video**

Illustration 10-2: Internet use can be synchronous or asynchronous.

two or more people can post text-based messages for everyone in the chat to read and respond to. Some of the available applications allow for the use of a common sketch-pad and also allow for drawings to be posted so many people can collaborate at one time. A caution concerning chats is that when the chat is over, like an unrecorded phone call, the messages posted to the chat may be lost. The use of the internet for synchronous audio/video conferencing will continue to grow. As applications move to the desktop and connectivity bandwidth increases, we will all use the internet as our audio/video medium just as we have grown to use the telephone.

There are two major asynchronous internet applications in business marketing:

- **Email** - is the use of text based communications delivered from one computer to another. It can also be delivered to multiple recipients at the same time using a customer or prospect database. Email delivered indiscriminately to thousand or millions of email addresses, called *spam*, is the electronic equivalent of true junk mail delivered to totally unqualified individuals.

  Business has become more and more dependent upon email as a primary communications vehicle. The asynchronous nature of email allows people to communicate with each other when it is convenient. As you read this book, fellow employees, customers, or prospects can leave you detail messages at your email address. Even more convenient is the ease with which you can respond or distribute the original message and/or the response to others. The most critical aspect is that the originator of the message can mail you at their convenience even though you may not be available. And you can respond at your convenience when they might not be available.

- **Static and Database-served World Wide Web Sites** deliver graphics, text and allow the user to interact with information presentations using a client-server computing model. Users can access information by filling in blanks, making selections and accessing text-based or database-served information. The information is delivered to the user via web pages, available whenever a user wants to access them. Companies are making more and more information about their products, services and businesses available. Unfortunately, many of the web pages are poorly designed and don't have a specific objective.

As you consider expanding your use of the internet, both synchronous and asynchronous communication can be used independently or integrated. How synchronous and asynchronous communications are combined depends on your needs. Can your communications be done in batch mode asynchronously or process mode with everyone at the same time synchronously? Some applications will require batch while others need process type applications. The determination of batch or process is part of the internet planning and evaluation process.

Internet - Intranets - Extranets

The internet is a global computer network providing information to users using standard communication protocols and the client-server computing model. Web sites and other information servers currently number in the hundreds of thousands and users in the hundreds of millions. The internet has also spawned two derivatives, intranets and extranets.

An intranet uses internet technology inside a company for internal communications. Intranets are not available to people outside of the company network. Intranets take advantage of e-mail and Web-based communication for internal use. Users can receive and send e-mail to the larger internet while signed onto these internal networks but outside users have no access to the web-based information on such a private network or intranet.

Extranets use the same internet technology for larger private audiences. Many utilize password protection to restrict access to the particular people or organizations the network is designed to serve. An example of an extranet is an on-line lead/customer management system that restricts access to sales people that have an assigned ID and password. As time goes on this may become one of the most valuable approaches to using the internet. Customer information, sales history and product pricing and availability can be made available to customers. By using a unique password or identification number (ID) the customer can access specific information related to them. Based on the password, your systems can provide special pricing and promotions to that specific customer. In addition, customers will be able to perform their own customer service functions like order status and tracking, service inquiries and other related functions.

Extranets can also be a valuable resource for some internal functions. Colleges and universities can make grades and class schedules available to specific students. Financial institutions will be able to provide on-line services that go far beyond those already available. Companies can provide salespeople access to the extranet where they provide information on leads and customers.

Internet Strategic Applications

The internet can change the relationships of the various business partners in the supply chain (Illustration 10-3). You can link suppliers with the front and the back office and deliver information to customers on-demand. Each distribution channel participant provides and receives relevant information and updates information relevant to others in the chain.

For example, ABC manufacturer of household appliances uses the internet to store, update and make available shared information to various members in the distribution and supply chain.

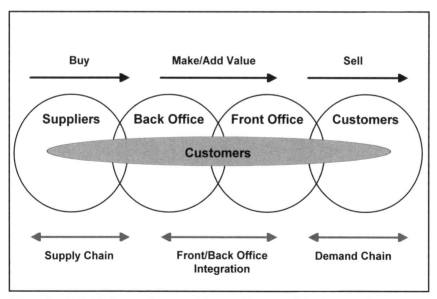

Illustration 10-3: The Internet has potential to provide connectivity from suppliers to users.

ABC maintains operational, dimensional, repair and maintenance information on their appliances on the internet. The information can be used by the company's customer service group as referral and reference information for inquiries. Distributors and retailers can use the information for customer service and technical support. Designers and people decorating their homes can use the information for planning. Service activities can use the information for repair support and training data for technical support personnel.

ABC's on-line information can be made available as part of any business partners' website within the distribution and supply channel. The partner does not need to develop, maintain or update the information. ABC manages and updates the information ensuring the brand, product and quality of the presentation through the channel all the way to the ultimate consumer. The partner does not incur any added overhead duplicating ABC's information, and they don't have to be concerned with the currency of the information on their own company website.

Information gathered on-line about the ultimate customer, end-user or OEM by ABC can also be shared with all partners within the channel. This sharing of customer information tends to improve the understanding and effectiveness of all the channel partners. By improving the under-

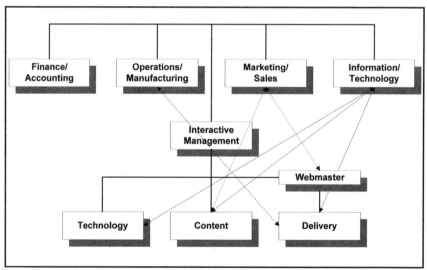

Illustration 10-4: Strategic applications of the Internet will require a new organization structure.

standing of customers at all levels of the supply chain, each channel partner can improve their individual performance as well as overall customer satisfaction.

Organization Structure

There are three areas of responsibility for effectively using the internet:

- Content - the information provided and the interactivity between your company and the various users.

- Technology - the hardware and software available to support the content and the connectivity to the internet.

- Delivery - presentation of the content and interactivity between users and the company, using available technology.

How these three responsibilities are assigned creates challenges and problems for many organizations. Unfortunately, where you assign the responsibilities of the internet within a company will often dictate the level of success you experience.

Since the internet deals with computers, the natural tendency is to have the head of Information Technologies (IT or whatever you call the computer department) responsible for your company's use of the internet. Experience teaches us that website maintenance and updating quickly becomes an unbudgeted burden for the IT department. In order to offset the additional costs, IT is more than happy to share costs by allocating them to other departments. This process tends to create rancor and dissatisfaction within the other departments who don't see any apparent benefit from the internet.

Marketing is typically responsible for content and often becomes the other primary department selected to handle internet expansion. However, marketing is seldom in the business of dealing with technology and therefore cannot independently ensure the conversion of marketing content to an internet presentation. In addition, marketing is not staffed or trained to deal with the dynamics of day-to-day website management. Ultimately, however, marketing has to work with IT to ensure successful implementation and management of the web site.

Delivery is often the responsibility of the webmaster. Though this is an evolving and misused title, it can best be applied to an individual within a company who is responsible for delivery of web communication. It is up to the webmaster to work with IT to understand and purchase technology that is necessary to deliver the requirements that marketing has established. The webmaster is also responsible to marketing for the conversion of content and interactive strategies to the internet as well as gathering information from the internet. Where the webmaster resides and to whom the webmaster reports can be a difficult decision. Unfortunately, many companies don't understand the far reaching implications of the internet and relegate webmaster reporting as just another technology decision.

As part of the IT organization, the webmaster will assume technology duties assigned by IT management. Typically in IT, the webmaster simply becomes a marketing aware programmer. Internet decisions tend to take the flavor and focus of the information department with little emphasis on communicating a marketing and sales message.

If the webmaster is part of the marketing department, the internet becomes one of the communications managers like the direct marketing manager, the trade show manager, or the advertising manager. Because the internet relies heavily on technology and technical enhancements, the webmaster will often have to politic with the IT department to get support. In this position the internet is underutilized as a strategic opportunity. The internet can become a go-to-market strategy or channel on a global scale. Relegating it to the status of a marketing medium rather than a strategic medium does not allow it to be properly exploited.

The webmaster should report to an executive level with enough authority to support national and, if it applies, global policy. This level of reporting may seem extreme until you consider the impact the internet can have on your overall success. It can provide all the communications services of a company from lead acquisition to customer acquisition and expand to enhance the lifetime value of customers.

As you can see, implementation of the internet crosses many department and practical reporting structures within most companies. There is a significant dependency on marketing, sales, IT and operations in order for your expansion of the internet to be successful. The internet can support and expand sales, service and customer service on a global basis with no increased variable communications costs. What other activity can have as much impact within your company? Organizations need to recognize the impact this new medium can have and elevate the function and reporting to a high enough level to facilitate success.

Database and the Internet

The internet has two important relationships with the database:

1. The internet serves as a giant database containing millions of pages of information. This huge database of information is available to anyone, twenty-four hours a day, seven days a week.

2. Internet browser and supporting technologies allow direct access to virtually any database by any user, assuming proper security, worldwide.

As a database, the internet is the most extensive electronic resource of information and options ever provided to the human race. It is no wonder that many people are perplexed and intimidated by the vastness of the resource. Searches for a product or service using commercial search engines can yield thousand of locations that mention that product or service. Finding exactly what you are looking for is difficult when you aren't specific enough in your requests. Search engines and other directory and context-based technologies are improving every day, but at this point, the hardest part of Web communication is attracting initial and lasting relationships with users.

If you're selling custom carpets, you cannot expect a user to find your custom carpets if they search the internet only for the word "carpet." In this search, every page with the word *carpet* on it will be identified. If the user instead searches for custom+carpet, the search will be reduced to perhaps 20% of the original number of pages they have to review.

Your customer and prospect's ability to find your company, products, and services depends on their skill, the capabilities of the many internet search engines and directories and your integration of the internet into your promotional activities. It is much easier for a customer to be given a specific Web address (called a URL) or email address to contact you than for a customer to try and find you on-line.

Be proactive with customers and prospects alike. Provide web and email addresses on all promotional materials. And to really drive traffic, make specific offers for those that use the internet. Typically, it is less expensive for you to deal with people on the internet and you should encourage electronic activity. Don't be bashful in offering discounts and other incentives for transactions initiated on the internet.

The Web browser can serve customers and prospects by allowing them to access whatever database you want to make available. The overnight delivery companies allow customers access to their tracking system to reduce customer-tracking inquiries. The growth of the internet is going to force us to consider making our internal databases available to our customers. Customers want information immediately and are willing to incur additional expense and even do more work to get that information. It is almost unbelievable that customers doing their own tracking inquiries are spending more money and time and are happier. They find security in knowing the data is available when they want it without dealing with a customer service person.

You could have the same impact with your customers if order tracking or billing is an issue for them. If these issues create customer inquiries, give your customers access to their billing accounts on-line. Technologies make the delivery of database information practical and inexpensive on the web. Whenever you have a person reading information from a printout or a terminal and delivering it to your customers, put that information on-line and directly reach that other person elsewhere in the company. This is how you hire your customers to provide their own customer service. You will probably be surprised at how receptive customers are to the additional effort and how loyal they'll become to your company.

The same technologies that allow customers access to information can deliver updated information back to your database. For example, you can allow a customer to update a bill-to address because the accounts payable department has moved. This mundane change of address can be accomplished very easily by the customer thus reducing your cost of service. By working directly through the internet (even if you put an audit on the change before you allow it to be permanent), paperwork and the number of people involved can be significantly reduced.

In this example, billing the correct address can also improve cash receipts by as much as one week to ten days simply because bills are not sent to the wrong address.

Moving information among many company databases is another opportunity of the internet. Applications can be built that access all company databases (legacy to relational) to provide decision support that has been dreamed of but never delivered. Web-based technologies can reach into proprietary databases and retrieve data and deliver it to managers quickly and efficiently. The availability of off-the-shelf analysis software for specialized decision support allows timely utilization of the information. These technologies can save thousands and even millions of dollars in large organizations by reducing custom programming for decision support, and reducing the need to move to a single enterprise-wide database.

Measurement

A visitor to any website provides a great deal of information that can be measured and collected for analysis and customization of presentations. The key to web measurement is to determine what measurements are important for decision making. Many marketers fall into a trap of over measurement simply because there is so much data made available on each site visitor. The data trap is alluring since marketers have imagined acquiring such in-depth data in other media but have only been able to surmise or observe it there. We suggest you use the same judgment you would make evaluating all data. Explore all available data until you determine the three or four data points that provide information on the visitor's behaviors that moves them to become a customer.

The computer serving the website can gather all types of data:

- The server where visitors came from. For example there may be 500 visitors from one of the AOL servers. This is interesting but provides no profile information about the individual visitor. To gain marketing information you can request that the visitor complete a form or questionnaire. As in all good direct marketing, an offer of some type will increase the number of people who provide information.

- Point of entry - the page a visitor used as the entry page to the site. It could be the home page. It could be a link from a search engine to a key word page. The best entry page is when you are running some type of program that is driving people to a specific page so you determine how many people arriving on the site are a result of that particular promotion.

- Pages visited during the visit and length of time on each page. This information can provide insight into the pages that the market considers valuable. Frequency and duration indicate the number of visitors that viewed the page, and how long they spent reviewing whatever is on the page. This information can also be misleading. A visitor could access a page and take a phone call, thus giving the false data that time was spent reviewing the page.

- Links - the way a visitor moved around the site from one page to the next. This information is useful in designing better user interfaces and pathways to important information.

- Hits - a hit is a file download by the web server. It documents a page access plus the graphics files included on the page. Accessing a page with five graphics is counted as six hits. Average hits per person vary from site to site depending on the average number of graphics per page and the number of pages a visitor accesses. It will be worthwhile to develop a rule of thumb for your site that indicates the number of visitors based on the number of hits divided by the average hits per visitor. The easiest way to determine the average hits per visitor is to monitor the number of users who access for a month, and divide it into the number of hits.

The real measurement of the internet is not based on the electronic data. It is based on the same standards as all direct marketing: cost per qualified lead, cost per sale, sales per visitor, sales per hit. Measuring the internet on a cost per qualified lead and revenue basis put it in the media mix for comparison. As in all measurement the issues are: what are the costs for development, monthly upkeep and/or variable cost of the contact?

Measurement reflects the true value of the internet to the business-to-business marketer. The internet will become the business-to-business medium for these reasons:

1. The cost of contact is virtually zero.

2. The internet is global for the same cost as national.

3. The 7/ 24 / 365 availability of information for customers.

4. The flexibility afforded the marketer to adjust strategies.

5. The movement through and support of channels serving end users, OEMs, and consumers.

Internet Creative

When developing an internet website, consider these four components:

1. Markets and audiences served.

2. Objectives for the site or section of a site for each market or audience.

3. Structural design of user movements from page to page within the site.

4. Content of the pages.

How well a marketer understands their markets can be seen by what appears on the *Home Page*, the first page of a website.

A home page that has a tangle of links, buttons, bangles and flashing graphics indicates the website is being managed by a non-marketer. It is being managed either by IT or by an administrative person given the responsibility for the website. Often IT and admin personnel lack the understanding of the importance of questioning and interviewing. The home page should include the initial questions put to a visitor to determine the purpose of their visit. It is absolutely necessary to move a visitor to their realm of interest in as few clicks as possible. A guide to keep in mind is three clicks to value. This guide will help keep your site easy to use and focused from the point of view of your prospects.

We recently redesigned a home page for a public utility that provides electricity and gas to various markets in a region of the country. Their home page was a mess. Every product manager and service manager wanted links from the home page. The result was a home page that made little sense to anyone, except the product managers. We began by reviewing the markets served: industrial, small business, consumer and investor. Visitors to the site were in one of these four market groups. By reducing the home page presentation to these four major categories, the home page became more readable and allowed for the company to use the small amount of available space on a computer monitor for special promotions.

A good sales person knows that you can't begin to sell until you understand what the prospect wants to buy, so each new relationship begins with a series of questions. An effective website is structured the same way - questions whose answers will help deliver useful information. The home page asks the first question - who are you? Based on which link visitors select identifies which market they are from. In the case of the utility company, a visitor who elects to go to the industrial section can be assumed to be an industrial user. The home page in the industrial section can offer a second set of questions by presenting options to the visitor. Within two clicks, the visitor can be viewing information that is of specific interest to them.

Four issues must be constantly considered when marketers guide creative development and evaluation of a web site, section, and/or page.

1. Each section/unit/page of the website must serve a market.

2. Each section/unit/page must have an objective.

3. Each section/unit/page must be structured to support the market being served.

4. Each section/unit/page must deliver messages visually and textually to communicate the objectives.

In the case of the utility company, the section created for the industrial market can be much more technical and present information in terms of much larger budgets than the section developed for the consumer. In both cases a visitor to either section has information needs that the utility company must understand and fulfill while achieving the objectives of the company. The industrial user can have a much more technical set of options as part of the structure and content. The consumer who lacks understanding of what electricity is and how much it costs, is presented with a non-technical structure with few choices. The utility can guide the consumer through the learning process through its presentation.

When designing a website it is important to understand that each page can be the arrival page by a visitor. This can be intentional - when you make a special offer and publish a web address that brings a responder to a certain page on the site. It can also be unintentional - when a search engine links visitors to your page based on key words. Because of this intentional or unintentional access to a page on the site, it is important to have obvious navigation options that can bring a visitor back to the home page or take them to a section that is of interest. In the case of the utility company, the navigation is the same as the major markets identified on the home page. A visitor can move quickly to an area of interest from any page on the entire site.

Navigation is important to give visitors options. This will keep them on your site as they seek interest areas. Good navigation will also keep them from leaving your site out of frustration after not being able to access an area of interest quickly and easily. With millions of pages of information available, visitors do not want to understand your logic. They only want what they came to your site for as quickly and as easily as possible.

Developing and Executing Internet Strategies

Internet deployment requires a sound business proposition to be successful. The internet will not fix a flawed business proposition. For example, if the leads you are developing for the sales force are of low quality, distributing them on the internet does not make them better. Poor quality leads delivered to your sales force is a waste of time and money via any medium including the internet. In similar manner, products and services that have no existing markets will not perform well on the internet.

When developing internet strategies there are three levels to consider: Strategic, Tactical and Administrative. Each of these levels can be approached using a few steps.

Strategic - using the internet as a channel for new and existing markets that may replace existing channels requires:

- Vision of Potential - understanding the internet as more than a communications medium and envisioning it as an interactive relationship medium.

- Resources/Vendors - necessary to accomplish the vision.

- Tactics/Actions - what needs to be done to realize the vision.

The issues to be addressed in a strategic plan can include supporting current go-to-market strategies using the internet. Supporting a distributor channel by providing on-line inventory is an example of advancing the current relationship. The plan can also include revolutionary use of the internet introducing new go-to-market approaches (ecommerce). Making repair parts available to the end user direct from the manufacturer might be a revolutionary approach because it changes the relationship the manufacturer has with the end user market reducing the channel relationship. Eventually, all manufacturers and service providers that sell through channels will make what they sell available to their markets directly. Examples of this are PC manufacturers that currently sell direct to customers without any channel relationship and airlines that allow us to be our own booking agents on-line.

Tactical use of the internet -involve delivering day-to-day value to people in the markets served. We call this Customerization™--using the internet to enhance customer relationships in support of existing channels or as a complement to current methods. Customerization involves presenting information and interactive processes specifically tailored to the needs of the customer. Such efforts must automatically update based on every single contact with the customer creating a truly one-to-one direct relationship. Customerization requires a detailed understanding of the customers' needs and wants and the customers' preferences in interacting with the systems and processes of your company. Often times what you decide customers *should* want is not what they do want. The meshing of these gears has been the job of the sales force (inside and outside). On the internet, there is no sales force to provide the alignment necessary for a positive relationship between you and the customer: it is up to you.

A planning approach might include these sections:

1. Markets/Customers - defined by segments.

2. Process(es) - current relationship systems.

3. Information Access - customer and company information needs.

4. Interactivity - information delivery processes on-line.

5. Security - for customer and company.

Administrative - use of the internet involves internal business administration, front and back office support, and creation of better communications with suppliers and channel partners. Enhancing existing business relationships by moving current processes on-line can be relatively easy. Since there is already a relationship and a process that can be defined, moving onto the internet is merely a conversion of medium.

Planning and deploying the administrative strategy is the easiest to accomplish because all those involved already have a business relationship as employees, suppliers or partners with vested interests in the relationship. Moving from traditional processes to internet based processes is more a training issue than anything else. Resistance can be expected whenever there is any change in procedures and practices. Moving onto the internet is no exception.

Promoting Your Website

Having a website is of little value if it is not used by prospects, customers, channel partners, investors, vendors and employees. The quickest groups to develop utility are employees, vendors, and channel partners. By delivering easy-to-use information, these markets become rapid adopters. One company we worked with created instant use by simply putting a current employee, partner, and supplier phone directory (with email addresses) on-line.

Promoting your site to the markets you serve can best be done through the internet and by using external media. Through the internet a website can be posted to the various search engines in the hope that people with specific interests will access the site. Cross links can also be set up with other sites where common customers and prospects might visit. Such a link could be established with a trade association. Banners (advertising on the other websites pages) can be placed on other sites as cross-link barter or for a fee. While banners have proven effective for some consumer marketers delivering high volume of visitors, business-to-business marketers should be more interested in quality of visitors not quantity of visitors. Linking can make a site busy, but not effective, in accomplishing the sales objectives.

Another internet based promotional opportunity is email. Sending email to customers and prospects delivering an offer that can be fulfilled using a special web address is a very cost effective way to use your site as part of your promotional programs. It is vitally important, however, that you only send email to contacts, with whom you have a relationship. Unsolicited email messages, called *spam*, are not acceptable to most internet users. The combination of email with the world wide web(WWW) as a fulfillment delivery vehicle will become more widely used as we become conditioned to responding on-line.

The best way to promote your website is to put your web address on all marketing materials and programs. Like the toll free number, the web address needs to be prominent so market members can make their own decision to seek you out through the web. Experience has shown that 75% of customers acquired on the internet are new contacts. Even when the same people had been repeatedly contacted by mail and phone. At a recent focus group with engineers, we learned that the engineers use the WWW as the primary source of information even if they have a complete product brochure in their hands. The engineers just wanted a big web address to go to. Promote your site everywhere you can, even at trade shows.

The Internet Summarized

The internet is a rapidly growing tool that will become the primary medium of business-to-business marketing. Companies can be at different levels of internet marketing, but there is no return on investment (ROI) on the internet until the level of interactivity is reached. Initial internet ROI will be enjoyed in the cost reduction possible by hiring the customer to do their own customer service. Customers are happier to answer their questions on-line at their convenience. Increased revenue and longer lifetime value of customers are the next levels of increased internet ROI.

The internet has two useful applications for marketers: the World Wide Web and email. The WWW is passive, delivering color graphics, text, video and sound on demand when visitors access a web page. Email is active and can be delivered to customers and prospects with whom a company has a relationship to cause a desired behavior. Just as postal mail is used, the internet technologies can also be used in three ways: Internet - available to everyone; intranet - inside a company only; and extranet - allowing only people with approved ID and passwords to have access to a larger network.

The internet provides a giant database of information accessed using a web browser. The same browser technology allows all users to have access to all types of databases within a company. Users can retrieve information from and deliver information to the database. This use of the internet will grow over time eventually become the most common business-to-business application of the medium.

Internet measurement should be based on the same business measurement as other media: acquisition of qualified leads and sales. Measurement of hits, page accesses, and movement through the website are important for website development, but not medium evaluation. Creating the website, like all marketing media, should be based on markets and objectives of the relationship with the market segment. Attention needs to be given to structure and content depending on the needs of the markets served.

Planning and executing the use of the internet has three levels: strategic, tactical and administrative. A strategic use of the internet is when it is used to create new or replace existing methods of moving goods and services to end users, consumers and OEMs. Tactical use of the internet involves the day-to-day relationship between the company and the customer. We call this Customerization. Administrative use of the internet is using the medium to support suppliers, business partners and employees. This use of the internet is the easiest to accomplish because of existing relationships and the vested interest of the participants.

Promoting the website is best accomplished by putting the web address on all marketing materials. Promotion through the use of search engines is random and cannot be controlled. Other methods of linking on the web are useful but can be expensive. The best way to attract your customers to your web site is a targeted promotion using the web as the response device.

Glossary

Access Time: The time it takes a computer to locate a piece of information in memory or storage and to take action, i.e., the "read" time. Also, the time it takes a computer to store a piece of information and to complete action, i.e., the "write" time.

ACD: *See Automatic Call Director.*

Action Devices: Items and techniques used in a mailing to initiate the response desired.

Active Buyer: A buyer whose latest purchase was made within the last 12 months. *(See also Buyer.)*

Active Customer: A term used interchangeably with "active buyer."

Active Member: Any member who is fulfilling the original commitment or who has fulfilled that commitment and has made one or more purchases in the last 12 months.

Active Subscriber: One who has agreed to receive periodic delivery of magazines, books or other goods or services for a period of time that has not yet expired.

Actives: Customers on a list who have made purchases within a prescribed time period, usually not more than one year; subscribers whose subscriptions have not expired.

Additions: New names, either of individuals or companies, added to a mailing list.

Add-On Service: A service of the Direct Marketing Association (DMA) which gives consumers an opportunity to request that their names be added to mailing lists.

Address Coding Guide (CG): A guide which contains the actual or potential beginning and ending house numbers, block group and/or enumeration district numbers, zip codes, and other geographic codes for all city delivery service streets served by 3,154 post offices located within 6,601 zip codes.

Address Correction Requested: An endorsement which, when printed in the upper left-hand corner of the address portion of the mailing piece (below return address), authorizes the U.S. Postal Service, for a fee, to provide the new address of a person no longer at the address on the mailing piece.

ADRMP: *See Automatic Dialing Recorded Message Player.*

A.I.D.A.: The most popular formula for the preparation of direct mail copy. The letters stand for Get **A**ttention, Arouse **I**nterest, Stimulate **D**esire, Ask for Action.

Alphanumeric: A contraction of "alphabetic" and "numeric". Applies to any coding system that provides for letters, numbers (digits), and special symbols such as punctuation marks. Synonymous with Alphameric.

ARS: *See Automatic Route Selection.*

Assigned Mailing Dates: The dates on which the list user has the obligation to mail a specific list. No other date is acceptable without specific approval from the list owner.

Assumptive Close: When a communicator assumes the customer is going to buy and begins asking questions about the order. *You use twelve ribbons per year. Would you like them shipped monthly, or quarterly?*

Audience: The total number of individuals reached by a promotion or advertisement.

Audit: A printed report of the counts involved in a particular list or file.

Automatic Call Director (ACD): A computerized approach to handling inbound calls. The ACD directs calls, in the order they are received to an inbound communicator. If all communicators are busy, the ACD plays a tape recording and directs the call to the next available communicator. This system typically will generate extensive production reports.

Automatic Dialing Recorded Message Player (ADRMP): A computer that automatically calls customers and prospects and plays a tape recording. Some machines have interactive capability and can record information. Many states are considering or already have enacted legislation curtailing the use of these machines. The ADRMP machines have the capability to sequentially dial random telephone numbers and should never be used in this manner.

Automatic Route Selection (ARS): An automated approach to routing telephone calls via the least cost route

considering time of day and day of week. Typically, the system will route the call over the least expensive available route.

Average Order Size: A simple arithmetic formula used to establish the average order size. The total revenue generated from a program divided by the total number of orders will establish the average order size.

Avoidable Expenses: Dollars that a prospect can avoid spending if they purchase your product or service.

Back-End: The conversion of a direct marketing respondent to a buyer, and a buyer to a repeat buyer. Also, the activities to complete a mail order transaction. Can define the measurement of: a buyers performance after he has ordered the first item in a series; prospects who become leads; performance toward purchasing. (*See also Front-End.*)

Back Test: Often described as a "retest" or "confirming test." For example, a list was tested, and the response was within an acceptable range but was not good enough to order a large quantity. To reconfirm the results, the list will be retested.

Bad Pay: Also referred to as "nonpay." Subscription or membership offers which are "bill me" (charge orders) and which subsequently must be cancelled due to nonpayment.

Batch Processing: Techniques of executing a set of computer programs/selections in batches as opposed to executing each order/selection as it is received. Batches can be programmed or created manually by collecting data in groups.

Batched Job: A job that is grouped with other jobs as input to a computer system, as opposed to a transaction job entry where each job is run individually to completion.

Bill Enclosure: Any promotional piece or notice enclosed with a bill, an invoice or a statement not directed toward the collection of all or part of the bill, invoice or statement.

Binary: Involves a selection, choice or condition in which there are two possibilities such as the use of the symbols "0" or "1" in a numbering system.

Bingo Card: A reply card inserted in a publication and used by readers to request literature from companies whose products and services are either advertised or mentioned in editorial columns.

Bit: A single character or element in a binary number (digit). The smallest element of binary machine language represented by a magnetized spot on a recording surface or a magnetized element of a storage device.

Bounce Back: An offer enclosed with a mailing sent to a customer in fulfillment of an offer.

BPI: *See Bytes Per Inch*:

BRC: Business Reply Card.

BRE: Business Reply Envelope.

Breakeven: The point in a business transaction when income and expenses are equal.

Broadcast Media: A direct response source that includes radio, television and cable TV.

Broadside: A single sheet of paper, printed on one side or two, folded for mailing or direct distribution, and opening into a single, large advertisement.

Brochure: A high-quality pamphlet, with specifically planned layout, typography and illustrations. This term is also used loosely to describe any promotional pamphlet or booklet.

Buckslip: A separate slip attached to a printed piece containing instructions to route the material to specified individuals.

Bulk Mail: A category of Third Class Mail involving a large quantity of identical pieces which are addressed to different names for mailing before delivery to post office.

Burst: To separate continuous form paper into discrete sheets.

Business List: Any compilation or list of individuals or companies based upon a business-associated interest, inquiry, membership, subscription or purchase.

Business-Person: Telemarketing; A person who will be contacted at his office or place of business, usually during the business day.

Business Planning: Putting on paper all the facts you have at your disposal.

Buyer: Someone who has purchased from the company. (*See also Active Buyer.*)

Buyer (1982-1984): Indicates that these people purchased from the company at one time during one of these years.

Byte: Sequence of adjacent binary digits operated upon as a unit and usually shorter than a computer word. A character is usually considered a byte. A single byte can contain either two numeric characters or one alphabetic or special character. A group of bits, usually eight, that stores a piece of information. Computer memory is measured in bytes: 32K means 32,000 bytes.

Bytes Per Inch (BPI): Characters represented by bytes per inch.

C/A: Change of Address.

Call Detail Reporting (CDR): An automated approach to capturing and reporting on the detail telephone activity by extension in a business. In essence, CDR creates a detail phone bill by extension.

Card Deck: A collection of 3" x 5" cards gathered in a wrap, bound together or placed in an envelope.

Carrier Route: Grouping of addresses based on the delivery route of each letter carrier. The average number of stops is 400 but does range from under 100 to 3,000. There are about 180,000 carrier routes in the United States.

Carrier Route Pre-sort: Refers to pre-sorting of mail (usually by a letter shop) to carrier route by zip code and preparing it to specifications established by the U.S. Postal Service.

Properly executed, the mailing so prepared receives a discounted postal rate.

Cash Buyer: A buyer who encloses payment with order.

Cash Rider: Also called "cash up" or "cash option" wherein an order form offers installment terms, but a postscript offers the option of sending full cash payment with order, usually at some saving over credit price as an incentive.

Catalog: Any promotion that offers more than one product. Frequently, a catalog is described as a book or booklet showing merchandise with descriptive details and prices.

Catalog Buyer: A person who has bought products or services from a catalog.

Catalog Request: (Paid or Unpaid). One who sends for a catalog (prospective buyer). The catalog may be free; there may be a nominal charge for postage and handling, or there may be a more substantial charge that is offer refunded or credited on the first order.

CBX: Computerized Branch Exchange. (*See also PBX.*)

CDR: *See Call Detail Reporting.*

Cell(s): In list terminology, a statistical unit or units. A group of individuals selected from a file on a consistent basis.

Centrex: A service offered by most local telephone companies which provides the features and functions of a PBX, but the actual equipment is installed in the phone company's central office, rather than at the customer site.

Cheshire Label: Specially prepared paper (rolls, fanfold or accordion fold) on which names and addresses are printed to be mechanically affixed, one at a time, to a mailing piece.

Circulars: General term for printed advertisement in any form, including printed matter sent out by direct mail.

Cleaning: The process of correcting and/or removing a name and address from a mailing list because it is no longer correct or because the listing is to be shifted from one category to another.

Closed Face Envelope: An envelope that is addressed directly on the face, and does not have a die-cut window.

Coding: (1) Identifying marks used on reply devices to identify the mailing list or other source from which the address was obtained. (2) A structure of letters and numbers used to classify characteristics of an address on a list.

Collate: (1) To assemble individual elements of a mailing in sequence for inserting into a mailing envelope. (2) A program which combines two or more ordered files to produce a single ordered file. Also the act of combining such files. Synonymous with merges as in Merge/Purge.

Commission: A percentage of sale, by prior agreement, paid to the list broker, list manager, or other service arm for their part in the list usage.

Compile: The process by which a computer translates a series of instructions written in a programming language into actual machine language.

Compiled List: Names and addresses derived from directories, newspapers, public records, retail sales slips, trade show registrations, or other sources, which identify groups of people with something in common.

Compiler: Organization which develops lists of names and addresses from directories, newspapers, public records, registrations, and other sources, identifying groups of people, companies, or institutions with something in common.

Completed Calls: An outbound call in which the target had been contacted and had made a decision concerning the offer. The prospect either accepted the offer, rejected the offer, requested additional information, remained uncertain, or refused to complete the call and, in essence, refused the offer.

Completed Cancel: One who has completed a specific commitment to buy products or services before cancelling.

Comprehensive: Complete and detailed layout for a printed piece. Also: "Comp," "Compre."

Computer Compatibility: Ability to interchange the data or programs of one computer system with one or more of other computers.

Computer Language: A generic term for the codes used to give computers instructions. COBOL is a computer language.

Computer Letter: Computer-printed message providing personalized, fill-in information from a source file in pre-designated positions. May also be full-printed letter with personalized insertions.

Computer Personalization: Printing of letters or other promotional pieces by a computer using names, addresses, special phrases, or other information based on data appearing in one or more computer records. The objective is to use the information in the computer record to tailor the promotional message to a specific individual.

Computer Program: Series of instructions or statements prepared to achieve a certain result.

Computer Record: All the information about an individual, company, or transaction stored on a specific magnetic tape or disk.

Computer Service Bureau: An internal or external facility providing general or specific data processing services.

Computerized Scripting: Software which displays appropriate script copy on a cathode ray tube based on the responses entered into the terminal by a communicator.

Conditioning: Sustained selling activity directed toward a prospect by both marketing and sales.

Consumer: Telemarketing; A person who will be contacted at his residence, usually during evening and weekend hours.

Consumer List: A list of names (usually at home addresses) compiled, or resulting, from a common inquiry or buying activity indicating a general or specific buying interest.

Continuation: The next step after a list test. If the test proved responsive within established financial parameters, the list should be reordered.

Continuity Program: Products or services bought as a series of small purchases, rather than all at one time. Generally based on a common theme and shipped at regular or specific time intervals.

Continuous Form: Paper forms designed for computer printing that are folded, and sometimes perforated, at predetermined vertical measurements. These may be letters, vouchers, invoices, cards, etc.

Contribution: A term that describes the amount of gross profit made by a specific activity. In essence, it is the gross profit of a project after allowing for cost of goods and cost of selling including commissions

Contributor List: Names and addresses of persons who have given to a specific fund-raising effort. *(See also Donor List.)*

Controlled Circulation: Distribution of a publication at no charge to individuals or companies on the basis of their titles or occupations. Typically, recipients are asked from time to time to verify the information that qualifies them to receive the publication.

Controlled Duplication: A method by which names and addresses from two or more lists are matched (usually by computer) in order to eliminate or limit extra mailings to the same name and address.

Controlled Subscription: *See Controlled Circulation.*

Conversion: (1) Process of changing from one method of data processing to another, or from one data processing system to another. Synonymous with reformatting. (2) To secure specific action such as a purchase or contribution from a name on a mailing list or as a result of an inquiry.

Co-op Mailing: A mailing of two or more offers included in the same envelope or other carrier, with each participating mailer sharing mailing costs according to some predetermined formula.

Copy: The words and graphics used to communicate offers to a market.

Cornercard: The return address information printed in the upper-left had corner of an envelope.

Cost Per Inquiry (C.P.I.): A simple arithmetical formula derived by dividing the total cost of a mailing or an advertisement by the number of inquiries received.

Cost Per Order (C.P.O.): A simple arithmetical formula derived by dividing the total cost of a direct marketing campaign by the number of orders received. Similar to Cost per Inquiry, except based on actual orders rather than inquiries.

Cost Per Thousand (C.P.M.): Refers to the total cost-per-thousand pieces of direct mail "in the mail".

Coupon: Part of an advertising promotion piece intended to be filled in by the inquirer or customer and returned to the advertiser.

Coupon Clipper: One who has given evidence of responding to free or nominal-cost offers out of curiosity, with little or no serious interest or buying intent.

C.P.I.: *See Cost Per Inquiry.*

C.P.M.: *See Cost Per Thousand.*

C.P.O.: *See Cost Per Order.*

CRT: Cathode Ray Tube. A screen used for display of computer information.

C.T.O.: Contribution to overhead (profit).

Customer: Individuals who have purchased products or services from you.

Data: A representation of facts, concepts, or instructions in a formal manner suitable for communication, interpretation, or processing either manually

or automatically.

Database: The structure for storing and controlling the relationship information between a company and its customers. Within direct marketing, a database will provide a means to contact a group of prospects, a method to measure respondents to the direct marketing effort, a method to measure purchasers, and a method to provide continuing communications.

Deadbeat: One who has ordered a product or service and, without just cause, hasn't paid for it.

Decoy: A unique name especially inserted in a mailing list for verifying usage.

Delinquent: One who has fallen behind or has stopped scheduled payment for a product or service.

Delivery Date: The date a list user or a designated representative of the list user receives a specific list order from the list owner.

Demographics: Socio-economic characteristics pertaining to a geographic unit (county, city, sectional center, zip Code, group of households, education, ethnicity, income level, etc.).

Dialings: The total number of times a communicator dialed the phone attempting to make outbound telephone calls.

Dimensional Mailings: Generally large mailings in a three-dimensional sense; they are packages or fat letters that have a tendency to get put on the top of a prospect's mail pile.

Direct Access: An access mode in which records are obtained from, or placed into, a mass storage file in a non-sequential manner so that any record can be rapidly accessed. Synonymous with Random Access.

Direct-inward-dialing (DID): A telephone capability providing individual's direct lines to the their office's, while still permitting calls to go through the company switchboard.

Direct Mail Advertising: Any promotional effort using the postal service, or other direct delivery service, for distribution of the advertising message.

Direct Marketing: An organized and planned system of contacts, using a variety of media, seeking to produce a lead or an order. It requires the development and maintenance of a database, is measurable in costs and results, and is effective in all methods of selling.

Direct Marketing Association (DMA): The primary trade association for direct marketing.

Direct Response Advertising: Advertising, through any medium, designed to generate a measurable response by any means, such as mail, telephone, or telegraph.

Directive Questions: Questions which guide a customer's talking that cannot be answered with a 'yes' or 'no'. *Who do you get your various cleaning supplies from now?*

Disk Processing: In data processing, data is stored in tracks on a rotating magnetic surface. A movable arm is directed to a specific track location. As the rotating surface passes under the access arm, the required data is read.

Displaceable Expenses: Dollars already being expended for similar or like services that can be eliminated if they purchase your product or service.

DMA: *See Direct Marketing Association.*

DMA Mail Preference Service: *See Mail Preference Service.*

Donor List: A list of persons who have given money to one or more charitable organizations. *(See also Contributor List.)*

Dummy: (1) A mock-up giving a preview of a printed piece, showing placement and nature of the material to be printed. (2) A fictitious name with a mailable address inserted into a mailing list to check on usage of that list.

Dupe: Duplication. Appearance of identical or nearly identical entities more than once.

Duplication Elimination: A specific kind of controlled duplication which provides that: no matter how many times a name and address is on a list, and how many lists contain that name and address, it will be accepted for mailing only once by that mailer. Also referred to as "dupe elimination" or "de-duplication" or "merge/purge."

E-mail: An electronic, text-based mesaging system using a standard set of Standard Mail Tranfer Protocols that provides universal usage of the system. Using a client-server computing model these messages can be transferred between any networked computers and can serve as vehicles for attached files as well.

Editing Rules: Specific rules used in preparing name and address records that treat all elements the same way at all times. Also, the rules for rearranging, deleting, selecting, or inserting any needed data, symbols and/or characters.

Envelope Stuffer: Any advertising or promotional material enclosed in an envelope with business letters, statements or invoices.

Exchange: An arrangement whereby two mailers exchange equal quantities of mailing list names.

Expire: A former customer who is no longer an active buyer.

Expiration: A subscription which is not renewed.

Expiration Date: Date a subscription expires.

Field: Reserved area in a computer which services a similar function in all records of the file. Also, location on magnetic tape or disk drive which has definable limitations and meaning: For example, position 1-30 is the Name field.

File Maintenance: The activity of keeping a file up-to-date by adding, changing, or deleting data (all or part). Synonymous with list maintenance *(See also Update.)*

Fill-In: A name, address or other text

added to a preprinted letter.

First-Time Buyer: One who buys a product or service from a specific company for the first time.

Fixed Field: A way of laying out, or formatting, list information in a computer file that puts every piece of data in a specific position relative to every other piece of data, and limits the amount of space assigned to that data. If a piece of data is missing from an individual record, or if its assigned space is not completely used, that space is not filled (every record has the same space and the same length). Any data exceeding its assigned space limitation must be abbreviated.

Flip-card: A method of scripting in which the script copy is printed on randomly accessible pages which can be "flipped" to display the next logical portion of the script based on the response of the customer.

Forced-Choice Questions: Questions which force the customer to make a decision. *Do you want your order shipped on the 10th or 15th?*

Format: The vehicle used to deliver an offer to a market: mail, phone, print, or broadcast.

Former Buyer: One who has bought one or more times from a company but has not purchased in the last twelve months.

Free-Standing Insert: A promotional piece loosely inserted or nested in a newspaper or magazine.

Frequency: The number of times an individual has ordered within a specific period of time. *(See also Monetary Value and Recency.)*

Friend-of-a-Friend: Friend Recommendations. The result of one party sending in the name of someone who might be interested in a specific advertiser's product or service; a third party inquiry.

Front-End: Activities performed to produce responses to a direct marketing program and the measurement of those activities.

Fulfillment: Delivering the offer made in a direct marketing promotion.

Full Print: The addressee's name and all of the body copy are generated by the printer.

FX: Foreign Exchange. A telephone technique of having an exchange added to your network that is not in the same exchange as your business. This approach can have a significant impact on phone toll charges.

Geo Code: Symbols used to identify geographic entities (state, county, zip code, SCF, tract, etc.).

Geographics: Any method of subdividing a list, based on geographic or political subdivisions (zip codes, sectional centers, cities, counties, states, regions).

Gift Buyer: One who buys a product or service for another.

Gimmick: Attention-getting device, usually multi-dimensional, attached to a direct mail printed piece.

Guarantee: A pledge of satisfaction made by the seller to the buyer and specifying the terms by which the seller will make good his pledge.

Hot-Line List: The most recent names available on a specific list, that are no older than three months. In any event, use of the term "hot-line" should be further modified by "weekly," "monthly," etc.

House List: Any list of names owned by a company as a result of compilation, inquiry or buyer action, or acquisition, that is used to promote that company's products or services.

House-List Duplicate: Duplication of name and address records between the list user's own lists and any list being mailed by him on a one-time use arrangement.

Inbound Telemarketing: The systematic handling of a call from a prospect or customer, resulting from a message seen in another medium.

Incompleted Calls: Outbound calls in which the caller was unable to speak with the prospect or customer because either the prospect didn't answer, was not available, or the line was busy.

Indicia: A symbol imprinted on the outgoing envelope to denote payment of postage.

Influencer: In the business-to-business environment, a person who is involved in the buying decision process but is not the decision maker.

Inquiry: One who has asked for literature or other information about a product or service. Unless otherwise stated, it is assumed no payment is required for the literature or other information. *(Note: A catalog request is generally considered a specific type of inquiry.)*

Insert: A promotional piece inserted into an outgoing package or invoice.

Installment Buyer: One who orders goods or services and pays for them in two or more periodic payments after their delivery.

Inter-List Duplicate: Duplication of name and address records *between* two or more lists, other than house lists, being mailed by a list user.

Job Description: A general definition of a job and its responsibilities which enables management to compare the job with other jobs within the company, and establish a relative level and value.

K: Used in reference to computer storage capacity, generally accepted as 1,000. Analogous to M (1,000) in the direct marketing industry.

KBN: Kill Bad Name. Action taken on undeliverable addresses (nixies). You KBN a nixie.

Key: One or more characters within a data group that can be used to identify it or control its use. Synonymous with Key Code in mailing business.

Key Code (Key): A group of letters and/or numbers, colors, or other markings, used to measure the specific effectiveness of media, lists, advertisements, offers, or any parts thereof.

Keyline: Any one of many partial or complete descriptions of past buying history coded to include name and address information and current status.

Label: Piece of paper containing the name and address of the recipient which is applied to a mailing for address purposes.

Layout: (1) Artist's sketch showing relative positioning of illustrations, headlines, and copy. (2) Positioning subject matter on a press sheet for most efficient production.

Lead: *See Referral*

Least Cost Routing: A feature on a PBX telephone system which automatically selects the least expensive route for a telephone call to travel based on distance, other calls, and the time of day.

Letterhead: The printing on a letter that identifies the sender.

Lettershop: A business organization that handles the mechanical details of mailings such as addressing, imprinting, collating, etc. Most lettershops offer some printing facilities and many offer some degree of creative direct mail services.

Lifetime Value: A measurement of the long-term dollar value of a customer, subscriber, donor, etc. This figure is essential when evaluating initial costs to bring in a customer against the lifetime proceeds.

Line: The extension or line of a telephone system within a company. Lines connect telephone instruments to the outside trunks usually through a PBX or key system.

List: Mailing List. Names and addresses of individuals and/or companies having in common an interest, characteristic or activity. The customers or prospects to whom a marketing program will be targeted.

List Broker: A specialist who makes all necessary arrangements for one company to use the list(s) of another company. A broker's services may include most, or all, of the following:

research, selection, recommendation and subsequent evaluation.

List Buyer: Technically, this term should apply only to one who actually buys mailing lists. In practice, however, it is usually used to identify one who orders mailing lists for one-time use: a List User or Mailer.

List Cleaning: The process of correcting and/or removing a name and/or address from a mailing list because it is no longer correct. Term is also used to describe identification and elimination of duplicates on house lists.

List Compiler: One who develops lists of names and addresses from directories, newspapers, public records, sales slips, trade show registrations and other sources for identifying groups of people or companies with something in common.

List Exchange: A barter arrangement between two companies for the use of mailing list(s). May be, list for list, list for space, or list for comparable value - other than money.

List Maintenance: Any manual, mechanical or electronic system for keeping name and address records (with or without other data) up to date at any specific point(s) in time.

List Manager: One who, as an employee of a list owner or as an outside agent, is responsible for the use, by others, of a specific mailing list(s). The list manager generally serves the list owner in several or all of the following capacities: list maintenance (or advice thereon), list promotion and marketing, list clearance and record keeping, collection of fees for use of the list by others.

List Owner: One who, by promotional activity or compilation, has developed a list of names having something in common; or one who has *purchased* (as opposed to rented, reproduced, or used on a one-time basis) such a list from the developer.

List Rental: An arrangement whereby a list owner furnishes names to a mailer, together with the privilege of using the list on a one-time basis only (unless otherwise specified in advance). For this privilege, the list owner is paid a royalty by the mailer. "List Rental" is the term most often used although "List Reproduction" and "List Usage" more accurately describe the transaction, since "Rental" is not used in the sense of its ordinary meaning of leasing property.

List Royalty: Payment to list owners for the privilege of using their lists on a one-time basis.

List Sample: A group of names selected from a list in order to evaluate the responsiveness of that list. *(See also List Test.)*

List Segmentation: *See List Selection.*

List Selection: Characteristics used to define smaller groups within a list (essentially, lists within a list). Although very small, select groups may be very desirable and may substantially improve response; minimum set-up costs, however, often make them expensive.

List Sequence: The order in which names and addresses appear on a list. While most lists today are in zip code sequence, some are alphabetical by name within the zip code; others are in carrier sequence (postal delivery); and still others may (or may not) use some other order within the zip code. some lists are still arranged alphabetically by name and chronologically, and in many other variations or combinations.

List Sort: Process of putting a list in specific sequence or no sequence.

List Source: The media used to acquire names: direct mail, space, TV, radio, telephone, etc.

List Test: Part of a list selected to try to determine the effectiveness of the entire list. *(See also List Sample.)*

List User: One who uses names and addresses on someone else's list as prospects for the user's product or service; similar to Mailer.

Load Up: Process of offering a buyer the opportunity of buying an entire series at one time after the customer has purchased the first item in that series.

M: Refers to a 1000 measurement unit.

Magnetic Tape: A storage device for electronically recording and reproducing, by use of a computer, defined bits of data. Processing via computer tape is restricted to sequential processing of the information.

Mail Date: Date a list user, by prior agreement with the list owner, is obligated to mail a specific list. No other date is acceptable without specific approval from the list owner.

Mailer: (1) A direct mail advertiser who promotes a product or service using lists of others, or house lists, or both. (2) A printed direct mail advertising piece. (3) A folding carton, wrapper, or tube used to protect materials in the mail.

Mailgram: A combination telegram-letter, with the telegram transmitted to a postal facility close to the addressee and then delivered as first class mail.

Mailing Machine: A machine that attaches labels, addresses envelopes, inserts printed pieces into any style envelope, affixes postage to mailing pieces and otherwise prepares such pieces for deposit in the postal system.

Mail Order Action Line (MOAL): A service of the Direct Marketing Association which assists consumers in resolving problems with mail order purchases.

Mail Order Buyer: One who orders, and pays for, a product or service through the mail. Generally, an order telephoned in response to a direct response advertisement is considered a direct substitute for an order sent through postal channels.

Mail Preference Service (MPS): A service of the Direct Marketing Association wherein consumers can request to have their names removed from, or added to, mailing lists. These names are made available to both members and non-members of the association.

Margin: The gross profit on sales after subtracting cost-of-goods from the gross revenue.

Marketing: All activities which move goods and services from seller to buyer.

Master File: File that is of a permanent nature or regarded in a particular job as authoritative, or one that contains all sub files.

Match: A direct mail term used to refer to the typing of addresses, salutations or inserts onto letters with other copy imprinted by a printing process.

Match Code: A code determined either by the creator or the user of a file for matching records contained in another file.

Match Fill: Having the letter body copy typeset and preprinted by a printer to achieve the appearance of a fully personalized letter. The address, salutation and perhaps some specific information in the body of the letter are added during computer printing.

MOAL: *See Mail Order Action Line.*

Monetary Value: Total expenditures by a customer during a specific period of time, generally twelve months.

MPS: *See Mail Preference Service.*

Multimedia: The use of a variety of media in promotional efforts such as direct mail, space, TV, or radio.

Multiple Buyer: One who has bought two or more times (not one who has bought two or more items, one time only); also a Multi-Buyer or Repeat Buyer.

Multiple Regression: Statistical technique used to measure the relationship between responses to a mailing with census demographics and list characteristics of one or more selected mailing lists. Used to direct mail to the best types of people or areas. This technique can also be used to analyze customers, subscribers, etc.

Name: Single entry on a mailing list.

Name Acquisition: Technique of soliciting a response to obtain names and addresses for a mailing list.

Name-Removal Service: Portion of Mail Preference Service offered by the Direct Marketing Association wherein consumer is sent a form which, when filled in and returned, constitutes a request to have the individual's name removed from all mailing lists used by participating members of the association and other direct mail users.

Need: A problem that a prospect has to address.

Negative Option: A buying plan in which a customer or club member agrees to accept and pay for products or services announced in advance at regular intervals unless the individual notifies the company, within a reasonable time after each announcement, not to ship the merchandise.

Nesting: Placing one enclosure within another before inserting them into a mailing envelope.

Net Name Arrangement: An agreement, at the time of ordering or before, whereby the list owner agrees to accept adjusted payment for less than the total names shipped to the list user. Such arrangements can be for a percentage of names shipped or names actually mailed (whichever is greater) or for only those names actually mailed (without a percentage limitation). The list owner may or may not provide for a running charge.

Nixie: A mailing piece returned to a mailer (under proper authorization) by the postal service because of an incorrect, or undeliverable, name and address.

Non-volatile: A telephone automation application in which the call can continue if the computer fails to perform properly.

No-Pay: One who has not paid (wholly or in part) for goods or services ordered.

"Uncollectible," "Deadbeat," and "Delinquent" are often used to describe the same person.

Novelty Format: An attention-getting direct mail format.

Nth Name Selection: A fractional unit that is repeated in sampling a mailing list. For example, in an "every tenth" sample, you would select the 1st, 11th, 21st and 32nd records, or the 2nd, 12th, 22nd, 32nd, records and so forth.

OCR: *See Optical Character Recognition.*

Offer: The terms promoting a specific product or service. The proposition made to customers or prospects to elicit a response.

One-Time Buyer: A buyer who has not ordered a second time from a given company.

One-Time Use Of A List: An intrinsic part of the normal list usage, list reproduction, or list exchange agreement in which it is understood that the mailer will not use the names on the list more than one time without specific prior approval of the list owner.

Open Account: A customer record that, at a specific time, reflects an unpaid balance for goods and services ordered, without delinquency.

Open questions: Questions designed to get a customer talking that cannot be answered with a 'yes' or 'no'. *Who do you get your various cleaning suppliers from now?*

Optical Character Recognition (OCR): Machine identification of printed characters through use of light sensitive devices.

Order Blank Envelopes: An order form printed on one side of a sheet, with a mailing address on the reverse. The recipient simply fills in the order, then folds and seals it like an envelope.

Order Card: A reply card used to initiate an order by mail.

Order Form: A printed form on which a customer can provide information to initiate an order by mail. Designed to be mailed in an envelope.

Outbound Telemarketing: A direct mail message being delivered over the telephone. The communicator is fully scripted.

Overflow Calls: Calls from people who dialed an 800 number and encountered a busy signal making it impossible to get through to the company they were calling.

Package: A term used to describe all of the assembled enclosures (parts or elements) of a mailing effort.

Package Insert: Any promotional piece included in a product shipment. It may be for different products (or refills and replacements) from the same company or for products and services of other companies.

Package Test: A test of part or all of the elements of one mailing piece against another.

Paid Cancel: One who completes a basic buying commitment, or more, before cancelling the commitment. *(See also Completed Cancel.)*

Paid Circulation: Distribution of a publication to individuals or organizations which have paid for a subscription.

Paid During Service: Term used to describe a method of paying for magazine subscriptions in installments, usually weekly or monthly, and, usually, collected in person by the original sales person or a representative of that company.

Paid Subscription: *See Paid Circulation.*

PBX: Private Branch Exchange. The equipment used to switch telephone calls within a company. Most PBX units are computerized and handle many telephone related functions. Some vendors refer to their PBX's as CBX meaning Computerized Branch Exchange.

Peel-Off Label: A self-adhesive label attached to a backing which is attached to a mailing piece. The label is intended to be removed from the mailing piece and attached to an order blank or card.

Penetration: Relationship of the number of individuals or families on a particular list (by state, zip code, SIC code, etc.) compared to the total number possible.

Per Interaction (P.I.): A payment method in the telemarketing industry. The user contracts with a telemarketing service bureau and agrees to pay for services on a per interaction basis. The per interaction can be per completed call or per order.

Personalization: Individualizing of direct mail pieces by adding the name or other personal information about the recipient.

Phone List: Mailing list compiled from names listed in telephone directories.

P.I.: *See Per Interaction.*

Piggy-Back: An offer that hitches a free ride with another offer.

Poly Bag: Transparent polyethylene bag used in place of envelopes for mailing.

Pop-Up: A printed piece containing a paper construction pasted inside a fold and which, when the fold is opened, "pops up" to form a three-dimensional illustration.

Positive Option: A method of distributing products and services incorporating the same advance notice techniques as Negative Option but requiring a specific order each time from the member or subscriber. Generally, it is more costly and less predictable than Negative Option.

Postal Service Prohibitory Order: A communication from the postal service to a company indicating that a specific person and/or family considers the company's advertising mail to be pandering. The order requires the company to remove from its own mailing list and from any other lists used to promote the company's products or services all names listed on the order. Violation of the order is subject to fine and imprisonment. Names listed on the order are to be distinguished from those names removed voluntarily by the list owner at an individual's request.

Post Card: Single sheet self-mailers on card stock.

Post Card Mailers: Booklet containing business reply cards which are individually perforated for selective return, to order products or obtain information.

Premium: An item offered to a buyer, usually free or at a nominal price, as an inducement to purchase or obtain for trial a product or service offered via mail order.

Premium Buyer: One who buys a product or service to get another product or service (usually free or at a special price), or who responds to an offer of a special product (premium) on the package or label (or sometimes in the advertising) of another product.

Preprint: An advertising insert printed in advance and supplied to a newspaper or magazine for insertion.

Pressure: The disparity felt by business as a result of face-to-face selling expenses increasing disproportionately to pricing and other cost items.

Private Mail: Mail handled by special arrangement outside the postal service.

Program: (1) A sequence of steps to be executed by the computer to solve a given problem or achieve a certain result. (2) A sequence of direct marketing activities that identify a direct marketing effort to sell products or generate leads.

Programming: Designing, writing and testing of a computer program.

Promotion: The further development and encouragement of prospects and customers to purchases one's products or services without the aid of a sales representative.

Prospect: (1) A name on a mailing list considered to be a potential buyer for a given product or service, who has not previously made such a purchase. (2) That group of prospects that meet your predetermined qualification criteria making you want to include them in an ongoing marketing program.

Prospecting: Mailing to get leads for further sales contact rather than to make direct sales.

Protection: The amount of time, before and after the assigned mailing date, that a list owner will not allow the same names to be mailed by anyone other than the mailer cleared for that specific date.

Psychographics: Any characteristics or qualities used to denote the lifestyle(s) or attitude(s) of customers and prospective customers.

Publisher's Letter: A second letter enclosed in a mailing package to stress a specific selling point.

Purge: The process of eliminating duplicates and/or unwanted names and addresses from one or more lists.

Questionnaire: A printed form to a specified audience to solicit answers to specific questions.

Question Close: A question asked with the intent of getting the customer talking about why he is reluctant to buy. *Sir, if you agree that this system will satisfy your need, and I believe you do, is there any reason to delay?*

Random Access: An access mode in which records are obtained from, or placed into, a mass storage file in a non-sequential manner so that any record can be rapidly accessed. Synonymous with Direct Access.

Reached the Re-call Limit: A record had been attempted a pre-established number of times, and having reached its dialing attempt limit, was considered consumed.

Recency: The latest purchase or other activity recorded for an individual or company on a specific customer list. *(See also Frequency and Monetary Value.)*

Referral: (1) That group of prospects that is of such high quality that it should be referred for immediate handling by a salesperson or customer support organization. Sometimes called leads. (2) Usually derived form the Friend-get-a-Friend program, where a member is offered a record or book to suggest the names of friends who might be interested in joining the club.

Reflective Questions: Questions that cause a customer to consider a statement he made or a possible thought which was unexpressed. *Do you feel that automatic shipments limit your flexibility?*

Reformatting: Changing a magnetic tape format from one arrangement to another, more usable format. Synonymous with Conversion (list or tape).

Regeneration: Repeated attempts to get a prospect to respond through direct mail and telephone selling once these prospect have indicated an interest in your product or service.

Renewal: A subscription that has been renewed prior to, or at, expiration time or within six months thereafter.

Rental: *See List Rental.*

Repeat Buyer: *See Multiple Buyer.*

Reply Card: A sender-addressed card included in a mailing on which the recipient may indicate his response to the offer.

Reproduction Right: Authorization by a list owner for a specific mailer to use that list on a one-time basis.

Response Rate: Percentage of returns or inquiries from a mailing.

Return Envelopes: Addressed reply envelopes, either stamped or un-stamped as distinguished from business reply envelopes which carry a postage payment guarantee included with a mailing.

Return On Investment (ROI): The evaluation of return on invested capital. In direct mail, often loosely described as the return (income) based on the dollars expended in a direct mail campaign.

Return Postage Guaranteed: A legend imprinted on the address face of envelopes or other mailing pieces when the mailer wishes the postal service to return undeliverable third class bulk mail. A charge equivalent to the single piece, first class rate will be made for each piece returned. *(See also List Cleaning.)*

Return Requested: An indication that a mailer will compensate the postal service for return of an undeliverable mailing piece.

Returns: (1) Responses to a direct mail program. (2) Returns of products shipped to customers on free or limited trials that are not purchased.

RFMR: Acronym for Recency-Frequency-Monetary Value Ratio, a formula used to evaluate the sales potential of names on a mailing list.

R.O.I.: *See Return On Investment.*

Rollout: To mail the remaining portion of a mailing list after successfully testing a portion of that list.

R.O.P.: *See Run Of Paper.*

Rough: Dummy or layout in sketchy form with a minimum of detail.

Royalties: Sum paid per unit mailed or sold for the use of a list, imprimatur, patent, etc.

Running Charge: The price a list owner charges for names run or passed, but not used by a specific mailer. When such a charge is made, it is usually to cover extra processing costs. However, some list owners set the price without regard to actual cost.

Run Of Paper (R.O.P.): Also Run of Press. (1) A term applied to color printing on regular paper and presses, as distinct from separately printed sections made on special color presses. (2) Sometimes used to describe an advertisement positioned by publisher's choice in other than a preferred-position for which a special charge is made.

Salting: Deliberate placing of decoy or dummy names in a list to trace list usage and delivery. *(See also Decoy or Dummy.)*

Sample Buyer: One who sends for a sample product, usually at a special price or for a small handling charge, but sometimes free.

Sample Package: Mailing Piece. An example of the package to be mailed by the list user to a particular list. Such a mailing piece is submitted to the list owner for approval prior to commitment for one-time use of the list. Although a sample package may, due to time pressure, differ slightly from the actual package used, the list owner agreement usually requires the user to reveal any material differences when submitting the sample package.

SCF: *See Sectional Center.*

Script-on-paper: A method of scripting in which copy is typed on pages and posted or available at the communicator station.

Script-on-record: A method of scripting in which the script is printed directly on the unit record.

Sectional Center (SCF or SCF Center): A postal service distribution unit comprising different post offices whose zip codes start with the same first three digits.

Selection Criteria: Definition of characteristics that identify segments or subgroups within a list.

Self-mailer: A direct mail piece mailed without an envelope.

Sequence: An arrangement of items according to a specified set of rules or instructions. Refers generally to zip codes or customer number sequence.

Sequential Processing: Type of information storage, reading one item at a time, having to move through all the preceding records to get the next record in sequential order.

Sheet-fed Forms: During computer printing using a standard cut form as opposed to continuous forms. Also referred to as cut-sheet forms.

SIC: *See Standard Industrial Classification.*

Silent Monitoring: Listening directly to a phone call while at least one party has given permission to allow a third party to listen.

SMSA: *See Standard Metropolitan Statistical Area.*

Soft Close: *See Trial Close.*

Software: A set of programs, procedures and associated documentation concerned with operation of a data processing system.

Solo Mailing: A mailing promoting a single product or a limited group of related products. Usually it consists of a letter, brochure and reply device enclosed in an envelope.

Source Code: Unique alphabetical and/or numeric identification for distinguishing one list or media source from another. *(See also Key Code.)*

Source Count: The number of names and addresses, in any given list, for the media (or list sources) from which the names and addresses were derived.

Split Test: Two or more samples from the same list -- each considered to be representative of the entire list -- used for package tests or to test the homogeneity of the list.

Standard Industrial Classification (SIC): Classification of businesses, as defined by the U.S. Department of Commerce.

Standard Metropolitan Statistical Area (SMSA): Major metropolitan areas as set forth by the government.

State Count: The number of names and addresses, in a given list, for each state.

Statement Stuffer: A small, printed piece designed to be inserted in an envelope carrying a customer's statement of account.

Step Up: The use of special premiums to get a mail order buyer to increase his unit of purchase.

Stock Art: Art sold for use by a number of advertisers.

Stock Formats: Direct mail formats with pre-printed illustrations and/or headings to which an advertiser adds his own copy.

Stopper: Advertising slang for a striking headline or illustration intended to attract immediate attention.

Strategic: use of direct marketing; the long term efforts and results that will be experienced.

Strategies: Definitions of long term goals.

Stuffer: Advertising enclosures placed in other media such as newspapers, merchandise packages, or mailings for other products.

Subscriber: Individual who has paid to receive a periodical.

Suspect: The name of a business in business-to-business direct marketing.

Syndicated Mailing: Mailing prepared for distribution by firms other than the manufacturer or syndicator.

Syndicator: One who makes available prepared direct mail promotions for specific products or services to a list owner for mailing to his own list. Most syndicators also offer product fulfillment services.

Tabloid: A preprinted advertising insert of four or more pages, usually about half the size of a regular newspaper page, designed for inserting into a newspaper.

Tactical: use of direct marketing; how you will implement direct marketing with the current approach to selling.

Tactics: The things one does to execute a strategy.

Tag: To mark a record with definitive criteria which allows for subsequent selection or suppression.

Tape Density: The number of bits of information (bytes) that can be included in a specific magnetic tape. Examples are 556 BPI, 800 BPI, 1600 BPI, etc.

Tape Dump: A printout of data on a magnetic tape to be edited and checked for correctness, readability, consistency, etc.

Tape Layout: A simple "map" of the data included in each record and its relative, or specific location.

Tape Record: All the information about an individual or company contained on a specific magnetic tape.

Tape Recording: A type of monitoring in which a phone call is tape recorded while both parties are aware of the taping, and there is an audible beep present at least every 15 seconds during the recording.

Teaser: An advertisement or promotion planned to excite curiosity about a later advertisement or promotion.

Technical Difficulties: A broad description of records that had been attempted and for some reason, were not able to be contacted. These records will not be attempted again

Telecommunications: (1) Data transmission between a computer system and remotely located devices via a unit that performs the necessary format conversion and controls the rate of transmission over telephone lines, microwaves, etc. Synonymous with Transceive. (2) The management and control of the routing that a voice or data communication takes when leaving one location and traveling to another.

Telemarketing: A medium used to perform direct marketing using a scripted or message-controlled communicator to deliver a direct marketing message over the telephone.

Telephone Line: The extension or instrument connected to the telephone system within your business.

Telephone Preference Service (TPS): A service of the Direct Marketing Association for consumers who wish to have their names removed from national telemarketing lists. The name-removal file is made available to subscribers on a quarterly basis.

Telephone Switch: A computer designed to control the telephone activity within a business. Phone calls are received or routed automatically. Often referred to as a PBX, private branch exchange, or CBX, computerized branch exchange.

Telesales: Telephone selling where the communicator has open dialogue with the prospect. Typically the communicator is a qualified salesperson.

Terminal: Any mechanism which can transmit and/or receive data through a system or communications network.

Test Panel: A term used to identify each of the parts or samples in a split test.

Test Tape: A selection of representative records within a mailing list that enables a list user or service bureau to prepare for reformatting or converting to a form more efficient for the user.

Tie-In: Cooperative mailing effort involving two or more advertisers.

Til Forbid: An order for continuing service which is to continue until specifically cancelled by the buyer. Also "TF".

Time Sharing: Multiple utilization of available computer time, often via terminals, usually shared by different organizations.

Tip-on: An item glued to a printed piece.

Title: A designation before or after a name to more accurately identify an individual.

Title Addressing: Usually refers to functional titles used in compiling business lists, where there is no individual name.

Token: An involvement device, often consisting of a perforated portion of an order card designed to be removed from its original position and placed in another designated area on the order card, to signify a desire to purchase the product or service.

Town Marker: A symbol used to identify the end of a mailing list's geographical unit. Originated for "towns" but now used for zip codes, sectional centers, etc.

TPS: *See Telephone Preference Service.*

Traffic Builder: A direct mail piece intended primarily to attract recipients to the mailer's place of business.

Trial Buyer: One who buys a short-term supply of a product, or buys the product with the understanding that it may be examined, used, or tested for a specified time before deciding whether to pay for it or return it.

Trial Close: A question that forces a customer to indicate that he is interested in pursuing one's offer. *How many will you be needing?*

Trial Subscriber: A person ordering a publication or service on a conditional basis. The condition may relate to: delaying payment, the right to cancel, a shorter than normal term and/or a special introductory price.

Trunk: The telephone line connecting a business to the telephone company local central office. Typically a company will have dedicated inbound and outbound trunks.

Uncollectible: One who hasn't paid for goods and services at the end of a normal series of collection efforts.

Unit of Sale: Description of the average dollar amount spent by customers on a mailing list.

Unit Record: A form designed to record information about individual calls to make it possible to sort, tabulate, and print records and reports.

Universe: Total number of individuals that might be included on a mailing list; all of whom fit a single set of specifications.

Update: Recent transactions and current information added to the master (main) list to reflect the current status of each record on the list.

Up Front: Securing payment for a product offered by mail order before the product is sent.

UPS: Acronym for United Parcel Service.

Variable Field: A way of laying out list information for formatting that assigns a specific sequence to the data, but doesn't assign it specific positions. While this method conserves space, on magnetic tape or disk, it is generally more difficult to work with.

Verification: The process of determining the validity of an order by sending a questionnaire to the customer.

Volatile: A telephone automation application in which the call cannot continue if the computer fails to perform properly.

WATS: Acronym for Wide Area Telephone Service. A service providing a special line allowing calls within certain areas to be called at significantly lower rates.

White Mail: Incoming mail that is not on a form sent out by the advertiser. All mail other than orders or payments.

World Wide Web: A network of servers storing information and providing transactions in a graphical user interface that can be accessed by any network user utilizng a Web browser software client. Linking of information between files and pages creates a Web of information and sites.

Window Envelope: Envelope with a die-cut portion on the front that permits viewing the address printed on an enclosure. The "die-cut window" may or may not be covered with a transparent material.

Wing Mailer: Label-affixing device that uses strips of paper on which addresses have been printed.

Zip Code: A group of five digits used by the U.S. Postal Service to designate specific post offices, stations, branches, buildings or large companies.

Zip Code Count: The number of names and addresses on a list, within each zip code.

Zip Code Sequence: Arranging names and addresses on a list according to the numeric progression of the zip code in each record. This form of list formatting is mandatory for mailing at bulk third class mail rates, based on the sorting requirements of postal service regulations.

Related Books and Articles

The following books are excellent reference sources that can be very helpful in learning more about all facets of direct marketing.

Baier, Martin and Stone, Bob

How to Find and Cultivate Customers Through
Direct Marketing, 1996
NTC Books
ISBN: 0844236667

Benson, Richard V. Secrets of Successful Direct Mail, 1991
Passport Books
ISBN: 0844232947

Bettger, Frank How I Raised Myself from Failure to Success in
Selling, 1992
Prentice Hall Trade
ISBN: 067179437X

Bohn, Richard N. Sales Automation Software Compendium , 1995
The Denali Group
ISBN: 1885413009

Brandi, Joanna Winning at Customer Retention, 1995
Lakewood Publications
ISBN: 0943210410

Brown, M.T.   Making Money with Telephone, 1982
                          Future Shop
                          ISBN: 0930490010

Debonis, Nicholas, J. and Peterson, Roger S. and Vitale, Joe
                          AMA Handbook for Managing Business to
                          Business Marketing Communications, 1997
                          NTC Business Books
                          ISBN: 0844235954

Donath, Bob and Dixon, Carolyn K. and Crocker, Richard A. and
Obermayer, James W.
                          Managing Sales Leads: How to Turn Every
                          Prospect into a Customer, 1994
                          NTC Business Books
                          ISBN: 0844235997

Emerick, Tracy and Gasteiger, Stacy
                          Desktop Marketing with the MacIntosh, 1992
                          Brady Publishing
                          ISBN: 0132036134

Executive Office of the President
Office of Management and Budget
                          Standard Industrial Classification Manual, 1987
                          National Technical Information Service
                          5285 Port Royal Road
                          Springfield, VA 22161
                          Ord #: PB 87-100012

Gnam, Rene   Direct Mail Workshop, 1989
                          Prentice Hall, 1989

Goldberg, Bernard A.   How to Manage and Execute Telephone Selling,
                          1997
                          Direct Marketing Publishers
                          ISBN: 1879644053

                          The Lead Generation Handbook, 1992
                          Direct Marketing Publishers
                          ISBN: 1879644029

Gosden, Freeman F.   Direct Marketing Success: What Works and
                      Why, 1989
                      John Wiley & Sons
                      ISBN: 0471513288

Haas, Robert W.   Business Marketing: A Managerial Approach,
                      1995
                      South-Western Publishing
                      ISBN: 0538847422

Hatch, Denny and Jackson, Don
                      Tested Secrets for Direct Marketing Success,
                      1997
                      NTC Business Books
                      ISBN: 0844230073

Hodgson, Richard S.   The Greatest Direct Mail Sales Letters of All
                      Time: Why They Succeed, How They're
                      Created, How you Can Create Greate Sales
                      Letters, Too!, 1995
                      Dartnell Corporation
                      ISBN: 085013238X

                      Direct Mail and Mail Order Handbook, 1988
                      Dartnell Corporation
                      ISBN:0850131162

Hughes, Arthur M.   The Complete Database Marketer; Second-
                      Generation Strategies and Techniques for
                      Tappiing the Power of Your Customer Base,
                      1995
                      Probus Publishing Company
                      ISBN: 1557388938

                      Strategic Database Marketing: The Masterplan
                      for Starting and Managing a Profitable,
                      Customer-Based Marketing Program, 1994
                      Probus Publishig Company
                      ISBN: 1557385513

Hunter, Victor L. and Tietyin, David
> Business to Business Marketing: Creating a Community of Customers, 1997
> NTC Business Books
> ISBN: 0844232300

Leighton, Richard J. and Regnery, Alfred S.
> U.S. Direct Marketing Law; The Complete Handbook for Managers (The Libey Business Library), 1993
> National Book Network
> ISBN: 1882222024

Lewis, Herschell Gordon
> Direct Marketing Strategies and Tactics: Unleash the Power of Direct Marketing, 1993
> Dartnell Corporation
> ISBN: 0850132207
>
> Sales Letters that Sizzle, 1994
> NTC Business Books
> ISBN: 0844235474
>
> World's Greatest Direct Mail Sales Letters, 1996
> NTC Business Books
> ISBN: 0844235709

Jackson, Rob and Wang, Paul
> Strategic Database Marketing, 1994
> NTC Publishing Group
> ISBN: 0844232327

Kobs, Jim
Profitable Direct Marketing, 1991
National Textbook Company Trade
ISBN: 0844230294

Libey, Donald R.
Libey on Customers, 1993
National Book Network
ISBN: 1882222008

Libey on Change; Superforces and Socialforces in the Marketing Future, 1994
Libey Publications
IBSN: 1882222075

Nash, Edward L.   Direct Marketing: Strategy, Planning, Execution, 1994
McGraw-Hill
ISBN: 0070460329

Database Marketing: The Ultimate Marketing Tool, 1993
McGraw-Hill
ISBN: 0070450539

Ogilvy, David   Ogilvy on Advertising, 1987
Random House
ISBN: 039472903X

Peppers, Don and Rogers, Martha
Enterprise One to One: Tools for Competing in the Interactive Age, 1997
Currency/Doubleday
ISBN: 0385482051

Posch, Robert   Complete Guide to Marketing and The Law, 1988
Prentice Hall
ISBN: 0131609041

Ries, Al and Trout, Jack Marketing Warfare, 1997
McGraw-Hill
ISBN: 0070527261

Roman, Ernon and Knudsen, Anna
Integrated Direct Marketing, 1995
NTC Business Books
ISBN: 0844233498

Shepard, David   The New Direct Marketing; How to Implement a Profit-Driven Database Marketing Strategy, 1994

Irwin Professional Publishers
ISBM: 1556238096

Stone, Bob

Direct Marketing Success Stories: . . .and the
Strategies That Build the Business, 1995
NTC Publishing Group
ISBN: 0844236659

Successful Direct Marketing Methods, Third
Edition
Crain Books, An Imprint of National Textbook
Company, 1986.

Stone, Bob and Wyman, John

Successful Telemarketing, 1993
NTC Publishing Group
ISBN: 0844232963

Successful Telemarketing/Opportunities and
Techniques for Increasing Sales and Profits, 1992
National Textbook Co Trade
ISBN: 0844232955

Strunk, William, Jr. and White, E. B.

The Elements of Style, 1979
Allyn & Bacon
ISBN: 0024181900

VanVechten, Lee

The TSR Hotline, 1995
Direct Marketing Publishers
ISBN: 1879644045

The CSR Hotline
Direct Marketing Publishers

Wunderman, Lester

Being Direct: Making Advertising Pay, 1997
Random House
ISBN: 0394540638

Index